SEE YOU IN FRANKFURT!

PETER WEIDHAAS

See You in Frankfurt!

Life at the Helm of the Largest Book Fair in the World

TRANSLATED BY LAWRENCE SCHOFER

©2010 LOCUS PUBLISHING, LLC
100 Park Avenue, Suite 1600
New York, NY 10017
LOCUS-INTERNATIONAL.COM

All rights reserved.

First edition, 2010

No part of this book may be reproduced, stored in a retrieval system, or transmitted in any form or by any means, including electronic, mechanical, photocopying, microfilming, recording, or otherwise (except for that copying permitted by Sections 107 and 108 of the U.S. Copyright Law and except by reviewers for the public press) without written permission from the Publisher.

First published as *Und kam in die Welt der Büchermenschen*
©2007 Christoph Links Verlag

Fire by Vishnu Khare appears courtesy of the author.

Printed in Taiwan.

ISBN 978-0-9842824-0-1

Contents

Here Come the Book People…	7
The "Berlin Pit"	11
A Surprising Choice	17
Out into the Shoals	39
Massaging the Media	51
My First Fair	58
China	66
In the Land of Magical Realism	74
Little House in the Rhön	84
The Year of Latin America	90
Struggles over Relocating	97
Did Somebody Say Communist?	106
A Growing Fair	114
Tribute to Hermann Schulz	123
The Third World Tells a Story	135
Decisions, Decisions	151
You Wish to Write on India, Sir?	162
Impressions	184
The Collapse of Real-Existing Socialism	210
Guests of Honor	224
Where Do We Put Everybody?	250
Death to Rushdie!	266
A New Design and the Results	278
The Neverending Rushdie Affair	289
Reform by Coup d'état	312
Losing Control of the Fair	326
The New Gutenberg Galaxy	340
Asia	352
Drawing Up the Balance Sheet	370
Afterword	386
Index of Names	389

*It is not love that makes the world go round, but doubt. That is the grand price of freedom.
If you struggle against that doubt, you will live in bewilderment. But if you can live with it—Life is an adventure.*

PETER USTINOV

Here Come the Book People...

If you follow the banks of the River Main as they wend their way through the German heartland, at a place not far from where the waters feed into the Rhine you will find a shallow crossing used centuries ago by the Frankish army. This *"ford of the Franks"* bequeathed its name upon the city that still occupies this very spot: Frankfurt am Main.

This is the place where hundreds of thousands of eager visitors converge every year, coming by plane, by train, by automobile, now and again by bus and by streetcar. Due to its location between North and South and between East and West, for over 1,000 years this is the place where people have come to see, to understand, and to buy and to sell. What we are talking about here is the Frankfurt Fair.

In the ninth century Frankfurt was the capital of the Kingdom of the East Franks. The nobles who came seeking an audience with the King did not come alone. Each of them traveled with a mighty entourage that had to be tended to. Their presence attracted the local farmers, who carted their fruits and other agricultural produce from the countryside to the city in order to offer them up for sale. Soon there arose a market for those traveling retinues, and this marked the origin of the Frankfurt Fair.

In the years that followed, more and more tradespeople and craftsmen came once or twice a year to the city on the River Main, which hence became a pivotal market and place of commerce for all of Central Europe. In 1147, at the time of the Hohenstaufen dynasty, the prosperous city of Frankfurt became the site of the coronation of the German kings.

In 1150, Eliezer ben Nathan from the nearby city of Mainz, and one of the leading rabbis of his time, spoke in his commentary on the Talmud of Jews who "come to the fair of the non-Jews." As an example of such a "fair of the non-Jews," he pointed to the one that was held in Frankfurt. That document is the earliest record we have of such a "fair" which names this city. Then in 1240 there followed the famous "fair privilege," a certificate of safe conduct to the Frankfurt Fair issued by Emperor Frederick II in Italy during the siege of Ascoli.

From 1450 to 1764, for more than 300 years, Frankfurt was in fact the leading commercial center for the book trade that the innovations of Johannes Gutenberg (whose print shop was in nearby Mainz) had made possible. Frankfurt was a book center not only for Germany but for all of Europe. Printers came from Antwerp, Basel, Paris, Venice, Amsterdam, Kraków, London, and from many German cities, but so did the authors of the books being traded there, such as Johann Reuchlin, Erasmus of Rotterdam, Philipp Melanchthon and Giordano Bruno.

After the catastrophe of the two world wars and the collapse of the criminal Hitler regime, during which time the lack of peaceful trade and cultural exchange made such commercial expositions unthinkable, in 1949 two Frankfurt book dealers revived the old fair tradition and founded anew the *Frankfurt Book Fair.*

The Frankfurt success story that they kicked off inspired the creation of new book fairs all over the world, all based on the organizational principles at Frankfurt, which was considered a model for presentations everywhere—in London and in Moscow, in Cairo and in Beijing, in Mexico (Guadalajara) and in Bologna.

This success did not happen by itself. After all, post-war Germany, the site of violent Nazi rule, was not the ideal place for a gathering of book people from around the world.

One day in 1967, the author of this book found his way into this "World of the Book People" and became enraptured by it. I too was marked by German history, and had to fight a running battle with a typical German identity crisis; I now bound up my life with an exposition that was struggling no less fiercely for its own identity. For 32 years I wrestled this thousand-armed and many-headed monster, much as Laocoön of antiquity fought with the sea-serpents, who in the end strangled him to death.

How this struggle evolved for me, but also how the Frankfurt Book Fair "found its soul," as a French publisher once put it, is the story of this book.

※

On a blustery autumn day, I find myself hurrying through the streets of Frankfurt, late for an appointment and somewhat out of breath. I hustle along the historic *"Buchgasse,"* our famous Book Lane which still harkens back to the medieval book fair. Here I can trace the footsteps of Johannes Gutenberg, who more than 550 years ago hurried along this very street in order to meet one of the market ships from Mainz on the river bank. A moment later I am rushing past the Frankfurt shopping street and making my way through Hauptwache Square.

All of a sudden a couple catches my eye, locked as they are in animated conversation among the steady stream of passersby. There is nothing exceptional in their appearance—he in his mid-50s; she, much younger. What grabs my attention is a single book jutting conspicuously out of the man's jacket pocket.

I am always curious when I see people reading, people with books, whether in the park or on the subway or at the beach. I always try to steal a quick glance at the title that they are engrossed in. That way, if only for a moment, I am able to pull these book lovers out of their anonymity. That is why, on this occasion, I edge somewhat closer to the nameless couple. The man's jacket pocket is obscuring most of the title, but the name of the author suddenly leaps out at me in bold letters!

I recognize the book and its author—not just an author, but a dear friend whom we have lost. A cold flood of memories washes over me. Something deep inside cautions me to withdraw from my reminiscence, to turn the page...

For the ancient Greeks, who stand firm at the base of our cultural memory, the mother of the Muses and the goddess of memory was Mnemosyne. The following anecdote has been attributed to Simonides of Keos, the first storyteller of Western history:

About 500 years before the Common Era, he was sitting at a banquet table with many other guests when someone called him out of the banquet hall. Scarcely had he left the room when the roof of the hall caved in and killed all the people who were sitting at the table. Their relatives found the bodies mutilated beyond recognition. The poet, however, could help them. Thanks to his memory, he remembered where the individual guests had been sitting. And so he transformed the unrecognizable bodies back into individual people.

No roof has fallen in on these reminiscences. Still, my memories of contacts, events, acquaintances, friendships and enmities have been covered over by a multiplicity of novel experiences and new encounters, as well as by the repression of painfully endured episodes. Like Simonides of Keos, here I remember the many book people whom I have met, and I give them the names that belong to them.

It should also be told that all of these people, whenever luck delivered a happy reunion or chance encounter in some far corner of the globe, always bid goodbye to each other with the joyous cry, *See you in Frankfurt!*

The "Berlin Pit"

My first excursions into the vast world that awaited me unfolded in the Berlin of my childhood, in the lots overgrown with patches of wild brush between the housing blocks on Africa street, where my parents were happy to send me off to play.

It must have been in the spring of 1942. With some very strenuous shoveling, the "big boys" of the neighborhood had dug a hole perhaps six feet square and almost three feet deep in the sandy soil. All day long we little ones had eagerly watched the strenuous "men's work." We had even tried to pitch in a bit with our toy shovels and tiny pails, but in vain. We were no match the older crew with their big shovels.

Finally the hour of completion struck, the hour of the long-awaited dedication of the grandiose structure. The opening ceremony was properly arranged, with the participation of all the children living in the neighborhood. They all stood together in the pit, and together evaluated the magnificent work.

Screaming and yelling, all the children milling about jumped into the ditch. The little ones were lowered down, or were let down by some of those already inside. Me too—though I was one of the smallest ones, I experienced this community service. I thought myself lucky and secure, and I pushed right away into the middle of the hole. Warmed and protected by the bodies of the other kids, I stood just like them and looked up in expectation of the celebration, which was now to come.

But up there on the outside, on the edge of the secure community, unrest was spreading. Something had happened, something that the leaders of the enterprise had not foreseen. The pit was filled up to the edges with little people, all looking up, and there stood the *"An-führer,"* the *ringleaders,* the ones who had led the entire enterprise and had set the pace—they stood there with legs apart and with their arms akimbo, fists pressed into their hips (as customary then!). They were standing outside the pit, and inside there was no more room. Everyone was standing pressed against one another, looking up in fright. Somebody had to get out so that the *"Anführer"* could get in.

I held my breath. I made myself even smaller than I already was, and tried to be as invisible as possible. But still the sentence of excommunication struck me—"Hey you, *peewee,* in the middle!"

Everybody looked around, including me, although I already knew that I was the one he was pointing at.

"You, with the funny hat—get out!"

The others, relieved, pushed me to the edge where I had to extend my hand to one of the big shots, and with one swing he pulled me out of the comfortable community and put me on the edge of the pit. Bawling loudly, I ran away.

It wasn't only the experience of the "Berlin pit" that made me a loner, but this image very early on marked my later path in life, which was always characterized by a great desire for community. As I ran crying along Africa Street to our apartment, I had left behind what I wanted the most—belonging to a group that created an identity.

Later I ran through the world many times—practically "bawling" out my individuality, taking on my singularity in a renewed fashion—repeatedly renewing the experience of the "pit," when communities that I wanted to create or to which I wanted to belong were not suitable for me to identify with—my parents' house, the church, the school, the youth groups, the Scouts and hiking clubs in which I invested my entire youthful energy. In fact I was seeking to belong to a group, a nation, to a culture, to my German culture.

I was born before the war. Still, I didn't become a conscious member of the society into which I had been deposited until a few years after the armistice, when I confronted with horror the terrible crimes that had been perpetrated in the name of that cultural circle, and by the people who belonged to it, the culture into which I had been on the verge of integrating myself.

Today, more than 60 years later, when I remember the experience of the "Berlin pit," I suddenly realize that this formative experience of my childhood had not only started me down a contentious, go-it-alone path, but that in the Berlin of those years, threatened by bombs and cowering under a brutal dictatorship, this children's game truly did symbolically satirize the events of the day. You can't tell me that children from ages 3 to 9 or 10 don't fathom what is playing out in the world of adults! The game with the pit, with the cowering children looking for "the People's Community," with the *"Führer"* above them, was an accurate reflection of the state of mind of Berliners in those dramatic days. Fear did not only mean having to flee into the cellars to escape the nightly carpet bombings; for we had already long been cowering under the menacing rule of the Nazis. The only escape from *that* terror was by seeking out a safe community in which to bury one's guilt and salvage what was left of common humanity.

Looked at from that point of view, my socialization was typical for the time in Germany. My drive to community and the contradictory construction of the individual, both of which determined my development, were ordained by the times and by the special relationships in the Germany of the Nazi dictatorship and the war. It's no wonder that as a young man I first considered myself a radical, and had to oppose this recent German past of conformity through coercion, in which the individual counted for naught.

I got into the German book trade through very indirect paths. After sticking it out through a strenuous three-year apprenticeship with a Duisburg book dealer, I broke away from this community of professionals and pursued a short study period of mass psychology in Nazi Germany, at a very special small college in the Swiss mountains.

Love for a Danish woman then took me to Copenhagen. With the aid of an energetic study of the Danish language, and with evening courses in book publishing technology at the Graphics Art Institute and then a job in a Danish bookbinding house, which quickly brought me to the position of a production manager, I tried—once again—with great effort, to become an acknowledged and respected member of a community. This time it was the community of the tolerant and endearing Danish bourgeoisie, whom I admired and loved.

I was nearly to succeed in this effort, and after getting engaged to that beloved Danish woman I was even offered a partnership in the bookbinding company. A well-adjusted life in small, friendly Denmark was beckoning me, but I had no choice but to climb my way out of that ditch, and traveled instead to the book fair in Frankfurt to look for a job among the many publishing houses as a production manager.

The year was 1966. In Copenhagen I climbed into my old VW Beetle and traveled to the Danish–German border near Flensburg, still relaxed and calm. From there I moved south on the German highways with the aggressiveness that prevails on those roads, and I became increasingly tense. I can still picture myself taking the western exit from the freeway and rolling on toward Frankfurt, which even then was a Mecca for "book people." On the way I had picked up a hitchhiker who was striving toward the same goal. It took us many agonizing minutes to find a parking space, and to find our way to the Fair. We both approached the big hall shyly and curiously. Inside throngs of publishers and book dealers circled among the stands loaded with thousands of books that met their many interests. This was an active and multi-layered community, one whose members varied significantly by skin color, sex, clothing and disposition, but which somehow managed to cohere as a group, and even speak a common tongue—though the languages one heard were mostly incomprehensible. Something bound these people together, they who from the outside looked so different and acted so differently from "normal" human beings.

What I experienced here was a community of individualists, who wrote books, produced books, sold books, read books—books of fantasy, books of science, books for study, for use, for enjoyment, useful books, useless books, picture books, children's books, photo books—books for reflection, books for enjoyment, provocative books, political books—and ugly ones too, stupid ones, seductive ones, and even repulsive ones (though one didn't know where to draw the boundaries, and these books were accepted and defended on the principle of freedom of expression). It was my discovery of this species of "book person" that made my first visit to the Frankfurt Book Fair so noteworthy.

With regard to my quest, I got lucky at this Fair very quickly. I found what was for my qualifications a well-paid job as a production manager at the scientific and medical specialty publishing house of Georg Thieme in Stuttgart. After I completed my move from Copenhagen to Stuttgart, I soon began my new job there.

I got ever closer to the "Frankfurt pit," but this time nobody grabbed my arm to pull me out. Rather I had brought myself close to the "world of book people." For the next year and a half, I was to work industriously and devotedly on the technical aspects of medical specialty books, in planning, calculating, organizing projects for printing houses and book binderies and managing and monitoring them, until the particular book was ready in three copies on the publisher's desk. He was someone who certainly rarely spared his criticism. Nonetheless, I had brought all the books in my area along the arduous path from manuscript to finished product. As a production manager, I had taken on a sort of midwife function. I felt myself responsible for every one of these newborn books—and was as proud of them as if I had written them myself.

I took a decisive step in the summer of 1968, when I joined the organizational team of the Frankfurt Book Fair, and from then on for seven years I managed exhibitions of German books around the world. A busy travel period began, which allowed me to become acquainted with the world that produced, marketed, and read books. Stays that lasted months in foreign countries in Latin America, the United States and in Asia alternated with specific assignments across the map of Europe. It was akin to small-scale military maneuvers for the Frankfurt Book Fair. I got to know one foreign book market after the other in my little ship of 1,000 to 4,000 German books that comprised the book exhibits. For this task, I had to acquire technical organizational skills for setting up exhibitions in the most diverse spaces, and to lead a team of employees hired in the host countries. I appeared on television and gave radio and newspaper interviews. All the costs had to be monitored and supported with good receipts, since the auditing department of the public funder, the Foreign Office of the Federal Republic of Germany, was merciless. I tried to understand the cultures in which I wanted to introduce German knowledge, and fast became interested in their literature as well. I learned how to be a representative and how to cut a good figure in front of ambassadors, ministers and government officials. I acquired the ability to deal with and to communicate with great authors, politicians and intellectuals.

It was the most comprehensive training for the post of a director of the Frankfurt Book Fair imaginable, although naturally that was not the intended goal of my activity while presenting German editions abroad. Nobody imagined, and certainly not I, where this career would lead.

But then came that day in the summer of 1973. To the astonishment of all the people who had followed the discussion regarding the successor to Sigfred Taubert, then current director of the Book Fair, I, the youngest among the applicants, was chosen to lead and to develop the Frankfurt Book Fair starting at the beginning of 1975.

After a further 26 years and 2 months, I finally got out of the big black chair at the Fair director's desk, where at first I had settled down so hesitantly. Now I moved to make a place for my successor, Lorenzo Rudolf from Switzerland. For a good quarter century I had devoted myself intensively to the community building aspects of this historic exposition. I had overcome my childhood trauma of being excluded from a community, and had devoted my entire strength to the furthering of this community. My internal drive and my self-generated energy arose from the post-war Berlin of my childhood. I had been shaped by the contradictory forces of a desire for personal security and a rebellious urge to find the path out of the "Berlin pit," all the way down to my new appointment in Frankfurt. I had acquired broad knowledge in matters of books and the book trade, in national and international literature and culture, and I was well-equipped in the areas of book marketing, representation, administration and organization. Was that enough?

A Surprising Choice

The Supervisory Board of the Frankfurt Book Fair had not made its decision easily on that hot day of July 3, 1973, in the airport hotel. All the members had committed themselves to a unanimous vote for the successor to Sigfred Taubert, who was the Fair director at that time. Conditions had also been laid down like those at an election for the Pope. The first test vote resulted in an overwhelming majority for Taubert's favored candidate, Dr. Müller-Römhild. Only a single person on the committee refrained from that vote. It was the chairman of that illustrious circle, Dr. Matthias Wegner, at that time director of the Rowohlt Publishing House in Hamburg. He had stuck to his word, given to me before my trip to Finland at the beginning of the year, that he would support me at the election for the new director.

In the second round, one man joined Wegner, a man whose anarchic playfulness I soon came to know in greater detail, Ulrich Staudinger from the Munich publishing house of Ehrenwirth/Schneekluth. The will and the eloquence of these two men succeeded in gaining another member in each round of voting. The last bastion that fell, so it was reported to me, was that of the conservative publisher from Parey, Friedrich Georgi, who for some years thereafter made his initial skepticism toward me known in the meetings of the Supervisory Board, through his hypercorrect monitoring and his quibbling cross-examinations.

And so the choice fell on the youngest of the candidates, which was surprising to many people, in particular to me myself. A bit of the blame for this was probably the general uncertainty brought about by the stormy days of 1968, which at the Frankfurt Book Fair in particular had shaken noble convictions and conservative principles. A representative of the New Age should take over the controls. And that person had finally been made out to be me.

Sigfred Taubert wanted to resign at the end of the year 1974, but there was no interregnum, no in-between period, in which the old director slowly handed over the reins and the new one gradually took charge. A few newspapers and magazines briefly honored Taubert's services for the Book Fair, and showed themselves to be astonished at the young, faceless successor. The *Frankfurter Allgemeine Zeitung* published photos of the old and new directors of the Frankfurt Book Fair, side by side, in order to emphasize the difference, and the American magazine *Publishers Weekly* wondered aloud in an editorial about the red turtleneck sweater and the leather jacket of the new incumbent. Still, all the excitement over the changes in the Exposition and Fair Company (the *Austellungs- und Messe GmbH,* which runs the Fair) quickly petered out, and everyone carried on as if nothing had happened. It was visibly quite difficult for old Taubert to depart from what had constituted the last 16 years of his life. He held his cards close to his vest, and he selfishly protected his authority in a way that made it appear that he had not voluntarily decided to leave, but as though he was being driven out.

    I took myself back to my exposition office some 200 yards away from Taubert's, and immersed myself even more concentratedly in my work.

    No one spoke anymore about the imminent change, and had Sigfred Taubert not celebrated his departure repeatedly with cheese and red wine, I fear that we would have completely forgotten the coming event of his replacement. And so I returned to my military-like practice maneuvers, using as a model all I had learned in the past five years about books, countries and people.

    I wanted to free myself from the practice phase with three large exposition projects. They would at the same time serve as examples of my masterwork. I thought that I knew how one could do it, and I wanted to show that book expositions could be completed successfully in such difficult places as London, Rome and New York, cities in which our ponderous and austere medium of the book had to make its way against a rich set of cultural offerings. I undertook to prepare for all three projects. Carefully and with great concentration, I worked on each of the three, with the first in Great Britain.

I took the railroad to Ostend, and from there I went by ferry to Dover and continued on with the train to London's Victoria Station. I enjoyed this ride, which I had once done in 1957 as a hitchhiker. At that time I traveled around for several weeks in the British Isles; I wandered around the Scottish Highlands, and I climbed Ben Nevis. I looked forward to my return, and pressed my face against the train window, trying to conjure some picture from memory out of the roads running alongside the train or from a passing village. Once I arrived in London, I left my suitcase unopened in the hotel and immediately strolled down Tottenham Court Road to Piccadilly Circus.

Then came the shock of what lay behind London's glitzy culture—a "druggie" lying on the street, and a policeman, who completely ignored him. All of a sudden the depressing impression of the decline of Europe came over me—it was as though I were observing the wax figures in Madame Tussaud's museum. All the people who streamed past me seemed to be hankering after something else. In a daze, I walked through the unreal scenery of this puppet theater of the absurd. After I had crossed Hyde Park, I was attracted to a rousing though somewhat aggressive speaker at Speakers' Corner. This Nigerian gentleman, whom everybody called Sammy Daki, cursed the English as "hypocritical impotent Fascists." The people who were being cursed looked on and smiled.

The next morning I tried to make some contacts, first with the German Embassy and the branch office of the Goethe Institute, later with Mrs. Wolff of the German book dealer Interbook. Then I went on to some English book dealers, including Foyles Bookshop, and to some English publishers—Sir George Weidenfeld, André Deutsch, John Hitchins at Penguin; Mr. Heyde and Mr. Russell at Collins; John Beer, Charles Pick and Nigel Viney at Heinemann; Clifford-Simons of the National Book League; then with the red-nosed, fuzzy-haired character Martin Ballard of the Publishers Association, and finally with the British Council and the British Library Association. In the days following I met with a few writers, students, professors, theater people and artists.

Afterwards I felt myself in shimmering and exuberant London in a way that I had felt as a hitchhiker in the 1950s, and I suddenly realized that somehow something had changed. Many contacts were extraordinarily easy to achieve; lots of people were immediately ready to receive me, since they were uninhibited in their curiosity about the new "Frankfurt Circus director."

So it was with the thin, dark-haired John Beer of Heinemann Publishing House, a man of a serious and penetrating gaze. This 51-year-old Czech Jewish émigré and his family lived quite unconventionally in a high-class commune made up of mature British personalities—architects, lawyers and judges. At first he cautiously invited me to a bar for a glass of wine to feel me out. He didn't feel any resentment against the Germans, he said, but he would really like to know who these new Germans were. Later, when I had apparently passed the test quite well, there followed an invitation to his "commune," an old English building, in which the various families lived in their own flats but in which the drawing rooms, the kitchen, the living room and the library were all used jointly. I considered this invitation to be a sort of medal, and the earnest John Beer later became a most important friendly English contact, who always got involved as a mediator whenever there were problems with the British publishers.

Then I met the charismatic Lord George Weidenfeld, head of Weidenfeld & Nicolson, in his office. He was also a Jewish émigré, in this case from Vienna, and one who had been raised to the peerage by the Queen in 1969. He was a friendly listener, and he immediately supported my project for an exposition. But here too I couldn't avoid the impression that I came across after careful inspection as a somewhat ill-mannered, chattering young man from Frankfurt yammering away about his plans for his London book exposition.

Lord Weidenfeld was a convinced internationalist, somewhat of an exception in the English publishing world, and an early and enthusiastic participant at Frankfurt. He had never missed a Frankfurt Book Fair, not a single one from the first to the fiftieth, as he reported 25 years later as a guest speaker at the 50th Jubilee Fair in Frankfurt: *My motives for entering and remaining in this profession were my unbridled enthusiasm for the cross-border, international tasks of the publishing profession, and for the link that has been forged between different worlds, that between my adoptive country, Great Britain, and Europe, and here above all to the cultural area of my German mother tongue.*

Here I had met someone who with great dignity represented the goals and visions that I myself hoped to assume in my freshly acquired post. I wished to carry these visions further, though not as a publisher, but rather as a mediator, and above all as an ally in our shared endeavours.

This was a time when Willy Brandt was campaigning for a foreign *cultural* policy as a third bulwark of foreign policy, and so each visit to a German embassy would invariably turn up some surprisingly striking personalities in the post of cultural expert. Dr. Lohmeyer, a gray-haired, extraordinarily industrious woman, was a splendid specimen of the type. She set up meetings and encounters for me with unflagging energy and poise. In cooperation with the director of the Goethe Institute, Dr. Schulz, she had already planned a German Month, a German cultural festival with concerts, theater and appearances by authors. A German book exhibit fit into this very well, and "if the German Publishers and Booksellers Association would make available its books and an advertising budget," the recently appointed director of the Frankfurt Fair should only be so happy to take on the planning and marketing of the operation.

From the viewpoint of a cultural promoter, in many ways London was difficult terrain, as were Buenos Aires, Paris and New York. Every day hundreds of theaters, movie houses, concerts, festivals, variety shows and event planners offered a colorful variety of divertisement, sometimes of outstanding quality, and as a result the public was quite spoiled for culture. That is why an attractive and not too tiresome advertising campaign was par for the course for any exhibition that hoped to draw a crowd.

In Dr. Lohmeyer's apartment we discussed the problem with the then very well-known German painter of the so-called *Köpffüßler* group, Horst Antes. After a long, cognac-punctuated night, the three of us developed what we thought was an irresistible notion to call the German month "Germany is a Puzzle." Later this topic and the way it would look were discussed at great length on various levels—at the Goethe Institute in London, at the Foreign Office in Bonn, at the exposition department in Frankfurt, and finally, in February 1974, by the British partners of the German Month. It was turned down.

We remained true nonetheless to the basic idea of the "Puzzle." In the end we developed a description for the book exhibition and for the entire German Month with a play on the words "many German facets":

GERMANY FACETS
GerMANY FACE S
GerMANY FAC TS

In London, Dr. Lohmeyer's had put me in touch with Mr. Cashfield, manager of the Royal Festival Hall, an important nexis of culture in central London. The contract that we concluded for the use of their magnificent ballroom turned out to be critical for the success of our project. Here in London some 35,000 people visited the exhibition; another 12,000 came in the cities that followed, Glasgow and Edinburgh, and finally 3,500 in Dublin.

I had begun to consider this work with the exhibitions to be a kind of art. The local conditions, the people and their social needs, and the information on offer were the raw materials of this art. This may seem vague, but in the years that followed I applied myself ever more diligently to this creative aspect of my organizational work. Yes, indeed—successful organization was a piece of art, and it called for a process of originary creativity as did any other work of art. It was just that the material used was more fluid, less predictable, and less concrete. The entire construct in the end is only successful for an intangible moment, and unites for only a short time all the relationships and the feelings of human beings that have come together on a rare and harmonious occasion. In my work with the Fair that came later, I was to experience the exceptional possibilities, but also the stark limits, of such a conception of organization.

In Italy, the country where presumably no one reads—a situation that was confirmed repeatedly, and in a resigned fashion, by Italian publishers and book dealers—the book belonged to one of the most unattractive offerings that one could make to an Italian. Now a German book exhibition needed to find a public.

I traveled to Rome and Milan and let myself be overtaken by the Italian ambiance. I repeatedly stumbled over German cultural representatives and institutions, and finally found a topic for exhibit that addressed at least half of Italian society; that is, its women.

The idea came from Inge Feltrinelli, the widow of the legendary publisher Giangiacomo Feltrinelli, who a year earlier had been found dead next to a high tension pylon near Milan. Dr. Götz Martius from the German Embassy in Rome, likewise a convincing and engaged cultural attaché, flew me to Milan specifically to meet Inge, whom he had visited at dancing lessons while a young man, at a time when Inge Feltrinelli was still named Inge Schönthal. At that time she had no notion of the great publishing business, but was preparing herself to become a talented photographer of international renown.

We visited Inge at midday in her old townhouse, where a surly concierge did not want to admit us at all. To be sure, the owner, who had been listed among the great international publishers with his release of Boris Pasternak's *Dr. Zhivago,* Lampedusa's *The Leopard* and Che Guevara's diary, had only recently died, and had left behind him great social and political turmoil.

Giangiacomo Feltrinelli, roué, eccentric, a millionaire member of the underground, who wrote letters to the Red Brigades, and who may also have made explosives, had recently placed himself in the ranks of those who stood at the ready over fears of a military *putsch*. The CIA, as well, had taken notice of this "representative of Fidel Castro and the Cuban revolution" in Europe.

His funeral, in which my German colleagues Heinrich Maria Ledig-Rowohlt and Klaus Wagenbach had participated, and which Uwe Johnson later described so impressively, had taken place in the not too distant past. One had to have empathy for the protective reflexes of the growling "Cerberus" at the entrance to what remained of the Feltrinelli family kingdom. When we finally were able to get in, Inge Feltrinelli greeted us with great warm-heartedness and with the enthusiasm which later became her trademark at all the receptions and meetings with publishers that were yet to come. She adopted me immediately as one of her many, many friends, and right away latched on to my project for an exposition. She offered me suggestions, telephoned, set up connections—all during a light lunch.

That's the way she was, and that's the way she remained over all the years in which I had contact with her, both in Frankfurt and elsewhere. George Weidenfeld was later to remark of Inge Feltrinelli that she was the "epitome of royalty and warm-heartedness." I was not the only one in the world of international publishing who was amazed at her lively interventions in the book trade, which were never merely reserved for those who had proven themselves a success. When suddenly at an extremely crowded cocktail party she took you by the hand and drew you clear across the room through the crowd to someone whom you absolutely *had* to meet, that was clearly something like a mother's care. Once, during an exposition, she even got me a beautiful Italian necktie because she didn't like my "boring" German one.

Finally, however, what awaited me was the true challenge, the greatest one for me as a creator of exhibitions. A grand German book exhibit needed to find a public in the United States of America. A German book exhibit in the U.S.A., the land of movies and television, the inward-looking world opinion leader—*could it succeed at all?* At the same time, the U.S. formed the third-largest contingent of exhibitors at the Frankfurt Book Fair. It was thus time for me to get better acquainted with the U.S. book trade.

On this trip I laid the foundation for my quite personal relationship to the U.S., which from then on always remained somewhat problematic, and which in my tenure at the Book Fair continued to present headaches. The U.S. exercised a strong but negative fascination for us, the rabble-rousing youth of recent years. We, the ones who had experienced our political socialization in the events of 1968, generally wanted nothing to do with this country. The U.S. was an "imperialist power," that was certain, and was an extraordinarily menacing state. We preferred to occupy ourselves extensively with the victims, those whom this country of "blind rage" had left behind in Vietnam, in Guatemala, and once again recently in Chile. We were convinced that Pinochet would never have been able to carry out the *coup* in Chile without the strong support of the CIA.

On the other hand, we were not blind to the fact that the "culture" from "over there" was exerting ever stronger control on our lives. We too tended to consume pre-packaged mass-market goods and mindless American entertainment. Increasingly, the political perspectives that had shaped our inclinations of 1968 faded away, and ceded their place to the "right" way to see the world.

What came to my mind was the well-known Canadian scholar of media Herbert Marshall McLuhan, who in his sensational book *The Gutenberg Galaxy* had announced the end of the age of the book. He called current (North) American civilization the most strongly shaped and polished culture in the age of the book, a claim that made me stand up and listen but left me confused. The medium of the book had molded American society most strongly by promoting a linear mode of thinking and an economy of specialization, with the subsequent partitioning and reformatting of all social sectors. McLuhan argues that, by 1800, the leveling power of the alphabet was even more effective in America than in Europe. He notes that from the very beginning, America took the technology of book printing into the areas of education, industry and politics, and was repaid with unprecedented potential for unifying the work force with consumption. He felt it had not been correctly recognized that literacy plays a basic and archetypal role in the construction of an industrial economy.

I was getting closer to this point of view, and had thus found a way to approach this country, which I now wanted to visit for the first time, though to be sure I was still anxious and full of prejudices, though equally driven by an insatiable curiosity.

On March 17, 1974, after an unusually rough and stormy

flight over the Atlantic, I was hit in the face by an ice-cold Washington wind. The first Americans whom I encountered in my initial gropings for knowledge appeared as though deaf, dumb, and blind, and completely isolated from one another. Was this some mocking confirmation of my prejudices, that the very first person I met in Washington was the otherwise very friendly but legally blind Dr. Baumhof from the German Embassy? Even with Dr. Price of the Library of Congress, who invited me for dinner, I could not get rid of the feeling that I was not being taken seriously. Only in the evening at the hotel bar, where the bartender said he had learned his trade at Columbia University, could I relax with a few beers and glasses of *ouzo*. Nonetheless, a pattern had been set that would repeat itself every day that I was in America.

Finally—my first time in New York, the quintessential experience for any visitor to America. Here, among the mighty primeval architectural outgrowths, the "skyscrapers," I crept around for several days like an insect at the feet of towering primordial trees. A perpetually smiling Dr. Russell, cultural official of the German General Consulate, had me put up in a curious ten-dollar hotel on East 51st St. I went by foot up Fifth Avenue all the way to the Goethe Institute on East 83rd St., and then back down Park Ave. to the area near the PAN-AM building, where the General Consulate was housed.

Fascinated by the gargantuan architecture that surrounded me, I never stopped craning my neck. My eardrums were near bursting with the crippling white noise of this metropolis. Something happened to me that I had not expected—if you let go of the eyes as your dominant sensory organ, then your all-inclusive sense of hearing rises up in a sea of decibels and practically carries you away! For the first time I became aware of the dominance of the eye in our cultural relationships, and gradually began to understand what McLuhan meant with his characterization of the European–American culture as a culture of books, of reading and of seeing. Had I thus found a key to getting closer to this American civilization, which seemed so unintelligibly similar to many other civilizations found in the Southern Hemisphere?

I could scarcely get any rest at the Pickwick Arms Hotel.

This second-rate flophouse was used to accommodate hardship cases who could not be taken care of elsewhere. One door down there was some crazy old lady. I never saw her, but I could hear her every night. Well after bedtime she would preach at the top of her voice: "And Jesus came down from the heights, on Easter he came to us, and the people stretched out their arms and called to him: *Give us dollars, dollars, dollars!*" And then she went up into a tremolo and screamed hysterically, *"Dollars, Dollars—give us dollars!"*

When I took the elevator to the lobby after another wakeful night, I found an old man dancing with arms extended, singing a crazed melody, "It's snowing, it's snowing—I love it when it's snowing!" Unnerved, I went into a coffee shop for breakfast. But everywhere on the streets I ran into the same odd people, all speaking to themselves. Was this America?

On Washington Square an African American sashayed up to me. "Do you like grass?"

"Oh yeah, man!" I answered jokingly. "What have you read of him?"

People were apparently quite accustomed to running into crazies everywhere, since my dealer friend pulled back very cautiously, holding his arms out in front of him for protection and begging me to "take it easy."

I had put up my headquarters in the German Department of the Rizzoli Bookstore on 5th Ave. Mr. Meinerz, a German book dealer clerk, had offered me his help over the telephone. From here I'd planned my expeditions. I began with the Germans. The book dealer Gerald Fuchs sat in a small, quite shabby one-room bookstore on lower Broadway, and was totally paranoid that someone would steal some secret from him.

Old Mary Rosenberg raced about in an enormous jumble of books, bills and prospectuses in her dimly lit bookstore on the first floor of drab, ugly building on 72nd St. Here she grabbed an invoice out of a dusty pile of papers, over there she piled up a mountain of books, and complained unceasingly that the young book dealers in Germany wouldn't last more than a few months with her.

I was introduced to the director of the German Department

in the Rizzoli Bookstore, Miss Stella Hershan, but she couldn't speak of anything other than a thick book on Metternich that she had written and which was to come out any day now.

Only in Adler's Foreign Bookshop did I find in Ruth Soika, a sensitive, engaged Jewish woman, someone with whom I could carry on an extended conversation. And that is what I did right away, and invited her to a Chinese restaurant. However, what she reported about business with German books was hardly encouraging.

At the *Aufbau,* the old German-language daily newspaper, I met Dr. Steinitz and Howard Wista—here conditions were cramped, everything covered in dust, pessimism reigned. It was even sadder at the other German-language newspaper, the *New Yorker Staatszeitung Herold,* which appeared only weekly. At night, screaming from the room next door; during the day, conversations which hardly merited the name. Everywhere I met agitated and depressed people.

Thereupon I turned my attention solely to the Americans. Elisabeth Geiser, employee of the Bowker Publishing House, a long-time visitor to Frankfurt, an acquaintance of Taubert, stayed quite formal with me. Her president, Richard Zeldin, made an effort to talk to me for five minutes. On the other hand, boredom poured out of the eyes of Arnold Ehrlich, the editor-in-chief of *Publishers Weekly.* André Shiffrin at Random House listened to me for a few minutes, sunk in thought, but he said scarcely anything and at the end wished me good luck. I didn't even get past the waiting room for Peter Mayer at Avon Books, even though I had an appointment. With Sally Wecksler, literary agent and long-time participant at the Book Fair, my headaches began to become so strong that I was looking cross-eyed. What did I want here with a German book exhibit, for God's sake? I drank a whiskey sour and then another one in a small bar somewhere between 3rd and 8th Avenues.

At Harper & Row I had wanted to shoot a few photos for an article in the *German Publishers Weekly* (*Börsenblatt*), but I couldn't get permission because the manager wasn't there. At the Tish House, where I sounded out the possibilities for an exhibit, I experienced a typical American snub. I had hardly gotten inside when I found myself out on the street! Only at the Loeb Student Center directly on Washington Square, yes indeed, we could get exhibition space—$3,000 rent under such and such conditions. O.K., I simply agreed. However, when I came back the next morning, there was a new manager. Now it cost $6,000, and this was not permissible and that wasn't allowed either.

And Henry Marx, Jewish émigré and director of the Goethe Institute, and correspondent of *Die Welt,* talked and talked. And Dr. Russell from the General Consulate smiled. They were both extremely overburdened.

After this depressing string of dead-ends, I had the luck of meeting a man who, with his stoic disposition and broad knowledge of New York—not least of all his insights into the Germans in this incomprehensible city—saved me from collapsing into complete defeatism: Professor Volkmar Sander of New York University. He was the chairman of the German department, to which the Loeb Student Center also belonged. He took me home with him; he explained; he interceded.

This smiling little Professor, always full of understanding, put me in touch with Wieland Schulz-Keil, a one-time Suhrkamp editor, who had extensive contacts among the downtown Manhattan intellectuals and came armed with an astonishing Rolodex. He introduced me to Michael Roloff, a young German editor living in New York, who was also a Suhrkamp alumnus. The two of them declared their readiness to accompany me through what was, for me, the impenetrable jungle of New York. Their readiness would prove decisive.

My connection with Volkmar Sander and his charming wife remained unbroken until he retired in the mid-'90s. Together we both later steered many an exciting exposition project through the perils of this city, including the German Book Fair of 1983. Without him I would certainly have failed pitifully in my first attempt at conquering New York.

Everyone engaged in the active life of the city seemed to be under tremendous pressure. The American ideology of success made these people into streamlined pile drivers. The light of success dominated their vision. *"First-come, first-served!"* as Peter Mayer used to shout when he became the head of Penguin. Everybody wanted to be the best and the brightest. There was no room for any reflection on other things, and definitely not about something as ephemeral as a book exhibit, certainly not one in an unloved foreign language, and from Germany at that!

"What can I do for you? How can I help you?" These were the simple introductory remarks, not unfriendly ones, that kept greeting me on my excursion through this country. However, when I began to explain what a book exhibit was, friendliness was over, and after a few minutes I found myself out the door. "Not interested, thank you! Lots of success in your endeavors!" A hint of a smile, and that was it for me. I would have liked nothing more than to abandon my senseless undertaking of a German book exhibit. But I couldn't go back. Any capitulation would have had devastating consequences for the future.

That's the way it went—reasonable doubts about this fair were simply not allowed. Besides, we had *subsidies;* optimism was the order of the day! Anyone who sucked at the money excreting teats of the public subsidy cow defended his place as if his life depended on it. He would celebrate "success" after "success." He had no other choice. I couldn't help but be depressed by this, seeing as my approach involved meaningful dialogue with the broad public, which simply wasn't possible here. Perhaps in Europe such an approach was also becoming an illusion. But here it had always been an illusion! It quickly became clear to me that I must lower my demands and concentrate on American society's niche interests. I therefore chose two peripheral groups who, I thought, might be receptive to our initiatives.

First of all, I naturally reckoned on people who were engaged with the medium of the book, who might approach our book expositions with open minds—library members, students, the intellectual classes of professors, journalists, artists, book dealers and publishers.

In addition, I anticipated a certain modicum of interest among German Americans, plus students and teachers of the German language. Hitherto, we had never particularly taken into consideration any German immigrants. However, German Americans were hardly a marginalized group, but rather an integral part of American society.

According to the data of the Census Bureau of March 1972,

more than 25.5 million of the 205 million Americans traced their origins back to a German source. After the Americans of English origin, the German element with its 12.5% of the total population was the largest group, even greater than the very large ethnic groups of Irish, Hispanics and Italians. The problem was that these German Americans did not form a homogeneous community. That became quite clear once I was able to update my knowledge about the various streams of immigrants originating in Germany.

If we omit the first German immigrants, the Mennonites (1683), Christian Anabaptists who settled first in Pennsylvania and made early appeals for the abolition of slavery, the real wave of German immigration began in 1820 and continued well into the 20th century. Germany with its some 6 million immigrants outnumbered all other nations. This stream of people consisted primarily of small farmers, artisans and laborers, but also included the first political refugees, those revolutionaries who had failed in 1848. This group was numerically rather small, but because of its intellectual and cultural attainments wielded political influence that could not be ignored.

This was a situation similar to that of the immigrants who came between 1930 and the end of the 1950s. This includes those who had been persecuted politically and racially, numbering about 100,000, a concentrated mass movement of university types and influential scientists, who held sway in America's scientific, cultural and political life to an extent that has yet to be fully appreciated. In addition, the large number of *"volksdeutsch"* immigrants, those who in 1937 had been living outside the borders of Germany in eastern and southeastern Europe, had been brought "home to the Third Reich." They too had been enticed by American immigration laws between 1948 and 1950, turning their backs on their homeland, which was in ruins, and following the call of the promised land.

People said that all these immigrant groups had integrated very quickly into American life and had forgotten their German origins. The theme of the "American melting pot" was a favorite slogan. This slogan was, however, more wish than reality. It was precisely in the period of my visit that one could observe the ethnic groups in the U.S. beginning to rediscover their particular heritage and to nurture it. This applied not only to the spectacular pronouncements of the African-Americans or of the Spanish-speaking Chicanos or Indians, but also to the Irish, the Poles, the Italians and the Germans.

Despite this rich ancestry, it didn't escape me that present interest in the German language (and Germany) was declining. This was not a development limited to the Germans, but was part and parcel of America's changing attitudes toward the Continent. Europe had lost its fascination. It was no longer the old home country with its history, its humanism, its romanticism. "Europe has in many respects become so much like us," a number of the Americans I spoke to sighed.

Modern American literature still sparkled at that time with an almost total absence of European themes, quite the opposite of works like Dos Passos's *1919*, Hemingway's *Farewell to Arms*, *Death in the Afternoon* or *For Whom the Bell Tolls*, Sinclair Lewis's *Dodsworth*, Scott Fitzgerald's *Tender is the Night*, Henry Miller's *Tropic of Capricorn*, or Thomas Wolfe's *Of Time and the River*, all models that in one way or another had taken up the American confrontation with Europe.

I thought I discovered another phenomenon in my American contacts. If McLuhan was correct with his oft-quoted thesis about America as a civilization of the book, then at this moment in history, in the early to mid-1970s, it seemed that electronic media, primarily television, had already supplanted the printed word as the primary carrier of information. The foreign observer of these contemporaneous changes could not help but note a number of crisis-laden phenomena in the American cultural landscape. The completely apolitical "hippie movement," which then stood at its zenith, could have been a reaction to this change. What was this generation after? Once again McLuhan: *The TV child expects involvement and doesn't want a specialist job in the future. He does want a role and a deep commitment to his society.*[1]

I saw another sign in the increasing interest in demonic and paranormal phenomena. This seemed to be symbolized in its

---

1. Marshall McLuhan, *Understanding Media* (New York: Signet Books, 1964), 292.

most striking form by the great success of the book and film *The Exorcist*. I couldn't rid myself of the impression that a mighty social change was making its way here, one that held everyone I met in its grip. Somehow none of the people I spoke to seemed to be quite centered or to be at home with themselves. Only on later trips did it become clear to me that the pressure and the demands of American society to focus on one's career or the simple struggle for survival were so strong that everything else was subordinated to this goal.

This trip gradually came to a head in a crisis for me as well. With my own doggedness, I fought to become aware of and understand the relations all around me, and I sought despairingly for anchor points for the project that I had undertaken. It seemed hopeless. My contacts kept shrinking even as I reached out frantically to find new ones. Every time I opened my mouth I saw the same question bobbing up behind their eyes—*Is he bringing me yet something else to invest in? No!*—"Thank you. When you have something else, please let me know." I visited theaters and cinemas. I combed through bookstores. Night after night I read magazines, newspapers and books. I kept going.

In Boston, I finally found in the Boston Public Library good exhibit conditions, and in its director Philip J. McNiff an engaged partner who was open-minded in the traditional way to matters of culture. I knew that here we would achieve the necessary number of visitors.

In Chicago, on the other hand, I could scarcely find an appropriate exhibition place. To be sure, the public library was not uninterested in the project, but one couldn't be sure that a planned renovation of the library would not take place at exactly the time of the exhibition. I therefore transferred the exhibit to Milwaukee, which was overwhelmingly German by heritage, and an hour and a half away by bus.

Finally Atlanta. In Atlanta I was at the end. Once again the same kinds of conversations repeated themselves. Atlanta in the past two decades had developed into one of the most important business hubs in the United States, and had a certain weight of its own as an African-American intellectual center. Nevertheless—the public library was in a desperate state, and the university did not have any appropriate exhibition space. The German part of the original colonization of the Southeastern states had indeed been significant, but the more recent German immigration was small. Because of the cultural level of the German associations, which limited themselves to Oktoberfest and similar activities, I excluded them as a target group for our exhibition.

After a frustrating day in which I hated my job and despaired of my ambitions, I always sought out the last human refuge that attracted many of my fellow business travelers with its comfort and care, probably for similar reasons. There we stood at the bar of our hotel until well past midnight, drinking daiquiris, whiskey sours, gin fizzes, beer, often all mixed together, celebrating our momentary friendship—the auto dealer from Detroit, the meteorologist from Seattle, and me, "the crazy book man from old Germany."

Even these evenings followed a pre-set pattern. "Hi, how are you? How's your business going?"

You could hardly get up to the bar when the friendly greeting would come, "Call me Jim, Joey, or Frankie!" and one would be plunged immediately into descriptions of home life— "My wife told me..., I said to my kids..."

Or else you had to listen to stories of business success—"I made 200 bucks today."

The bartender would nod sympathetically while he polished the glasses or mixed a new drink, and my broad-shouldered drinking companions painted a picture of a desirable American world, in which only success and happy families existed. But the longer the evening lasted and the more drinks ran down our gullets, the more clearly did the dark reality penetrate into the dim light of the bar. The successful auto dealer suddenly stood there on the verge of ruin; on top of everything else his wife was alienated from him, and his charming daughter was a drug addict. And the wife of the meteorologist had breast cancer, and he had a sexual need that he had to satisfy with women of the street.

I had a night like this behind me when in the morning I looked out of the window of my hotel room in Atlanta onto a sad American urban landscape—an unfinished cement-block wall, beside that the remnants of some structure that had been razed and turned into a parking lot; on the left, a stretch of asphalt street on which one of those big American limousines passed by back and forth as if in slow motion, and behind that more windowless walls. The picture radiated emptiness and loneliness. It could have been painted by Edward Hopper.

I stood at the window of my hotel room; a dreadfully boring hotel weekend lay before me. Headaches and self-loathing tormented me, as is common after a night of heavy drinking. Then I thought about my earlier love Birgitte, the Danish woman who shortly before our planned marriage had left me and had married an American "friend." I got interested in finding out how she had made out in America. She was living in Dallas.

I went right over to the nearest public library, asked for the telephone book for Dallas, and looked up the telephone number of that Albert H., who had frustrated my life's plan and had seduced the woman whom I thought I loved like no other, and brought her all the way to America!

Oh, how often had the loss of those years robbed me of sleep! How often had I asked myself how my life would have unfolded had I married this heavenly Danish being, as we had planned? Why had this relationship taken such an abrupt and humiliating turn? What were my mistakes, what had I forgotten to do, what were my errors? I still had not gotten over the loss and the injury to my feeling of self-worth.

I got on the next plane to Dallas. Albert was waiting for me at the airport. Silently he drove me downtown, where we were to pick up Birgitte, who was working in a department store as a salesperson. We stood at the rear entrance of this temple of consumption and had nothing to say to one another.

Then I caught sight of her. She came up to us both, smiling, swinging her hips, in the middle of a group of giggling and noisy salesgirls.

Time stood still! My pupils dilated. Everything else became a blur. It seemed to last an eternity. She was walking and smiling, walking toward me with a big smile.

At first I didn't feel anything. Breathing a sigh of relief, I thought—*an average woman among other women, the fascination has stopped. Well good thing you came. Now you're free!*

But then she started coming closer, smiling, closer and closer—it seemed to last forever! Then it happened—three steps away from me she was suddenly transformed. From among the faceless American salesgirls emerged the woman whom I had loved.

I stood there stiffly as she hugged me and pressed her kisses onto my cheeks. Something that I had long suppressed burst out in me. I mean, something exploded! *Great God in heaven, if only you hadn't come here!* I struggled to keep my composure.

The next few hours passed as though in a trance. Albert had left for a football game that he didn't want to miss. He must have understood that something was going on here, and he was standing in the way. Birgitte and I walked through a park in Dallas where children were playing, as we had once done in the Swiss town of Chur. As I had done then, I refrained from touching her. And she chattered on next to me in that Danish singsong that I so loved. Once again I was burning brightly, and I had to work very hard at keeping my emotions in check.

She talked and talked—about the difficult life here, about her bad decisions at that time, about her unhappy marriage. Then she suddenly stood still and pressed up against me. After a weighty, thoughtful pause, in which I felt her breasts rise and sink, she said, "Let's begin again!"

I stood there as though struck by lightning. Up until that moment everything was still a beautiful memory, a muddy stream of long forgotten feelings. Now standing right next to me was the past, from which I had wanted to completely separate myself. Without speaking, I went a few steps further. My insides were raging, but I knew what I would answer.

"My love, you can't step into the same river twice. Even a love has its history. You have to grab it when the time is ripe. Unfortunately we missed that. Now I have a wife and children, and you are here in America and have a husband. Life has gone on!" That's approximately how one should answer in such a situation, and that is how, in fact, I did answer.

That night in the hotel I had an unusual dream. A train, riding on swaying tracks on thin, wobbly pillars, was rolling through the mountains. Suddenly it fell with a huge crash, along with the tracks and the supports, into the ravine. In the morning I awoke with a feeling of liberation, but also of deep, painful sadness.

I continued my American journey to Houston. Shortly thereafter Birgitte got divorced, and a year later married another man in the same city. I never saw her again.

Still, I wrote to her once on the following evening in the Houston hotel in a strongly emotional state. I felt a sweet pain here. Something had broken through, something that I had always intentionally concealed from myself. I loved, I could keep loving, and... I could say "no."

We had parted a second time. I felt myself free, finally completely free for my marriage as well, which I had contracted in the meantime. Now I would return home a new person. Once again a trip had transformed me. All of this I wrote in that letter to Birgitte, an ill-fated letter as it later turned out. I did not write to my wife, since I feared that she would misunderstand the situation.

Which, in fact, she did, when I returned to Frankfurt some weeks later. I had made a detour to Mexico, where I was involved in the opening of an exhibition that I had prepared during the previous year, and I gave a lecture at a publishers' seminar before completing my U.S. trip with visits to Los Angeles and San Francisco.

I stepped out through the proper door at the Frankfurt airport, as always with uneasy expectations of what might have happened during my absence, but this time also with the joyful conviction that I had completed a great liberating act for my marriage. There standing before me was my wife Dora, like an avenging goddess with an opened letter in her hand. This was the reply that Birgitte had sent to me as an answer of burning love to my farewell letter, addressed to the Houston hotel that I had long since departed. The hotel had forwarded the letter to me at my home address

I was unable to calm the untamable wrath of my Latin spouse. That lasted for days, and in the end I had to remove everything from our apartment that was a reminder of my Danish period. But something in me was smashed, a still cherished, silent hope of saving this marriage, in which I had invested so much hope and desire. It lasted a few years more, until I finally closed the door behind me.

The professional results of this trip? In that country where, as the saying goes, everything is possible, book exhibits were not an efficient way to launch a cultural mission. Here one can only be heard if he dangles the prospect of a lucrative business venture, or if the product to be presented has a high entertainment value. This entertainment market, however, was marked by extremely tough competition, and only the blockbusters got any attention. In light of this our modest offering could not make headway. But our retreat into the niche markets at least in the end was able to satisfy the bean counters at home—2,600(!) visitors in Washington, 6,500 (after all) in New York, 18,000 (who could have imagined?) in Boston, 7,500 (the Germans) in Milwaukee, 11,100 (a miracle) in Atlanta, 8,300 in Houston (hoo-ha), 9,600 (not bad) in Los Angeles, 7,800 (even here) in San Francisco—altogether some 72,300 visitors. For myself, measured against the effort, this was far too few. I would never again attempt to fulfill my mission of spreading culture with the book exhibition in the back rooms of public libraries. What did this effort cost? I'd rather not say.

Out into the Shoals

Unsure of myself, I cautiously approached the first Book Fair that I was responsible for. It seemed as though I were sliding in a light shell onto a black sea, whose depths and storms I was unfamiliar with.

I got to thinking about my father, that father who was always convinced that I would "never amount to anything." After some 25 years of unquestioning service as an engineer for a large firm, fate had surprisingly named him director. His desk was exchanged for a larger one. He got new, more expensive drapes, a different colored rug for his office, all the ritual signs of power which mark small differences in a global firm.

Well, after a few days all the racket was over. The decorators appeared once more, tore out the carpet, pulled down the drapes, and carted the big desk away. A power shift at the head of the company had brought in new management. They had other ideas and quickly canceled my father's appointment. Although he had never been career hungry, the old man never got over this experience. A short time later he got sick from cancer and died.

Here for the first time I identified with my father, whom I had fought with bitterly while growing up. If only what he suffered would not happen to me! I swore to myself that nobody was going to do that to me. In the background there resonated something of revenge for the sufferings of my poor father. Some of my expectations had been affected by his "appointment as a director." I moved cautiously, and I waited for the blow to fall at any moment.

And it came, scarcely three weeks after I had taken my place at the bigger desk of my predecessor. Siegfried Unseld, the mighty and difficult Suhrkamp publisher, did not take it lightly that the new young man at the head of the Book Fair had found fault with his earlier work, and let his feelings be known with a devastating three-page critique. The letter was delivered to me—with the hint of a smile—by the general director of the German Publishers Association (the *Börsenverein des Deutschen Buchhandels*). With the patronizing air of a good buddy, he showed me the document that was addressed not to me, but to the current chair of the supervisory board Ulrich Staudinger, with copies to be sure—and this was a bit vicious—to the director of the German Publishers Association Rolf Keller, to "state minister" Arnold in the Foreign Office (who was not in fact a minister of any sort, but only the manager of the cultural department), to Mr. Fehr, of the management board of Inter Nationes, and to Hans Hermann Kahle, general secretary of the Goethe Institute.

The letter was teeming with reproaches against the exhibition work that was going on, work that I was known to be responsible for. In particular Unseld hammered away at the book exhibit in France, which had just recently been opened, *Une societé vivante–eine lebende Gesellschaft*. The exhibit was said to have "no focus," and left "the book trade visitors completely confused." A book exhibit, "which merely lines up book after book, and in very crowded conditions at that, is a dead exhibit because it frustrates every visitor." It seemed "as if the organizers had never learned anything of modern exhibit techniques." The choice of the books to be exhibited "was completely obscure, and often absurd." One could only label the presentation as "set up on the higgledy-piggledy principle." He summarized his exhibit criticism thus: *I consider such an exhibition to be senseless. It does not serve the purposes of the German book in France; it does not give any picture of our living society, and it does not speak well for the German language or for German interests. It is certainly not an effective element of German cultural policy. I can only imagine what this exhibit cost all of us.*

One could certainly think about our admittedly somewhat exotic activity abroad as one wished. We ourselves often had second thoughts about the purpose and goals of these exhibits, but in the end we were convinced that an inter-cultural dialogue would succeed through the medium of the book. The delivery of such a fundamental reproof by an apparent professional to the hands of the Foreign Office, which extensively promoted these exhibits—that would place their continuation in undeniable jeopardy.

As the novice at the head of the Fair, but also the one who was directly responsible, the questioning of this work by its major financial supporter might be reason enough to send me a pink slip and show me the door, particularly since I had not yet had an opportunity to prove myself in my leadership position and could only point to what I had done previously. Now came this savage criticism of the exposition.

The director of the Publishers Association, whom I had barely gotten acquainted with, had come to me in such a friendly manner and had surreptitiously allowed me to be involved in what was being said in the illustrious circles of our organization about me and my work. After all, this letter had not been directed either to me or to him, and he saw himself in a kind of supervisory role over me. He had his reasons, which were not purely of collegial sympathies.

In general, I was astounded. The departure of Sigfred Taubert had left a power vacuum, which I really did not want to fill. Weren't power and its outer signs suspect and unacceptable to me because of the way these tended to corrupt people? At the moment, I could hardly sit in the great black leather chair behind Taubert's desk, let alone make my leadership abilities clear with an enormous pounding of my fist on the furniture! Focusing sternly but gently, I had set about analyzing the existing structures of the Fair. Here I wanted to make a start; there I wanted to convince others. I believed that with my abilities I would win recognition as a leader in my new position. However, after these first weeks, I began to have an inkling that I would scarcely have time for that.

First of all I had to understand that in this company everything had been tailor-made for my predecessor. There were no other structures. This applied to the Fair and to the organization of work within the team. Barely was the master out of the house when the internal struggles for influence and mandates began. Taubert's assistant Manfred G., who had understood himself to be his master's voice and the second-in-command at the Fair, began to clash with Franz-Josef Fenke, who, as the one responsible for the technical flow of the Fair, wanted to push his way into that post as assistant. The power struggles also broke out in my former department. Ronald Weber, who by way of his seniority had stepped in as my successor in the department, had to defend himself against strong attacks by a power-hungry colleague Ingo-Eric Schmidt-Braul. He soon overcame Weber, who in the end ceded direction of the department.

To my great astonishment, my predecessor Sigfred Taubert now reappeared in the office, and demanded work assignments for himself. The Supervisory Board, without my knowledge, had concluded a consulting contract with him for five years, and now Taubert, who had not been having an easy time of it since his departure, wanted to fulfill this contract and thus facilitate the transition to retirement.

That letter came fluttering into this setting amidst my hesitant behavior, accompanied by whispered comments by the head of the Publishers Association. At that moment everything became crystal clear. I could not do this job casually, as a competent technocrat. What was happening here was only the beginning, the beginning of the decline into collapse. I instinctively knew that a fundamental question was being put to me that would decisively influence my future in this company—a question of power.

The question of power is posed to anyone who wishes to manage, whether he wishes to lead a military group, a religious sect or a business organization. I was not a person who loved power. Power was repugnant to me. I had always mistrusted power and battled against it whenever it had appeared in my life, in the form of demands from teachers, politicians and ministers, or from my father. From one point of view, my entire youth had been a clash with power. I wished to be able to survive as *primus inter pares,* a first among *equals,* if I were to devote myself to such an organization and to merit the position that had been assigned to me.

In a social system in which power is open to all, the posts which confer power will, as a rule, be occupied by men who differ from the average in being exceptionally power-loving, wrote Bertrand Russell in his famous treatise on the nature of power in society, published in 1938.[1] He adds immediately thereafter a description of what was then the new type of powerful personality in the large business organizations, the so-called "executive," as it had been bequeathed to us from the United States: *The typical "executive" impresses others as a man of rapid decisions, quick insight into character, and iron will; he must have a firm jaw, tightly closed lips, and a habit of brief and incisive speech. He must be able to inspire respect in equals, and confidence in subordinates who are by no means nonentities. He must combine the qualities of a great general and a great diplomatist; ruthless in battle, but a capacity for skilful concession in negotiation. It is by such qualities that men acquire control of important economic organisations.*[2]

Well, even with a massive overestimation of my abilities, I would never have been able to conform to this ideal picture of a business leader. Besides, I did not want to match this image. Till now I had only committed myself to my new role halfheartedly. If I hoped to avert disaster and traumatic failure, and to forestall the tragedy that overcame my father, now I had to "seize power," whether I liked it or not. I had to make it clear with absolute decisiveness that I was a factor to be reckoned with. This decision could only mean desiring success with all my might and with my total commitment, by shaking off ambivalence and becoming absolutely resolute.

Several times in my life till then I had prescribed the kind of decisiveness that I felt in those early February days of 1975. I took on and occupied the position of general director of the Exposition and Fair Company (*Ausstellungs- und Messe GmbH* or AUM) and that of the director of the Frankfurt Book Fair, even though there were still many things in this role that were still incomprehensible to me, unacceptable, or even odd.

I lay awake for three nights after the Unseld letter. My most all-encompassing feeling was one of insecurity. Thoughts of flight came first, followed by philosophical arguments about the true meaning of my life. This is the state that a person gets

1. Bertrand Russell, *Power: A New Social Analysis* (London: Allen & Unwin, 1946), 12.
2. *Ibid.*, 46.

into when everything comes at once, when an entire host of ideas, a stampede of sensations cause one to seek salvation by running away. Who then gives the command of *Stop!* Who can bring a halt to this wild horde of considerations?

In my case it was the chasm before me, the anxiety of failing—and the anger over my father's fall. It was quite clear to me that I had maneuvered myself into a situation that in my heart of hearts I really did not want. But once I was in it, failure was not an option. *What had happened to the old man wasn't going to happen to me!*

I had to decide to become the "Director" of the Frankfurt Book Fair. And so I did. More quickly than expected, I positioned myself in that big black leather chair! The Unseld letter had come at the right time. He had challenged me early on by putting my position in question. If he had not emerged, I would have certainly continued to act as I had for quite some time. How long would that have been successful?

I got a copy of the letter before the company director disappeared again with his copy, and set about sending a properly improper answer to the complaint that was not directed to me.

Siegfried Unseld had made my task easier by being completely wrong on the facts. My clarification took up four pages, and ended with a call for somewhat more solidarity in our industry—I couldn't leave that out! Naturally I sent it to the same distribution list that Unseld had used.

I had always shied away from this tool of distributing copies and had rarely used it, although this sending a "FYI copy" was justifiably a favorite means in business for getting one's way, for disparaging others, and for battling hierarchies. In this case I couldn't do without it; my hand was forced.

There naturally followed an agitated back and forth, since the "proper channels" had not been maintained, and since I, impudent and cocky as I was, had dared to answer such a letter that had not been addressed to me. Nonetheless, after a hastily called round of discussions, the scene quickly quieted down again. People had been made aware that I was not "predictable." In other words, *you had better be careful!* I had sent up an important signal that was clearly understood.

Siegfried Unseld never held my "emancipation proclamation" against me, even though it had clearly come at his cost. It turned out that he had been angered about an announcement in the *German Publishers Weekly* (*Börsenblatt für den Deutschen Buchhandel*) of the exhibit in the U.S., in which two former Suhrkamp editors, Wieland Schulz-Keil and Michael Roloff, whom I had approached in the U.S. as contact persons for the American book scene, had been mentioned as my co-workers. Both of them were at odds with Unseld, and that had been the emotional trigger for his audacious letter.

Now I had truly pounded my fist onto my big writing table. It was only a beginning, though I didn't get any tougher, but just continued to move along swiftly. Otherwise nothing had been resolved. All the same problems persisted, and other than myself, few people around me had noticed the change.

When Sigfred Taubert reappeared the next day, I asked him not to set foot in our offices for a year, giving a short explanation that I had to take control of the enterprise. With eyes wide with surprise, he left, and for exactly one year to the day he did not reappear. Now I could analyze and bring some order to the muddle that I had found around me.

My predecessor was not a systematic person; his strengths lay elsewhere. When Sigfred Taubert took over the Book Fair in 1957, it was about to develop from a German book dealer fair into an international professional exhibition. Taubert had dedicated himself to this development with all his strength and enthusiasm. Over the course of the years, he had spread a network of personal friendships over the book world, and in so doing had created world-wide connections to Frankfurt, all of which strengthened one another.

He had thought of this continually growing Book Fair as his own family, and had added the newcomers to those who were already there. His style as the head of the Frankfurt Book Fair was that of a liberal, open-minded patriarch, who every year gathered his many family members around him. His greatest service consisted in building up and stabilizing this Frankfurt center. Now participation was growing, and as it grew, Taubert's embrace was soon no longer adequate to grasp, maintain, or even to promote all the new facets and characteristics of this exposition.

In the Taubert era the Frankfurt Book Fair had become an international fair for rights and licenses. The publishers who came from afar to Frankfurt sought out other exhibitors in order to do business with them; they did not come for the customers walking in off the street. In light of the growing scope of the exposition and its needs, we now had to create procedures for support, such as help in finding business associates. Our well-constructed catalog, oriented to bibliophiles, and the simple stall numbers alone were not sufficient for orientation. Communication systems were needed; paths had to be shortened; conference rooms and meeting sites had to be created. In this regard the infrastructure of the Frankfurt Fairgrounds had little to offer.

The characteristic quality of Taubert's leadership was strong emotion. That's the way he got his co-workers to do everything to solve the problems that emerged. The colleagues did their best to solve the problems as well as they could. And that's how the team in the building on Kleiner Hirschgraben Street had come to be Taubert's family. He ruled with a not quite care-free atmosphere of "voluntary" fitting in. "Trust" and "Disappointment" constituted the premises of Taubert's leadership style. That's the way he could manage the ever more quickly growing child prodigy called the Frankfurt Book Fair for so long. Now, however, this hitherto so well-behaved child was suddenly developing new traits, which extended well beyond a closed exposition for one business sector. Something new had emerged as a result of the student demonstrations of 1968—the "social relevance" of the Book Fair was discovered. And on the way my esteemed predecessor was practically torn apart, because suddenly his control mechanisms no longer worked.

Taubert's departure marked not only the end of a generation, but also the end of an epoch at the Book Fair. For years on end many of the participants in the Book Fair would look back longingly at something that had ceased to exist—the Book Fair as one big family of the book business. The Fair had achieved its size as a multi-layered event, with business significance, but also with a cultural import that called for professional structures and easier ways of doing business; in short, a definite product offering from the organizers. I began to understand what my task in the coming years would be.

This task appeared gigantic to me. It was no longer the black, unknown sea, in which I was helplessly being tossed about without compass or sextant. Suddenly it became a mountain rising up in front of me, one that I wanted to chip away at with my toy shovel. Where should I start? Where would be a logical place to begin? I decided simply to start. My approach did not consist of producing a completely new fair in the first year of my being in office. I went to work and submitted the Fair to a thorough review, item by item and element by element.

The first item was to attend to all the correspondence with the exhibitors, to be worked on with my experienced graphic artists and friends, Reinhard Schubert, Klaus Janorschke and Tom Röder. Here, in recent years, a wild variety of official forms had grown up, so many that one could hardly get through them. For each new need of the exhibitor, a new form had come into being. We tightened up and assembled related information; we put it all in order, and then we created three information groups bundled together as supply, information and services. The invitation to the 1975 Book Fair for the first time gave our correspondents a clearly laid out offering of services.

What applied to communication with the exhibitors was no different from the case of straightening out admissions. There were 21 types of admission tickets—special tickets for students and soldiers for a limited time, total fair passes for apprentices in the profession, for workers at the fair, for private visitors, exhibitors, book dealers. There were complimentary tickets for full-fair entry and complimentary cards for single visits, press cards, tour cards for half an hour, *etc*. I reduced this hodgepodge of admission tickets to eight types, and was thereby able to score a publicity coup that was not to be underestimated. Since I deleted many of the cards with special prices, I was able to reduce the individual entry prices by one half without causing any loss of income, something that immediately was played up by the press to the reading public as a new policy. It was commented on very positively.

I do not want to describe the many steps forward that I took against the looming mountain. As soon as I finished working on one problem area of the Fair, new problems opened up, which I thought had to be taken care of. In the course of things, the people around me in the Association and in the business sector seemed to look ever more skeptical and more disturbed.

A new target of attack by my critics was the supposed destruction of the "Good Old Fair" by "foolishness," which I supposedly wanted to impose. A letter came in from a former chairman to Mr. Staudinger, the current chairman of the Supervisory Board:

Dear Mr. Staudinger,

*I am writing to you from my skiing vacation, somewhat disturbed by a notice in the newspaper (*FAZ** of March 6) about plans to sprinkle the Fair with all kinds of advertisements. That is what they say about the new thematic program, the Woman in Literature (what a worn-out cliché!) and the topic of Latin America.*

I have been hearing how the enemies of our Frankfurt—and these are many and mighty—say to their people: "What do you care about a South American Fair in Frankfurt?" And this South American production? Who in the name of God is going to buy anything other than South Americans? This is really not a fair, but a cultural exposition. And "accompanying literature discussion groups and film weeks"—these are the cultural management notions (what notions!) of my honorable friend H.H.† *He is still laughing about it. Nobody is really going to come to Frankfurt for these "reading circles," but lots of people who are in Frankfurt will have their Fair work destroyed by these groups.*

And then "The Woman in Literature"—oh God! Is this supposed to mean "belles-lettres," or does this include gynecology and "the fashionable garden"? And in belles-lettres? Is there any without a woman? Does this mean old maids, transvestites and Lolitas? Or does this mean the woman as author?

This is really not a topic at all, at least not for a fair, at which belles-lettres make up at the most 25%. We go to the Fair to exhibit books and to sell them. Otherwise nothing! What do these completely

* FAZ—*Frankfurter Allgemeine Zeitiung*
† *H.H.*—Hilmar Hoffmann.

unoriginal ideas have to do with anything other than result in messing up the running of the fair?

Hopefully, dear Mr. Staudinger, you can prevent this.... What's going to happen to our beautiful, great, old successful fair in the face of such tomfoolery?

In friendship...

What was it that disturbed our former Chairman, who had done so much for the Fair? The Fair had grown out of its innocence as a part of one economic sector. Through the events of 1968, it had grown into something with cultural, social and political meaning that was not apparent to those book dealers who knew and loved the old Fair and wanted to keep it the way it had been. The discussions and the arguments of the people of 1968 were, for them, merely an occupational hazard to be overcome. And then everything would again be the way it used to be.

This was however impossible, for something had come out of the heated discussions with the literary producers of those years—the critical public.

At the 1965 Fair, barely 100 journalists came to file reports, but then their number grew in the wake of the public events of 1968 to 1000, increased in 1972 to 3,000, and by the middle of the 1970s had grown to 5,000 reporters. This concentrated media power stayed on, but the students who cared about the content that the media had once reported on had disappeared. The Fair as the good old trade exposition, such as the one that the upset letter writer wanted to retain, had grown brittle, and in its commercial structures of unending display booths presented little of value to report on.

As a result, the reporters grew increasingly frustrated, more aggressive and more critical. They went to those who merely wanted to carry on commerce, and asked them about the cultural significance of the Fair. This time marked the beginning of the strategically prepared bestseller campaigns for the biographies of prominent people, which was quite dramatic in the case of Muhammad Ali. A conflict broke out here that couldn't be resolved on its own. Each of the two approaches, that of the book trade and that of the media, was convinced of the value of their own approach, but they talked right past each other.

The result was a generally critical picture of the book trade as painted by the media, a negative view which radiated out from the Book Fair and contaminated the whole world. The business sector and the Book Fair had an image problem! Like all the other people responsible for the Fair, I had followed this development for the past two years attentively and with increasing astonishment.

I remember one meeting of the Supervisory Board with a dozen journalists in the big conference hall of Radio Hesse. It was the exact same story. The higher-ups at the Fair argued in a moralizing tone: "But you can't just... but you also must..., look around at art, religion, science. It's not all bestsellers!" And the journalists: "You can't tell us what to write. You represent special interests, and we report what we see!"

It was clear to me that we had to accept the public as participants in the Book Fair as well as serve the previous classical participants, the publishing houses who exhibited and the professional trade. We had to offer some content that was not primarily oriented to business interests. And we had to deal with and guide the press.

This was the moment of birth of topical themes for the Book Fair, which I wanted to start in the following year with the exposition of "Latin American Literature." During 1975 I had prepared several programs for the "Year of the Woman," partially as a test run and to get experience.

The excited resistance in the main melted away when it turned out that the presentations of topical themes in no way altered the character of the trade fair, or barely touched it, while on the other hand something had been added to the Fair that resolved our image problem. It was the right answer to welcome the active participation of the public in the Book Fair. At any rate, this is what the experiences with the topical theme of "Latin America" showed clearly in 1976.

Massaging the Media

Was there really anybody who knew the Fair and who knew just what it needed? *Oh yes,* there were plenty who knew. Everybody knew what the problem was. Everybody knew what ought to be done! Everyone, it seemed, except me. Long-time exhibitors naturally knew it before everyone else, as they envisaged just what a perfect Frankfurt Book Fair would look like—*from their point of view*. Even though the conceptions of a German literary publisher might be diametrically opposed to those of a foreign scientific publisher, all of them always went on about "we" and "us," and demanded for the entire Fair what really only served their own selfish interests.

Who else knew it? The professional public, the German book retailers. They desired to be taken more seriously at the Book Fair. They stuck tenaciously to the idea that the Fair was made for them alone, which in fact had initially been the case. They were, after all, the ones who wanted to sell everything that was exhibited there. They were driven by a basic dissatisfaction. Above all, they didn't like all those foreigners, not to mention the small left-wing publishing houses that were sprouting up all over the place and causing unrest.

Naturally the press and the media also had all the answers. They had retreated to a critical stance from which they painted everything that happened in those years at the Fair as a money-grubbing vulgarization of literature and culture, especially when it came to the latest bestsellers and the larger-than-life biographies. It was among the representatives of the press that one could most clearly discern the lingering resentments and crushed aspirations of 1968.

Of course my colleagues also knew what to do, since they had been with the Fair longer than I had. Here Manfred G. in particular stood out, as he gave me clearly to understand that

I would be a lost soul without him and the other co-workers whom he claimed to speak for.

The group that combined in itself all the knowledge about the Book Fair and had resolutely institutionalized it all was the executive committee, in the form of the Supervisory Board, that had undertaken to guide me. According to the German law of corporations, a supervisory board actually has only a limited influence and only limited rights over management. Here however things were different.

Since the German Publishers and Booksellers Association (the *Börsenverein des Deutschen Buchhandels*) was the sole owner of the Exposition and Fair Company (the *Austellungs- und Messe GmbH,* or AUM), this particular supervisory board also acted as the general shareholders meeting, and it could naturally function and reign as it pleased. And it did so with the sublime conviction that it embodied the book trade in its totality, and that it would take care of its needs and rights against a business management led by "God knows what."

In this way, a quite independent and self-deceiving sense of reality obtained among these nine gentlemen of the board—six German publishers, two German book dealers and a German wholesale book dealer. At that time, three quarters of the exhibitors came from abroad, but their interests were not represented at all. I was the only one who could speak up for them, which occasioned a fundamental conflict between me and the executive committee.

Why should I beat around the bush? In this company there was not just one management board that administered affairs, and not just one council that monitored finances and set the framework in which one could freely act. There were here two management boards, which eyed each other with distrust and used all kinds of procedural tricks to try to gain the upper hand in the exercise of power and influence. Quite apart from the running of the Fair, it was this never-ending power struggle that in the following 25 years consumed all my energies, and again and again led to explosive crises. The history of my management of the Frankfurt Book Fair is a history of my clashes with this supervisory board.

Every appointee of the German Publishers Association attempted to bring the Frankfurt Book Fair back into the arms of its parent, that German Publishers Association. This in fact occurred after my departure through a reform of the association by way of a new holding company. A conflict of this magnitude could never have arisen simply out of the petty-mindedness and inflexibility of a particular manager. At no moment could the years-long conflict between the association people and me be reduced to the logic of personal differences (not to say grievances).

Every living being tries to be a unity. The goal, the expression of the unity that is achieved, is one's identity. This is no different for an organization than it is for an individual. From my point of view, the Book Fair was a living organism, one that was continually striving for a unified and integral identity. In the same way one can, and should, consider the German Publishers Association as the organ of expression of the German book trade. Such organisms strive to find themselves and to assert themselves, just as individuals do. It was here that the defects of the arrangement showed through.

It was in 1964 that three powerful publishing personalities (Dr. Alfred Metzner, Friedrich Georgi and Dr. Caspar Witsch) freed the Book Fair organizational office from its internal dependence on the German Publishers Association and prescribed an independent course. They recognized that the Fair, with its international tasks and goals, had to hammer out a new path, divergent from the one marked out by the national goals of the Publishers Association. The German Publishers Association declared itself the parent company of the new, independent institution, the AUM (which I headed), and let it go its own way with an independent set of bylaws—though to be sure with a whole series of reservations. Such a parting of the ways never occurs freely and without internal struggles, since all entities have a will of their own and a voracious ego. They unwillingly gave up something that at one time they had regarded as their own. This is no different in institutions than it is with unreasonable parents. It requires a strong, rational and responsible intent on the part of the parents and/or just as strong a desire on the part of the still maturing body whose future is at stake. In the case of the AUM, it was thanks to the broad vision of these three men in the German Publishers Association that the Book Fair finally was set on its own weak legs with the mission of "Find your way by yourself!"

At that time, in 1964, it was a difficult struggle of persuasion against the hard-line faction in the German Publishers Association in order to take this step. Soon enough, the arguments were forgotten that had led to the founding of the AUM and the freeing of the Book Fair from the internal network of relationships and interests in the German Publishers Association. The subsequent representatives of the Publishers Association did everything that they could to prevent the independent development of this new institution, and to restrain it as tightly as possible in favor of the goals and wishes of the members and the executive committee of the German Publishers Association, goals and wishes which often were personally motivated. In later years, some people even attempted to reverse the decision and to again take the splendidly developing Book Fair Corporation under their own wing.

It was true that my predecessor Sigfred Taubert also had suffered under the constraints of this situation in trying to make independent decisions for the Book Fair, and in attempting to implement them against the demands of the members of the Publishers Association on the Supervisory Council. But with me—and I couldn't help but be suspicious that I had been chosen for the succession as an ostensibly manipulable young man—they thought from the very beginning that they would have to prevent any ambition for self-sufficiency of the Frankfurt Book Fair. As early as 1973—when I had not even been installed and was still working with my U.S. book exhibit—a first, seemingly amateurish "reform" attempt by the German Publishers Association to dissolve the AUM and to integrate the organizational structures of the Frankfurt Book Fair into the German Publishers Association fell through.

When I finally took office, it was soon clear that the struggle for the independence of the leading book fair of the world's publishing trade was now up to me, and that it would be quite toilsome. I was hindered in this task in that even during my seven-year period of belonging to the company, I had no clear idea of what was happening. Before I could even orient myself, external demands crashed down upon me.

Nonetheless, I accepted the challenge. As I came to understood that these blows were not directed at me personally, but rather directed at my function as the new bearer of the unloved independence of the Book Fair, I quickly came to identify with the goals and conditions of the Fair. My own identity and that of the Book Fair, which was under attack, became one. My own personality solidified as I went about strengthening the Book Fair. A very tight, close bond grew between me and my job. I had become a part of the Book Fair. I completely justified the name "Mr. Frankfurt," which was later bestowed on me by many foreign exhibitors. I became the Book Fair itself. Its limbs were my limbs; its pains were my pains; its goals were my goals.

These were the conditions prevailing as I set about raising the first Fair "of my own" out of the baptismal font. I stood before this "Colossus," and intuited how particular interests threatened to capture me. I wanted the Fair to grow of its own will and find its own way. There had to be some point from which the means, the growth tendencies and the zones of stagnation of the Fair could be recognized from the inside, not from the point of view of vested interests, but also not from some pre-set position prevailing over the entire project.

I knew very little about the mode of functioning and the interconnections of this mammoth exhibition, and even less, so it seemed, than all the people around me. And so I threw myself into the work. I saw myself identified with the object of my desire and made it the very fabric of my life. While I continued to work on the Fair, I was working on myself. That made me enormously focused in my decisions. This meant that I could develop my plans out of an inner necessity, and link them with existing conditions. For me, my work on the Fair turned into a creative act.

This attitude, however, also made me enormously vulnerable. I suffered because of the conflicts with the Supervisory Board. Each time my nerves were wildly irritated, and I could not objectively deal with whatever topic we were arguing about. I took everything "personally," since every attack on the Fair was at the same time an attack on my life's work. I showed myself to be quite competent at getting what I wanted with this attitude, since everything that I expressed came out of a unified whole. But what needs, what pains, what despair I suffered because of this tight psychological bond, which ultimately depended on factors that were beyond my control.

As I set about managing the annual "creation" of the Book Fair, I quickly realized that I had no tools for speaking out. The Book Fair had no organs for expression or instruments of communication with its customers; it had no publicity for its business sector. It had no access to the press or the media. Except for the invitations that were sent out, there were no possibilities for contact with the outside. The origin of the Book Fair was the general book trade magazine of the German Publishers Association, the *German Publishers Weekly* (*Börsenblatt*), and contact with the press was controlled by the press department of the German Publishers Association. Yes, indeed, not even the design of the annual Book Fair advertisements or of the catalog cover lay within our authority.

The battle for in-house control of the graphics for the Fair publicity lasted ten years. Up to that point the tasteless overlay of the Book Fair logo on the chosen color of the year were the rule for public signboards. Only in 1987 did the German Publishers Association, through the Supervisory Board, finally allow the AUM to replace the established Book Fair logo overlaid on the German Publishers Association logo. So I gave every one of my four graphic artists the task of designing a sign that retained our logo under the company name, and would sit playfully alongside the Publishers Association logo. The four designs were seductively colored, humorous and eye-catching. I presented all four designs to the Supervisory Board, which, as in the preceding ten years, did not want to choose any of them. I finally decided simply to accept all four. From this time on, each year our graphic artists designed several signs, which we used alternately.

At the time of the separation of the Fair office from the Publishers Association and the founding of the AUM in 1964, dealings with the press remained the domain of the communications department of the Publishers Association. If it was simply a matter of saving costs, as was claimed, or whether the higher-ups in the Association wanted to preserve their influence by silencing the Fair Company, is something that will never be known for certain. However, the struggle for an independent, professional management of the press went on for a full 20 years, and it was only in 1995 that it was possible to make the arrangements I thought necessary.

More and more, the negotiations degenerated into a power struggle. I began to clash with the Publishers Association right then in 1975, when for the first time I set up a dedicated journalists' corner, which I asked one of my charges to mind. In the 26 years of its existence, the Fair had never thought it necessary to make any specific arrangements for the journalists covering the Fair. I was actually thankful for this omission, and had made a writing cubicle of a few old Fair walls. I put some typewriters in, connected a few telephone lines and served free coffee. For the first time, the entire press corps at the Fair felt themselves accepted as a group. They were no longer made to feel that only the select few with special access to the press spokesman of the German Publishers Association got all the leads.

Internally I appointed someone as a "press consultant," as the people "over there" in the German Publishers Association might call it, but we weren't allowed to use this name, and actually we had no right to have such a person at all. We called him our *clandestine* press chief, whom we intended gradually to put in place as the director of a true communications department. Over 20 years passed before we reached this goal, and a number of very capable people were worn out in this position or early on called it quits: Doris Oberländer, Karin Hoffmann, Michael Fenderl, the Australian Diet Simon, Helmut Muth, and finally Helmut von der Lahr. The last-named was openly introduced as "press assistant of the AUM," though only provisionally, and was only responsible for the foreign press. At this time too, at the beginning of the 1990s, we struggled with the Publishers Association over who would stand on the podium and moderate the opening press conference—the press spokesman of the Publishers Association or our own spokesman. Year after year, I was involved in clashes with the German Publishers Association; I had to keep rebounding from such scuffles. Early on, it became clear that this was a struggle for power and influence, a matter of defining the path that the Book Fair would follow.

My First Fair

"The image of the Frankfurt Book Fair is problematic!" That was the message that I emphasized at the meeting of the Supervisory Board taking up the issue. I started up a "Welcome Newspaper." Titled *Welcome To Book Fair City,* 20,000 copies were sent out to all exhibitors, distributed to bookstores throughout the country, and displayed in all the Frankfurt hotels. The newspaper was actually a brochure set up in newspaper style, and gave information in English and German to visitors, including practical tips on restaurants, entertainment, cultural programs, how to get around, and general information about the Fair. The brochure was extraordinarily successful. It had been made according to the most contemporary principles of design. With Manfred G. in charge, we had developed this publication ourselves in-house with a good deal of effort and enthusiasm.

The big reception for guests of the Frankfurt Book Fair was spread out among rather sterile cocktail receptions at the municipal theater. I took it upon myself to create a new feeling of community, and at the same time I planned an assault on the negative image of Frankfurt itself. The conditions for overnight stays and for leisure time had plagued the Fair with horror stories. These included the building of the Frankfurt subway in the 1960s, which transformed the city into one giant construction zone; the hotel prices, which during the Fair periods reached dizzying heights; the poor service in hotels, restaurants and public transportation; the poor food—at that time there were essentially only German restaurants, with very little international fare.

I had the idea of acquainting our guests with the cultural offerings and other interesting sights of the city during an evening reception. I began to speak with the directors of the museums. Negotiations with the Städel Art Museum foundered over insurance issues after months of discussion, but I was finally successful in obtaining the Senckenberg Natural History Museum for the soirée. This evening became quite an event. Conversations under the giant dinosaur skeletons never ceased. It was also documented in photos sent out by the local newspapers and the world media that the "Dinosaur Fair" was also offering happy times, fun experiences and a personal touch.

At the same time I began to deal with the understaffed reception for foreign delegations, which was a general event sponsored by the city of Frankfurt and the German Publishers Association, by moving it to the Senckenburg Museum. For the first time, I allowed someone from the Soviet Union to speak for the foreign delegations, the director of the State Committee for Publishing (Goskomizdat) in Moscow, Irakles Chikrishvili, who was very gratified at being allowed to represent the total body of exhibitors.

The improved price structure for admission and more transparent lines of communication with exhibitors were only the beginning of a package of innovations. In cooperation with Frankfurt's cultural director, Hilmar Hoffmann, we took over the historic Römer City Hall to put on what people came to call a "literature circus," a kind of talk show featuring authors. This "circus" enjoyed a 20-year run at the Book Fair. All in all, what was new in substance and style that first year was very well received, as evidenced by the many letters from the expanded circle of participants. I could not have expected more for this first Fair under my leadership. It had again grown by 136 exhibiting publishers to 2,387 individual exhibitors, plus 1,652 participants at shared stalls.

For the opening in 1975, I had thought of something special without letting the Supervisory Board in on all the details. The chairman Staudinger had been informed, and had expressed no objections. I wanted to break up the exhausting program of speeches with a literary interlude supported by some spiffy music. I assigned this task to the renowned Brecht director Peter Palitzsch, who showed off Bertolt Brecht at his best with some rousing songs and poems presented by actors from the Frankfurt Theater. However, there was a hitch. We had forgotten the piano, and as a result there was a refreshing pause in the fancy Festival exposition as two workers in their blue overalls shoved the instrument, mounted on a squeaky dolly, through the surprised public gathering, and then with fulminating grunts heaved it onto the stage. Then the actors appeared. At first everything seemed to go well. The good-natured audience had put on its liberal face and became engaged with the joy of the literature: "Aha, that was Brecht, let's see what's coming now!"

But that's all there was, only Brecht. I had assumed that Brecht was already a German classic, and that at an international literature meeting in Germany one could certainly allow oneself to let a modern classic have the last word.

I was wrong. The faces of the honorable festival company became grimmer and grimmer, especially that of the right-wing conservative federal Minister of the Economy Hans Friderichs of the Free Democrats, who had been the introductory speaker. When he jumped up and started to rush out during the Brecht poem *Questions from a Worker Who Reads*,[1] I gave Palitzsch a signal to end the presentation after that text. It was obvious to me that I had miscalculated.

It was then that I had my first major altercation with the "Supervisory Board," which felt itself deceived. Members did not take me at my word that what was involved here was nothing more than a literary presentation and an attempt to enliven the often sterile opening reception. Instead they supposed that I had opened the gates wide with my supposedly "Socialist" philosophy. I was absolutely astounded at the almost hysterical attacks by some members of the Supervisory Board, who shouted at me like madmen. It was clear to me that I had transgressed the required offering of "balance" in such situations. In the future I would not be able to afford such naïvity.

In addition, there were other problems in the world that now disturbed the contested "Peace of the Fair." In Spain, the slowly disintegrating regime of the old and enfeebled dictator

---

1. A well-known poem by Bertolt Brecht. The first verse: *Who built seven-gated Thebes? / Books tell but the names of Kings. / Did the kings ever haul quarry? / And Babylon, many times razed, / Who rebuilt it each time? / In what houses of gold-glinting Lima did the builders live?*

Francisco Franco reared its ugly head once again by having five young men executed for belonging to an underground organization opposing a regime that had survived long past its time. Franco, who died a month after the Book Fair, had ruled the country as a dictator for 40 years; between 1940 and 1944 alone, he had 190,000 people executed.

The *Caudillo* had also led Spain into economic ruin. At the time of the Fair, everyone was ready to believe that the worst was over and that the tender seedling of democracy in Spain was ready to sprout. The world, and particularly the still very politicized students, who had put up with Franco for so long, now came together in uproar over the executions. Demonstrations took place all over Europe, including at the Book Fair, which had been sensitized by the events of 1968. I was completely in sympathy with this expression of opinion, but I also had to protect the persons and property of our exhibitors and ensure a smooth exhibition. My problem lay less with the some 150 student protesters, who wanted to occupy the stall of the Instituto Nacional del Libro Español, but rather with the police, who after the events of recent years still had a civil war street-fighting mentality. The old-timer group commander Wilchek considered me to be a closet Leftie, to be kept under close surveillance. I simply could not get rid of this image. So I placed myself between students and the police cordon, and I worked to prevent one side from provoking the other, until after about two hours the whole thing dissolved by itself.

Since I was held fast at this Spanish booth, I could not be at the Soviet Union booth at the right time, where on the same afternoon a Maoist group tried to break into the stall area. The staff of the booth, made up of Soviet officials and employees of the Brücken publishing house that imported Soviet literature, attempted to prevent the occupation, and a hand to hand fight ensued. The German director of the booth, Mr. Meyer from the Brücken publishing house, was beaten and injured. Manfred G., my problematic employee, had hurried over there instead of me, and with his lack of sensibility was unable to restrain himself from telling off the director of the Soviet copyright office (the VAAP), who was wildly cursing the "Fascists," by saying, "We decide who is a Fascist here!"

That very evening I, together with the assistant director of the Book Fair, the attorney Franz-Wilhelm Peter, had to listen to a sharply worded protest from the Soviet delegation, led by Irakles Chikrishvili, who held ministerial rank. Later we received this protest in written form.

The following day, a *German Publishers Weekly Extra* appeared, which in the opinion of the Soviets gave a completely false report and ignited their mood a second time. I was forced to have a long conversation on Sunday morning with the members of the Soviet group and with the representatives of the Soviet Embassy, who had in the meantime arrived, during which I expressed the regrets of the management of the Fair and agreed to a proper clarification in the *Publishers Weekly*. It was true that our Soviet friends were very sensitive, but on the other hand the exchange of rights in Frankfurt was extraordinarily important for them, as it was for us as customers. Their share in the sales in the legal business was estimated to be several million dollars a year, and climbing.

On the evening of that same Sunday, the confrontation that I had feared between the police and some demonstrators took place. According to the police report, the demonstrators had intended to tear down the Spanish stall. The police sprayed the crowd with Mace and took three persons into custody for "review of their identification papers." Since one of those booked was an employee of Saarland Radio, there were strong reactions by the other representatives of the press. The billing of the "literature circus" in the town hall that evening was hijacked and turned into a protest meeting, where people demanded the immediate release of the three people who had been detained for questioning. I attempted with all my might to get an explanation from the criminal police about the case and eventually to achieve a release. Late on a Sunday evening, this was an undertaking that could try one's patience. Finally, at around two o'clock in the morning, the employee of the Saarland Radio was released. At close to 6 AM the other two persons were freed from custody.

Since a group led by some employees of the Neue Kritik publishing house wanted to occupy the press center for a press conference about the affair, I quickly forestalled the intervention of the police by making a separate conference room available to this group of journalists.

My relationship to the police became increasingly strained. I was not successful at getting a clear explanation for what happened, while the police on their side felt provoked by the reports in the daily press. At the end of the Fair, I tried to calm things down somewhat in a conversation with Mr. Vogel, the Frankfurt police commissioner.

I was sitting in my office chair at my desk in the director's office of the Fair, trying to relax a bit between visits of delegations, greetings of politicians and complaints from publishers. All of a sudden, with no warning, his fists punching the air with jabs and uppercuts, barging in came the "Sportsman of the Century"— so crowned by *Sports Illustrated* and the BBC—Muhammad Ali (*né* Cassius Clay), the greatest boxer of his time.

"The Greatest" looked quite grim. He grimaced, *What am I supposed to be doing here?* Behind him a whole baggage train of photographers crammed in, their flashbulbs lighting up the air. He did them a favor and posed with some fierce moves. Then he became somewhat friendlier, but still not really charming, and greeted me with a powerful handshake. He towered over me. After a few minutes he was gone, and with him that babbling gaggle of photographers. Calm was restored. Franz-Josef Fenke, the technical director of the Book Fair, had found him outside in the corridors and had piloted him in to me in order to do me a favor.

This was the year of memoirs at the Book Fair. Muhammad Ali's *The Greatest* was launched. Franz Beckenbauer was looking for an audience for his book, *Someone Like Me;* Klaus Kinski presented his confessions, *I Am So Wild About Your Strawberry Mouth.* Gina Lollobrigida was prancing about in the exhibition halls. Hildegard Knef was still advertising for her *The Gift Horse,* while Max Frisch portrayed his love late in life in his autobiographical *Montauk*.[2]

---

2. *Franz Beckenbauer*—German soccer star. *Klaus Kinski*—German actor. *Gina Lollobrigida*—Italian actress and sex symbol. *Hildegard Knef*—German actress and singer. *Max Frisch*—Swiss architect and novelist.

After five and a half days, it was clear that once again it was a very satisfactory fair in all areas. The business results for the exhibitors had improved by more than 40%, and we had a satisfaction rating of 88%. The general opinion—a splendid Fair. Basically the mood had become much better. Could I be so presumptuous as to attribute this at least in part to my innovations, which generally came off very well?

I let it go at the fact that the Fair had been successful. At such expositions we always dealt with a blinding strobe-light of opinions, feelings, true successes, attitudes, relationships, changes in the weather, accidents, good and bad books, good and bad information, a bit of business, a bit of an exchange rate situation. Out of all this a judgment was brewed, a positive one or a negative one. As much as I tried in the years to distill this brew and to understand what led to a good or a bad fair, I never succeeded in understanding what did it. Only one thing was quite clear to me after my first Fair—one had to take account of the feelings that ran through the heads of all the Fair participants, because this was as important and as much a component of the presentation at the Fair as were a perfect offering or booth matériel that was up to spec.

It was an important task to work on the mood of all the participants, and for that we needed a good relationship to publicity, that is, the press. This became my goal for the next year, one that I wanted to work on.

Not everybody found the Fair so gratifying, as was proven to me by a derisive piece of doggerel that Jo Hebsacker of the Ensslin Publishing House put in the *German Publishers Weekly* several weeks after the Book Fair. Once again this made clear how certain people in the German book trade had failed to appreciate the transition of the Frankfurt Book Fair to a *World* Book Fair.

Moments at the Frankfurt Book Fair

You have to praise the Fair header
Since he was elevated by one who thought better

Over our little company stage,
The spot was really no match for his age.

And tho he's in the trade organization's pay,
He sees the world quite differently than they.
The global scope of all he addresses
Assures his name in the printing presses.

Public attendance (an inflated figure)
Helps him paint a rosy picture.
Ten old German business leaders at work
Have found him to be just an outsider, a jerk.

And a few come from New York
To help him pop the champagne cork.
For him the Third World is hot,
Something that our dear Germany is not.

The "joker in the deck" is quite sly,
Since our paper makes him look quite a guy.
But some like me see right through this trick,
And can't stand the sight of his little clique.

So we'll soon see how it will all turn about,
How Frankfurt's dance card is filled out.
Let he whose nod to tradition is less than pure
Sit for a while in his own manure.

We've truly never witnessed such conceit,
Just wait till we put him in the hot seat.
Let's just hope he isn't too hare-brained
To learn how the Fair should be maintained.

O colleagues in the German book trade
Express your opinion about what he has made
So that our aim for our good fair
Becomes the goal everywhere.

China

Sigfred Taubert had been negotiating for two years with the Embassy of the People's Republic of China in Bonn regarding a return of the Red Chinese publishers to the Frankfurt Book Fair. They had stayed away since 1957, and their condition for return was unambiguous—exclusion of publishers from "the Chinese province of Taiwan." There was a small group of exhibitors from Taiwan who put in an appearance at Frankfurt on an irregular basis, but the exclusion that was demanded so clearly violated the absolute freedom from censure at the Frankfurt Book Fair—a freedom that had been strongly defended even during the wild events of 1968—that negotiations had come to a standstill. I inherited this unresolved problem, and threw myself energetically into renewed negotiations. I wanted to bring the Chinese to the Book Fair, and beyond that I wanted to travel to China myself. Mao Zedong was still alive; the Cultural Revolution had just collapsed; and a great fascination radiated out of China, especially since so little was known of the actual conditions of life there.

Then an opportunity opened up, and I grabbed at it. For the first time, the Federal Republic of Germany was setting up a German technology exhibit in Beijing (*Techno-Germa*). Although the Chinese coupled the presentation of a German book exhibit in China with what would be for them an acceptable solution to the Taiwan problem, early on I had arranged with the German organizer of *Techno-Germa* for a small book exhibit of technical and architectural literature. I used this occasion to apply to visit Beijing. I was surprised to receive in return an invitation for the visit of a "German book dealer delegation" in Beijing from Guózi Shūdiàn (the China Publications Center), which was responsible for the foreign book trade of the People's Republic.

I was overjoyed, though somewhat confused. Could I now travel alone and appear in China as an official delegate of the German Publishers Association that ran the Book Fair? The invitation to the Publishers Association was passed on, which meant that there would be a broad discussion of who could travel and for what purpose. Such a discussion would mean principally questions of status with regard to the composition of the "trip cadre." I knew that this trip would be no mere showing of the flag and shaking some hands, but a first, difficult contact with a recalcitrant partner, for which I wished to achieve some useful results for the Book Fair. I therefore chose the rest of the delegation with some care, and as a companion I invited the Munich publishing director of the Hanser Publishing House, Joachim Spencker, who at that time occupied the position of chairman of the foreign trade committee in the German Publishers Association.

On August 30, 1975, we flew with Air France via Karachi to Beijing. The party included Uli Bechler, our colleague who was to be in charge of the exhibit. Liu Chuanwei, with whom I was later to develop a decades-long and oddly cautious friendship, greeted us with several colleagues at the old Peking Airport, where before everything else we had to sit in the big hall on a leather bench and drink a serving of Chinese tea. Liu at that time was director of the European Department of Guózi Shūdiàn. Due to his excellent knowledge of German, he served from then on as our interpreter. He and his superior, Wang Yongshen, put us up in the state-owned Peking Hotel.

Here we immediately had to give our hosts a somewhat rude lesson—namely, that Europeans do not like to be housed together in a double room. At dinner, when Spencker and I tried to be alone, we were the ones who had to learn a lesson. After several repeated requests for a bottle of Chinese wine, we were brought a porcelain container resembling a shoe-shine can. It reeked. But driven by a fatal curiosity, each of us drank down a little glass of this devil's brew, which took our breath away. This rice drink was called Maotai and was about 140 proof. That container, which we never touched again after that first round, later stood for a few years in my office in Frankfurt, still giving off its rank smell.

The trip was very strenuous—an intensive mix of sightseeing, banquets with many courses and many toasts by the Chinese (where the two of us had to respond with *"Gānbēi"* at every toast, before downing each glass of Maotai), endless lectures, cultural events, and, always interspersed among the negotiations, something about the "Taiwan question."

First in Beijing, and later in Shanghai, we visited one after the other—the scientific publishing houses, the Forbidden City, the Xinhua press agency, the Great Wall, the Ming graves, the art house Róng Bǎo Zhāi (the workshop of the "four treasures of study"), the home of the Chinese revolutionary poet Lu Xun, a Chinese department store, a printing company, a regional book dealer, a regional committee, a handkerchief factory, the apartment of a working class family, a people's commune in the country, an engine factory, a carpentry shop, a forge, a kindergarten (in which the little round children's faces kept calling for *"Shú-shu* [Uncle] Spencker"), a hospital, an acupuncture clinic staffed by "barefoot doctors," an underground water complex, a six-person peasant family, an animal husbandry ranch for cattle, swine and poultry, the Peking Opera, and finally the 15th century garden of a finance minister.

We both tried hard to make a good impression, to attentively follow the lectures about the revolutionary method of raising pigs, and now and then to pose intelligent questions. Because of the mental effort, the food and the alcohol, sometimes we were completely out of it. One person would pay attention and show interest; he would ask questions, while the other one dozed and tried to relax a bit. Our Chinese hosts were relentless. Punctually at 7:30 AM they showed up at our unlocked room where they usually had dropped us off well after midnight.

The continual tension to which we were exposed required an escape valve. On the ninth day of the trip toward midnight we were coming out of an opera, the *Red Chair*.[1] We were exhausted, but as on every other evening we sat down with our hosts for another final glass of beer. This time some ice cream was added. I desperately was looking for a topic to talk about,

---

1. *Investigation of a Chair* was one of the last new-style Peking operas of the Cultural Revolution.

and finally began to explain in a tedious manner what a paperback book in Germany was, thinking they might know of our pocketbook series RO-RO-RO. Liu Chuanwei listened to me patiently with his constantly earnest grin, when suddenly his face lit up. "And," (he began every sentence with an "and"), "and I know... *lololo!*"

Something welled up in my diaphragm, something that wanted to go up, wanted to come out! Spencker seemed to be experiencing the same thing. A real laugh, a guffaw, was on the verge of coming out, but out of politeness to our hosts we didn't allow it.

Calmly, Liu continued on: "We *learry* like to get *mole lololo!*"

We couldn't hold out any longer. An avalanche of laughter was descending upon us. We quickly left the restaurant, clutching our stomachs, as though our guts were bursting, while our disturbed Chinese handlers hurried right after us. At the entrance of our rooms we came to a stop. "It's nothing," said Spencker, in an effort to calm down our companions. "It's nothing. I'm now going to put on my samurai [he meant to say *kimono*] and go to bed."

"But Spencker, that's not called a samurai; it's called a *samovar*," I wanted to say, and then we both couldn't hold out any longer. We collapsed snorting with laughter in the next room. We threw ourselves on the floor, laughing and gasping for breath. We rolled around on the rug, dragged ourselves up by grasping on to the edge of the bed, and then fell down again, panting and giggling when we saw each other's red, tear-swollen eyes. Two mature representatives of an advanced cultural society were breaking down in barnyard laughter on the floor of a Chinese hotel room. Our Chinese companions retreated quietly in what must have been complete shock.

It was hard to explain this behavior. It must have been the only channel left for our emotions after days and days of intense, agonizing concentration. Afterwards things went better for us, and our Chinese hosts never referred back to this episode.

Even though our Chinese counterparts had always expressed themselves derisively in German regarding their Communist neighbors to the north (this was the period of the hot border conflict between China and the Soviet Union), I had planned my trip home from China via Moscow. Wang Yongshen and Liu Chuanwei were quite moved in taking care of me when they brought me to the train station. Wang personally stowed my luggage in the compartment. They kept warning me about the "barbarians" in the north. Li Paotung and the rascally interpreter Wang Chengchung of the Import Corporation had come along. So had Joachim Spencker, who was flying directly home. He waved to me, somewhat sadly, now that our joint adventure had come to a close.

Obligingly, our Chinese counterparts had accepted a proposition that would allow their participation at Frankfurt. I had intimated that the publishing houses from Red China as well as those from Nationalist China be listed in the catalog, in the signs over their booths, and in the directional signs as "China." Neither the "Republic of China" (the official name of the government that ruled Taiwan) nor the "People's Republic" were to appear, but simply "China." And with that both parties came to an agreement, and both would continue to claim to represent the true China. I boarded the train to Ulan Bator knowing that I had landed a historic "deal," and that we had, so to speak, reunited China. The agreement lasted for many years, though these days the Taiwanese present as "Taiwan."

Slowly the train pulled away. I had my own compartment with a bed, a thick, crumpled-up pillow and a shoddy lamp. The train steamed through flat plains country, and only in the area of the Great Wall did steep mountains arise, partially concealed by the fog, as seen in old Chinese paintings or woodcuts. Small settlements passed by on the plain. People stood around and looked at the train with some curiosity. Once in a while a child waved. The white sun glared down from an empty sky.

After a twelve hour journey, I emerged from my cozy compartment in Erlian, and under a splendid starry sky walked up and down next to the tracks. In a shed, the rail car was lifted up high by a crane and the chassis was transferred to a narrower guage. Three hours later the train left China. The night was cold. The car was unheated. In the morning I ate breakfast in a cold Mongolian dining car. The waiter greeted me in German with a resounding *"Guten Morgen!"* The landscape that was passing by remained the same—slightly hilly steppes, here and there a few yurts and small herds of cattle.

In Ulan Bator I was greeted by Mr. Gombosuren, whom I knew from the Mongolian participation in Frankfurt. In the hotel room of the state hotel Ulan Bator, he gave me a bowl of *kumis* (fermented mare's milk) as a greeting, and quickly said goodbye, with the explanation that the State Theatre was closed today. The following day, the Assistant Minister of Education was to honor me with a meal in a yurt.

On my second day I was pacing up and down in front of the hotel long before the appointed hour. I had gotten through the day reasonably well, strolling about the city and visiting a museum. I must acknowledge with regret that the pedestrians stampeded along mercilessly, as though they were still moving like nomads on the steppe. To avoid the slalom of people coming down the sidewalk, I returned to the hotel. There, despite a number of attempts, I was not successful at ordering something to eat from the Mongolian waitresses, who were outfitted with starched aprons and swaggered about on tall stiletto heels. Since I spoke neither Mongolian nor Russian, they looked at me with distrust, and even when I quickly switched to English, French, or German, they stared right through me. And so toward evening I was quite hungry and frustrated as I paced the street, waiting for the Minister. Soon enough, or so I thought, I was to leave this unfriendly city and get acquainted with the steppe and with life in an authentic Mongolian yurt.

The Minister came with the tardiness that is so common here, accompanied by several bureaucrats, and greeted me in a friendly manner. However, instead of inviting me to get into his big black Volga, he took me by the arm and, to my great astonishment, steered me back into the hotel. We crossed the hotel lobby, got into the elevator, and got out on the top floor. There stood a wooden ladder, leaning up against an open skylight, peering out onto the star-studded Mongolian night sky. Politely, the Minister let me go first, and hesitantly I climbed up.

There before me on the roof of the hotel I was greeted by a festively lit-up state yurt. We sat down comfortably onto the spread-out fur blanket, and toasted each other with Mongolian vodka. The first deputy of the Education Minister, Achmet, was the person responsible for the state publishing houses, as was the custom in all the Socialist countries. Lying there on the animal skins, we began a professional discussion about Mongolian publishing and the Frankfurt Book Fair, a discussion that with the increasing consumption of vodka soon turned to general human and philosophic themes. The same long-legged Mongolian waitresses who had refused to serve me at noon now zealously brought out tasty soups and Mongolian meat dishes. I wondered how they kept their balance on that steep ladder.

The next morning I was given a hasty tour of the palace of the last Mongolian emperor, a rundown cloister, a state printing house and, on the run, the Museum of the Revolution. So that I could be acquainted with the broad country, the steppes and deserts of Mongolia, in the Ministry of Culture I was led into a movie theater and shown a one-hour propaganda film about beautiful Mongolia. Somewhat the worse because of a slight fainting feeling—Ulan Bator was located almost a mile above sea level—I was then crammed into a very small automobile with five other men, all wearing black leather coats, and raced to the airport.

There we learned that the Aeroflot plane was to arrive only several hours later, perhaps five hours, perhaps more. We squeezed back into the car. The driver sped straight across the landing strip and over the gentle hill behind it. The car drove straight as an arrow until the wheels stopped turning at the top of the hill. When we could go no further, we all got out. Some people gathered some dry camel dung and lit a fire with it. I wandered in the meantime a bit off to the side over the meadows and plucked a bouquet out of the dying edelweiss. Up here they grew like wildflowers. Then we all sat down around the fire. The men told stories, which Gombosuren translated poorly into English. We waited for a long time, wrapped in our blankets until the lights of the landing airplane lit up the broad Mongolian night sky.

Scarcely had I returned to my office in Frankfurt when I was off again to China's ally in Europe at that time, Albania. For more than ten years my predecessor sent annual invitations to participate in the Frankfurt Book Fair to a mysterious address of the Albanian publishing organization in Tirana, but we had never received an answer. During all those years, Albania was one of the most isolated Communist people's democracies, in which the adherance to Maoist principles was a case of being more royalist than the king. To want to get to Albania was something that would generate only enervated headshaking among my contemporaries. I, however, was of the opinion that if we wanted to be a Book Fair for the world, then we needed to have a European country that was known even to me only from the Karl May adventure book *In the Land of the Skipetars*. I wrote a letter to the only person in that country who could freely decide, to the dictator Enver Hoxha himself. And what do you know, two weeks later there appeared in my office two representatives of an Albanian trade office in Vienna, and we quickly came to an agreement on trade. This was 1975, and for many years thereafter the Albanians ran a triple booth, one that from the very first year was filled with curious people (Kosovo Albanians, who were working in West Germany). As a result, from the beginning we had the booth watched by our security guards for fear that demonstrations would be organized there. However, the only visitors were Albanian-speaking people who wanted to take this rare opportunity to sample the offerings of their cultural fatherland.

In the Land of Magical Realism

Max Frisch said, "An accident is something that is long overdue that finally hits you." For many years I moved about in the literary world of Franz Kafka. I dug into all his stories, his diaries and letters, until I had finally had enough of the obsequiousness and assimilatory tendencies of the main character K, and was on the lookout for a new, completely different world. And so I hit upon Latin America, this tragic culture, something that grew out of conquest and destruction of the cultural identity of its Indian peoples, the Aztecs, the Maya and the Incas, by the European conquistadors from Spain and Portugal. This was just the thing for finding an identity for someone like me, who, like Kafka's hero K, felt guilty but did not know why. The two cultural streams of the oppressed and the conquerors are still locked in a battle over values and influence in Latin American *Mestizo* society. They are still far from creating a homogeneous view of the world for the peoples who live there.

How could this not fascinate me? I was looking for something that had left me, that would fill in the deficits in my identity, and I had uncovered in their wake an attractive, controversial mode of life and culture. The Broken, the Unfinished, the Struggle for the meaning of reality, in which much that is human but also much that is magical stirs, fascinated me both in Latin American literature and in the Latin American people whom I met at my expositions in Buenos Aires, Montevideo, Córdoba and Santiago de Chile, as well in later trips to Mexico, Central America, the northern reaches of South America and Brazil.

There are two different ways to grasp a foreign country, a foreign culture, a foreign society, a foreign language. One way goes through literature; the other, through love.

When I first set foot on this continent, I was quite susceptible to both forms of adaptation. Boundlessly curious and open to everything that I ran into there, I was soon consumed by a powerful passion for a woman from Córdoba, in Argentina, someone marked by strong Indian features, and who on the basis of her powerful and exotic personality quickly drew my interest and then aroused my love. After only a few days I had decided to take her and her one-and-a-half-year-old daughter to Germany, to my ponderous fatherland, to live with me.

In the years that followed, both in trips abroad and here at home, my dedication to the study of the Latin American continent never flagged. I felt myself guided by Latin American literature, which was published only sporadically on the German book market and was barely noticed, and which for the time being I could only read in German. The German reader could find very few aids in getting into a literature which seemed at first to be strange, magical, mythical, quite surrealistic, and often even baroque-sounding. In the 1960s various editions existed of the works of the great stimulator of the new Hispano-American literature, Jorge Luis Borges; of the two Nobel prize winners, the Guatemalan Miguel Ángel Asturias and the Chilean Pablo Neruda; and various titles by the Paraguayan Augusto Roa Bastos, the Cuban Alejo Carpentier, the two Mexicans Carlos Fuentes and Juan Rulfo, and the Argentine Ernesto Sábato. On my first visit to Argentina, Sábato had introduced me to the fascinating life of Buenos Aires through his book *On Heroes and Tombs*.

As part of the wave of politicization related to the student protests and the youth revolution of the end of the 1960s, the revolutionary situation in the states of the southern continent hit you right between the eyes. We took account of the political drive of the Latin Americans, and raised the charismatic prophets of the new age to the rank of idols, from Camilo Torres[1] to Che Guevara and Ernesto Cardenal.[2] However, it soon became clear that the interest in Latin America had a mere surrogate character. The interest was fanciful, and whenever it appeared it was superficial and on the surface only. The surest

1. Camilo Torres (1929–1966): Colombian priest and Marxist guerrilla.
2. Ernesto Cardenal (b. 1925): Nicaraguan priest, liberation theologian and poet.

indicator of this was that very little attention was paid to the most reliable sources about the change of consciousness in Latin America, namely the self-discovery of the Latin American authors visible in the common traits of a literature that they themselves were devising.

In this regard, it is worthwhile to trace the story of the reception in Germany of the Latin American author, the Colombian Gabriel García Márquez, who like no other embodied the magical realism of Latin American literature in his stupendous work, *One Hundred Years of Solitude*. Immediately after publication, his books became global bestsellers, and were blessed with sales of several hundred thousand copies. In Germany, García Márquez first appeared in 1966 in a small novel in German translation, known in English as *In Evil Hour* (*La mala hora*), published by the East Berlin Aufbau Publishing House. The book was immediately taken under license for West Germany by the Sigbert Mohn Verlag in Gütersloh.

Still, this book was a flop in both parts of Germany, since, as Sigbert Mohn wrote to the head of Aufbau, Fritz-Georg Voigt, "... its completely unsatisfactory sales do not even cover the cost of storage, let alone promise any profit...." The book was sold at clearance. The East German publisher tried another book, *No Letter for the Colonel* (*Coronel No Tiene Quién le Escriba*). Since this too was unsuccessful, the Aufbau Verlag gave up.

In the meantime, the West German Kiepenheuer und Witsch got interested in the author, and in 1970 published García Márquez's masterwork, *One Hundred Years of Solitude*. This time the West German–East German exchange went the other way. In 1975 the Aufbau Publishing House took a license to publish this book.

As the author once noted, he writes as his grandmother told stories, and does not analyze events. Nonetheless, or perhaps precisely because of that approach, like no other book the novel contributed to a "spiritual identity" of the splintered continent. Both in the Spanish motherland and in the United States, especially because of its success in Latin America, the book was a sensation. In France, the Académie Française in 1969 named it the best foreign novel. Otherwise the reception outside of Latin America was restrained. In Germany, García Márquez did not make the bestseller list until the time when the Frankfurt Book Fair chose Latin America as its special topic in 1976. In the six years up until this marketing event, the Cologne publishing house sold only a few thousand copies, and the resonance among the general public was muted.

My personal enthusiasm for the discovery of a new literary continent was somewhat hyperbolic and quite boundless. This was a time when I was still not convinced that the job in Frankfurt would be a lifetime career for me. I immediately began a plan for forging my own publishing house, in which I would introduce to the German language all these wonderful books that were still available in great numbers. I wanted to make available to myself personally and to my German countrymen this powerful literature. An intensive correspondence ensued between me, the "wannabe" publisher, and some Argentine authors, such as Adolfo Bioy Casares, Antonio di Benedetto, and the then very well-known and important translators Wolfgang A. Luchting, Maria Bamberger, and the former translator of Gabriel García Márquez, Curt Meyer-Clason. The last-named met me by accident on my very first visit to the Latin American continent when we were in the same hotel in Montevideo, and immediately at an evening meal of steak and *chimichurri* gave me a session of private tutoring about the Hispanic and Brazilian authors whom he had translated.

The whole fairy-tale publishing house project silently collapsed once I had finally reckoned the costs involved. Along the way, I learned how one makes books, and overrated myself in my excess eagerness to sell them on the German market, but I lacked the funds for such a venture. The two things, a Latin American family and a publishing house for a Latin American literature—both were not feasible. And so of these two I stuck with the family. Still, the idea of being a facilitator for foreign literatures, to develop their richness and exotic nature for us in Germany and in Europe—this notion had gotten its claws into me, and I could not scrap it from my plans for the future.

My next attempt to bring Latin American literature closer to the reading public occurred when the Book Fair and the German book trade in general got wind that they had a serious image problem, due principally to the over-commercialization of literature. In planning the first topical program of *Latin America* at the Frankfurt Book Fair, I had prescribed for myself a grand outing to the *Cono Sur*, beginning in the middle of November 1975. By the end of December I wanted to visit nine Latin American countries, and convince them to bring their publishing houses and authors to the Book Fair in Frankfurt in the fall of the following year, with the aim of making their art and literature known the world over. I was armed with a film about the Frankfurt Book Fair and a Spanish-language stump speech that I could revise as occasion demanded, all intended to convince publishers to participate. I planned on going to Colombia (Bogotá), Venezuela (Caracas), Cuba (Havana), Mexico (Mexico City), Peru (Lima), Bolivia (La Paz), Uruguay (Montevideo), Brazil (São Paulo) and Argentina (Buenos Aires).

This was a very strenuous trip, with lectures, TV appearances, press interviews, lots of official banquets, lots of alcohol, all with temperatures I was not accustomed to of around 104° Fahrenheit, and with elevations ranging from sea level to 12,000 feet above sea level (La Paz). The most strenuous thing for me was my internal tension. I was in Latin America, and—how can I say it?—I wanted to be a Latin American. I wanted to take hold of Latin America from the inside; my enthusiasm for being there was unrestrained. René Pacheco, Director of the Historical Commission of the Cuban government, invited me with my companion Manfred G. to Fidel Castro's box seats in the theater for classical ballet (Tchaikovsky's *Swan Lake;* we were later treated to Lorca's *The House of Bernarda Alba* and Strauss's *Salome*). When the prima ballerina Alicia Alonso enraptured the public into storms of applause, the kind that we have only at soccer matches, tears came to my eyes about this successful mix of the European cultural patrimony with the Latin American temperament.

On the other hand, my shock was great when, in a Bolivian café, the Jew Peter Levi spelled out that the friendly gentleman at the table next to me was the old Nazi and one-time SS officer Klaus Barbie, *alias* Altmann. Barbie had been sentenced to death several times, most recently in 1954 in Lyon, for a massacre in St. Genis-Laval and for many executions in the Montluc Prison in Lyon. Here was the "Butcher of Lyon," sitting as an innocuous passerby, an arm's length away from me, enjoying himself with his bodyguard in unabashed contentment. Since 1964 he had been active as a consultant for the Bolivian military government. Beate Klarsfeld, the representative of the International League Against Anti-Semitism and Racism, had dug up this fugitive in La Paz and had publicized his stay and his activity worldwide, something that did not seem to disturb him at all as he sat there and savored his coffee and laughed.

So it popped up again, this burdensome question of identity that I was seeking to escape from in Latin America. Wasn't I one of them; wasn't he one of us?

I got up and left. Peter Levi, at that time secretary of the Bolivian Book Association, himself a child of immigrants, with whom I was to be bound by many years of friendship, had himself become such a Latin American that he could live with these contradictions without any problems. He followed me smiling.

Leaving Cuba, I landed in Lima in an old Aeroflot Ilyushin jet with a hard landing from one hundred feet up. "Damned tractor drivers," cursed the mainly Russian passengers while shaking their fists at the pilot's cabin. However, the landing was also difficult in a more than literal sense. To be sure, I was able to roll out my program just like everywhere else, but my inner conflicts put me to the real test. After a restless night of thought, I shaved off my moustache and looked at a new face in the mirror. That night ideas poured out of me, and I wrote half a dozen pages, which later (1981) were published by the small but discriminating Berlin publishing house of Fietkau:

habits

I'd like to rise up
to get out of myself
to become someone else
or perhaps to be really myself

I swim in my own flesh
a dead bird
in an oil contaminated-sea
dead habits

choke me
first here
then there
my existence lurches everywhere
a trademark
a concept
painted once
stamped once
understood once

outside
where the wind shakes the palms
there
where night still
has deep holes in it
where anxiety lasts
and love vents itself
where the pelican in its dive
cuts through the air
there in the song
there in desire
there
I am no longer

In Mexico, the charismatic publisher of Siglo Veintiuno, Arnaldo Orfila Reynal, invited me for a little cocktail on the roof of the publishing house. This important contact to Orfila had been arranged by his right-hand woman—or should I say his "left-hand woman"—Concepción Zea, whom I had met at one of the publisher seminars for the Central American region put on by us and the Friedrich-Ebert Foundation[3] in San Juan (Costa Rica). Orfila, who was already well into his seventies, was the most impressive publishing personality in Mexico, perhaps even in Latin America. Born in Argentina (from Córdoba!), he had initially directed the Argentine branch of the Mexican state publishing house Fondo de Cultura Economica, housed in Buenos Aires, and in the end had been tapped to become the head of the company in Mexico.

3. The *Friedrich-Ebert Foundation,* named for the first president of the Weimar Republic, promotes scholarship and democratic education.

He had immediately resigned his new post when the state censorship or the censorship within the publishing house of Fondo, which were essentially the same thing, wanted to forbid him from publishing the work of the U.S. anthropologist Oscar Lewis (Illinois), consisting of a book of interviews with the poor Mexican peasant Jésus Sánchez and his four children, Manuel, Robert, Consuelo and Marta, titled *The Children of Sanchez*. He then founded the Siglo Veintiuno, which in a short time became the most important publishing house for contemporary Latin American literature and politics.

Orfila introduced me to the Cuban Alejo Carpentier and the widow of Salvador Allende, who had been killed in the Pinochet *coup d'état* in Santiago de Chile in 1973. He also introduced me — and this actually might have been the goal of my entire Latin American trip — to Gabriel García Márquez. My meeting with him, however, was extraordinarily disappointing. Referring to the hopes of the imminent Latin America Festival of literature in Frankfurt and to the question of whether he would come to Frankfurt to lend some glamor to the exposition by being its leading light, he answered curtly, "You and your publishers over there are all exploiting capitalists. I'm not going to support you!" And with that he turned away to speak to the other people present.

Later I returned to my hotel and spent the night until 3 AM drinking half a dozen margaritas in the hotel bar. I had never suffered such a snub in Latin America.

García Márquez's new novel *The Autumn of the Patriarch* (published in Spanish in 1975, in German in 1978) had just appeared. The story started out anew with the discovery of the dead dictator in a palace now inhabited by cows and birds. Only after the vultures appeared did the downtrodden people dare to enter into the site of divine power.

The Mexican author Carlos Fuentes came out with his book *Terra Nostra* (German translation 1979), a monumental novel, whose theme included the tension between the real history of Spain and Latin America and the unrealized historical opportunities. The book ended with an apocalypse in Paris. I was not able to convince either of the authors to come to Frankfurt. Before I could tackle the question of the leading figure for the

Latin American authors at Frankfurt, which was absolutely a question of identity, I was engulfed in a quite personal problem.

To be sure, I seemed to be successful during this trip in convincing the publishers of the countries I visited to come to Frankfurt, but my personal desire to find security in this strange world and to find a new identity for myself was driving me toward an unavoidable fiasco. In Buenos Aires, the last stop on my trip, my intensively driven personal search for a foreign, non-German existence for myself came to a head. A deeper and deeper depression, which I could not explain to myself, seemed to signal that I would not be able to find what I was seeking so desperately. In the little Hotel Dorá on Calle Maipú, in which I stayed since my first Buenos Aires trip in 1968 and which made me feel at home, I booked a telephone call back home to my Argentine life companion to tell her of my feelings of desperation. It was really a cry for help, but I couldn't reach her.

During the day I continued my professional discussions with complete equanimity, but at night I lay awake with my troubled psyche and waited for the telephone connection to my Latin American wife in my faraway homeland. When I finally was able to reach her after 25 hours, the painful process had already passed its peak. Dora complained at length about the children, about conditions in Germany, about her loneliness. I stared straight ahead for a long time after hanging up the receiver, looking at the shadows on the ceiling of my room, until the dawn washed away these light games.

I had gotten closer to a way of life, a culture of endearing and powerful people. I had life around me to gaze at in adoration, a life I had learned to love, but I could not hide out. It was now finally clear to me that my life lay elsewhere, far away, on the other side of the Atlantic, where I had been born.

And once I had gotten back, and the Frankfurt Book Fair was pouring all its new releases over me, I wondered not a little bit whether the question of my origin and identity, as well as the resolution of individual problems and conflicts, were not only mine, but also those of many important authors in this literary year.

Thus Elisabeth Plessen, in her novel *Mitteilungen an der Adel* (*Reports on the Aristocracy*), confronted her aristocratic family, principally her authoritarian father. The writer Christa Wolf, living in East Germany, describes in her novel *Kindheitsmuster* (*Patterns of Childhood*) her early experiences under National Socialism in a city that is today in Poland. She did not conceal that the "Third Reich" had exerted a certain fascination on her as a young girl. *Patterns of Childhood* was an attempt to get free of the mold of her generation and to test it critically. Another book was devoted to the personal and social search for identity of 20 million African-Americans. The black American Alex Haley used the programmatic title *Roots* for a mixture of reports of facts and fiction to create a history of his family since 1750. I personally had found no homeland, no orientation in another country and no other culture. But when I returned to Germany, I no longer felt myself alone in my search for answers to questions like *What am I? Where do I belong? Which of my roots may I accept? Where is my cultural homeland? Where is my personal homeland?*

Little House in the Rhön

Well, while rummaging about in all these memories, I am in my little old cottage in the Rhön region, which I acquired just at that time, in the middle of the 1970s. I sit here, half lying down, my feet on a footstool, in a comfortable, somewhat worn wingback chair under the steep wooden roof of an old cottage in the hilly country of the Rhön. Dry fruit wood crackling in the green tile oven encloses me in a healthy, sheltering warmth. The roof rafters creak under gusts of pounding autumn wind. In my imagination, I am sitting in the wood-paneled cabin of a windjammer, a model of which the friendly Vassily Sokolov had given me on my first visit to the St. Petersburg book fair. It now adorned the chimney mantelpiece in a glass case, as though I were an aging captain who for years had traveled on the seas in such a sailboat, and now and again remembered with a sigh his exotic excursions and adventuresome deeds.

Outside, beyond the window, life is raging in the fall-colored leaves, which move along the stream around the meadow in a broad semicircle. The autumn wind whistles and shakes the cottage, which is nestled against the embankment like a little wild duck. Beyond the Arnsberg Mountain, which stands upright as a dark background over the shaking ash trees, shreds of blue and white clouds leap out. Now and then a single sunbeam breaks through the clouds and lights up the still green meadow and the red, yellow and green leaves that waver on the branches.

I look up from my book and quickly draw on my pipe so that it doesn't go out. I read further in the novel of a young Polish author whom I had become aware of through the presentation of Poland at the Frankfurt Book Fair in 2000, Andrzej Stasiuk's *Dukla*. In this book, the still young Polish author describes the age that is also overtaking me. Outside, through the windows, the wisps of clouds have lost their blue. The Arnsberg Mountain stands out, threatening and black, before the somewhat brighter sky, over the dark inky clouds, always changing, moving to the east. Night is falling over the little valley.

In 1976 I had the opportunity to acquire this little cottage with its mighty walls, over three feet thick, and the barn next door. With my tent-house, I now moved my family of five from the nearby camping site, where we had been spending our summer holidays for three years, into the garden, thick with fruit trees, between a little stream and the house. The structure itself, falling down and covered with mildew and fungus, had been built more than four centuries earlier as a fulling mill, which I began to renovate, rebuild, and fit out with my own hands.

This project has been going on to this very day. First of all, I quickly removed the workbench and a chaotic workshop, in which wires and electrical scraps were piled up next to the half empty cans of paint and dried-out brushes. For the moment the project of *The Little House in the Rhön* has been completed. I have been back and forth to this place, experiencing my "retirement," looking back.

"The Little House in the Rhön" was a place where I could rest and retreat from the battle, from the everyday cares of the office, a place to unwind from intellectual labor, a place away from the pressure of decisions, of travel and of creating new projects. Every time, nature and the little house were waiting for me and beckoning me. When I came here on one of my free weekends, about a two-hour drive from Frankfurt, my head felt relieved because of the distance from the scene of all the activity, and the place hugged me tightly right away.

Half an acre of yard to be mowed, raked up, and trash taken away; the bushes and trees, which enclosed the doors and windows of the house like a Sleeping Beauty's castle, had to be cut away. The stream had eroded the bank and carried it away. The bank had to be shored up with rocks from the water. The trees that had fallen over had to be sawed up and chopped to pieces. The martens, which we could not get out of the barn, had gotten into the roof of the house and had ripped out the fiberglass insulation. The storm had taken off part of the barn roof. The wooden posts of the garden fence were battered, and the fence had partially collapsed. The moles had turned the meadow into the surface of the moon, and the snails had nearly finished devouring the flowerbed.

Nevertheless, I swung myself onto the roof, repaired the chimney and opened the roof windows, broke stone blocks out of the wall and installed doors, put in water pipes, laid bricks, plastered, painted, installed wooden panels. This was work absolutely different from what I did in Frankfurt. On Sunday evening or at the end of the vacation stay, I left a construction zone, only to take up hammer and saw again after two or six weeks. And this lasted for 10, even 15 years, actually down to the present day. However, for me this was rejuvenation, an alternative, and—as I gradually understood—it also neutralized what I was calling my "identity problem." Finally I found what I had sought with such despair as early as 1975 in Latin America, a place to be at home, a homeland—relaxation, security.

This "identity problem" broke out at the beginning of the 1950s. For purposes of re-education, the schools took us 10- to 12-year-olds to films about concentration camps, which often went on for hours; these may have helped bring on the "identity issue." There we had to experience how mountains of bodies of murdered prisoners were shoved by bulldozers into sandy pits, tumbling down with lifeless limbs like discarded dolls. There— emaciated, speechless people looked at us through the camera with big dead eyes, smoldering with dread. For minutes on end we had to look at piles of eyeglasses, mountains of shoes, which at one point living people had worn. We had to sit and watch the causes of this craziness in close-up: the concentration camp guards, men and women in worn-out German uniforms, run-down forms with lifeless and patently evil faces.

We said nothing. We didn't cry, and we didn't laugh. Silently we left the cinemas, which had often before given us adventure, action, fantasy, diversion. We remained silent because we didn't know what we were supposed to do with these images. Nevertheless, those dreadful eyes were fixed on our young souls, and compelled us youth, just on the verge of puberty, to seek out the authors of this horror in our environment, in our teachers, and in the values preached by the society into which we had been born.

Suddenly my disobedience against the German authorities

burst out, against my father, against my teachers, against the church and government, against all those who wanted to tell us post-war Germans what to do and where we should go. They were simply the old authorities with the same spirit that demanded obedience. It was still the old authoritarian German spirit that had brought so much death and destruction in the name of the German nation. My youthful reaction was defiance and disobedience. In the end I ran away from all those Germans older than I was.

It took a number of years until I finally came back via some tortured paths. The uprising by the generation following me in 1968 helped me here, but actually my return lasted my entire adult life. It was difficult for me to put down roots in Germany. For me, the "dominant culture" was ruined by those very people who, lodged in some "heroic" past, were meant to epitomize the essence of Germany. A deep resentment against everything that defined itself as German made it practically impossible for me to get involved with people in this country. For years after this outburst, when I had already taken a leadership role in a "state supporting position," even when I had advanced to being a German "cultural ambassador" and tried to make my peace with everything that more recently had gone under the name of German culture, I still felt myself more at home when I was abroad than when I was here.

On the thorny path back to the German Motherland, back to *Novemberland* and the landscape of historical contradictions that Günter Grass evoked, "The Little House in the Rhön" suddenly became a protected home port. In 1975, when I returned from Latin America, I planted my walking stick in this primeval German soil. I finally allowed myself to do this; I did not follow many of my generational comrades by flying away to Tuscany or to Spanish Ibiza. Here, only a few miles from what was then the border between East and West Germany, here in the rough German Rhön, where people said that there were nine months of winter followed by three months of cold weather, here under an often dramatic sky of clouds, among the petty bourgeois German people and the strong, ponderous but friendly German peasant faces, I dug in.

It was from this house as well that I had to drive out the past, though only in short bursts. In the house that I had purchased there lived a rather poor family, a slovenly scrap dealer with his wife and young son. He paid 75 Marks a month rent. Somehow I had to find a way to get rid him and his family because I wanted to use the house for myself and my family. Unexpectedly, I found myself in the role of a landlord, an "exploiter," who was robbing a poor family of its abode. I felt very uncomfortable with myself.

When I knocked on the door of my tenant for the first time, the plump scrap dealer opened the door and asked me, the new owner of the house, to come in, all the while acting too subservient for my taste. In this sparsely arranged kitchen there was a stove, a table, two chairs and a broken-down sink. The man cleaned up a bit and began to talk.

"My wife is also quite famous."

Somehow he had heard that I was a "famous director from Frankfurt." He leaned back as far as the rickety chair would allow and proudly announced, "She was at one time a guard in a concentration camp." Now he leaned forward, and his powerful bad breath wafted into my face.

"And I'll tell you one thing—the Hungarian Jews, they were O.K. They helped my wife—afterwards! But those Polish Jews, they were pigs, real swine!"

The hairs on the back of my neck stood straight out. All I wanted to do was to get out of there. These broken-down shapes in their worn-out German uniforms, with their malicious but subservient expressions, walking straight out of the concentration camp films of my youth, all just like the wife of the scrap dealer, who just then came into the kitchen.

I worked out a deadline for the scrap dealer to move out in the next two weeks, and I offered him a little fee to help him move. That did the trick. And then as quickly as I could, I got out of the house which would soon be mine, and which would help me gradually to overcome the problem of my German identity.

Actually the experience with the "Berlin pit" had given me a taste of what later occupied me as an adult—the difficulty of belonging somewhere. But now I have learned not to seek my homeland elsewhere, in other cultural spheres. I learned that I was a German, and that I could find an understanding of myself only here in my association with these people. I also learned that we today can only be German because we reject that which the Nazis had held to be German.

Outside the windows, night has fallen. I get up to put wood into the oven. Now I have moved from my reading into brooding. The complete darkness that envelops the house gives me a calm security. Here I sit and look back. In an edgy way I suck on my pipe, which again threatens to go out.

The Year of Latin America

Ruppert Schmidt, a clever fellow, always ready for a joke, was a book dealer from the Rhine city of Offenburg, quite close to France, and the owner and director of the Offenburger Dokumente Verlag. Schmidt had joined the French Resistance during the war, and since that time had maintained good contacts with French intellectuals, contacts which he had used since 1946 to promote the introduction of literature from Germany into France. Through him, I had established contact with the great Argentine author Julio Cortázar in Paris, and after a short period of hesitation he expressed willingness to take over the role that I had originally intended for Gabriel García Márquez. As it soon turned out, Cortázar's name was a big drawing card on account of his literary works being known by practically every other living Latin American author, but also because of his exemplary political stands. Cortázar, an Argentine living in Parisian emigration, had spoken out decisively against the Argentine military, which in April 1976 had taken power in Buenos Aires and was on the verge of removing from its past anything that appeared leftist or critical of the new *junta* regime. Cortázar was also physically a larger-than-life figure, with his calm face under a frizzy beard.

We were successful in gathering behind Julio Cortázar almost all the important names in Latin American literature, such as Juan Rulfo (Mexico), Mario Vargas Llosa (Peru), who agreed to speak at the opening of the Book Fair, Jorge Amado, Osman Lins, Thiago de Mello (Brazil), Sergio Ramírez (Nicaragua), Eduardo Galeano (Uruguay), Manuel Puig (Argentina), Manuel Scorza (Peru), José Donoso and Antonio Skármeta (Chile), Adalberto Ortiz (Ecuador) and others.

Juan Rulfo was the author of only two books, *The Burning Plain* and *Pedro Páramo,* both written before the war but which appeared in German only in 1953 and 1955. These books were considered classics of the new Latin American literature, since the author employed an experimental style of storytelling in a masterly way, something that was becoming common in the literature of the continent only in the 1970s. I was soon bound to him by a hearty friendship. Rulfo, even then a convinced proponent of moving slowly, appeared as early as one week before the Book Fair in Frankfurt, and stayed on afterwards for another two weeks, which he spent principally with us, at our home, and with other friends.

Jorge Amado, the father of countless novels about his town Salvador da Bahia, was the creator of the most widely read novel of Brazilian literature, *Gabriela, Clove and Cinnamon*. Amado, whom I had missed very much in Bahia for my book exhibit in 1971, had the peculiarity of never getting on an airplane. He crossed the ocean by ship.

José Donoso's novel *The Obscene Bird of Night* had fascinated me long before the Book Fair. In a park, Don Jerónimo founds a society of cripples and human monsters. Don Jerónimo himself finally gets into the park, but as a non-cripple he is considered by the inhabitants of the park to be too ugly. He is therefore killed. In this world of dread, which Donoso lays out, this is the symbol of the subjection of the helpless individual, violated by outside forces—a book that leaves a deep impression.

The Chilean Antonio Skármeta made a name for himself in Germany as a young author primarily by his homage to the Chilean poet Pablo Neruda: the novel (and film) *Ardiente Paciencia* (which became the basis for Michael Radford's *Il Postino*). Skármeta became a friend of our house. Later, when he had returned to Chile, I often met with him when I spent time in Santiago. Many years later he returned to Germany as the Ambassador of Chile.

With *Open Veins of Latin America*, Eduardo Galeano had created a penetrating historical survey of his continent from its discovery down to the present. Our introduction of Galeano at the Fair made his book a sensation in Germany, and since then its stature and popularity have only grown. President Hugo Chávez of Venezuela has called *Open Veins* "a monument of Latin American history." In 2009, the book was once again catapulted onto the bestseller list when Chávez presented a copy of Galeano's famous work to the new American President, Barack Obama.

Back then at Frankfurt, Galeano and his wife soon were numbered among the good friends in my Latin American family, in that during the Book Fair they also got involved in our practical problems, such as babysitting.

A great misfortune befell Manuel Scorza from Peru, who died in a plane crash on a return flight from Europe in 1983.

I personally had just been able to read the two very significant debut novels of the Peruvian author Mario Vargas Llosa, *The Green House* and *The Time of the Hero*, both of which "express the sociological reality of Peru and Latin America," as my earlier teacher in Latin American literary affairs, Günter W. Lorenz, used to so dryly express himself. The second novel, *The Time of the Hero*, was both brilliant and very complex in its narration, and was seen "as a milestone of the new Latin American novel." According to Donoso, it contributed to the splendid "boom" of Latin American literature.

These authors, and a few more like Manuel Puig from Argentina, Thiago de Mello from Brazil, Arturo Uslar Pietri from Venezuela and Augusto Céspedes from Bolivia, represented *Latin America 1976* at the Frankfurt Book Fair, and thereby set off a boom for Latin American literature in all of Europe. And if some other Latin American author, due to previous engagements or scheduling conflicts, could not be there that year, that same person arrived in Frankfurt later on in the years after the Frankfurt Fair presented its Latin America topic. Here I am thinking of Octavio Paz, Carlos Fuentes and Ernesto Cardenal.

Some were not completely satisfied with the choice of lead authors. One day after Cortázar's name appeared in the German press, the new Ambassador of the Argentine military *junta*, who was confined to a wheelchair, was rolled into my office, and relatively undiplomatically gave me to understand that Cortázar, that "terrorist," was not acceptable to his country and must be immediately disinvited. As a "substitute," the Ambassador suggested that Jorge Luis Borges was available, and that his travel and expenses in Frankfurt would be underwritten by the Argentine government. Now Jorge Luis Borges was without doubt a great author, but he had been stigmatized for once having greeted the military in Argentina. Later, he distanced himself from them. I told the Ambassador "no" in just as decisive and undiplomatic a manner, basing my position on the fact that the invitation to a literature festival in Frankfurt is entirely the choice of the organizer and not of governments, who in general do not participate in the organization of such events.

The Ambassador, however, was a particularly hard-headed sort. In the following weeks he visited me in my office two more times. Our conversations differed not at all from the preceding ones, though they became increasingly aggressive. Finally the Ambassador, pushed by his silent aide, on leaving my office shouted out some threats that I naturally did not take very seriously—"You'll soon see the results of your position, *you'll soon see...*"

As a matter of fact, a few weeks later I received a telephone call from Günter W. Lorenz, who was working as a journalist and who had authored the books *Dialogue with Latin America* and *Contemporary Literature in Latin America,* a man with whom I had twice traveled through Argentina and Brazil. He had learned through contacts at the *Clarín* newspaper that the military authorities in Buenos Aires had sent some people to pass on a "thank-you note" to the "Communist nest" at the Frankfurt Book Fair.

The thank-you note was delivered, if only after the successful conclusion of the Latin America Book Fair. One Sunday evening, as I returned with my family from my weekend in the Rhön, I found that the entry door of our Frankfurt apartment had been broken down. As we timidly entered the apartment, we discovered complete chaos. The book shelves had been ripped off the walls; chairs and tables had been overturned; furniture had been destroyed. Strangely, nothing had been stolen except for a black leather coat, even though money, passports and jewelry were lying in my unlocked desk. The police found no clues and no fingerprints. Rather, they dealt with me and my somewhat chaotic mixed family with increasing distrust as we told them of our suspicions. Coincidence, or really a "Thank-you note"? A few days later I found my car in the courtyard with its tires slashed.

The Argentine military dictatorship affected my family and me even after that, quite independently of the topic of the Book Fair. My wife Dora could no longer travel to her country, and increasingly our friends and acquaintances, and even family members, were disappearing forever, even those to whom one could hardly attribute a left-wing orientation. Many intellectuals tried to leave the country. I learned that Eduardo Galeano, publisher of the Buenos Aires left-wing cultural magazine *Crisis*, had been detained and was in great danger. Through my good contact at the German Embassy in Buenos Aires, the cultural attaché Dr. Gottfried Arens, I was able to have him, together with his wife, receive an official invitation and tickets to Frankfurt for the Book Fair, something that put him in a good position to leave the country.

The situation was somewhat more difficult for Daniel Divinsky and his wife Kuki Miler. This publisher couple of Ediciones de la Flor had already been put in jail because of the publication of a children's book, *Five Fingers Make a Fist,* which they had bought at one of the prior Frankfurt Book Fairs from the German Basis Publishing House. Some friends figured out where the two were in prison and sent me the information. Through Gottfried Arens I sent an official invitation for the two of them through the German Embassy to the spokesman of the military *junta,* General Videla. Gottfried Arens brought the tickets with his own hands to the Divinskys in prison, and they flew directly from there to Frankfurt. After the Book Fair, they traveled to Venezuela, where they lived until the end of the military dictatorship.

Practically all the countries that I had visited in 1975 sent delegations from publishers, and displayed the products of their publishing houses in joint booths, often exhibiting for the first time. Only Cuba laid down conditions, and thus excluded itself from the one-time opportunity of presenting its country, its authors and books, in common with all other Latin American countries. In the following year, however, the Cubans also appeared in Frankfurt, and from then on were permanent participants in the Frankfurt Book Fair.

The special topic had a nice effect on the Fair, even if the presentations didn't run perfectly according to plan. Dieter E.

Zimmer of the weekly *Die Zeit* in particular criticized the two big literary presentations in the Congress Hall. I put this down to my inexperience in putting on a dramatic program, at least when important authors were involved. With real excitement, I had invited the heroes of Latin American literature to a not too fancy dinner in the mayor's room at the Fair. Around that square table there soon heated up a vigorous discussion among Manuel Scorza, Juan Rulfo, Julio Cortázar, Sergio Ramírez, the Chilean-German poet and coordinator of the program Federico Schopf, plus Curt Meyer-Clason, the moderator of the program that was to follow. I was really looking forward to seeing what would happen at the public appearance, but alas, the heroes were tired. Somewhat listless, and at least worn down from eating and drinking wine, they got up, satisfied with what they had already said, and strolled over to the nearby exposition hall. The discussion there was much less impressive to all those members of the public and of the press whom I wanted to bring closer to this literature—600 people had come. The Brazilian poet Thiago de Mello stepped out in front of the podium, dressed all in white, with an unruly beard and long, wavy hair, and in a Jesus-like pose, with arms outstretched, proclaimed his revolutionary message to the people of Latin America. Nobody else dared to contradict him, but simply confirmed what others said. The moderator Meyer-Clason did not intervene; Vargas Llosa said nothing. José Donoso, quite angry, left the podium and the room shouting, "Shame! Shame!" The other presentations by the very few German specialists in Latin American literature suffered clearly from the fact that the moderator, the writer and president of the writer's federation, Carl Amery, who had let himself be convinced by me to take on this role, clearly didn't understand anything at all about the material.

Nonetheless, all of this did not mean a total failure for the topical program. The newspapers and the media reported objectively and profoundly about the authors, the conditions in Latin America and the literature being offered here. The goal that we had set ourselves was reached—the books were translated, and the splendid boom in Latin American literature was set off among us as well.

And one more thing—the negative press reports about the

bestseller dominance at the Book Fair quieted down. What I especially took pleasure in, as the head of the Fair, was that the negative image of the "Frankfurt Moloch," that sacrificial altar on which nothing cultural or literary took place any longer, disappeared from the heads of the other participants in the Fair, including those who were not particularly impressed by the presentations on special topics. The self-assessment about the business done by all the participants increased by 13% in the area of "Good to very good," according to a survey taken after the Fair. This made clear how much participation in the Book Fair depended on the feelings of those participating and on their emotional readiness to assess their participation as positive or negative. After all, the actual number of publishers in this year, as proved by other factors, had not grown.

In the spring of the year before the Fair, I had invited the German publishers of Latin American literature to my office for a preparatory discussion. Those who came, a pitifully small group at that time, naturally were led by Siegfried Unseld of Suhrkamp. He showed up with a delicate young woman, Michi Strausfeld, whom he had recently hired in order to build up his Latin American program. She was dark-haired and charming, holding a degree in Romance languages and living in Spain. In the next quarter century she was to become the most important agent of Latin American literature in Germany. She became for me as well a consultant of special importance for all matters relating to Spain and Latin America. Something was added to this by the fact that we had lived in the same city in the Ruhr area at the same time, and that she, while waiting for the bus in Duisburg opposite the train station, had pressed her nose against the shop window of the book dealer while I was inside setting up a display for the publisher Suhrkamp. Gerhard Beckmann of Goverts was also one of those involved in Latin America, as well as a comrade-in-arms from the Deutsche Verlagsanstalt publisher—that's the way it was then! What I remembered most from this meeting was someone of my age with a walrus moustache and leather jacket—the publisher of the Peter Hammer House in Wupptertal, Hermann Schulz, with whom from that moment on I developed a deep fraternal friendship.

74 The transition between my predecessor, Sigfred Taubert, and myself lasted over a year and a half. He had directed the Fair for 18 years, and the transition did not go perfectly smoothly, but in the end passed without any great tensions.

1974   Following official protocol: For the first time I was able to conduct the German Federal President Walter Scheel around the Fair. He was accompanied by the Hessian Minister of Economics Heinz-Herbert Karry, who in 1981 was murdered by shots into his bedroom, presumably by members of the Red Army Fraction.

1975   There was quite an outcry at the first Book Fair that I was entirely responsible for. For the opening program I asked Peter Palitzsch and his actors' troupe to present songs and poems by Bertolt Brecht. This brought on the accusation that I was spreading Socialist ideas.

75 Cassius Clay, *alias* Muhammad Ali, "The greatest boxer of all time," was a surprise guest in my office. Next to him I seemed like a featherweight. That was the year he published his autobiography to great public interest.

76 The official opening of the Book Fair with the focal theme of Latin America. The guest speaker was the Peruvian writer Mario Vargas Llosa, who was later a presidential candidate in his country.

1976 In the year of the military *coup* in Argentina, the Argentine national bookstall wa occupied by students demanding the release of one of their comrades, who had been arrested in Buenos Aires and was threatened with death.

1977 The president of the International Community of Booksellers Association (ICBA the American Russell Reynolds, surprised me with an award of the *Monumento del Lib* It was important to me over the years that book dealers as well as publishers should al feel at home at the Fair.

1977 Private meeting on the outskirts of the Fair with the Dutchman Fekko Snater. We bonded over memories of our time together at a publishing house in Stuttgart. At my side, Dora (my spouse at the time).

1977 The intervention of the Book Fair was successful in getting the Argentine publishing couple Daniel Divinsky and Kuki Miler of Ediciones de la Flor in Buenos Aires out of an Argentine military jail, and bringing them to Frankfurt. After the Fair they went into exile in Venezuela.

1978 A critical exhibition designed by the Book Fair on the topic *The Third World in German Children's Books 1967–1977* unleashed vehement discussions among publishers of youth literature. The logo for the children's year at the Frankfurt Fair, the "smiling potato" was designed by a three-year-old.

1979 The difficult puzzle of where to put everybody every year was the task of Franz-Josef Genke and his team, here in a discussion about location with representatives of two publishing houses in India.

1979 Meeting the Dalai Lama during his visit to the Frankfurt Book Fair.

Strolling around the stalls of the publishing houses. The first days of the Fair are reserved for professional visitors, but the doors are opened on the weekends to the general public.

Struggles over Relocating

Like its predecessors, the 29th Frankfurt Book Fair in 1977 broke all records—177,870 visitors were drawn in by 279,000 titles from 4,534 publishing houses (9.1% more than in the previous year) from 74 countries. For the first time, we attempted a census of the throngs of visitors with a questionnaire. We found that the professional visitors comprised 37% of the total, and the general public 59%; in all 17% of all visitors to the Fair came from abroad. Although the sale of rights went well, and though the U.S. exhibitors even spoke of the most successful Frankfurt Book Fair ever, for most people it was simply "business-as-usual." Needless to say, while the exhibitors celebrated their successes, the newspapers wrote it off as just a trifle "boring."

Just in that year there was no "special topic." Initially, these special programs were planned on a two-year cycle. After Latin America in 1976, for 1978 we prepared the next topical year, *The Child and the Book*. Obviously something was missing in the years without a theme, something that could leave a mark on public opinion. Profitable bestsellers, which always caused a furor, were hardly to be found that year. Anyway, wasn't it the journalists who in earlier years had decried all the hustle and bustle surrounding the memoirs of actors, boxers and celebrities?

The press was now recognized as an integral participant in the Book Fair, with its numbers growing larger every year (1976: 2,375; 1977: 3,500; 1978: 4,000). As organizers of the Book Fair, we had to take their needs seriously, just as we did the demands of the other groups—the exhibitors, the book dealers, the librarians and the general public. In 1977, 3,500 journalists had appeared in Frankfurt to report on the premier international book exhibition. Some 3,000 of these visited the improvised press center on the second floor of Hall 5, and leafed through the presskits. The press center, however, was hopelessly overcrowded from mid-morning on, with many journalists looking for a little place to write in the corridors or on the benches by the shabby lawn. The task of the hour was to provide adequate working conditions for the press corps. However, we were hindered in this task, as the bylaws of our parent, the German Publishers Association, decreed that all press activity at the Fair was the sole responsibility of the publicity department of the Publishers Association, and was not to be handled by us.[1]

A very irritating back and forth stretched out over a decade between the management of the Fair and the top management of the Publishers Association. The controversy gave birth to a number of restrictive policies, none of which were workable because the media naturally sought out those of us in charge at the Exposition and Fair Company (the AUM), including me as director. However, this operating company was owned by the German Publishers Association, which would have liked to be the place to go to, but the press did not cooperate. (In the opinion of the Publishers Association, the AUM was to function simply by putting on a trouble-free, technically satisfactory exposition. The analysis of what went on with the Fair should in every case remain with the "owner," meaning the German Publishers Association.)

With the newly organized press activity, we were not concerned merely to explain and to interpret our activities for the emancipated representatives of the writing, recording and interviewing press. More than that, we wanted to facilitate the work of the press corps, which numbered 3 to 4,000 members, to supply them with plenty of leads and rooms for interviews, to have speeches translated, as well as to find them places to relax, to get something to eat, places to store their equipment, and help in the form of press liaisons who could speak their

---

1. Under German law, corporations are composed of a management board responsible for daily operations, with a Supervisory Board exercising general oversight. Final decisions lie with the general shareholders meetings. The Frankfurt Book Fair was managed by the Exposition and Fair Company (AUM). However, this company had only one owner: the German Publishers Association. Thus, as the single shareholder, the Supervisory Board felt a greater entitlement to authority. (The Frankfurt Fairgrounds Company was the official owner of the fairgrounds, and thus the landlord of the Book Fair.)

language. Finally, the goals of the entire international Fair had to be communicated, and not only the goals of the German section, whose interests were the main priority for the German Publishers Association.

After three years of wrangling over various solutions for the press, the conflict escalated beyond hope when a new press spokesman, Dr. Jörg Seelbach, signed on as head of the publicity department of the German Publishers Association. Seelbach got around the conflict quite well and avoided taking a position between the top management of the Publishers Association and the management of the Fair. He was successful in making a technically superior set-up on the third floor of Hall 7, which was somewhat out of the way, but better than the dubious, jury-rigged press center near the offices of the Fair management. Here it remained, though not without the top management of the German Publishers Association expressly stating: *It is not the primary responsibility of the public relations department to gather information, but rather it is the duty of the Fair management to provide such information; one should plan on any information from the management of the Fair being transmitted hourly to the press center.*

So went the nerve-wracking little game between the German Publishers Association and the Fair. Even at a distance everyone knew how hectic things were for the management during the Fair, and what problems always cropped up, and could recognize the futility of such requirements. Even today, I'm really piqued when I think back on this! The Fair management had to be on hand for the participants of the Fair, whether they were exhibitors, foreign delegations, or journalists, and could not march in hourly rhythm to the public relations department of the Publishers Association. However, I had to swallow this pill. The whole thing naturally did not work. Besides that, the new press center was in no way really capable of serving the needs of the ever-growing number of journalists.

Our goal was to develop the Fair into an operation that functioned well for all participants. We had to cut back on setting up a real press center, but there were many other areas where structural improvements and structural changes were pressing tasks.

The Frankfurt Fairgrounds Company, owner of the fairgrounds that were rented to us, was at that time offering a quite unsatisfactory product. There was a shortage of infrastructure at the Fair in almost all areas. Not only did the fairgrounds lack a press center with the right equipment, in fact there really was no modern equipment to speak of apart from the bare exhibition halls—no rest areas or benches for tired visitors; no conference rooms for our ever-contentious professional public. Refreshment areas were quite deficient—among British exhibitors, the saying was that when they were hungry and were lining up at one of the bratwurst stands, "The *Wurst* is yet to come." What were called "exhibition halls" were really "aircraft hangars" set at some distance from one another. After many complaints to the management of the Frankfurt Fairgrounds Company, these halls were finally connected to one another with laughable tin roofs, so that in bad weather participants moving between the halls could at least feel minimally protected. There was no internal telephone network, and as a result we had to apply for a new, separate telephone connection for every booth (this was 1977—there were no cell phones yet)—quite an expensive proposition. There was not even any cabling in the halls for loudspeaker announcements, so that our technicians every year had to lay very expensive wiring. The transportation problem was not solved; no subway connection and no urban train reached the fairgrounds. We could not understand why the Book Fair had to pay the city of Frankfurt for the signs directing visitors to the streetcar lines traveling to the fairgrounds.

I pestered the management of the Frankfurt Fairgrounds Company. All those letters that I wrote to the municipality and to the Fairgrounds Company resulted in no improvements, apart from the red tin roofs. It didn't make any difference to the authorities in Frankfurt, and I finally decided to timidly go public with our dissatisfaction. I invited the Supervisory Board to come to Düsseldorf for its February 1978 general meeting, while the fair was being held there, and I merely reported the invitation to the press. This invitation was actually directed to my own Supervisory Board, so that its members could take a look for themselves at the most modern fairgrounds in Germany. At the same time I wanted to emancipate myself from the niggling role that I was playing *vis-à-vis* the fine folk at the Fairgrounds.

In the end, the meeting in Düsseldorf took place without me. As a result it escalated into the first big campaign for moving the Frankfurt Book Fair out of Frankfurt. I was sick at the time. A few days before the meeting of the Supervisory Board, I had had myself jabbed in the behind all at once with two cholera inoculations that should have been given several days apart, all because right after the meeting I wanted to travel to India and China. As a complication, a fever set in, not very high, but in the E.R. the doctor just gave me more shots, which induced a strange paralysis of my bite. For several hours, an enormously heavy weight pressed against my jaw, and I couldn't open my mouth. My little daughter kept coming into the bedroom and asking me, full of curiosity, "Are you dead yet?" I could only shake my head.

On the day before the Düsseldorf meeting I had to give up. I called my assistant, Manfred G., and Uli Staudinger, the chairman of the Supervisory Board, to my bedside and gave them the necessary information. Once everything was taken care of, I had a numb feeling—for the first time I had to pass. Was my strength no longer up to the job? At this point the figure of myself as the great functionary, which I myself actually mistrusted, began to crumble.

The supposed reason for my refusal to participate in the Düsseldorf meeting came from the fears of a doctor who had been called in and warned of a heart attack. However, on the inside, I judged the decision another way. This was the feeling of simply not being able to carry off my task. It was as though I were standing before the peak of the mountain, with one hand already on the top, and it was gradually beginning to slide away. Now I was numb. I didn't expect anything. I wasn't afraid of anything.

I had probably worked too hard, neglecting my spiritual life as well as my private life. Even in my own surroundings I was simply standing around, without anything to hold onto, isolated, if I could no longer be active.

I had done everything possible for a proper agenda for the meeting. Still, I slipped into a crisis that originated in my strenuous efforts to get everything right at the Book Fair. There were urgent needs that I had recognized and that I thought had to be met immediately.

In terms of the process of decision-making and approvals, the meeting must have been a fiasco. The major reason for this was that the two people to whom I had entrusted information, the assistant manager and the chairman of the Supervisory Board, could not satisfy the extensive questions of the Board. On top of everything else, the chairman of the Supervisory Board came to the meeting around noon on the second day after a long Düsseldorf night. He had already been replaced by one of the other members, something that he ignored when he finally got there and took over the management of the meeting. In the end the Supervisory Board decided that something had to be done now. They sent a three-person delegation to my sick bed in Frankfurt to inform me that, effective immediately, I should look for and hire a second director.

These three gentlemen, the chairman of the German Publishers Association, the chairman of the Publishers Committee and the chairman of the Supervisory Board, hurried to Frankfurt from Düsseldorf immediately after the meeting, and with great wheezing struggled up the worn-out wooden steps onto the third floor of our somewhat rundown old apartment building in the Frankfurt west end. I took one look at the serious *mien* and dark hats coming in, and with sarcastic irony realized that they composed my "firing squad."

These gentlemen were very careful in trying to convince me that the new person would reduce my work overload, and intimated that I was probably suffering from the too great demands of my office. This set of excess demands could only be resolved with a division of responsibilities. Silently, as though I still had my lockjaw, I accepted the "verdict."

At the municipal elections of 1977, the citizens of Frankfurt had voted out of office the Social Democratic Lord High Mayor Rudi Arndt (Dynamite Rudi), and in his place had chosen with an absolute majority the ever smiling Walter Wallmann of the Christian Democrats (CDU). "Dynamite Rudi" had gotten that nickname for purportedly saying that the ruins of the opera house, still not rebuilt, but which still bore the epigram "To the Beautiful, the Good, the True," should be dynamited and replaced with a modern building. (Critics of the time, in reference to the Frankfurt reputation of being nothing but business, suggested that the epigram should be "To the Beautiful Goods for Sale.")

Walter Wallmann, the smiler, a liberal conservative, was more inclined to preserve the past. He gave the people of Frankfurt their *"Gude Stubb"* old-town historical area by having the Römer Square redone in its medieval style. He worked with the experienced Social Democratic cultural commissioner Hilmar Hoffmann, and gave him a free hand in building up the "Museum Riverbank Section." Now, this new head of the city and the fairgrounds, someone ready to build, was set upon by the provocative press with reports of a campaign to move the Frankfurt Book Fair away—as though he were also the chair of the Supervisory Board of the Frankfurt Fairgrounds Company. To all of us at the Book Fair, it was quite clear that a Frankfurt Book Fair without Frankfurt would be an impossibility, no matter how bad the conditions were. Still, the press had a sensational story, and milked it for all it was worth. The Supervisory Board and the AUM could only issue denials, and avoided saying anything at all that would in any way be for or against the idea of moving away.

To be sure, there were a number of voices on the Düsseldorf side. Director Schoop grabbed the lifeline that we had waved in front of his nose, and held on to it tightly. In the end there was a fierce competition between the cities for the Fair. Book dealers and publishers from Düsseldorf and Cologne also raised their voices, and formed a lobby within the German Publishers Association for the big city on the Rhine.

In May, there was an inspection of the Frankfurt Fairgrounds by the Supervisory Board of the Exposition and Fair Company, in which I also participated. By its strong presence at this meeting, the city of Frankfurt made known how seriously it took the discussion regarding the fairgrounds. Despite the fact that a meeting of the municipal authorities was taking place at the same time, the Lord High Mayor Dr. Walter Wallman came to the meeting, along with his personal adviser Dr. Alexander Gauland and City Councilman Hilmar Hoffmann. Everybody who was anybody in the Fairgrounds Company showed up—company director Dr. Peter Graf von Wedel; the assistant company director Alfred K. Schnorr; the director of the headquarters and chief negotiator Kurt Beyer; Karl Roth, director of the technology section at headquarters; Emil Schmidt, director of administration and personnel at headquarters; Kurt Erbach, from the technology department; and Günther Reymann, head of the press division. The inspection took place in streaming rain, and as a result the lack of roof coverings was felt quite painfully at first. After that, a Fair bus was used.

At the final joint meeting in the Lord High Mayor's office at the Fair, Graf von Wedel took the floor. There is no doubt that the head of the Fairgrounds Company at that moment meant his calming words to mean something different, and that he did not grasp how painful the consequences would be. "We are very interested in putting you at ease and keeping you happy. We are clearly keen on your remaining. Please be assured that we will do everything in our power," he said, and then, "We will not content ourselves with mere words!"

Whereupon our chairman responded in a curt military manner, though in the mumbling Swabian dialect, "You have to take our demands seriously!"

Now was not the time for polite, soothing words. The last sentence from Graf von Wedel had that character, and immediately people jumped on the outrageous conditions: The huge distances between exhibition halls. The walkways lacking any covering. The awful food. The absence of cabling between the halls. The all too small press center, though it was helpful for the moment. The reception barracks for the professional visitors in Hall 5A. (A shouted remark from Ulrich Staudinger: *"It reminds you of Checkpoint Charlie!"*) The less than appetizing atmosphere in Fair Hall West. The egregious fact that more than half a million square feet of the fairgrounds could not be utilized for the Book Fair because other exhibitors had built permanent stands. The utterly deplorable parking situation that got more desperate by the year.

The director of the Frankfurt Fairgrounds Company once again gave a painful answer, "Our campus is physically still quite reasonable," a remark that met with only negative headshaking from our side.

And then Walter Wallmann took the initiative by saying, "I agree with you that something has to be done!" This comment from the Lord High Mayor was, as it soon turned out, also a political program. In the years that followed, Walter Wallmann made sure that the entirely amiable but unproductive management staff of the Frankfurt Fairgrounds Company was removed and replaced by managers from the southern sugar industry, who were hard as nails. He was successful in putting through investments in the infrastructure of the Frankfurt Fair of some 750 million Marks, and as a result, after a few years, the Frankfurt Fair had a very modern campus with large new exhibition halls, all connected by conveyor belts, and a technical infrastructure that made it one of the most sought-after fairgrounds in the world.

Walter Wallmann, whom people applauded for this accomplishment, in later speeches referred without vanity again and yet again to the origin of his successful activity for the Fair, namely the threat that the Frankfurt Book Fair would move away.

Because of this success, in 1986 I once again used the instrument of a threat to move, when the Fairgrounds wanted to raise our rental fees by 160% (over a period of 10 years). Since I would have had to pass on these annual increases to our exhibitors, I would have gotten into an area of prohibitive charges, and was left with no other choice than to answer this demand with naked threats. Once again I was lucky that this campaign, this time with Munich as the place to move to, ended successfully. I owed the successful conclusion to the fact that the Lord High Mayor Wolfram Brück lost the election, while the feisty Dr. Horstmar Stauber left the directorship of the Frankfurt Fairgrounds Company.

The successor to my successor, Volker Neumann, did not have as much luck when he tried to play the same game a third time in 2004. He got crushed under the political wheels, something that cost him his job a year later.

Did Somebody Say Communist?

The 1970s ended with the collapse of all the hopes of the "Left" that had been aroused by the events of 1968. In what was called the "German Autumn" (1977), an urban guerrilla group called the RAF (*Rote Armee Fraktion*—Red Army Fraction) escalated into a political terrorist organization with the kidnapping and murder of the president of the national employers federation, Hanns Martin Schleyer. Even in the months before this, the federal attorney Siegfried Buback and the banker Jürgen Ponto had fallen victim to the assassins of the Red Army Fraction. On October 13, 1977, Palestinian terrorists hijacked the Lufthansa "Landshut" flight on its route from Mallorca to Frankfurt, first going to Aden and then to Mogadishu (Somalia), where they demanded the release of eleven RAF prisoners from German jails. After the storming of the hijacked airliner in Mogadishu and the freeing of the hostages by the German border guard special unit GSG 9, three terrorists who had been condemned to life imprisonment—Andreas Baader, Gudrun Ensslin and Jan-Carl Raspe—committed suicide in their cells in the Stuttgart Stammheim prison.

A vociferous "student movement" had grown up in 1968, a movement that at the time ruled the streets. The movement grew out of the "Extra-Parliamentary Opposition" (APO) against the Vietnam War, the emergency laws of the Grand Coalition in Bonn, which encompassed both the Christian Democrats and the Social Democrats, and the movement against the rigid structures of the universities and against the public amnesia regarding Germany's Fascist past. The radical core of the APO loudly preached the construction of a socialist society. In the 1970s, the student movement declined in strength, and split into political groups and sects. Some of these groups, such as the RAF, chose a path of illegality and terror. From then on, being a left-winger meant bearing a special stigma. Left-wing teachers, even left-wing mailmen, particularly in the 1970s, were covered by the official "employment ban" that disqualified any person belonging to political parties considered to be radical. The search for the "leftists," who were to be excluded from having any influence on society, did not spare me or my tasks at the Fair.

On November 4, 1977, the Straubing book dealer Karl Pielsticker posed this question in an emotion-laden letter to the chairman of the German Publishers Association Rolf Keller: *Is the left-radical political propaganda to continue at the Fair, or are there still people at the top of our Publishers Association who once and for all can decisively put an end to this stuff? I hope you will set the Fair director straight.*

Pielsticker was referring to a comment of the Passau publisher Martin Teschendorff, who in the *German Publishers Weekly* of October 28, 1977, had resignedly warned of all the left-wing bazaar-type activity at the Fair.

The Marburg book dealer Wilhelm Braun-Elwert pursued me for several hours every day during the Fair in 1978, so that I finally made myself scarce and directed the Fair from my car. Braun-Elwert was obsessed with "tipping me off" to all the hard-line Leftists and the numerous left-wing publishing houses, who "were stirring up trouble at the Fair and should be excluded."

Everything that had the mere outward appearance of being "left-wing" was denounced and persecuted, and preferably chased out, by the majority conservatives, not to mention the "right-wing" propertied interests. In response to the new spirit of the times, and as a result of the many insinuations and attacks, I asked myself what I actually was. The question of whether I was a left-winger, a Red, a Socialist, had never been posed to me before. This occurred only during the virulent times of the 1968 APO demonstrations. At that time I was classified as *right-wing* by the students and demonstrators, who labeled me a "liberal asshole" or "in the pay of the exploiters." In my life up to that time, I had always defended myself against being classified or labeled by anyone from the outside, whether it be for my worldview, for my religion, or for my ideology. Still, it could not be denied that I was receptive to certain feelings of unease about the present state of our society.

> It is
> a groundhog, a hibernator
> it sweats
> and never laughs
> it does not even smile once
> it has only a metallic sound
> it does not stir
> it does not move
> it has death as a result
>
> I met it
> at the hothouse
> of local politics
> in the padded cells
> on the executive floors
> I also climbed the political Olympus
> and found
> what was dreadful
> in the midst of democratizing
> gods.
>
> Then I shit flowers
> from pure despair
> I kissed life
> wherever I found it
> and threw myself into the sand
> that cooled me down
>
> But hibernation
> overcame me
> my breath grew cold
> single-minded and flat
> my walk
> hypocritical, my
> embraces at night...

The author "Nachtigall" (*Nightingale*) was someone I connected with in the 1950s, and who accompanied me in my youth through all my bewilderment and wanderings with his small, unpretentious poems. He spoke to me from the heart, or rather, from the gut. He marked out what I was suffering from, what I still feared to admit. He became for me an escape valve without which I would have become sick from the pressure bearing down on me from all sides. Nachtigall was my *Alter Ego*.

Granted, what I did on the outside often said that I was one of those "Reds," who should now be segregated from proper society. Had I not begun the director's post in a red turtleneck sweater and a leather jacket, which occasioned a snide remark from the American magazine *Publishers Weekly*? Had I not shown whose spiritual child I was by planting songs and poems of Bertolt Brecht in the first Fair for which I was principally responsible? And my original sympathy for the uprising of the students was not to be overlooked. And then my work for the Chilean victims of the Pinochet *putsch* in the left solidarity groups! And my use of the familiar *"du"* for "you" instead of the proper *"Sie"* in conversation where I worked, all this equalizing activity…

I never wanted to be anybody else than the person I was, but this constant reproach of "being a lefty" got on my nerves. I could never act naturally in the world of business, even if the book business had more liberal and left spirits than elsewhere. It was my impression that, as a "lefty," I had to do more than other nobodies. I suddenly got an inkling of the position of women, who had to do more in order to make their way in the world of men. The world in which I wanted to exert myself all of a sudden turned out to be just the way it was before — conservative, right-wing, authoritarian, happy to defame anyone who was different, who did not think like all those people who considered themselves the majority.

I had welcomed the emergence of the students against the ideology of the 1950s, which appeared to me and to many others to be strongly marked by authoritarianism and even by the Nazi idols who had been overcome — and yet I was not a member of the generation of 1968. In general, opposition interested me more than did the establishment, whether it was in Brazil or in the Soviet Union.

The authors whom I read included Marx, Mao and Ernest

Mandel.[1] I was interested in their alternative ideas regarding the existing economic and social system, and besides that I wanted to know just what Socialism *was*. Was this enough to be a lefty? If "left" meant seeking more existential and social freedom, then I certainly wanted to be a left-winger; but I also did not want to have the free expression of literature limited. To exclude the left-wingers from the Fair was censorship, just as was the demand not to allow "right-wing" publishing houses. It was always important to me that the entire political spectrum of opinion be represented at the Fair, whether it be of the left or of the right, whether for military autocracies or for socialist dictatorships, whether liberation fronts or police states. The only criterion for participation in the Frankfurt Book Fair should be that the exhibitor present his own books, that everyone follow the democratic rules of discourse, and not use force against opposing parties.

What drove me personally was the different opinion I had about authoritarian behavior. One could of course ascribe this to my political outlook, since the spirit of the times also showed such a split attitude toward ever more demanding authority, "one that finally would act vigorously and put an end to the left-wing drive," as opposed to "anti-authority," and thus left-wing. When I had to fire an employee of the Exposition and Fair Company because he no longer fit into the team (we called that the "bullfrog disease"), many times I suffered from the same thing. Here I had an individual as well as a class-specific conflict. With the individual I had an ongoing debate. The class-specific item came from the sense of being torn out of the *petite bourgeoisie,* which had quickly adapted to imitating those above it because it could not develop its own ethos. In order to get away from this, this class made the punishing Superfather the driving motor of its activities. Protestantism, Hitlerism, which was also a *petite bourgeois* escapism, and the current terrorism were all manifestations of the same basic problem, namely, the hopelessness and the emptiness of the middle class and of the *petite bourgeoisie.* We the children of Luther, we the children of

1. Ernest Mandel (1923–1995); Marxist theorist, Trotskyist, leader of the Fourth International and author of *Late Capitalism.*

Hitler, we the Wandering Hikers and the German fraternity men, we the Mahlers, we the Baaders, we the Meinhofs, we the Ensslins,[2] were only reacting, and really coming to the wrong conclusion.

If you entertained such thoughts, then it seemed natural in the spirit of the times to be a left-winger. Such a left-winger, not tied to any political party, not hemmed in by any ideology, but a free and critical thinker—I was such a left-winger, and that's what I wanted to be. That's why I did not defend myself against the blanket charge that first came out, first moderately from my own sector of the economy, and then later directly at me.

The true Left, put on the defensive, starting in 1978 became involved with the controversial "Third International Russell Tribunal on the Situation of Human Rights in the Federal Republic of Germany." Sixteen foreign jurors, almost without exception left-oriented personalities, concerned themselves with the situation in an avowedly democratic state, in which certain events led one to fear the possibility of a slippery transition to an authoritarian regime—so went the official announcement. At the center of all this was the practice of the aforementioned "employment ban," that is, the refusal to take on applicants for the civil service on the basis of "well-founded doubt as to their loyalty to the Constitution."

An earlier tribunal, also named after the British philosopher and pacifist Bertrand Russell (1872–1969), had condemned the United States in 1967 for numerous war crimes in the Vietnam War. The topic of the second Russell Tribunal, meeting in Rome and Brussels from 1974 to 1976, was the issue of human rights violations by dictatorial regimes in South America. That the third such tribunal should now put on its agenda the political situation in the Federal Republic of Germany was something that aroused indignation among politicians and among wide

---

2. *Horst Mahler,* former member of the Red Army Fraction (RAF), recently convicted of hate crimes. *Andreas Baader,* RAF leader convicted for a string of robberies and bombings. *Ulrike Meinhof,* journalist and RAF co-founder; her role in Baader's prison-break helped coin the term "Baader-Meinhof gang." *Gudrun Ensslin,* RAF co-founder and leader. Baader, Meinhof and Ensslin all died in prison.

circles of the West German public, but it must be seen as a reaction to the growing hunt for lefties in our society.

We ourselves got involved in this fracas in the spring of 1978 with our book exhibit in the Netherlands, *The German Book Today*. One of the Dutch opening speakers for the exhibit in Groningen, Prof. Lolle Nauta, lecturer in philosophy at the University of Groningen, was disinvited by the German Embassy in the Netherlands when it became known that he had agreed at the same time to participate in the Russel Foundation's Tribunal regarding the Federal Republic of Germany. The participation of Lolle Nauta, who belonged to the left-wing of the Dutch Labor Party, was a subject of much controversy in the Netherlands, and subjected Lolle Nauta to a lot of criticism. Much of this turned into solidarity, however, when public opinion learned of Germany's overreaction. Big headlines appeared in the Dutch press, quoting a spokesman of the German Embassy, who, when asked why Lolle Nauta had been disinvited, had explained, "The Federal Republic of Germany cannot allow itself such masochism!"

This actually insignificant affair around the opening of a German book exhibit escalated when the Dutch speaker at the opening of the first exhibition site in Rotterdam, André van der Louw, the mayor of the city, canceled his participation in the local opening out of solidarity with Lolle Nauta.

There was a big blow-up when Martin Ross, foreign language editor of the De Arbeiderspers publishing house, who had been invited to give a speech at the opening of the exhibition on *The German Book in the Netherlands,* announced to the German general consul Dr. Hans-Ludwig W., that in his speech he would go into the current political events surrounding the invitation to Nauta. W., as the individual in charge of the cultural department of the Foreign Office, had been responsible for several years for providing the financing of the international book exhibitions. He was a person who made the comment, which was making the rounds among us, that he would rather have a tank than 16 book exhibits. He sent an ultimatum to Ross to leave this out, and according to what Ross later said, himself still visibly angry, W. had acted in a very authoritarian manner. He declared that during the conversation W. had simply turned around and did not want to have any discussion. To Ross's argument that he was strengthening the impression that censorship was being exercised, W. simply did not reply.

This continued during the Ross lecture that occurred afterwards. W. sat in the first row next to Martin Mooij, the director of the Rotterdam Kunststichting, which had given substantial support to the comprehensive program surrounding the exhibition. When Ross began to speak about the disinvitation of Nauta, W. ostentatiously turned around, put on a sour face, and carried on a stage whisper conversation with his neighbors. Among other things, he is said to have asked Mooij if there was nothing to be done about these Ross appearances, a comment which was interpreted to mean W. would like to cut off the microphone. Ross, in great anger, left the exhibit after his speech. The next person to speak out about this affair was I myself. I had rushed off to Groningen, where I wanted to take over the part of Nauta in order to save what could be saved. In my speech I expressed it this way:

In books, the life of humans is reflected; what we have learned, what we have experienced; analyses and questions are brought together and transmitted. We know that you in Holland have lots of information about the Federal Republic of Germany. In your northern province, German television is received; German tourists visit your cities and the coast; you read German newspapers. And let us not forget that this view includes the experiences of the Second World War, as well as the experience of the terror that has crossed borders in recent days. The exhibition The German Book Today *would like to add another aspect to the picture that you have of us.*

The attempt at reconciliation was successful. In a closing interview in the *Universiteitskrant,* the Groningen daily newspaper, which had extensively documented the whole affair, Prof. Lolle Nauta finally said: *I had an extraordinarily pleasant discussion with Weidhaas. If it had depended on him, all of this would not have happened. I find it a crying shame that the exhibit has been so discredited, because it seems to be very good. I would like to go back there again.*

A Growing Fair

The Book Fair in 1978 took place amidst the constraints and limitations of the Frankfurt Fairgrounds, just as in every other year, and it was successful. That means that our exhibitors were successful. The Fair grew, but the exhibition halls did not grow along with it. Again and again we had to relocate people, something that met bitter resistance from those implicated. In 1978, it included the publishing houses from the group Science–Technology–Cartography, who were furious because they were moved from the common large hall, the current Hall 8, into the secondary Hall 5A. Of course, in paragraph 5 of the conditions for participation in the Frankfurt Book Fair, which every exhibitor acknowledged with his application, the following was clearly stated: *The completion of the Fair contract does not give the exhibitor any claim for being placed in a specific location, though the wishes of the exhibitor will be considered as much as possible regarding the location, neighboring booths, size and assignment to a group.*

Regarding the second half of this sentence, our little crew on Kleiner Hirschgraben Street did what it could. There were three women working under the technical director Franz-Josef Fenke, who every year by the end of June had to accomplish the miracle of a precision floorplan. Of the 2,428 correspondence associates, who had to be satisfied in this case, practically one-third had a special wish. This one wanted to be next to so-and-so and opposite so-and-so, but as far as away as possible from competitors, at the beginning of a corridor, not under a ventilator, definitely not against a wall or near the toilet, but also not near a pornographer, a political publisher, a religious publisher, a noisy booth, or a foreigner. It was clearly not easy to piece together that puzzle each year, but as the Fair got stronger, more and more often places that had been secured had to be abandoned and new arrangements made. Each time it was as though someone had stirred up a hornets' nest. Those who were really irritated buzzed around and wildly stung everyone in sight. Our task was to pacify those who were agitated, and to give them the feeling that the new location would prove just as satisfactory as the old.

The process always followed the same pattern. The particular exhibitors who were "extraordinarily satisfied" with their previous position wouldn't give it up for the world, since their loyal customers already knew precisely where to find them—these exhibitors put up a fight and protested most vehemently against being moved. The insidious word "ghettoization" made the rounds. One first had to check with the other exhibitors, while new exhibitors coming for the first time had to prove their worth at the Book Fair before they could be allowed into their favored section. The staff in our organization had to be skilled in the fine art of diplomacy. I always admired the people in the "Technology" department, who year after year met our June deadline for sending the Fair catalog off to the presses. My job in all this was to take care of the public discussion of the industry through articles in the *German Publishers Weekly* (*Börsenblatt*), interviews in other industry newspapers, such as *Buchmarkt* (Book Market) and *Buchreport* (Book Report) put out by Harenberg Publishers. These served as the mouthpiece for the most outspoken book dealers. Harenberg was always quite rude to us.

At the end of the day, I still had to deal with those companies that were exceptionally contrary and were not prepared to give way. They had to be convinced in long telephone conversations, which often ended in success, but not always. Sometimes it would happen that companies would be absolutely impervious to reason and would speak of a boycott. Finally, when they could get no support for such a thing from the other exhibitors, they would stay away, being sure to make a big deal of it in the press. A year later they were back. Sometimes the company representatives liked to share the fact that they had been in Frankfurt for quite a few years, and that they knew me well. I on the other hand rarely remembered them, but I always consoled myself and them with the comeback, "And a good thing too, since from among the large number of exhibitors I usually recall only those who gave me personal grief!"

There were of course many exhibitors who did not resist, and who accepted the guidance of the Fair administration and acted on it without argument. Roughly speaking, the exhibitor community was divided into thirds. One third was easy to handle and did what was asked; they rarely had a conflict with us. The second third was quiet as long as their interests were not directly affected; when that happened they were quite vocal. The last third included those who were always among the rebels. They were the difficult ones, the ones who always came up with new demands, the ones who were seldom satisfied and were always slamming their fists on the table. It goes without saying that those who were counted among this particular third were not always the same ones. One could surmise that the "tough ones," assuming that they were not manic grumblers, usually were numbered among the most successful exhibitors. The more modest ones, the ones who did not rebel, were as a rule not so successful. That's the way it was, but it did not make appeasing the troublemakers any bit easier.

In 1978, the science publishing houses had to be moved. We avoided a dispute about their placement by the time-honored tactic of ducking out of sight. Later, when we had to deal with much stronger exhibitors, say the Americans, we could no longer uphold our sovereign claim to dictate where people should go. The only truly accurate measure for our work was, in the end, success—that is, *How well did the entire Fair function?* Should one day it no longer be possible to satisfy the ones who protested, they would simply drop out. That was the conclusive sign that we had not succeeded in accommodating the interests of the participants in a balanced way.

This pattern was repeated even in the early 1990s, when the disputes with individual exhibitors grew into conflicts with whole groups or nations, whom we could no longer control once they became organized into conglomerations of aligned interests. In 1978 we had been successful in carrying out our reallocation as planned. After one year, when the new paths and structures had been accepted after the first few hours of the Fair, all those involved calmed down again. The Fair ran its usual successful course, as the questionnaires clearly showed.

One year earlier I had begun to give some of the groups participating in the Book Fair their own special meeting corner. In actual fact I had started this policy as early as my first year, 1975, when I set up a provisional press center under the adverse conditions prevailing at the time.

One year later it was the literary agents who would become more conspicuous with the start of their own center. Twenty-eight agents signed on in the first year, and more recently we had over 1,000 agents from 280 firms. Since then, every other international book fair has not been able to do without such a center for literary rights.

And then a year later the New York book dealer Mary Rosenberg—who at age 70 was still lugging her hefty prospectuses around the Fair and was highly sought out by publishers wanting to cut a deal—proposed that we set up a center for foreign retail book dealers. Over 350 retailers took space in the first year, and in the second year it was over 500. Soon there were over 3,000 non-German book dealers exhibiting at the Frankfurt Book Fair.

The centers were always set up according to the same model. There was an administrative counter, manned by our employees, armed with a directory of present attendees and the means to schedule appointments. A small food service gave the opportunity for modest business meals, and cupboards with locking doors gave space for storing belongings. Those who signed up at such a center earned an invitation for the following year, and they received advance marketing information and a guide for the next Frankfurt Book Fair. In this way we developed lasting relationships with participants in the Fair, who previously could be reached only through generic advertisements in the industry newspapers.

The success of setting up these centers had an effect on a larger group of participants, who until then could be approached only in very diffuse ways, even though they were quite important for our publisher-exhibitors—this was the group of librarians and document specialists. Through contacts with libraries, I learned that most librarians could not claim expenses for attending commercial expositions. We thus created a center for librarians and document specialists, run by two librarians under the direction of Dr. Werner from the University Library in Frankfurt, and with its own exhibitions of equipment for libraries. We offered expert lectures there, something that raised the status of this new center at the Frankfurt Book Fair to a professional conference for library and information science, which in turn would secure travel reimbursement for more than 2,800 librarians.

In the years that followed, the success of these really sensible centers caused additional centers to grow like weeds. Most of these lasted only a few years. The center for foreign book dealers naturally had to be followed by a center for German book dealers. This was taken up happily, even by the difficult retail clientèle. Later, when the retailer committee of the German Publishers Association took over the leadership of the center, it turned into a pure retail "restaurant," visited by 6,000 members year after year.

A center for the reading public near the children's book exhibitors was the answer to the worries of the book trade that reading was becoming a lost art for children. A graphic design center gave the group of illustrators and artists a refuge and a contact place. An East–West center and a North–South center took care of Fair publicity for the regional interests of otherwise often neglected publishing houses, book dealers and authors. The East–West and North–South centers finally combined into an international center. Afterwards the translators got their own center, an important and underpaid group who are so crucial for the international exchange of literature.

These centers were, in essence, social areas for groups that were not exhibitors, but who were quite important nevertheless, since they formed a target group who earlier had filled the corridors of the Fair as an amorphous public, one that could hardly be found by the exhibitors. These groups of book dealers, librarians, document specialists, literary agents, illustrators, translators and journalists could from now on be found at specific places and could be drawn into the business activities of the exhibitors.

Finding business contacts quickly was of extraordinary importance for all those struggling for success in a quickly growing book fair. We therefore examined the exhibitor group once again very carefully, and we determined that the directional system that we used was not in any shape to bring people seeking something to their destination with a concise, convenient communication formula.

I suggested to our working group the following, a format that was realized in 1979. Every booth was to get a new code number, consisting of the hall designation, an alphabetic corridor number, and within this corridor, depending on the location of the stall (left or right), an even or odd number. The Verlag für Deutsch of Munich, for example, which had its stand in Hall 8, Corridor H, on the right side numbered 725, on all the signs received the code 8 H 725.

Now we could do without consulting the comprehensive listing of the exhibitors with its long index of addresses and catalog information; and we were able to learn from the general alphabetical list or the country list the location of the booth that was being sought. We then soon shifted to printing a visitor's guide for the Fair, something in addition to the more comprehensive main catalog, a pocket guide that listed only the exhibitors by country. The large catalog was very well-received as a world-wide list of addresses of the international book publishing trade, and graced publishing offices around the world—and still continues to do so today, despite the electronic edition which has also been appearing.

The stalls, which were owned by the Frankfurt Book Fair, and which were stored and maintained at the Troschke Fair Construction Company, were shipped in to the fairgrounds every year two weeks before the Book Fair by several hundred truckloads from Troschke's storage sheds. They had been purchased in 1967. In the meantime, they had become out-of-date, unstable, and no longer suitable for the needs of the exhibitors. They also did not conform to a modern, ergonomic, cost-effective technology.

The system also consisted of a total of 23 components, of which 9 were "small parts," many of which were lost or had to be repaired at every Fair. The result was very high costs of acquisition, repair and construction. Besides that, the system lacked stability, and frequently had to be set up on the sometimes very uneven ground in the halls by using wedges underneath. The bookshelf hangers were also in part unstable if the hanging hooks had been compressed on the rails.

I convened a working group, consisting of our graphic artist, technicians from the Troschke Fair Construction Company, a company architect and colleagues from our technical department; at the beginning I also participated. I had learned from discussions with exhibitors and our technical personnel just what the users needed from our exhibit stalls, and I prepared sketches of three basic types of stalls, which were now to serve as the basis for the development of the new stall system.

- Basic type A: a stall open to the corridor with three exhibit walls.
- Basic type B: a wall of half height in front, so that the person in charge of the stall could also make eye contact with the public while sitting, though this was only in connection with a double stall of type A, so that free access to the stall was possible.
- Basic type C: like B, but with one half comprising a closed cubicle with a door, as a private meeting or storage room integrated into the stall.

The three types were then developed within the new stall system, which had many advantages compared to the old system. The components were reduced to 8 parts, a reduction of some 15. This new system no longer contained any small parts. Costs for acquisition, repair, storage, transport, and set-up and dismantling could be reduced. This was especially true for the transportation costs, since the individual parts, like flat plates and frames, were not unwieldy, and so fewer trucks were needed for transport. Fairground reconstruction evened out the floors. With its newly created cover frame integrated with light rails, the stall not only was well-constructed, but also self-stabilizing. The hanging hooks for bookshelves were done away with, since the shelves could be hung directly on the walls. All kinds of small improvements were added and tested.

Questionnaires were distributed to many places in the Book Fair, so that other Fair participants, even though not belonging to the publishing houses that were being tested, could participate in the assessment or critique of the new stalls. These questionnaires included a reference to things like the color of the stalls, the wall coverings, the seat cushions, the bookshelves and much, much more. The publishing houses who used the stalls were intensively questioned about their experiences.

The total functional impression was overwhelmingly positive. The colors tended to white and light gray. Criticism, when expressed, usually related to the "closed-in nature of the stall." This impression was probably fostered by the new layers of covering, which gave the impression of being an open but compact whole only when viewed from the front. This contrasted with the old stalls, which were completely open up above.

After this year of testing, we began to create the stalls in series, and year after year outfitted one or more exhibitor groups with them. The complete new outfitting of the Book Fair was completed after five years, though the financing of this new investment lasted more than seven years. It ran to over 35 million Marks, a sum that was experienced relatively painlessly through clever depreciation and a one-time increase of the stall price of 8%, and through other extraordinarily moderate increases. In this affair, the finance people from the Bertelsmann Verlag (Munich), as provided by Dr. Ulrich Wechsler, chairman of their Supervisory Board, were very helpful, and gave me the necessary arguments for an eight-year period of losses in this area for the annual financial statements.

The old stalls, matériel for around 5,000 units, had to be scrapped, since practically nobody wanted them. I offered the stalls for free to several fairs from developing countries such as Zimbabwe, as well as to China, since the Chinese were getting ready to put on their own book fair in Beijing, and Cuba. The only condition was that we not incur any transportation costs. Zimbabwe did not answer; Cuba took advantage of the opportunity and transported around 200 stalls with a sugar shipping freighter returning empty from Rotterdam to Havana. The Chinese reacted in a very peculiar way.

When I learned of the plans from my friends in Beijing, I

offered my help in setting up a book fair there on the Frankfurt model. They did not respond at all to my indirect though well-meaning offers. Now however, when I officially offered them our old stalls for free, they sent me a diaspora Chinese from Los Angeles, who, having scarcely come into my office, attacked me with his broad middle American accent, saying that the stalls were much too expensive and that what I was demanding would in no way be paid by the Chinese.

Quite apart from the fact that this man was quite unlikable, and given the way he was behaving, I leaned back in my chair and decided not to do anything to clear up this obvious misunderstanding. I listened to what this man, who was very zealous in his task, had to offer, and I understood after some back-and-forth that it was a matter of about a half a million Marks that he was turning over in his head. If one were to add in the transportation costs, that was naturally an exorbitant amount with which to burden the startup of the "Peking Book Fair."

However, since the man annoyed me very much, and since he had aroused my playful instinct, I entered into the negotiation game and played hard to get. At the end of the day we finally agreed on 150,000 Marks, which was a welcome bit of windfall profit after our extensive outlays for the new stalls. When the first Beijing Book Fair took place in September 1986, the organizers defended themselves from overseas attacks for charging such steep exhibition fees by countering that Frankfurt had sold them the stall matériel at too high a price!

Tribute to Hermann Schulz

Hermann Schulz, walrus moustache and all, whom I first encountered in May 1976 in my office at a meeting of the German publishers of Latin American literature, became my close friend, my comrade-in-arms. We got together in Wuppertal, where he had his publishing house, and in Frankfurt, and with our families as well—he had two daughters and a son—at my little house in the Rhön. Hermann arranged my contacts with the Evangelical Church, and as a result the founding of the Society for the Promotion of the Literature of Asia, Africa and Latin America became possible. He also took over the role of publisher for our workshops in Africa, Asia and Latin America, and always traveled with our team to the book dealers of the developing countries. On March 20, 1982, he received the Von-Der-Heydt Culture Prize of the city of Wuppertal. Here is my tribute to him:

Ladies and Gentlemen, Mr. State Secretary, Mr. Lord High Mayor of Wuppertal-Barmen, dear Hermann Schulz—

Much has been prophesied, spoken and written about the decline of the book trade and the publishing industry. The ugly word of a "book factory" is making the rounds, where literature is manufactured as nothing more than mere merchandise, subject solely to economic laws. Salability is the exclusive measure for judging manuscripts, and many publications appear that are "streamlined" and "slim," due to the agenda laid down by publishing houses. And, so some notorious culture pessimists tell us, naturally the publisher as a personality has died out, that individual who is truly engaged with culture and literature. Names like Kurt Wolff, Samuel Fischer, Ernst Rowohlt and

Peter Suhrkamp[1] are dropped only when nostalgia is evoked or when one tries to substantiate criticism of the practices of the larger publishing houses. Their managers, so the judgment goes, are interested only in the functioning of their companies, and in no way have any kind of cultural engagement.

I would like to rebut these reproaches by looking at the man being honored today: Hermann Schulz, *the publisher.*

Certainly the criticism I have noted about our profession contains bitter truths. Large publishing houses exist that have programs seemingly tailored only for the market. One should not play down the risk that certain important themes and subjects, if they promise no profit, will be refused or will disappear into the desk drawer. On the other hand, the large-scale publishing house has its positive side—the broad, multi-faceted recording of all areas of knowledge, life and culture would not be possible today without such a company. Often enough bestsellers provide financing for less popular titles, and such a product mix is the only chance of publishing difficult texts.

The result, since it is in fact human beings who work in the book trade and in publishing, is that without editorial and publishing activity, even the large publishing firm would not survive. Consequently, the claim that publishers as such no longer exist is really not tenable. It is just that the demands and the risks of this trade have changed—it is still quite daring to be a publisher.

Hermann Schulz is undoubtedly a publisher in the best sense, someone standing in the tradition of Kurt Wolff and other outstanding personalities. His engagement has been and continues to be with what we call "The Third World," where his constant search for important, readable, meaningful manuscripts has been bound up with this engagement, and with the affairs of those people who live in the "developing countries"—what condescension can exist in one expression! These are the regions, as we know, that as a rule draw the attention of governmental

---

1. *Kurt Wolff* (1876–1963): German publisher of Franz Kafka and Franz Werfel; later founded Pantheon Books. *Samuel Fischer* (1859–1934): Founder of S. Fischer Verlag. *Ernst Rowohlt* (1887–1960): Founder of Rowohlt Verlag. *Peter Suhrkamp* (1851–1959): Founder of Suhrkamp Verlag.

and church organizations; since these are distant places, they are used as playgrounds for verbal gymnastics. That a publisher should seek out foreign cultures and ways of life is something that occurs quite seldom.

Admittedly, the successful work of Hermann Schulz, seen from this perspective, might best be recognized by a foreign embassy, and not with the cultural prize of a German city. To compare him with other publishing personalities who have been honored, like Kurt Wolff, would be mere flattery, since the work of Hermann Schulz does not go beyond the fields sketched out here. Actually, however, what flows out of this work for individuals and peoples who are Other, who are strangers, who are beyond our cultural circle and our history is something of infinite value for our own identity; something extraordinary is done for our cultural survival.

Hermann Schulz is a German publisher. He did not make his living from some random, escapist-tinged turn to foreign ways of enjoying life, to foreign revolutions or to foreign mysticism. These kinds of things are well-known, unfortunately, and should not be prevented. No, the way of life and ethos of Hermann Schulz are inextricably bound up with German history and with the experiences of his generation; his work has an indissoluble connection with the desolate situation of the lives and spirits of people that one meets ever more frequently in the industrialized West.

Perhaps the best way to clarify his significance is to look at the biography of our prize winner. He was born in Nkalinzi, in what is now Tanzania, as the son of a Protestant missionary, and shortly before the outbreak of the war he returned to Germany. His youth was shaped by the turmoil of the war, by the exaggerated nationalistic educational ideals of the Germans, along with their overriding conviction that they were the chosen people, though a misunderstood one, a conviction that verged on hysteria. It was gruesome to grow up in the generation that Hermann Schulz belonged to, the generation that in the 1950s had to recognize what crimes were laid at the feet of this country and its inhabitants, this country into which he had been born and in which he matured from a youth into an adult.

I am not speaking here of some vague social psychological

phenomenon—I happen to share the same birth year as Hermann Schulz, and had to cope with similar experiences. At that time it was principally books that explained to us what had happened (not our teachers, who did everything they could to conceal recent history). In my case it was a book with the title *The Yellow Star*, by Gerhard Schoenberner. For Hermann Schulz it was a brochure put together by an author named Reinhard Henkys, who posed the provocative question; "Was it really so bad?" This booklet appeared from the Lettner Verlag, which no longer exists. Hermann Schulz found the brochure during his apprenticeship in the book trade and took it home.

I would like now to allow myself to speak in the plural, since our reactions and the developments were really quite similar, as we later found out. Our horror and shock were so great that neither of us wanted to have anything to do with this society. We reacted the way young people still do today—we ran away.

Hermann Schulz hitchhiked to Turkey, Syria, Jordan and Lebanon. In Turkey, he had a revelatory experience when he met a very vital woman, the 65-year-old Turk Fahriye Bükey. For nights on end he and she drank home-made *rakı* in the hazelnut forests along the Black Sea, and she let him participate in her rich life experiences. This strong personality, who has gotten lost to us today in our country, we can recognize in many of the books later published by Hermann Schulz.

Then came the day of returning home, the time when the reins that had been dropped were taken up again. In 1960 Hermann Schulz started with the Jugenddienst Verlag, which had been built up by Johannes Rau,[2] and in 1967 he took over the responsible position of director of the publishing house. The moment had arrived for him to tie together the two formative elements of his socialization, the dismay over his own origins and the hope that was fed by a vigorous foreign culture—perhaps best expressed in the exaggerated and personalized form, Hitler and the old Turkish woman!

There are good grounds to think that this was the time of the birth of the "publisher" Hermann Schulz. In that same

---

2. Johannes Rau (1931–2006): Social Democratic politician; President of the Federal Republic of Germany, 1999–2004.

year he was responsible for a publication by a writer who was then completely unknown, the *Latin America Psalms* of Ernesto Cardenal, appearing in German under the title *Cut the Barbed Wire*. In order to grasp the significance of this publication for Schulz's future work, we have to go into detail more exactly on how this book came to be.

Schulz had just prepared a novel by the Soviet writer Valentin Kataev as a radio play for the South German Broadcasting Service, when he read in the literary column in the Zürich newspaper TAT two poems by a certain Ernesto Cardenal. The poems denounced radio and loudspeaker propaganda as methods of repression. In the same way the Russian Kataev had described these techniques as means for exercising power by the German occupiers against his people. This concordance lit the fire of Schulz's interest.

The *Latin American Psalms* was the first publication by Cardenal. The book appeared in an edition of 500 copies in Colombia, and was known there only to a small circle of the initiated. This circle included the enigmatic personality Ștefan Baciu. As the Romanian press attaché in Berne, Baciu had defected to the West and was granted asylum in Brazil in 1949. He traveled the contintent, had noteworthy run-ins with Fidel and Che, and became an expert in Latin American literature and Surrealist poetry. Baciu had stumbled on Cardenal's *Psalms;* he translated two of the poems and used his good connections to have them published in the Swiss newspaper.

Schulz took up the hunt. From Zürich he received Baciu's address, currently in Hawaii. After a few return-to-sender notices, Baciu finally sent along a postal address in Managua. After waiting for weeks for an answer, which never came, Hermann Schulz went to the Düsseldorf State Library and in the international press listings looked up the address of *La Prensa* in Managua, the newspaper which at that time, under its editor Chamorro, was leading the resistance to the Somoza regime. At that time nobody in this country knew anything about Nicaragua. Remember, we are writing here about 1967, and it was only the earthquake of 1972 and later the successful revolution of 1979 that brought this Central American country into the headlines of the world press and into public consciousness.

Shulz's persistence finally paid off. The letter to *La Prensa* was answered by the poet Pablo Antonio Cuadra, a cousin of Cardenal, who gave an address on the Solentiname Islands, an archipelago in Lake Nicaragua. Cardenal, once contacted, sent the Colombian edition of the *Psalms,* which Schulz immediately had translated by Baciu. The three outside reviewers, whom the freshly minted publisher consulted just to play it safe, unanimously advised against publishing. Hermann Schulz, however, did not let himself be led astray. Just as his motivation could hardly be called political, he was not scared off by any economic risk; rather he was driven on by his moral conviction. The little book, which was offered for 3.50 Marks, came at the time of the beginnings of the student movement, and despite all prognoses sold rather well. Down to today 250,000 copies are in print. The *Psalms* at the same time established Cardenal's world renown, and the German publication made Cardenal quite well respected even in Latin America. Carlos Lohle, Cardenal's future publisher in Argentina, discovered the little volume in an Amsterdam bookstore and was thus made aware of the poet. Later Cardenal gave him all the printing rights for all publications in Latin America. As an aside—Lohle, originally a Dutchman, was trained in Leipzig as a book dealer, and thanks to his knowledge of German was in a position to rightly value the German translation of the poems. Don't let anybody say that there are no longer any publishers!

Little by little, the complete works of Ernesto Cardenal appeared in German under the editorial care of Hermann Schulz. In 1972, the publisher traveled for the first time to Nicaragua, to that country whose existence and whose people were known to him and which had come alive for him and many others only through books. These books, which owed their genesis to the engagement of a publisher, reach out to another world, one which is quite downtrodden, but which on the other hand has so much more to offer in strength and self-assertion than does our depressed Europe.

This trip was the beginning of a lifelong love for Nicaragua. Hermann's enthusiasm for the discovery was reflected through a book in which the publisher, here an author, reported under the title, *A Country like Powder and Honey,* based on his three-month stay there. Further trips to Latin America followed; the results of these excursions can be looked up in the publishing list of the Peter Hammer Verlag. The authors represented in this program from Latin America include Eduardo Galeano, Salvador Allende, Sergio Ramírez, Mario Benedetti, Nicanor Parra and Gioconda Belli, and from Africa, Francis Bebey, Ngũgĩ wa Thiong'o, Ousmane Sembène, Ahmadou Kourouma, Mongo Beti, to name only a few.

I put this speech down on paper during a business trip to India. Since India is for us a synonym for the so-called Third World, I have expanded my comments with a longer citation from the contemporary Indian author Nirmal Verma. Hermann Schulz will understand this as an encouraging nod for him to take on the literature of this subcontinent in the years to come.

Nirmal Verma took up the dilemma of Indian tradition and the crisis of identity among his countrymen, which had been exacerbated by the encroachment of the Western cultural politics of individualism and technological progress. He held that the self-autonomy at the center of European humanist thinking had resulted in a split consciousness in which the individual is fatefully severed from his or her culture and traditions. The development of Western civilization was a bold—even hazardous—attempt to overcome this division by grounding value in self-consciousness and making man the measure of all things. In India, on the contrary, no such split has ever occurred. As such, India has no history; its past is "lodged in the very heart of the present." For Verma:

This has given a paradoxical continuity to Indian tradition, in its immobility it flows into us, in us it again becomes eternal. It becomes difficult to separate oneself from myths, images and symbols...for these constitute the very framework which encloses the self of a person, the mirror through which he projects himself to the world out-side. We are total within its totality. Without it we become nothing.

It is precisely this complex nature of Indian tradition which has to be kept in mind in reinterpreting the basic ethos of Indian people....

It is not strange that we in India never had a concept of 'history' in the strict sense of the term, as it is used in the European context....
The basic mode of life in India remained substantially unaffected

through the continuous chain of external changes.... I am merely recording a fact which would become obvious if we compare the basic transformations in European consciousness at various moments of history, e.g., the decline of classical culture, the beginning of the Renaissance, the collapse of the Church authority and the final rupture brought about by the Industrial revolution and the two world wars.

No such cataclysms made inroads within the structure of Indian consciousness. And yet history did intervene, casting its shadow, if not on the dark mythical roots of Indian consciousness, then definitely on the surface, where man is continuously compelled to make adjustments with the changing reality.... We are desperately trying to recast our image in a hypothetical future, a future designed and fabricated for us by Europe. We never dared to question the validity of this hypothesis.... When some one did question it... it was realized that the challenges of a historical European Culture need not be relevant to us: indeed may be totally alien to a society which on entirely different terms has related itself to history, time and nature....

The difference lies in the very concept of change which has become a crucial element in the very making of modern western consciousness [where the] *future became the embodiment of perfection.... All future ideologies... speak in hostile terms against nature, constantly working to 'conquer' it... in utter disregard to man's essential needs.... But to destroy nature completely it is necessary to completely dehumanize man; for man himself is a part, albeit an alienated part, of nature. What is human in man is precisely the awareness of himself, his own nature. Man is nature conscious of himself... man has not yet been completely alienated from nature. Nature, once it partakes of human consciousness... penetrates into the moral categories of human experience—in short, it is transformed into the active principle of man's freedom. Culture is that precise area of intersection between nature and consciousness where necessity is fused with freedom....*

The British have gone, but the degradation continues for the simple reason that the colonial values of the rulers become the model we aspired to imitate. In our passion to 'civilise' ourselves we have imposed a uniform industrial pattern on a society which hitherto derived sustenance through diverse streams of thought, myth and tradition. The result has been disastrous.[3]

3. Nirmal Verma, *Word and Memory* (Vagdevi Prakashan, 1989), 91–96.

What I want to make clear with this citation is this—that authors of these ideas, whom we mindlessly and superficially shrug off as "Third" or "Fourth World," in the search for their own national and cultural identity may turn to sources other than the ones we find customary. This applies to Asian writers and poets as well as to their colleagues from Africa and Latin America.

They are all bound together with their European and North American colleagues by a world-wide feeling of crisis, of the wish to overcome a general anxiety that has taken hold due to the increasing loss of human identity. The means of conquering this anxiety are varied; those which writers and poets offer us are just as distinct as the cultural *milieux* in which their literatures take root. I am convinced that we, the people of the northern industrial nations, need these alternatives just as urgently as the people of the southern "developing countries" need our technology and our civilization.

I am also firmly convinced that the cultural situation in the "North" is far more dramatic than that which the Indian Verma has pointed to in his description of the decline from Greek philosophy to the current deformation of Western man.

I would venture the claim—and here I base myself on many years of critical interaction with electronic media, and on the profound analysis of the Austrian philosopher Günther Anders in his major work *Die Antiquiertheit des Menschen*—that man in the industrialized nations stands on the verge of sacrificing his autonomy to cold and inhumane machine culture, in which life is reduced to bare functions, just one more variable in the equation of existence. Even worse! This loss of autonomy is not imminent; it began long ago and is silently moving full speed ahead! People only exist in the calculations of "overkill capacity" in nuclear wargames, as subjects to be conditioned by detached behaviorists, as a market for product launches and sales targets; as statistical quantities, as computable sums reducible to binary numbers and software inputs. Humans as humans—that is an anachronism, and anthropocentrism has long been swept away by the primacy of the machine. Simulation has overtaken reality; every sign of human life–weakness or inadequacy, sadness or joy—is just a blip in the universe of information.

We must not insist on the error that the fundamental threat

lies in a few computers or data centers. It is much more the invidious combination of systems, including economic "drives," that allows this megamachine to arise. The process is not yet complete, but humans as individual and in groups are increasingly ordered according to this supersystem; we are being replaced by machines that are undeniably superior in terms of speed, intelligence and life expectancy.

But is this really so? We cannot forestall this development, as it is bound tightly with other economic forces. It is high time for us to awaken from our technological fantasies of omnipotence and free ourselves as human beings. We can try to change course. Or else we can continue to stumble forward like lemmings, handing over our consciousness to the magic priests of the machine world. Where this way might lead I dare not say. We are continually force-fed information that nobody needs, information that is devoid of all human vitality and at the same time divides us. It lends the greatest urgency to commonplace events, and draws us into a banality that has already become the unspoken consensus.

Very often I think that our situation is similar to that of the American Indians at the beginning of colonization. It is impossible to understand today why these great cultures collapsed in the face of a handful of Europeans. Was it perhaps the failure to assess the weapons and intentions of their opponents, or the the blind trust in their own gods and social systems?

Then the parallels would be striking. We and our contemporaries in the industrial world place trust in our anthropocentric blindness, in which people are content to be guided by machines and impersonal systems. Heidegger understood this, perhaps in an exaggerated manner, in speaking of the "Shepherds of Being," or as when Anders, following Heidegger, calls human beings the "shepherds of the world of products and gadgets."

Industrial countries, whether they lie in the East or in the West, are no longer constituted for the people living in these societies; they have overthrown humankind as an axiom. If the methods of dehumanization on this side and the other side of the Iron Curtain are different, still the belief in efficiency and in technical feasibility bind together the diametrically opposed ideologies.

Most of the cultures of the "Third World" have an advantage over us in that they have not reached this stage of dehumanization. The concept *developing country* has within it something else. The defective industrialization is what the *Third World* can thank for its human substance. The cold brutal attack of the colonizers is turned against this. In the opposition to foreign rule, the colonized have unearthed the deeper layers of their own traditions and culture as a weapon and as a means of protection.

What can we from the North learn from this? A thin ray of hope, as a way of working against the dehumanization, is given to us by literature, our own as well as that of foreign cultures. It is literature, such as it is, that will always dare to think of deeply convinced and convincing utopias. We must reach back to the source if we wish to survive as humans in our overdeveloped civilizations.

A concrete beginning would be that we, the people in the industrialized world, give up the "starving nations" cliché of our fellow human beings in the "Third World." We need to stop having such a high estimate of ourselves, and should come down from the podium of "Giving aid to the developing countries." It should at this point be clear who it is who needs humanitarian and developmental aid!

And to return to the theme—we need literatures that provide alternatives that we have not even dared to dream about for a long time. These literatures show us the way to forgotten sources of vitality, and they open up doors that we think have been closed for a long time.

One person who has opened such doors wide enough so that human beings and humanity can pass through is the publisher Hermann Schulz.

We have him to thank for this!

℘

I took the assignment of the tribute for my friend very earnestly. I holed up for a week in a small Indian hotel on the beach at Margão in Goa, a place where I had intended to relax. On the terrace of my bungalow, with my view every evening of the setting of the sun in the West over the Arabian Sea, I composed this text. In New Delhi I had gotten to know of Nirmal Verma at a reception, when someone had pressed into my hands a brochure published by the German Embassy titled "The Cases of the Banyan Tree," which pulled me right away into the depths of his thought.

When I made that speech, on that 20th of March, 1982, I could not take pleasure in the vigorous applause that followed after I had finished. During my talk, a vicious headache had overtaken me, so that when I had spoken the last word, I swayed away from the speakers' podium and had to be taken into an adjoining room.

What had happened?

As one can see without difficulty when reading this speech, I was not only honoring my friend Hermann, but I allowed myself to lay out my philosophy, my credo, something that had developed from my activity over the previous twelve years. What I said there was meant to acknowledge a conviction that was the engine of my inner goals and professional labors. It was not, as I first believed, the theoretical basis for everything that was on the agenda from now on; it was not the beginning of a completely sealed off *Weltanschauung*, but rather was a wordy conclusion of my own search for identity in things foreign. Three months later I left my Latin American family, thus ending an intercultural experiment in which I had temporarily hoped to find shelter, as well as my restless search for an alternative to my rejection of all things German. I could not and would not be the Other, so long as I had not taken on my roll of being who I was, a German, a European, a White Man.

The Third World Tells a Story

The Fair and its community of book people had become a total work of art, and I worked at it like a true artist. With no small measure of intensity I searched for the moment in which all elements—the exhibit halls, the walkways, the rooms—and the demands of the people themselves could be brought into perfect balance, where an air of satisfaction would flit across the faces of the crowd, if only for a moment. I was keen to go on repeating such moments.

For this "demiurgic" artistic role it was necessary that I know my material in great detail. Above all, the publishers were my employers. They formed the basis of this great exposition. Their goal was to make a name for themselves, to sell the rights to titles, to purchase new titles, to grab the attention of the public, to garner publicity and to exert influence. My ambition was to make Frankfurt the home for all these publishers from around the world. Here they were to be raised on high, observed, and made to feel welcome. Yes, and more than that—they were to identify with this place. If that were to happen, that would ensure the vitality of our entire operation. The Book Fair—why did they come other than for making connections, for showing off, for chasing profits, but also out of habit? Every year it meant making the trip (and bearing the costs!) only to endure a full five days of communion together, in non-stop, round-the-clock commerce. Of course there were a number of snide comments by exhibitors about what they were doing here, and now and then someone intentionally marched out of step and simply did not want to have anything more to do with this affair. This happened with the ambitious Diogenes publisher Daniel Kehl from Zürich, who succeeded in staying away from the Frankfurt Book Fair for four long years before he returned.

In point of fact, a total artwork with infinitely interwoven threads—the authors had to be presented properly; the right books had to be brought to public attention; the journalists had to be led to the real stories; the librarians had to be encouraged to make acquisitions.

And then came the book dealers. They were in a way intimidated because, as sellers of books, they were no longer the most important points of contact for the publishers. The Fair no longer promised any special discounts, and the book dealers had long since lost their monopoly of access to the reading public. They had been supplanted by department stores and supermarkets, and by the direct sales of the publishing houses themselves. Whereas orders used to come in at the Fair in time for the Christmas season, now those same orders were being posted a whole six months in advance by the field representatives or later via wholesalers. Still, the book dealers had to come to the Fair, cost what it may. It was really a question of self-image.

A number of years earlier I myself had been an apprentice book dealer, and was aware of the traditional significance of the book trade for the sale of books, for the safeguarding of literary, artistic, scientific and technical values in a world that had come to exist only through the medium of the book. For the book dealers, the Fair meant only a few late orders for Christmas or a chance to see the latest titles, in particular from the smaller publishing houses without field representatives. One could not simply dismiss them. After all, the retail book trade still held the greatest expertise in the commerce of books, even if its sales were shrinking and made up an ever smaller slice of the total market.

I was also consumed by a certain missionary zeal to communicate specific themes and subjects that I considered of value to this community. Out of my desire for experimentation and innovation, I immersed myself more and more deeply in the program of "special topics." For the second year with a special theme, we chose to address the publishers of children's books and youth literature, and their customers; this included children and youth as well as their teachers and parents. We decided here on a single set of axioms for the program:

- Children in our society are an oppressed minority.
- Children have a right to appropriate reading materials.
- Children have a right to the truth.

This sounded somewhat pretentious, but the shape of our program concentrated on the treatment of some very important questions, and opened the way for further critical approaches and educational activities. We aimed to deliver this with the exhibit *The Third World in the German Children's Book, 1967–1977*, which included some 900 titles organized by region, encompassing Africa, the Far East, South and Southeast Asia, Oceania, Australia, Latin America, travel books and comics about the Third World.

I had assigned the directorship of this project to the sociologist Dr. Jörg Becker, a trustworthy friend in Frankfurt and a well-known scholar in the field. However, another personality was to prove pivotal not only for this event but for the future of the Frankfurt Book Fair. For the execution of this critical exposition of children's books, I engaged Rosmarie Rauter, a member of the Institute for Children's Book Research, which was headed by Prof. Doderer at the University of Frankfurt. She revealed herself to be a very earnest and knowledgeable specialist, and from then on until her retirement in 2004 she served as the coordinator of all further thematic presentations and foreign programs. A canny sleuth, Rosmarie uncovered some 900 children's books, purchased them from book dealers, and sent them to our scholars for analysis. We had to acquire the books on the sly, without tipping off the publishing houses, since, if they had gotten wind of our project to uncover hidden racism in children's books, might have pulled those titles from the shelves. In fact, one of the bigger publishers of youth literature, the Schneider Verlag, did just that!

After the opening of this spectacular exhibit by the State Minister of the Foreign Office, Mrs. Hildegard Hamm-Brücher, the expected uproar ensued, since the publishing houses who were targeted felt betrayed. Some were simply aghast as to what kind of outdated colonial and racist images had percolated into their prized children's books. But the program forced the publishers to clean up their act, and was later highly praised. The reportage on the topic of "The Child and the Book" was overall very positive. Only the magazine *Bild* called it a "Child Unfriendly Book Fair," because we had not reduced the 2.50 Mark admission price for children.

Then in 1980 came *Black Africa—Africa, A Continent on a Path of its Own*. We had placed the search for identity at the center of this topic, for one of the first casualties in the conflict that bound the continent's fate to that of Europe was precisely the question of African identity. European colonialism had suppressed the development of this Africa.

We had hired as our African consultant Said Mzee, who came from the East African Publishing House in Tanzania and who had completed his education at the University of Bayreuth. The Nigerian sociologist J. A. Sofala describes the African as altruistic, rich in humanity and social consciousness, and with unspoiled morality. Said Mzee, whom I worked with very closely for a year and with whom I eventually undertook a four-week trip to Africa, was on the other hand a rather reserved African intellectual. He had all of that which was described by Sofala, but through his many contacts with Europeans or because he felt himself somewhat different as an intellectual, he had developed a cynicism which he used to amend this uniform picture of Africa. The identity problem of the African intellectuals seemed to be reflected in this figure of our consultant.

At first everything went relatively smoothly. We had set up a symposium on African literature in the council meeting room of the Römer town hall three days before the beginning of the Book Fair. Thirty invited African authors were to work honestly on the problems of exile and of the multiplicity of African languages. Again and again the African authors living in Europe had to defend themselves against the reproach of their colleagues back home that they had been alienated from their own cultures and had lost all sense of responsibility to the African reading public. Mongo Beti, a writer from Cameroon, called on German publishers not to give undue support to African authors living in exile.

The trauma of the Africans of being alienated from themselves, by the actions of whites, particularly the Europeans, broke out in the introductory symposium. The weedy South

African poet James Matthews, my personal guest, caused a sensation in the town hall with his dramatic display of startled and self-denigrating comments. Matthews found himself in a situation of "being banned" in South Africa at the time when I met him, a kind of house arrest after a long stay in jail in the *apartheid* state. Through good contacts in the German Embassy in Pretoria I was able to get Matthews a passport and permission for the trip to Frankfurt; I was able to do the same for another poet, Sipho Sepamla.

Matthews's appearance at City Hall included a singular cry: *I ask myself, what the hell am I doing here? I am a semi-literate person, and they put me in a luxury hotel. Am I being bribed? Like all the other European countries, this country has raped my own country. Are we being repaid for that . . . ? I am not a writer, I am not a poet, I am here to talk about the pain that I feel, the pain that is felt by my sister and my son. Jails are my home. . . . Do I write poems? No, I write feelings. . . . I can't write a poem about beauty, I know only my pain, the pain of my brothers and sisters. I am so confused about why I am here. Shit! Shit! Shit!*

If you think that these comments were the overwrought outbreak of an African poet, you would be wrong. Here the basic African feeling had broken out in the person of this diminutive South African poet, and it overflowed in front of an alien European public, who did not know how to deal with the unchecked hysterics of a guest. But the Africans who were present—they paid attention.

That's exactly what we were aiming for. We were not trying to present any summer-in-the-sun Africa from travel brochures. We had invited the Africans so that they would speak, honestly and without holding anything back, and that we, the whites, should actually listen. It was clear we would not be treated to polite chatter. The South African *apartheid* regime was there with a big contingent, but so were the black African resistance organizations ANC and PAC. I had made special efforts to bring these organizations. I was always proud of being able to bring political opponents into proximity peacefully—or at least relatively peacefully—in the company of the book world in the exhibition halls.

We wanted a dialogue, with Africa too. So it was not hard to understand why we witnessed increasingly strident demonstrations in front of a South African booth. We could not exclude the South African publishing world that was complicit with *apartheid,* although it was repeatedly demanded of us; our rules on freedom from censorship at the Book Fair did not allow that. Likewise, we were dead set against calls for the expulsion of the African resistance organizations.

The African discussion, which took up almost all my time in negotiations with the various African spokespersons, escalated to the point that the Africans themselves boycotted the Fair for one day, and on that day we had to do without the African presentations, visitors and exhibitors. After that the heat of the moment receded to the point where we could bring the Book Fair to an end more or less in the standard way.

Basically, we were very successful. The events of the Black Africa theme were intensively, if controversially, discussed in the press and in the media. This gave us publicity. People talked about Africa and showed interest in it. It also had a good effect on the commerce in publishing rights. Even if the authors did not seem to have bestsellers to offer, practically all of them returned home with contracts for the publication of their titles in other languages. A Muslim author from Senegal, Mariama Bâ,[1] hit the jackpot with her little book *Une si longue lettre;* at the Fair she was able to sign contracts for translations into 14 languages. Unfortunately she could not taste the full measure of her success. She died one year later.

All in all, 26 authors from 14 black African countries showed up in Frankfurt. At the opening ceremony of the Frankfurt Book Fair, Tchicaya U Tam'si (1931–1988) from the Republic of Congo (Brazzaville) made a very impressive speech that took up the topic of finding an African identity. The Nigerian Chinua Achebe (b. 1930), generally considered the "Father of modern African literature," was there; his 1958 novel *Things Fall Apart* is still the most meaningful attempt to present the penetration of colonialism and missionary work into the traditional structures of Africa. The Nigerian Wole Soyinka, later the intellectual voice of Africa, came to Frankfurt at his own expense. Nigeria

---

1. Mariama Bâ (1929–1981): Senegalese writer, activist and educator.

was also represented by V. Chukwuemeka Ike (b. 1931), Cyprian Ekwensi (1921–2007), Emmanuel N. Obiechina (b. 1931), the literary critic Abiola Irele (b. 1936) and Buchi Emecheta (b. 1944), then living in English exile. Ousmane Sembène (1923–2007) from Senegal had served as a soldier in the French colonial army and then lived for more than ten years in France. In the 1980s, he became internationally known as a novelist and important filmmaker. Arlindo Barbeitos (b. 1940), poet, and José Luandino Viera (b. 1935), poet and novelist, both from Angola; Gaston Bart-Williams (b. 1938) from Sierra Leone; the poet, novelist, songwriter and well-known singer Francis Bebey (1929–2001) and polemicist Mongo Beti (1932–2001), both from Cameroon; José Craveirinha (1922–2003), resistance fighter and poet from Mozambique; Nuruddin Farah (b. 1945) from Somalia; Euphrase Kezilahabi (b. 1944) from Tanzania; Ahmadou Kourouma (1927–2003) and the poet and Minister of Culture Bernard Binlin Dadié (b. 1916) from Côte d'Ivoire; Sony Labou Tansi (1947–1995) from Congo-Brazzaville; Lewis Nkosi (b. 1936), James Matthews and Sipho Sepamla from South Africa—these filled out the impressive list of African authors who participated in a very significant way.

I had tried to make the Book Fair into a dynamic forum for contemporary themes as presented by the international book market. The topical discussions that were set off by Frankfurt spread through the press and the media and out into the world. This could be attributed to the incredible growth of press participation in Frankfurt. The topical programs and the discussions of content that took place had the effect of creating the image that Frankfurt was the place where things were happening!

However, in Frankfurt itself there were other opinions. Rumors abounded, particularly among the members of the Supervisory Board of the Book Fair. There continued to be forces in the German Book Trade and Publishers Association that did not like the direction that things were taking. They hung on to the good old idea of the Fair as a family festival of the book trade and as a purely commercial exposition. On the Supervisory Board, which understood itself to be the institution responsible for the Book Fair, the feeling spread that the Fair was not successful at meeting the wishes and desires of the members of the Association. Ever more clearly contrary notions stood out as to what the Frankfurt Book Fair should be. The Supervisory Board then began to simply despair that it could not manage the director of the business, who from their point of view was out of control.

After the events that took place during the Africa theme Fair, a fundamental debate was undertaken by the Supervisory Board, and I was completely shut out of it. After the fateful meeting, however, the chairman of the Supervisory Board, with the chairman of the German Publishers Association by his side, had a discussion with me in which he informed me that the Supervisory Board, in the meeting that had just ended, had decided to renew the decisions made in Düsseldorf in 1978. This meant that they would hire a second business director for administration and finance who would be on a level equal to my own.

Astonished, I asked how this was to be done. "The previous supervisory board, as you know, already installed JK as *Prokurist* [a corporate secretary with signatory power] for this area."

The answer was loud and clear that I would have to somehow take care of this problem internally. The most important result of the meeting was that the Supervisory Board from now on would once again determine the policy of the company. That was also an astounding statement. I immediately protested against this formulation because it undermined me and seemed to subvert my authority; the Supervisory Board was venturing out of its sphere of influence; it was entering into areas that were not its concern.

When asked to give examples of their anxieties, the gentlemen explained that it had been mentioned in the Supervisory Board that I had prevented both Peace Prize winner Léopold Senghor and German President Karl Carstens from coming to the Fair.[2] This was surely a malicious insinuation invented by somebody; I clearly did not have that much power. And why should I exclude those two from the Africa Fair, when I was

---

2. *Léopold Sédar Senghor:* Poet and President of Senegal, 1960–1980; recipient of the 1968 Peace Prize of the German Book Trade. *Karl Carstens:* President of the Federal Republic of Germany, 1979–1984.

interested in having as many different voices as possible participating on this topic? I rejected this criticism as a ridiculous slander.

Yielding somewhat, the chairman emphasized that they were not thinking about a basic change in the Fair policy, but rather on a "course correction," and he magnanimously added, "The Supervisory Board is of the opinion that it can still work with you."

I was naturally incensed and said, "The Frankfurt Book Fair and the other activities of our company over the past six years under my direction have been very successful. I consider this behavior by the committee and its comments to be an unjustified vote of no-confidence in my policies for the Fair...." I floated the idea that I should resign. The two gentlemen tried to calm me down by maintaining that the chief matter of the two internal meetings (with the management board excluded) had been to find a new self-understanding for the Supervisory Board....

This was a really unproductive discussion. In order to be in control of the supposed problems that existed in the company, the chairman suggested, "You have to make clear to your *Prokurist* that he has no future here any longer. That 'little clown' has completely screwed up."

He actually said the *little clown*. Was the enraged chairman making a joke of the small body size of the *Prokurist*?

"Instead of spinning out all the numbers and rounding them to the nearest five percent in the Fair report, he should have been much more concerned with the costs of personnel." During the meeting "a knife opened up in the pocket" of the chairman. And: "As far as I'm concerned this can go on to the end of the year, but after that the 'clown' has to go!

"And another thing: The use of the familiar *Du* for 'you,' that You, Herr Weidhaas, introduced when you took over the management of the company, must cease immediately. There are employees who are not ready for that. The notion of solidarity which was supposed to be achieved in this way has not caught on!" Obviously there were channels to the outside of which I had had no idea (just as with the affair with Senghor and Carstens). But then apparently trying to be more conciliatory he said: "Doing away with the *Du* is of course your own decision."

At the end of the discussion he could not avoid giving an encore performance with an emphasis of how close we were to the German Publishers and Booksellers Association. He crooned that more care must be taken regarding the personal relationship to the German Publishers Association. "You have to go on a regular basis to the head of the company, to solicit him and to consult with him before the meetings of the Supervisory Board, of course without letting him have control over essential matters! The directors of the retail sales committee and of the publication committee also have to be consulted on a regular basis."

What was it that so agitated me about this Supervisory Board? Wasn't this the standard way that supervisors dealt with their subordinates? Couldn't you simply get rid of such forms of intercourse if you are talking to your top manager? And didn't the board chairman here signal that the board itself had a problem, since they believed that they weren't able to force their opinions on me?

We certainly had different conceptions of how the Book Fair should continue to develop. These nine gentlemen were all personalities who were accustomed to dictatorial power in their own companies. Here their ideas were not adopted automatically. On the one hand, they were not in complete agreement with one another, but on the other this business director was always finishing the race ahead of them by a nose. Every meeting, every session of the Supervisory Board turned into a power struggle. The gentlemen of the Supervisory Board wanted to lead and make decisions for the national federation that had given them their mandate.

For months I had worked on projects with my colleagues that we then presented to the Supervisory Board to get their approval. Every time it was a nerve-racking, nail-biting event. If the Supervisory Board should reject our proposal, we had a very bad hand to play. Time and energy were not sufficient to develop new plans for the next Book Fair. Nonetheless, the gentlemen on the Supervisory Board wanted to decide. They did not simply want to leave such central matters of Fair policy to the discretion of the business management. From our side we were under immense pressure from thousands of fair participants to prepare an exposition that would meet the needs, interests, goals and wishes of at least a majority of those who spent great sums to come to Frankfurt.

In the end, I took the view that I had taken over the job and the responsibility of the head of the business. As long as I was there, I would lead the company whatever way I saw fit. If someone else were wanted or if I should be unsuccessful, then they should show me the door and find somebody else. This was the basis of the offers of resignation that I made repeatedly.

Obviously, I didn't make it easy for the Supervisory Board, and they were very frustrated with me; but I could not allow the members of the committee to have the impression that I supported the decisions that they wanted. Our conceptions lay too far apart.

With hindsight, I can give a rational account, but at the time I was not a detached observer. Actually, I also wanted to see a happy end to these arguments. I always wanted to reach a compromise with the people who sat in judgment over me and my closest colleagues with earnest faces and wordy speeches. I fought consistently and stridently to carry out my ideas. Sometimes I had to take my defeats, and then I retreated and accepted my losses.

But I never gave up. On a four-week trip through Africa with our local expert Said Mzee, we met many African authors, who shoved their handwritten manuscripts at us; they had never before had the possibility of publishing their work. These authors had no chance at the large state printing houses, generally set up with development aid from Western countries, and which were equipped with very efficient Roland or Heidelberg printing presses. Domestic publishing houses hardly existed, nor was there any marketing or sales system in the country by which at least the printing costs for such a publication could be recouped. The printing houses were almost without exception used for printing official government documents, or for publishing the collected volumes of speeches of the state president, in gilt binding.

I wondered how one could get around this difficult situation. I had heard from some Dutchman about an initiative in Indonesia. Some people had set up a printing house and a book bindery, together with a computer for text processing, all packed in a single VW bus, which was sent throughout the country and manned by volunteers, and which created informational brochures on the spot. This was a time in which we witnessed a boom for so-called mini-press companies, which with modest technical means were able to print small editions of 1,000 to 1,500 copies for niche markets. I thought to myself that many such presses could also help our African colleagues to obtain publishing expertise with little money, and to build up a small market to cover their needs.

The Ministry of Development in Bonn warmed to this idea, and asked the Carl-Duisburg company to come up with a financing plan. That was the beginning of the engagement by the developing countries, now lasting over 25 years, of "indigenous publishing," which spread beyond Africa and even to Asia and Latin America.

Four colleagues formed the project team under a project director from the Exposition and Fair Company (AUM). They were usually Hermann Schulz from Peter Hammer Verlag, Wuppertal, marketing; Benno Käsmayr, a small publisher from Maro Verlag in Augsburg, who took care of the used computers, small printers and binding machines, and signed off on the finished product; Reinhard Schubert, the graphics expert from our Frankfurt Book Fair, responsible for layout and art production; the fourth person was the project director from the AUM. We began our adventure in Ile-Ife, Nigeria, still somewhat clueless. We then started with a series of workshops in Kenya and Zambia, each lasting about ten days. Each time a book was created together with the participants whom we invited. Finally, there were workshops as well in Nicaragua, in Colombia, in Thailand and in the Philippines, and then in the former Socialist countries after the collapse of their state book trade.

Whoever knows how to do something should share that knowledge. That was the simple moral principle of solidarity with developing countries, but it was no less important for the economic future of the Frankfurt Book Fair, which also needed international partners in the future. It shouldn't even be necessary to say that my supervisory committee did not really look on such an engagement as quite in the core area of our activity at the Fair. Still in the end no one was able to refute our reasoning.

A broader and even more comprehensive project grew out of the experiences that we had gotten in the two topical programs of Latin America and Black Africa. It grew primarily out of my personal attraction to the literatures of the southern continents, which were still rarely translated. I wanted to read in my own language the books of the heroes of Latin American literature, such as Mario Vargas Llosa, Gabriel García Márquez, Julio Cortázar, Juan Rulfo, Jorge Amado and many others. I knew what the German reader was missing if this literature remained inaccessible to him. In Africa and Asia it looked even worse. For whatever reason, German interest in these literatures was still minuscule, and the cost of translation and production were too high for the small printing runs that could be achieved with these books. Hardly any publishers were interested.

Thus the German reader remained deprived of the native notions of the thought, feelings, life, love and sorrows of a third of humanity on our common earth. In this way the powerful character that adheres in these poetries, a frank view of life and a will to survive, remains lost in our own, overly rational prose.

There were a few institutions that were interested in these literatures. The Evangelical Church supported publishing houses in producing a few titles, and the state gave a subsidy to the Horst Erdmann Verlag in Tübingen, but they only produced unattractive boxy books with titles like *Indonesia Tells a Story* and *Tanzania Tells a Story*. Neither the charitable efforts nor the state-mandated textbooks from the Tübingen publishing house could reach a broad public, though the products from Erdmann usually sat on the shelves of the German embassies to make a show of the readiness for dialogue. These books were seldom present on the German book market.

Since just about at that time the Tübingen publisher Horst Erdmann was sentenced to jail for accounting fraud, I saw the chance of moving along another path of communication, one that conformed to the market and at least aspired to reach the public. I was trying to get a "communication agency," which would use people knowledgeable in the relevant literatures, to recommend to publishers books from Africa, Asia and Latin America, help them see these books to market, and try to share some of the risk. In this way it would be easier to bring more of this literature to the market.

For that we needed money! The maintenance of an office, the financing of the reading tours for authors, payment for informational materials—for a catalog of *"Sources,"* which would list all the available translations from the three regions, ordered by the country of birth of the authors. We also needed basic financing for the quarterly that had begun to appear, *Literary News—Africa, Asia, Latin America*. We thought about a translation program, which would cover the costs of translating the original languages into German. Such a project had no source of income, for we had no product of our own, but were only helping others to have one. And so we needed supporters, sponsors!

Through the recommendation of Hermann Schulz, whose publishing house now and again jointly funded a few titles with the Evangelical Church of Germany, I met the journalist and author Ansgar Skriver, who was able to obtain an annual financial commitment from the Evangelical Church, which is still ongoing. After the recent disaster with all the subventions going to the Erdmann Verlag, the Foreign Office was now convinced to set up a fund to promote translations, for which there were also contributions from Pro Helvetia, the Swiss Arts Council. The Frankfurt Book Fair took over the remaining organizational costs and the fixed costs of the Frankfurt office.

This little publishing society tried to raise its own funds through a so-called readers club, "The Others' Literature," but it was of limited success, since the club stagnated at a membership of about 2,000 readers and could not be increased, despite various advertising attempts. Nonetheless, the receipts were enough to pay for the work of one office person who took care of club business.

I was not able to integrate the planned agency completely into the Frankfurt Book Fair, for the Supervisory Board would never have gone along with the idea. I gave them some superficial information about an Africa agency that we helped found, but one which would be an independent institution separate from the Book Fair and supported by outside organizations, the Evangelical Church and the Foreign Office.

In April 1980 I convened a meeting of 14 people involved in this matter—publishers, authors, cultural managers and cultural organizers—in the conference room of the Book Fair organizational office on Kleiner Hirschgraben Street for a founding meeting of a "Third World Book Agency." As usually happens, there was at first an argument over the name of the institution to be founded. What resulted was the not very electrifying but very characteristic name for our German organizational bureaucracy, "Society for the Promotion of the Literature of Africa, Asia and Latin America," a nonprofit organization that in its name seemed quite middle-class and modest. The aim was to attract further substantial donors, something that did not happen so easily.

This office, which is still housed in the building of the Book Fair, did extraordinary things in promoting literature under its three directors, Dr. Jörg Becker (1980–81), Günter Simon (1981–87) and Peter Ripken (1987–2007). More than 500 titles from southern regions have been put out by German publishers since the founding of the society. The catalog titled *Sources* has appeared multiple times and now exists as an online database, and includes more than just small, activist niche publishing houses of literature from the South. Large publishing houses as well soon got involved in the many literatures of these cultural regions and made possible literary voyages of discovery.

Three active members formed the management committee of the small organization, starting with Hermann Schulz as treasurer, myself as chairman, and the animated literary agent Ray-Güde Mertin, who devoted herself principally to Brazilian and Latin American literature, as vice chairwoman. In the person of the minister president of the state of North Rhine Westphalia, Johannes Rau, we had a political lighthouse within the management committee. Hermann Schulz, since 1968 the successor to Rau at the Evangelischer Jugenddienst Verlag in Wuppertal (thereafter renamed the Peter Hammer Verlag), had persuaded this high-ranking politician to be involved in this matter of the book. Johannes Rau took his membership in the "Society with the long name" seriously, and so in the 1980s there were a number of meetings of the management board in the house of the minister president in Düsseldorf.

Spreading knowledge about literature from other languages became more and more a basic credo for me. As early as 1968, on my first trip for the Book Fair Company, I had the formative experience of having my entry into an unknown country made easier by reading some literature from that country before I got there. On the flight to Argentina I read Ernesto Sábato's *On Heroes and Tombs*. Upon arrival in Buenos Aires, I was astonished to feel that I had actually already been in this city.

The central task of the Book Fair was to open up the various literatures to each other in an increasingly globalized world. The Book Fair as a medium made this exchange concrete. Where else, other than in an international Book Fair, could one open up the regional makers of books to each other? The 1990s were to show that even the omnipotent electronic media could not fulfill the task of exchanging books. Books needed discourse; they needed the personal knowledge of the foreign book people and their social and cultural background in order to migrate from one publisher to another. Books for sale could not be reduced to a simple commercial exchange. Book rights could not be negotiated on the basis of some simple data on fax machines and e-mail. This required the people who stood behind these things, people who met, got to know one another, engendered trust in one another, and spoke to each other a great deal. This was the thing that made sense for the fairs to do, to be a medium for the trade and the distribution of the book. This is something I wanted to continue working on.

Decisions, Decisions

The focal themes would have to meet the interests of an exhibitor group or of the public. Purely intellectual themes without a direct relationship to the activities at the Fair would be meaningless for the people meeting there and would thus be unsuccessful. The Book Fair was not a literature festival, nor was it any abstract cultural exposition, concerned only with lofty themes or with its own image. Here life took place in the form of business that was concerned with costs. We as organizers had to sensibly handle the question as to how much culture we could assume for this event and how much content could be absorbed during the hectic back and forth of the week's events. At the same time it was our task to put on a show for the interested public. A window had to be opened onto the world of the Fair. Furthermore, the offerings had to account for the interests of everyone involved. I always considered it a task grounded in reality, one which was distinct from the intellectual speculations of the many literary and cultural expositions on offer.

The topic for 1982, *Religion of Yesterday in the World of Tomorrow,* was targeted to all those who sought answers to the questions of their lives in books. Whether author or reader, the person sensitive to questions of religion, which lay among the deepest human probings, was the same person who read the book as a humane medium of communication. A history of religions was at the same time the history of the book.

We succeeded in creating a program that helped to break down anxieties, where religion could be discussed for its true significance for how we live together. We brought in the politician Erhard Eppler, the Protestant theologian Heinz Zahrnt, the Catholic professor Johann Baptist Metz, the poet and theologian Dorothee Sölle and the Jewish religious scholar Pinchas Lapide. The topic was greeted with delight by the media and by the public. It was probably the last thematic program that was universally considered a success.

The theme for the year 1984, on the other hand, could not be checked off as so "successful." To celebrate the theme of the year *1984* for the media and scientific clientèle of the Fair was obvious from the date, or so we thought. As early as 1980, when I was touring through Africa, I had this "original" idea of an "Orwell" year, which, as it later turned out, was not quite so original. From the start of the year 1984, the public did not lack for press and television coverage that analyzed existing conditions against the dark background of an Orwellian Dystopia. When we finally came out with our carefully prepared programs in the fall, the topic was completely old hat.

We also had not paid attention to the fact that the really existing Socialist countries, who were important participants in the Book Fair, still had Orwell's book on their index; they must have felt challenged and insulted by it. Even the American media theorist and critic Neil Postman, author of *Amusing Ourselves to Death: Public Discourse in the Age of Show Business,* who was a speaker at the opening ceremonies of the Frankfurt Book Fair, confirmed that the topic had been poorly chosen, and that instead one should have used Aldous Huxley's *Brave New World* for a critique of the media landscape.

The public fallout of this central topic showed us clearly the limits of our ability to purvey critical messages. In 1993, under the slogan "Frankfurt Goes Electronic," we took up this topic once again and handled it without criticizing the media. This resulted in much more positive coverage.

For me personally, however, the *1984* theme had a remarkably fine result on my friendship with a great human being, the bestselling author Robert Jungk, the "futurologist," as he was generally called. I had known him for a few years as a committed visitor to the Book Fair. As a committed reader, he took advantage of the Fair to gather hundreds of books, gladly given to him by publishers, which he then deposited in the waiting room of my office before carting them off to his hotel room at the end of the day.

Bob Jungk, who was very convincing in his belief in a positive end of history, was an enthralling story-teller and fascinating person who knew how to draw his listeners into his life-affirming convictions. He was a critical person, and in the general political scheme of things he therefore was considered to be on the Left. He tried indefatigably to attract young people to his "future workshops" and to win them over to the idea of meaningful work in a future society.

I look back with pleasure at the long conversations I held with him as we wandered along through the Salzburg meadows. I had signed up Jungk as the chief consultant for our topic *1984*. Actually, I regretted the topic if only because it didn't get us any closer to Jungk's vision. To experience the book person Robert Jungk—and he was the archetypal book person—at the Book Fair was a stroke of good fortune for us as organizers. In his autobiography titled *Nevertheless*, he described his relationship to our Book Fair:

Unlike the many who moan that it is all too stressful, too superficial, too confusing, too costly, and that they are never coming to this circus again, I love the Frankfurt days, overflowing with their many quick greetings, short conversations, hasty meetings, urgent appointments, extremely important promises, the ending and the opening of old relationships.... My boundless fondness for the Fair was increased by the experience of the rapid and almost effortless wandering from country to country, from continent to continent, from one cultural area to another. It was only a few steps from the stall of my Japanese publisher to that of the Italian, French, Brazilian, or American. I would go down only a few steps or walk only a few hundred meters from the elegant art book displays to the modest stalls of these scientific and business publishing houses. If only I had more time to rummage around everywhere.

At the evening get-together at Horst Krüger's or at Gerd Kalow's, or at a farewell party with guests from all corners of the earth in the apartment of someone being honored, and from the much beloved head of the Fair Peter Weidhaas, I could regularly hear the voices of well-intentioned people warning me, "You are overdoing it. You spread yourself too thin. Arrêtez un peu, mon vieux."

A short time later, the chairman of my Supervisory Board had to take notice of the remark of the "much beloved head of the Fair

Peter Weidhaas" on the occasion of a dinner in honor of my 25 years of activity at the company. He however went on, "...We don't actually love him, but we certainly treasure him!" This chairman was well-known and notorious for his eagerness to make witty phrases and his prowess at extemporaneous speaking. From his post as the chairman of the Supervisory Board of the Exposition and Fair Company, he made the following comment in the German Publishers Weekly, "There are enterprises, like the Frankfurt Book Fair, where you can't help but be successful!" All of us who work in the company were not pleased at this remark.

Ten years had gone by since the book exhibit in the U.S. in 1973. The Foreign Office wanted renewed activity of the German publishing houses in the United States of America, but in no way did I want to repeat what I had experienced the first time around. I had since learned that if you wanted to be taken seriously in the book circles of the U.S., you had to go about the matter differently than with formal book exhibits in the back rooms of public libraries. It was only translated books, with their particular cultural messages, that had a chance of making it through to the readers of this self-satisfied country.

I therefore got together with Professor Volkmar Sander, and we developed the project of the German Book Fair in "The Big Apple."

This project also had a second goal. In Frankfurt we had learned that international trade and book rights were the answer of the book trade to globalization. Frankfurt, with its Book Fair, was as global a book market as you could get. Although this event took place in Germany, and although German book publishers were numbered among the most avid purchasers of book rights and translators of foreign literature (around 14% of the German book production consisted of translated works), the interest of the German publishing houses in international business, in the sale of their own materials to the outside, was definitely stunted. Only about 30 to 40 publishing houses of the over 2,800 in our list of addresses of the German Publishers Association had their own export and legal rights divisions. We were able to convince about 280 publishers to get involved in foreign activities now and then. That's about all there was. Foreign business seemed to be too difficult. People would gladly handle the translation rights of their own titles if a request came from without, but for the publishers to do something about it on their own was not opportune; it was too expensive.

The licensing business was for the Frankfurt Book Fair the most important business factor to be promoted. The German Book Fair in New York, "Frankfurt on the Hudson," was to stimulate German publishers and to give them a platform to do something themselves in order to promote the rights to German books to our American colleagues.

We had to spend a great deal of time convincing 240 German publishers to come personally to New York. This number included many small publishers and book dealers; in total, 500 publishers were represented by 17,000 books.

We very carefully prepared this bilateral project. In addition to an American "advisory board," we set up group panels with well-known German and American publishers. For the group Fiction/Nonfiction, we had Christoph Schlotterer of Carl Hanser publishers (a man who unfortunately died very prematurely), together with Cornelia Bessie of Harper & Row. For Science/Professional books, we had Dr. Wulf D. von Lucius of G. Fischer Verlag and Klaus G. Saur, plus Jeremiah Kaplan from Macmillan of New York. For Art/Picture books: Dr. Andreas Bartels (DuMont Buch Verlag) and Paul Gottlieb (Harry Abrams).

These leaders also brought in the other important personalities from their particular areas of expertise, who then during the book fair discussed the common problems and possibilities of cooperation with a select professional public over a number of meetings.

The question was posed at the very beginning by the German publishers as to why so few new German authors were translated and brought to market in the U.S. An American publisher brusquely dismissed the issue with the remark that they had plenty of average authors whose books could be published only at very high risk. Paul de Angelis went even further and explained that the prejudices against Germany and German books had grown in America over decades and in no way had wavered, but had rather been reinforced. French and Italian literature found a much greater resonance in the States.

Klaus Wagenbach rebutted this by saying that the West German publishing industry had been subjected to growing Americanization. More and more people were speculating on books with quick turnover, which could be sold out after a year, as opposed to the general pattern in the German industry of keeping a title available for many years. In turn, the public was invited by the American publishers to say why American authors sold so well in West Germany. The answer merely supplemented what had been said before, that the post-war youth was Americanized and that the pressure of the culture and capital from "the Superpower" was very great.

On the second day, the discussion continued as to why the licensing exchange between the German and American publishers was in the main a one-way street. Each year some 3,000 were sold to Germany, while only some 300 made their way into the United States. The attempt to analyze this imbalance clarified some of the differences and inequalities.

The Suhrkamp publisher Siegfried Unseld, along with Christoph Schlotterer, supported the view that American editors did not limit themselves to pure editorial work, but were engaged in management to a much greater degree than their German colleagues; besides that, they were merely underinformed about the market for German literature. On the other hand, both publishers agreed on the superiority of information channels supplied by American literary agents and the U.S. professional newspaper *Publishers Weekly,* which at any time would say which titles were available in the U.S. and which were read regularly on an international level.

Albert Hall in the Sheraton Center Hotel, where we succeeded in creating a true Book Fair atmosphere with authentic Frankfurt Book Fair stalls, was extraordinarily well-attended in the four days of March 1983. As in Frankfurt, 35,000 visitors crowded through the halls, including about 20% from the professional public. We had thus fulfilled our mission to the satisfaction of the political circles who had entrusted us with this task and to the satisfaction of all participants. But how thorny this had been for me, how strenuous to bring this project into reality! I can still see our crew on the Sunday before the opening, with their heads drooping like *The Burghers of Calais,* in despair at the windy and rainy beach in Queens. We were all convinced that we would meet our Waterloo in New York in the coming week, that we would experience a total fiasco.

An influential group of New York publishers had been leaning on us quite hard for half a year. To be sure, in an attempt to bring all the American publishers into our project, we had created an "advisory board," consisting of important publishing directors such as Joan Manley (Time Life), Simon Michael Bessie (Harper & Row), Nicholas Chantiles (Times Mirror), Jeremiah Kaplan (Macmillan), Leo Albert (Prentice Hall), Robert Baensch (Springer New York), Roger Straus (Farrar, Straus & Giroux) and Mark Werner Linz (Crossroad and Continuum Books). There was still a group of some eight market dominant publishers who observed us distrustfully at every step, and commented critically in the industrial press. The American manager of our "German Book Fair," Rodney H. Clurman, recommended by Jeremiah Kaplan, whom we had contracted with to prepare our project on-site, turned out to be an absolute loser, who did not produce anything other than astounding bills on his expense account. I finally had to let him go, and in the last four months personally took over the preparations for the German Book Fair in New York.

Somehow we had the impression that these New York publishers were blocking our appearance in the heartland of their sphere of influence, or at least wanted to put obstacles in our way. Again and again we had to quickly defend ourselves against rumors that were spreading about our inability to pay our bills and about other irregularities. The firing of Clurman, an affair that he made noise about, led to other claims and rumors about the "invasion of the Germans."

As had often occurred previously, I felt myself challenged in my role as a German. Was it an accident that the group of American publishers who kept attacking us consisted exclusively of Jews? I refused to believe it; and yet the venom aimed at us could not be dismissed. Had they reacted in the same way to Italians, Dutchmen or Swedes? The comments that were spread about us were without exception of an emotional type, as we learned to our astonishment. Of our group, I understood this better than anyone, since I was a German who since his youth had been grappling with this problem.

I didn't get a chance to clear things up. We had to see it through, and we had to force the hesitating American colleagues to work with the Germans whether they wanted to or not! That wasn't simple, but we did it.

It was clear that I, as the head of the whole enterprise, could not simply roll up my sleeves and take over the marketing and advertising for the project in New York, and so I asked Robert Baensch, who had just lost his management position at Julius Springer/New York, to take over contact with the American publishers. I also hired one other person, Minette S., who understood the customs of New York, since for some time she had been working with Prof. Volkmar Sander on the cultural work of the German House at New York University. She began preparing the cultural expositions for the German Book Fair.

Günter Grass in an interview made some provocative remarks, which we published and paid for in a four-page insert in *The New York Times*. Ordinarily, foreign projects had a difficult time getting into *The Times,* but our publicity work in this case was so successful that it received extensive coverage. The interest stemmed primarily from his unsettling remarks. In the interview, Grass said, "I am convinced that Fascist tendencies have recently come out clearly in the United States among the so-called silent majority...." Grass made this comment in connection with the common American critical cliché that equated Germany with the Holocaust. His comment enraged the liberal reading public of *The New York Times* no less than the domestic right-wing press.

For quite some time I had been pursued by a correspondent of the Springer newspaper *Die Welt* not only here in New York, but also at home at the Frankfurt Book Fair and at various other foreign venues. His name was Alfred Starkmann, and he hounded us with his staunchly right-wing opinions. He continued to do so here, and finally his supreme master, his Excellency the head of the Springer concern Axel Springer, felt himself called upon in an editorial in his newspaper to label our efforts in New York a "sham enterprise..., a defeatist social orgy of 'progressive' American and German literary figures and self-appointed cultural functionaries."

At a panel discussion with an audience of over 1,000 people titled "The role of the writer in an endangered world," featuring the authors Günter Grass, John Irving, Joyce Carol Oates and Fritz J. Raddatz (the last substituting for the delayed Max Frisch), Grass laid another one on us by saying the following: For him as an author it was "rather normal to fight as a citizen in my country" because of the spirit of 1933. "This spirit of '33 is still alive, not only in Germany, but in your country as well!"

The American press, including *The New York Times,* latched onto this controversy between the great German author and his country's press, and created a degree of publicity that we otherwise would certainly not have attained. This whole audacious project turned into a grand success, which was featured both in the German press and on television.

New York had been a challenge, especially for me personally. When I returned home in the summer of 1982 after a long trip, concerned as usual as to what had happened at home, I found nobody there. The apartment struck me as a place not worthy to live in, a great emptiness. The dog was howling in the basement, for he had not been let out for quite some time. I tried to reach my wife Dora at the union, but was cut short by a secretary who said that my wife was in a meeting and could not be disturbed. I hung up. The dog, a strong black German shepherd that I had gotten because my wife was often afraid of people "out there," was nudging me and wanted to go for a walk. I felt really tired, and my head was hurting. It was clear to me that I could no longer cope with this two front war, where I was constantly being interrogated at work and at home about what I was doing. What I really wanted to do was to sink down onto the rug and go to sleep, to sleep as I have often done when I didn't know what else to do. But there was a dog that would not let me sleep—and besides, this method of overcoming problems had never brought me true solutions.

I got up slowly, talked gently to "Choco," took my two suitcases and carefully closed the front door of the house. I went to the office and moved into our guest room there.

It's true that I must confirm that this episode had a precedent in New York. The basis of my marriage with Dora, after the very emotional initial phase, had long ago become a mere duty. When love is no longer the stuff that binds people together, then other forces start to work, forces that lie dormant in the depths of one's soul: drives to domination and subordination and the fear of being wounded by the other person. A person reaches for a way to screen himself off, often at the price of a guilty conscience. More and more I had excluded my wife from my professional life.

It had long been clear to me that this relationship could not last, but because of the children and the general feelings of guilt in relation to this woman from the Third World, whom I had "seduced" into my cold world of prosperity, I had not been ready to break the chains.

Then in New York I met Minette, a youthful woman in her mid-40s, who had just dissolved her marriage to a diplomat. On the recommendation of Professor Sander, I had entrusted her with the care of the cultural program of the German Book Fair. There had been a few signals between us, a few friendly pleasantries, looks, nothing more. I still look back on her with pleasure, as she cycled down Fifth Avenue with her flying mop of hair and her bright coat flapping in the wind.

One evening she invited me to go with her on the subway to visit her friend Marlies in another part of New York. All of a sudden I recognized the danger to my life that had been held together by a makeshift lie. Actually I wanted to refuse her that evening, but I went on foot from the Sheraton Hotel to Times Square, where I was to meet her.

As we were on our way home from this friend, and it was becoming clear what was happening with us, she just said, "Shit," because she too was not seeking any new adventure after her recent separation.

From then on we were a pair. On one of the following weekends we took a trip to Montauk, a small coastal spot on the tip of Long Island. We wanted to trace Max Frisch's novel about his love in old age and to visit the places that were described in his novel. Since the beginning of the 1980s, Frisch had enjoyed a great popularity among readers and authors in the United States.

I had been able to convince Frisch to make an appearance at the German Book Fair, particularly since he was living in New York at that time. The "Lynn" in the Montauk novel actually was named Alice Locke-Carey, and Minette and I wanted to follow along with the famous author and his Montauk love at their parting scene.

It wasn't clear to me what moved Max Frisch six months later to invite me, Minette and a third person, a man with a beard whose name I don't remember, to come to a Christmas party at his loft on Prince Street. We didn't have any opportunity to communicate with one another. Instead, we had to experience a dreadfully painful and long drawn-out argument between Frisch and the blonde love from Montauk, Lynn, who was actually Alice. At the end the blonde lady left the apartment in an agitated state, and we too soon quietly made our exit.

Was this a bad omen for our new love? Neither of us was superstitious! Minette and I loved each other, and at the moment felt only liberation.

Awakening

The hull of muscles
that I am
breaks apart
and from the
gap between your shoulders
the bat emerges
and you stretch
in the morning fog
our night
breaks in two
I slip into
your muskox scents
I love you
I kiss
your mound of Venus
my death cramps
have worn me out
the sun is
bringing in
the day.

You Wish to Write on India, Sir?

To Writers Abroad
by Keki N. Daruwalla

You wish to write on India, Sir?
This way, please!
Let's trail the alley cat down the drain
choked with ash and eggshells. Have a care
the scum and the slime may soil your shoes!
Would you care to photograph
those urchins lost in their laughter?
You'd prefer, I think, a hangdog look
assertive ribcage, and mouth
caked with snot and grime.
The choice is wide, the space-clad sadhu
the lunatic in hessian
or the beggar with the running sore
It sure feels good, Sir
discussing pus-pockets
with a disinfected pen
on sterilized paper.

And now to the drought-land
soil dry as staghorn
and calf-mouths pleading with empty udders
Lean cattle circumambulating
fat, greasy sadhus screaming
for a ban on cow-slaughter!
Skeleton, Sir? There is none at hand!
Yes, filmed against this stubble backdrop
it would carry a lot of punch, as you say
But right now I can't even

> *turn out an honest corpse*
> *orifices acrawl with ants*
>
> *And then to the street crossing*
> *where the cobra sways*
> *to the wailing serpent-flutes*
> *A flash of coils in the basket*
> *as the charmer throws*
> *his turban over it to keep them quiet*
> *If you are looking for stench, sir*
> *You'll find it in his armpits.*[1]

The Indian poet Keki N. Daruwalla spelled out in this poem those "cases" that often skew the vision of a well-intentioned Western observer and allow him to retain his stereotypical views. I have cited only the first few stanzas here because it's enough to show what Daruwalla is reproaching us with. I later was able to introduce Daruwalla to the public in 2005 at the second round of a Frankfurt Book Fair with the special topic of India.

We spent a lot of effort and expense on preparing a dialogue between what India has to offer us and what our so-called interpreters offer (the representatives of the media and the world of publishing), but we met with only limited success. The reporters from our newspapers and our electronic media were not ready to pay attention and to comment appropriately, nor were the Indian authors ready to engage and neutralize the public's almost total ignorance. They willingly confirmed the clichés of a wretched, starving, impoverished India, and the clueless reporters on our side grabbed onto these childish offerings as oracular sayings.

I with my own romantic notions of India also had difficulty in penetrating the "sensitive inner being" of the country's authors. During the reconnaissance trip, which I went on for four weeks with Professor Dieter Riemenschneider as a consultant, I was only rarely able to break through the multi-layered Eastern reality and to overcome my Western stereotypes. To see what

---

1. Keki N. Daruwalla, *Collected Poems, 1970–2005* (Penguin Books, 2006), 9–30.

drives Indians in their innermost being was difficult. Our trip did not confirm our prejudices, but it did not completely do away with them, since the complex imagery and daily ordeals left me no room to reflect on what we were experiencing.

We began our voyage of discovery in Calcutta (now known as Kolkata). Calcutta is crazy; Calcutta is magical. Once you make your way through the dust, the masses of people and the streams of autos, you are happy to find refuge within the secure walls of a luxury hotel. Sometimes the city came upon me like a gigantic body in which thousands, nay millions, of people were streaming in. I experienced something exalted, but that probably came from me. Tranquility was something peculiar to the teeming and scurrying masses. I noticed that they were just living their ordinary lives, but for the visitors it was as though everything was on stage. You could feel the moment when you suddenly stepped into another city and into another life.

This seething cauldron welcomed me back again, but this time the big show was no illusion. It actually took place. The Pope had come. The city itself, however, was not any different, though a bit calmer, since a few hundred thousand people who live on the streets had concentrated in one place.

When everything had been completed for the evening for both Riemenschneider and me—receptions, discussions, dinner—we stepped out once again from the hotel into the black, evil-smelling streets, past the bodies lying huddled together asleep in the alleys. Here and there a little fire flickered; here and there another light, a human powered rickshaw whizzing by, trash, puddles, a tomcat mounting a female with ear-piercing yowls. Here everything was right on top of us. The upper body of a woman rose up out of a group of bodies and made a begging motion, but not really seriously, more as if in a dream, showing a slightly ironic smile. This was the way they communicated with people like us, dressed in our dark suits and ties.

Here everything is right on top of you. What would it be like if I were to sleep on the street, and to spend my nights against this damp wall? I looked very closely at every stone that was worn smooth, every puddle, at the branch growing out of the wall. If I were to live here, this would be my living space. The people lying here did not spend much of their life outside of this space. Here they breathed; here they begged, here they relieved themselves; here they loved; here they suffered; here they struggled—and every morning they woke up again next to the warm bodies of others.

In a dark villa in New Delhi an English lady had us for tea. Around a coffee table were sitting six old men who seemed to have come out of a film by Fellini. I took a seat on the sofa with my companion, Dipak Kumar Guha, opposite the others. All six looked at me and said nothing. A tall skinny man sat next to a short one, both bald. I noticed that everybody had giant ears. Their eyes looked at me but didn't stare; they rested on me. Only one of them was wearing Western clothing, a suit jacket and trousers; all the others were dressed in Indian garb. In order to overcome the painful silence, I began to talk about the reason for my being here and about the Frankfurt Book Fair; I began to explain the plans and expectations of the upcoming festival of Indian literature...

Hardly had I spoken a few sentences when the first one collapsed into himself, then the next one bent forward, and another one leaned back with his mouth wide, each of them against his neighbor—till all of them in variously twisted positions had fallen asleep, snoring loudly. One of them had turned his face so sharply that one eye looked up and the other one looked at me, and I almost snorted with laughter.

I didn't alter my tone of voice when I asked Dipak, "So, what now?" "Keep talking, keep talking!" he whispered to me. So I continued on talking as though I had an interested public in front of me. The English lady, who seemed to have been left over from the colonial era, had meanwhile tiptoed out of the room. My audience however gave an indescribable picture of madness, as they bent against each other, next to one another, bent forward, hanging back with distorted faces, all sitting opposite me. I really had to pull myself together not to be overcome by the comic nature of the situation. Finally I kept quiet.

The first one, whose dead, unmoving eye had remained fixed on me the entire time, woke up, sat up and without any further ado began to talk, presumably in Hindi, since I didn't understand a word. His neighbor, whom he had pushed aside when he stood up, was the next one to wake up; he shook himself conspicuously, jumped up, and barked, "You shut up, I'm talking!"

As we left, two of these gentlemen, the younger ones, guided us to the back seat of a little Nash Ambassador, got in front and acted as if we weren't even there. They told each other stories about women, laughed about it, doubled over with laughter and pounded each other on the back. Dipak, who had listened to the conversation that they carried on in Hindi, softly explained to me the dirty jokes they were trading. Not a word to us until we got to my hotel, the "Taj Mahal." Then the two of them jumped out of their seats, pulled open the doors of the Ambassador for us, and said goodbye with an exaggeratedly deep bow. We proceeded to go swiftly up the marble steps of the hotel in order to gain a certain distance from this singular experience.

Dr. Vogel, Mrs. Di. and Mrs. D. of the German Academic Exchange Service (DAAD) were the three female musketeers of German cultural policy in India. Dr. Vogel had expended a lot of effort in drawing together a circle of Indians, all of whom wanted to make clear to me that Indians were not in a position to contribute even a modest collection of books; we would have to do that ourselves. Vishnu Khare, the "embassy poet" (every embassy has such a guest who comes to all receptions) was there, as was the Hindi poet Raghuvir Sahay, who had already visited me once in Frankfurt. He had read my poems, which he had translated himself. I had a good conversation with him that evening.

Initially I held myself somewhat reserved to Vishnu Khare, since he was, as I thought to label him, an "embassy poet," that is to say a sort of Indian show poet, who is just invited to receptions. His poems, which I later read, showed that he was nonetheless a good poet:

Fire

*If they have grabbed hold of her
if her useless husband, her dissolute brother-in-law,
her lecherous father-in-law
have labeled her
a slut, a filthy swine, a whore
and they have worked her over with fists, kicks, and
 stomps
and her mother-in-law has burned the childless slut
with a red-hot iron
and if every punishment meted out for her guilt
has turned out to be too mild
and then they have finally decided
that only her demise can save the family honor
and they have bound her mouth
or otherwise have treated her as half dead
and they have thrown her in the bathroom,
with her howling like an animal, all curled up
and the match has been lit
by her trembling husband — trembling, aroused for the
 first time
whom she had betrayed
she was there, like a thrashing fish
thrown into boiling water
remembering from 15 years ago
the looks of her brothers, those petty crooks who were paid
 off
certain images returned
that the elderly man showed to your sister
one hot noonday she suddenly burst into the room
a 19-year-old silent boy
who lay down
She stuck her tongue into her maw
and tore the clothes from her body
as though she were going up in flames
and said
you, I have been burning for a long time
and besides I don't have much time.*

The publishers whom I now met were with few exceptions minor, poorly educated potentates, who hardly gave a visitor time to finish his sentence, and were always putting themselves in a good light so that they could brag about their connections and their past. Still, if you were to contradict them, a shadow of uncertainty would flit across their faces.

I tried to comprehend this weakness of ego that was evident in most middle-class Indians, often played out in the brashest of manners. Was this state of being immaturely wrapped up in oneself what had drawn me to India in my youth? Clearly Hindu philosophy had not encouraged Indians to acknowledge or divulge any raw, naked truths. The social order and the caste system integrated them into a set role, and they were unable to emancipate themselves or to "rise above it," as we in the West would say. This merging into karma, into non-existence, into nothingness, could scarcely be completed by an individualized, well-formed psyche. However, it was precisely this which we had striven for when we were growing up, this merger into a greater set of interconnections. Youth too had not developed their egos. Here is where the dangers for Indians lay in the period shaped by the West. Or perhaps they had an advantage in the age of new media, in which we are beckoned away from the real, and take on the roles of mere avatars.

I had the feeling of having really arrived correctly in "India," although I had hardly been a week in Delhi. In the morning I wanted to fly on to Benares, but happened to miss my flight because I had depended on an older flight schedule and had not asked about it at all. And so I gained an off-the-record rest day, after a strenuous week with many meetings in ministries and institutions. Without further ado I set off with my Indian companion Dipak Kumar Guha for Old Dehli and the Red Fort.

The first thing that impressed me there was a group of Tibetan "tourists"—small wrinkled old men, who once had fled Tibet with the Dalai Lama and who now lived here in India as refugees. Even in the heat they continued to wear the thick linen clothing and quilted jackets of their Himalayan homeland They eagerly wandered about in this Mughal fort; they looked at the ceilings; they felt the columns. They made a disconcerting impression on me, transporting me out of time and space.

Two green cockatoos were resting on a ledge of a wall. One of them was trying in vain to get into a crack in the edifice. A squirrel was running excitedly back and forth along the bark of a tree, the movement of its tail marking the rhythm of its agitated screech. Dipak took me away from a tree full of birds for fear I would get soiled on. In a little meadow between the walls some curious crested birds with long beaks were pecking away—"Woodblakers," as Dipak called them.

Then we were outside of the Fort in a neighborhood with many shops, overflowing with people, growling Vespas, bicycle rickshaws, buses and taxis. We both sat on a bicycle rickshaw while the bent-over back of the rickshaw driver heaved up and down in front of us. Stores upon stores—supply stores, bookstores, spice stores, flower stores—a lively inferno of people. I hardly knew what to look at.

Later we traveled by taxi across the broad tree-lined boulevards of New Delhi to our elite hotel, frequented only by the decked-out, big-bellied Indians who made up 0.01% of the population.

The Byzantinism of the local bureaucrats really tired me out. Every state secretary or under state secretary or simple secretary or whatever they were called were little gods. Now and again I was tempted to grab one of these subordinates by the collar and tell him to knock it off. But in addition to these "secretaries" there were also many "directors," "heads of departments," *etc.*, who all trafficked in subservience and the cult of personality. For every individual in private industry in India there were two government officials.

State Secretary Gupta's sigh of relief was audible when Minister Narasimha Rao took a positive attitude to our project and approved the trip to Frankfurt. Now the matter was much easier for him because at any time he could refer to the minister's approval.

Once again we were in Calcutta for the book fair there. The arrival in Calcutta, at night, the same as before, was a flight into a nightmare. First there was the struggle for a taxi as unknown people tried to drag you into their car. Then, in the shadows, I saw a soldier, quite embarrassed, but without lifting a finger, who indicated a normal taxi which I quickly got into. A driver who looked absolutely wild, wrapped up in rags, got behind the steering wheel. The car was a real junker, and it seemed that at any moment it would fall apart. A yellowish fog was sinking over the barely lit streets, from inhabitants burning cowdung as fuel in their little ovens in the cooler weather. I could see the hazy outlines of dogs, and everywhere on the sidewalks I noticed little piles that looked like trash or raked-up leaves. These were, however, people, men, women and children, the homeless who spent their nights on the "sidewalks." The streets themselves were practically empty. Here and there a figure darted by. My taxi did not make more than ten miles an hour. When I got out, we haggled over the fare again. A few adventurous characters grabbed for my suitcase. They carried it up four steps to the entrance of the hotel and then held out their hands for a tip. Then the glittering hall of the Oberoi hotel and—no hotel reservation. Waiting for an hour—it was midnight by now—but still no solution. Then back outside. A trip with another old taxi to the Hindustan International, a five-star hotel, but which in the meantime had lost a few stars from its crown.

Calcutta is an ever more "fascinating" community. The people living on the streets, some 100,000 of them it is estimated, sleep on the sidewalks. Two million were out in the slums. The beggars, the dirt, the traffic, the air pollution—and yet the community held together. The people here have enormous patience. The Indian background, the Indian philosophy.... It was to me unfathomable that not one person would get up and smash down everything that was standing. Unmitigated poverty existed alongside conspicuous consumption. "Change in Continuity"—that was the title of the Indian theme in Frankfurt; but where was the change?

We walked along College Street where are all the bookstores were concentrated. We visited the oldest bookstore in Calcutta, Dasgupta Book Dealer, which in the following year was to celebrate its 100th anniversary. Its shelves were made of mahogany worn thin, and a narrow, ornate wrought-iron circular stair led to the second floor. The 80-year-old Dasgupta, son of the founder of the firm, sat there in the midst of his dusty books.

His son, the third generation of the book dealer family, stood respectfully behind his father, whom I asked how he was able to look up whatever book a customer was searching for. He pointed at his head—"I have only this computer here! I know very well my holdings of a good 10,000 books."

Back outside in the glistening sun, messengers tripped around back and forth on the narrow, very crowded streets with piles of books on their heads that they had picked up at bookbinderies. For a time the street traffic completely froze. At the crossings the bicycles and human rickshaws, the antiquated streetcars, double-decker buses ripped open on the sides, Nash Ambassador taxis and ox carts all wedged against one another. Nothing was moving. "This will sort itself out soon!" someone said and leaned back to relax in his little scooter taxi.

While walking along this College Street, past the hundreds of books stalls, we discovered an old feudal townhouse. We were interested in visiting it since it was by chance the birth home of our publisher friend Bimal Dhur. His two nephews, who were running a healthcare institution there, showed us the still magnificent living room and bedroom, packed full of pseudo-art and knickknacks. Thoughts of the splendor of the one-time colonial power flashed before us once again, and gave the impression that nothing was real, at the most just a stage setting.

The book fair itself consisted of 800 tiny shops, some one story, some two stories, that were constructed with a good deal of fantasy. Fantasy, plywood, paint and line. A Potemkin book village, and people came full of interest, looked through the books, looked for answers to their questions, looked in the strange books for the other world beyond, which they had heard was quite beautiful. They had even reconstructed the old birth house of Dhur. This plywood building concealed the press center, which was in the back, in a walled garden on dark columns, naturally all out of plywood, containing a meeting room with 150 seats. All of this was not real; it could not be; this was a theatrical fancy.

On the last evening we sat on the veranda of a cricket club with several authors. The hospitality of the Indians was overwhelming and limitless. I had already downed three large glasses of an excellent Indian vodka. The fourth, which I could no longer drink, I poured out on the cricket field with the cry, "Long live India!" Dhur was completely drunk. Frantically holding onto the steering wheel of his little car, always on the wrong side of the road, he managed to get us back to the hotel.

As we landed in Bombay (now called Mumbai) coming from Hyderabad, we felt miserable, and the physical distress lasted for the next two days. The air pollution in Bombay took your breath away—literally. In the Oberoi Tower Hotel we always turned off the air-conditioner as soon as we entered the room, since the whole building felt like an icebox. At first we were chilled to the bone; later on we could hardly breathe. The hotel lay on the beachfront, which was named "The Queen's Necklace" in reference to the row of street lanterns that reached around the bay in a wide arc.

Bombay was the capitalist center of India. Everywhere skyscrapers shot high. In no other city could one see so many cars adorned with the Mercedes star. However, right next to the glistening marble of the skyscrapers, there lived the approximately 500,000 "pavement dwellers" in makeshift shacks that were hastily erected on the sidewalks. This was a city that had about 10 million inhabitants in the metropolitan area, with many exceedingly persistent beggars, who often gave you the feeling that they were professional panhandlers. Finally there were the arrogant "rice bellies," who walked around in the hotel, quite indifferent to the boring, faceless business people from the West and from Japan.

Slowly I became immersed in this colorful continent that was struggling just to survive. On this trip I experienced little in the Indian metropolises of a foreign way of life. I moved around exactly as I did in European cities. Of course the same exotic motifs kept appearing, especially if you searched with European eyes. The two of us, Dieter Riemenschneider and I, had not come here to reinforce our cliché-laden images; rather we were allies in the search for the other India, the one existing here and now. It gradually became visible, that India with its many structural problems, but also with modern, open-minded people—open-minded, but also shaped by their own traditions and philosophy, through which they might add a distinctly Indian accent to the common search for the way into the future. The India that had always appeared before my eyes, a rotting, depressed country with beggars, hunger, *maharajas* with turbans, lepers, with lots of dirt and lots of weird paraphernalia—that India suddenly receded, and I went through the streets taking notice of the normalcy of urban life, despite all the poverty, which could not be overlooked.

The car ride to Mysore, some 90 miles away, gave us for the first time on this trip the chance to see something of the countryside. The road on which we moved along at a very slow pace was populated by cows, water buffalo, goats, sheep, dogs, and certainly by lots of people. Always people, who used the streets to thresh their grain by spreading the grain on the ground and waiting for the traffic zooming by to separate the wheat from the chaff. Mysteriously turbaned figures, but also beautiful women, wearing colorful *saris* with white flowers in their smoothly combed-back pitch black hair, continued their work there, or else walked with gentle movements of the hip while balancing heavy loads on their heads.

The trip took us through a landscape of rice paddies, from which high barren rocks suddenly jutted up. It was harvest time, and the hunchback buffalo were dragging over-laden ox carts. On the fields too the wheat was "threshed" by having an ox drag a stone roller over the straw, following which the women would separate the grain from the chaff through a sieve. The traffic was quite an adventure. Everyone passed whenever he felt like it, and it often happened that someone traveling at high speed on his own side of the road came up against a vehicle in the same lane coming from the other direction. Twice our driver had to swerve off the road in order to avoid a collision.

In Mysore, the former palace of the Maharajas was lit with a million small lamps in honor of the "Kannada conference," a regional festival in the south Indian Kannada language. Everything was as kitschy as if it had been lifted from a travel brochure. Thousands of people were on the roads on the way to the presentations of the "Kannada conference." On this occasion the state had closed all the schools and all public institutions. We pushed through to the palace in order to see what was going on there. We saw only people. One Indian addressed us in Danish. Then we pushed ourselves through a fairground in a search of a book exhibit that we had read about in the newspaper, but without any information about the venue and the opening times. At midday on this Sunday we ate in the Lalitha Mahal Palace Hotel, formerly the palace of a *maharaja*.

Our impressions were so many and so overwhelming that when I finally got to Professor Narasimhaiah's place, I promptly fell asleep on a chair. Narasimhaiah was a sensitive though very conservative Karnataka scholar, who had been upset about a newspaper article that reported on the demands of some Karnataka writers calling for the abolition of the caste system.

The writer R.K. Narayan, already verging on age 80, whom we then visited in his house, in real life expressed himself just as heartily as he did in his books. (He presented to me two older German editions of his novels that I began to read even during the trip.) As his Japanese telephone rang very softly, he turned his head sideways and said, "It rings like a beetle in an envelope."

Radsha Rao was a figure who was a grand name of Indian philosophy, with a cerebral face, but also elsewhere a trace of a smile which marked not only a very sensitive person but also a vain one. The old man had a very friendly and open manner. He had been strongly impressed by French philosophy, but he also expected a great future for India. His presentation of Indian literature completely contradicted that of Narasimhaiah. He saw a great deal that was specifically Indian in Indian literature.

U.R. Ananthamurthy, only later visited in his house, was quite different. He was a progressive man of our age. If I had previously felt rather tense in the face of the three elders of Indian literature—R.K. Narajan, Radsha Rao and Narasimhaiah—and was afraid of putting my foot in it or of asking the wrong questions, with Ananthamurthy I felt completely at home, and we were able to chat without reservation.

My trip with Dieter Riemenschneider ended shortly before Christmas in Trivandrum. While he was returning to his family in Frankfurt, I waited for Minette at the airport so that we could spend the rest of the year together in the country that had drawn me in so completely.

We arrived in Suria Samutra, an octagonal house on a cliff directly over the sea, about 10 miles from Trivandrum. We had rented the house for 240 rupees a day. To get to the sea you climbed up a little path, about 50 yards, to a bay in which the fishermen cast their nets with a monotonic singsong. On the other side stood a newly built mosque on a tongue of land. In the morning before sunrise a big set of fireworks were shot off. On Christmas Eve we sat over the sea by candlelight. A peaceful and calm evening.

On the road from Trivandrum to Kovalam Beach we kept seeing a truly Indian type of women's work. Trucks delivering large mountains of basalt rocks to the doors of the houses, and the women in their beautiful work saris, often with flowers in their freshly combed hair, crouched in front of the mountains of stones and used little hammers to break the rocks into gravel. People did not pay much attention to the hard work of these gentle women, which they labored at for months from sunup to sundown. But the images themselves could represent the situation of the Indian woman.

The week in Suria Samutra was the most peaceful holiday that I had experienced in a long time. On the cliff in front of the house there stood day in and day out a meager black man with a white beard and a white turban, cleaning his seashells by shoveling them into a box, which he then lifted over his head and slowly let the contents trickle down so that the lighter sand was carried away by the wind. This man, so we learned, had killed two of his wives because they had betrayed him. After twelve years in jail he stood on the cliff every day and sifted his seashells through the sieve.

The last three days of our stay in Trivandrum, from December 30th to January 2nd, we put up in the Rokholm Hotel, a nice little inn on a cliff over the sea, but things did not go so well. It felt like we had lost our new-found paradise. Here, as on the so-called hippie beach next door, Kovalam beach, by which you could get to another hotel, international hippie tourism was the rule. Anyone who came who was not yet a hippie quickly got dressed up in Indian rags, loosened up, and smoked hashish.

In the evening we walked along the beach to the Kovalam Hotel, about half an hour away. On the way we met a beautiful orange-red sunset, and on the way back in the darkness our path was marked by the colored lamps in each hut along the beach-front. The whole thing was as though under a spider web of light. God knows this had an Oriental exoticism.

Not long after my return to Frankfurt I got the news that the Prime Minister Rajiv Gandhi was ready to receive me in New Delhi. Dina Malhotra, the charismatic publisher of the Sterling Press, had arranged this. So I hopped on the first plane back to India. I hoped that a powerful word from the highest representative would make our task easier in the Indian bureaucracy, so oriented to authority.

Dina Malhotra accompanied me to the discussion, which lasted 20 minutes, though we had to be present at the prime minister's palace three hours ahead of time because of all the security precautions. They tested our heart and kidneys. Then we stood somewhat humble in front of the door of the office of the great ruler of all India. Gandhi got up out of his chair behind his big desk and greeted us with a handshake, and said to us with a surprisingly gentle voice, "What can I do for you?" And later, "Do you want a photo with me?," which I naturally very much wanted to have, at least to have some proof of my connection to the very top of the Indian hierarchy. Not much more than this came out of this audience, at least not that I noticed. Later Rajiv Gandhi was assassinated.

India at the Book Fair once again occupied me. It was a vastness rushing upon me that I could hardly control. India's heaven of gods, so someone had once counted, included 341 million deities, an overpopulation almost as crowded as that down below on the Indian subcontinent. We didn't learn whether the gods communicated in as many languages as did the peoples of India. It was said that there were 1,600 languages, of which 16 were then recognized as official written languages, and in which most literary works were composed.

According to our plans, the Indian authors were to lead us through this seething cauldron of life, and I had invited 26 of the most important of them to our India Festival at the Frankfurt Book Fair.

The best known among them was the over-80-year-old Mulk Raj Anand (1905–2004), whose Gujarat language novel, *Untouchable,* had found a public of millions of people in India in the 1930s. His novel has also appeared in German.

Udipi R. Ananthamurthy (b. 1932) from Karnataka, one of the central figures of the Kannada language literature of that time, is known primarily for his novel *Samskara* (1965), which was translated into many Indian and foreign languages and was made into a successful film in 1970.

R. Thyagarajan (b. 1931) had been the head of the leading Tamil film studio in Madras (now Chennai) for 14 years. Day after day he sold colorful kitschy dramas about evil villains, seductive dancers and noble Supermen: "Until I noticed that my identity was breaking into 1000 pieces!" He resigned and became the best-known writer in Tamil.

Dilip Chitre (b. 1938), a writer in Marathi from Gujarat, wrote fiction and poems in two languages, Marathi and English. He also made a name for himself as a painter and film director who wrote his own screenplays and musical score.

Anita Desai (b. 1937), whose literary languages were English, Bengali and German, coming as she did from a German–Indian marriage, had published short stories, eight novels, and tales for children since the end of the 1950s.

Kamala Das (1934–2009), in her day the most important poet of India, is known in Germany by her book *My Story,* which appeared in German in 1982 from a Japanese publishing house. It is the story of the unrestrained poetic life of a woman who cared little for conventions.

Daya Pawar (1935–1996) is one of the most well-known authors of the so-called *Dalit* literature, the "literature of the oppressed," which has been composed primarily in Marathi since Indian independence.

Arun Kolatkar (1932–2004), by profession an advertising artist in Bombay, received the Commonwealth Prize for his book of poetry *Jejuri.*

Ajneya—Sachchidananda Vatsyayan (1911–1987), the old wise man among the invited authors. In 1934 he was sent to prison for anti-British seditious activities, but as a convinced anti-Fascist, he participated on the British side during the Second World War. Ajneya wrote in Hindi and sometimes in English as well. In his very comprehensive work he strove for an ideal synthesis of Indian and Western thought.

Mannu Bhandari (b. 1931) worked as an instructor at Miranda House, a college that is part of the University of Delhi. She wrote in Hindi. Her many novels and short stories are extraordinarily popular outside the Hindi speaking areas as well.

Vijaydan Detha (b. 1926) wrote in Rajastani and in Hindi, and convincingly combined domestic traditions with modern internationalism.

Mahasweta Devi (b. 1926) published more than 70 titles, primarily novels, in which the conditions of life and work of the society of the oppressed are authentically presented.

Nissim Ezekiel (1924–2004), professor of English literature at the University of Bombay, published a number of anthologies of columns and plays in English.

Sunil Gangopadhyay (b. 1934) for quite some time has been counted among the most widely read Bengali authors.

Qurat-ul-Ain Haider (1926–2007) wrote in Urdu, and was a convinced and convincing representative of the culture associated with that language. She also made a name for herself as a translator of Western literature into Urdu (Henry James, T.S. Eliot, Truman Capote).

Vishnu Khare (b. 1940), whom I unjustly derided as an "embassy poet," was a Hindi poet and critic, as well as a prolific translator.

Sitakant Mahapatra (b. 1937) was a well-known poet not only in his mother tongue of Oriya, but also in the pan-Indian context.

Rasipuram Krishnaswami Narayan (1906–2001), whom I had visited in Mysore, since 1935 had written over a dozen novels in English, as well as travel books, essays and retellings of Indian myths and legends.

Amrita Pritam (1919–2005) lived in Lahore up to the partition of India; after 1947 she lived in Delhi. Starting in 1936, she published over 50 books—collections of poetry, novellas, novels and essays—in Punjabi.

Raghuvir Sahay (1929–1990) had established himself as one of the innovative representatives of the new Indian literature; many think him the most original of these writers.

A.K. Ramanujan (1929–1993) was born in Mysore and wrote in the regional language of Kannada and in English. He lived in Chicago and was professor of Dravidian languages and linguistics at the University of Chicago.

Kabita Sinha (1931–1999) for some time has been a program producer in Calcutta for All India Radio. This broadcast experience gave her writing the character of good dialogue and good storytelling.

Vijay Tendulkar (1928–2008) was one of the most well-known playwrights and film writers of modern India. His literary work included dozens of plays, two collections of short stories, five pieces for children's theater and collections of essays.

I had invited this fascinating group of the best authors of India to Frankfurt—and they all came. I was driven by the hope that these 24-karat authors would find people interested in them, especially among the many publishers who gathered in Frankfurt. We had a booklet with samples from these authors titled *…down below, like Shesha, am I*. We also had arranged for a person to accompany each author, a "scout," as we called him, who was to create contacts with the publishing houses and otherwise to take care of the well-being of the guest. We didn't spare any expense. But all of this was not enough. Filled with a premonition of bad things to come, I wrote about the Indian authors in an article in the *German Publishers Weekly* before the Fair began: *When will the representatives of the media in our country free themselves from the clichés of the Western images of India,* The Tiger of Eschnapur,[2] *the picture of poverty and of the hungry masses?*

My fear that the erudite European understanding of literature would hack to pieces these proud exemplars of Indian writing proved to be justified. Our media organs hardly concerned themselves with the authors who had come; they instead worked over well-worn clichés. Only a few got into the litera-

---

2. *The Tiger of Eschnapur*—The title of a number of German films set in India, most famously by Fritz Lang (1959).

ture that was offered, and the legion of our Indian authors, who were in general good-natured and original personalities, did not feel themselves accepted, nor well-received, and felt lost in the hectic goings-on of the Frankfurt market.

Vijay Tendulkar had been invited in 1986, but did not visit Frankfurt until 1995, when he came to give a lecture about contemporary Indian *belles-lettres*. In 1996, 10 years after the India Festival, he echoed what must have been the cause for misunderstanding among his compatriots in 1986: *My expectation was that in Frankfurt I would have something to do with a literary affair, but what I found there was more a commercial than a literary event. It was my ignorance about the goals of this Fair that gave rise to such an expectation. I learned later that the Fair had always been a commercial event, where the sales and purchase of publication rights was a central issue, and not meeting with writers...*

We were once again confronted with the limits of our Frankfurt Book Fair in bringing so many providers of content from all regions of the world, writers whom we considered worthy of attention. As a pedagogical institution, our exposition did not amount to much.

Our presentation could have succeeded if we had been able to convince the representatives of the press who were present to support our goals. I had been very successful in the case of Latin America, but in the case of India the mechanism failed. Was it that the media were not given enough material by us, and that the exposition was poorly presented?

What could be done we certainly did: A three-day symposium on literature at the start in the Frankfurt Römer Town Hall, daily readings by authors in the original languages with simultaneous translations, presentations of music and dance, and last but not least the smells and spices of Indian cuisine which were to provide a sensory aspect to the professional public, the publishers and the media, and to the potential German readers.

At this first India fair, I had to learn painfully for the first time (I had put myself out to an extraordinary extent) what a press campaign meant and how helpless one could be when you were offered up as a target for the media. It was pointless to bring one's own arguments into a public discussion and hope that these would even be heard, much less accepted. The media seemed merely to crib from one another and create an echo chamber of opinion. They all blabbed about the great flop that we had suffered with the India theme. Tilman Jens did a film for German television in the series TTT—*title–topics–temperaments*— that quite irresponsibly pinned the source of Indian authors' frustration on the fact that they had been exploited by us and had not received enough to eat! *Have compassion for the poor!*

"It Would Be Better To Send The People Something To Eat," was the headline in the *Frankfurt Pflasterstrand*. The paper then cited a presumably cultivated publisher with a critical review of the so-called "Flop at the Book Fair."

A typical interview appearing in the *Frankfurter Neue Presse* on October 7, 1986, projected the image of a critically questioning organ of the press, as did many media at that time, but it really gave only hackneyed superficialities that were floating around in the news:

The Book Fair India Theme, a Debacle?
Under the Fair Dome: Ashamed and Helpless

QUESTION: *The theme of India, the central theme of this Book Fair, has become a horrendous disaster. It presented itself generally as an involuntary demonstration of literary seeking of political asylum. That certainly could not have been what you had in mind?*

WEIDHAAS: We have a totally different impression. For the first time we brought to Frankfurt a literature that is generally unknown here. The polemics with which we have been beat on the head in the past few days have more to do with the inability of the reporters to come to terms in so short a time with such a varied literature rooted in other cultures.

QUESTION: *But it was not only the reporters, but also the Indian guests themselves who stepped into the foreground. The discussions with them all have one result: helplessness, embarrassment, and the feeling of having been misused. Their strongest criticism is that they had no contact at all with authors from other languages, not even with the Germans. Couldn't you have coordinated that better?*

WEIDHAAS: We told the authors ahead of time what to expect here. The point of these topical themes is to present these authors of this literature to our public. They all had the possibility of doing this. That the authors now say that they felt themselves to be isolated is a strange contradiction. They do not say this to us, although that may have been out of politeness, but they heartily thanked us for everything and for all the great possibilities here. We also know what such a book fair means in terms of a hectic atmosphere and in human coldness toward others. True, an author, especially an Indian, could well overreact. But if you rely only on that and create a gigantic flop, that is something that I find shameful. And not only for the Indian guests, but also for those people who are posing the questions.

QUESTION: *Not so, my dear Mr. Weidhaas! The Indians, so far as the rumor goes, are leaving without any German publisher having contracted for a single publishing license with any one of them. Indian literature, so goes the argument, is too risky and too difficult. Instead of a central topic of India, it should rather have been "India—A Topic for Frustration." Don't you think so?*

WEIDHAAS: That just isn't correct. I know at least one person who completed a contract at the fair and of 40 titles that have already appeared in German or will be published as a result of this thematic Fair. That this can't happen so quickly is obvious. We wanted for the first time to open up public consciousness of this topic. We have here very representative authors from the various regions of India, but there is also the inability on our side to open up to strangers. You have to give this thing a chance. We have opened it up; we have shown what is there to be discovered here. More than that the Book Fair cannot do. I'm sorry.

QUESTION: *Well, people now think that those involved, the Indians, believe that the Fair leadership, except for the pocket money, the hotel rooms and the free transportation cards, was involved primarily with the intellectual side of the guests. I would like to read what some of those Indians have to say at home about their experience at the Book Fair.*

WEIDHAAS: I'd be very interested to read that, but in fact these criticisms don't make any sense. For every two authors we had a contact scout available day and night. We made sure that every one of the authors had at least three public appearances. I can only explain this to myself by saying that exhaustion after this marathon of the Fair has led to these controversial comments from a few authors. On the organizational side, everything went very well. And as far as the resonance among the public, at least in Hall 7 we had around 45,000 visitors.

QUESTION: *Insiders are already making jokes about what lightweight topic will come around next year: "Illiterates Without Any Books." But seriously: How do you want to make the Frankfurt Book Fair more attractive to other out-of-the-way cultures after this controversy over India? It seems that you have bargained away any trust in you.*

WEIDHAAS: We have apparently not been successful in making these literatures and cultures of people on the outside to be so appetizing that they can be swallowed down whole in this country. And based on the reactions I hear from you, I can now say that this will be the last topical Fair. I always considered this as a sensible supplement to the hustle and bustle involved in the Fair. If I can't succeed with this, I won't worry myself sick about it.

Impressions

Is time what we read from our watch? Do I still have time? Have I ever had time? Is history time? Did the alienation of people from nature and thus from God begin 500 years ago with that damned little pomander watch from Peter Henlein in Nuremberg? Our mechanical division into hours, minutes and seconds that we live with day in and day out, as though it were an inborn part of us, has alienated us from unending time, from the time of infinity. The flow of time has a simple division through natural rhythms, like day and night, sowing and harvesting. These ritual divisions of time gave people in earlier ages a framework, an approach, an orientation, something calming. Does the calmness of the people in India stem from the fact that they are still living in a completely different time?

When I look back on the line of my life through time, I see myself incapable of simply "seeing the past go by as in a revue." The time that I experienced was not a film that I could let spin out. It was also not a story that I wanted to relate exactly as it happened. When I look back on life as I lived it, there is no linear sequence. It consists of events that I experienced, of images, of aromas, of interrelated thoughts, of impressions.

In Colva (Goa, India) you can meet all the representatives of our sphere of culture—zoned-out hippies who have given up and whom you can recognize from afar by the way they meander. Then the family of Mr. Upright from the German equivalent of Middle America—their children screaming at the top of their lungs because they want to have their sandy hands washed off. And the No-future people, like Cornelius, the doctor. And then those Bhagwan charlatans in the bungalow next door—the German guru with his lover and his enraptured gang of young disciples. He used to be an official in the Communist Free German Youth in the old East Germany, then later a Maoist in Hanover, and now he is a pompous *guru*.

Still, the paradise of Goa makes you think about the basics of life—the long walks barefoot on the beach, the crabs that scurry away, love games in the warm seawater, where we were suddenly surrounded by squeaking dolphins.

One time, our rented motorbike would not start. A moment later a passing rider stopped and awkwardly looked at the problems with our bike.

Thoughts about a more humane civilization. In this capitalistic society it is the concern with ownership that keeps driving us forward. Dream of a new renaissance—architecture and technology suited to people, not oriented to profit!

A bicycle tour on the beach down to the Sal River, some 20 miles there and back—because of the tide and the rising water level, we kept getting pushed deeper into the sand on the beach. Just a bit away from the edge of the water the going was good, since the ground was as hard as asphalt, but farther off in the looser sand we could not go forward. Two German bike riders, who were traveling to the South without maps and wanted to get to Kerala. A miserable Alpine type, who had hepatitis. The little black child whom we named "The Little Prince."

Later, in the "restaurant," a wooden shack made of four posts, we ate fish and drank Kingfisher beer. I felt quite invigorated and energetic, and really living simply.

In 1987 I flew to Managua with Lutz Kliche to organize the first literature festival for the Minister of Culture Ernesto Cardenal. I had sketched this out with Ernesto at the last Frankfurt Book Fair, in the Wieland pub. Michi Strausfeld came along from Madrid. Cardenal came to meet us. I thought that he would be expecting the rock singer Wolfgang Niedecken, who was also on board the plane with his band, but he was waiting for me.

I met a lot of old acquaintances at the opening of the literature festival, which was inaugurated by Comandante Ortega with the attendance of the vice president and writer Sergio Ramírez, Cardenal and myself. In addition to the Comandante Tomás Borge, the revolutionary Minister of the Interior and hero of women, I met Roberto Díaz, the Guatemalan publisher;

Erik Blandon, a publisher in Nicaragua; Eduardo Galeano, my friend from the focal theme fair of 1976 and author of *Open Veins of Latin America;* Fernando Cardenal, Ernesto's brother; Klaus Höpcke, Vice Minister of Culture of East Germany, who used me as his interpreter; José Coronel Urtecho, the Nicaraguan poet; Federico Cruz, my friend and colleague from Havana; Gioconda Belli, the very beautiful "revolutionary" and author from Nicaragua; and Lutz Kliche, who had done all the organizational work for the book festival. The world press was heavily represented at this political hot point.

Others present included Walter Moutchia from Cameroon, head of the book center there; the KGB colonel Vassily Sitnikov, a friendly hard drinker from Moscow; Bob Baensch from New York; Gongor from Ulan Bator; the Brazilian publisher Alfredo Machado; the Argentine Hugo Brik; Fritz Gröning from the German Embassy; Peter Levi, then still with the Latin American Publishers Association in Bogotá; and Ana María Rodríguez, also from Bogotá. They were all friends and acquaintances whom I had worked with elsewhere in the world, and were all kindred spirits, people really interested in books.

In the late afternoon Ernesto Cardenal hosted a lively party under a giant leafy tree in front of the Ministry of Culture. Lots of local rum and cigars—tropically warm, but not too hot. We danced to salsa rhythms until late into the night. For the first time I felt something like a lucky feeling in my professional life!

On another occasion the professional gossipiness of my press spokesman once again led to speculations in print about moving the Frankfurt Book Fair, as in 1978, only this time not to Düsseldorf but to Munich. Once again this unleashed an avalanche in the press. Everybody got involved in the speculation—the German press service DPA, the Associated Press, the *Frankfurter Allgemeine Zeitung*, the *Frankfurter Rundschau, Bild, tz Munich,* television, radio. For days on end I had tried not so much to deny the rumor, because it could certainly help us in our difficult negotiations over costs with the Frankfurt Fairgrounds, but as far as possible to chalk it up to a "routine checking of the technical possibilities elsewhere." The plan in Frankfurt was to increase prices by 160% over a certain period of time. The head of the German Publishers Association had made contact with Munich with the clear intention of exerting pressure on our current hosts.

The argument about the fairgrounds had to be continued, that I understood, but there was nothing to the rumors about our moving away. Everyone on the Supervisory Board was convinced that we would stay in Frankfurt. Spurred on by the chairman of the Supervisory Board, the situation got worse step-by-step. It seemed that you could no longer go back because you would lose face, *etc.*

Is that how wars are begun? What kind of mechanism is this? Force, blackmail? For the two sides there was no alternative to "The Book Fair stays in Frankfurt!" I found that interaction with others at times like this was ruled by the law of the jungle; it destroyed former communal feelings, and all prior civil forms were given up as soon as one's own interests required it.

Despite my experiences in 1978, I was astonished at the public effect and the broad interest in this question. What was behind all this? Envy against the growth of Frankfurt or against the successful people at the Frankfurt Fair? Executive Director Horstmar Stauber? A question of party politics, or growing suspicion in the press against institutions that were growing ever more independent?

Whatever the reason, we "won" this moving-away campaign as well, though not because we had better arguments or because the people we were negotiating with in Frankfurt suddenly had a burst of insight. We won because the Lord High Mayor Wolfram Brück lost his bid for reelection as mayor. As the chairman of the Supervisory Board of the Fairgrounds he had identified himself with the demand to up the rent; now he softly and quietly disappeared from the Frankfurt arena. Our other opponent, the executive director of the Frankfurt Fairgrounds Horstmar Stauber, whom I had gotten to know and to appreciate from many negotiations over the years as a person with the "mentality of a prize fighter," a hard but fair opponent, just at that time decided to leave the Fair Company. His successor, the somewhat gentler Heike Markau, had no choice but to give up the price hike in order to put himself on a firm footing in his new position. I was able to call off the soundings in Munich.

Buenos Aires: Jorge Timossi from Havana greeted me with what I first thought was a cold face. In actuality, it was only with the greatest effort that he could overcome his sadness and deliver the news—Federico was dead!

My friend Federico, director of the Havana book fair, dead, murdered by a petty thief (as was reported) when he was in the apartment of a friend looking after things (I didn't believe these explanations). There are very many acquaintances in our profession, but very few friends. He was a friend. I loved him—a beautiful smiling relationship between men stretching across various political systems and practices.

We wanted to see and address only the positive in each other. It's obvious that other forces were at work in him and in myself, but I never saw them or experienced them in him. We reacted to one another positively, in a life-affirming manner, even joyfully. He had the advantage that I offered him as the "big brother" from Frankfurt, and he displayed an almost childlike, naïve manner toward everyone, whether he wanted to listen to them or not.

I never found him in a bad mood or depressed. Even in the worst of cases he was just very serious when certain circumstances required taking care of. A person full of the joy of life! There are few people like that. It's really a shame that it's only through loss that we recognize what a wonderful relationship we had. *My dear friend, the world and our lives are poorer without you! I feel a great pain on losing you, and at the same time I feel close to you in a way that wasn't clear to me while you were still alive.*

1988. Two dreams: My father takes over my weekend house without my agreement. I call him to account for this, and as a result an atmosphere of enmity grows up between us.

At a meeting Johannes Rau suddenly hits me in the face with a folder because I had gently mimicked him. Although I liked him, I felt myself quite insulted and left. On leaving, I let him know that I was now going to join the Christian Democratic Party (CDU). Later, Rau during a speech made gestures of reconciliation to me, which I deliberately ignored.

When Jaime Smolovich appeared in 1976 and presented himself as a friend of the Frankfurt Book Fair, everyone thought that he was a member of the Argentine Secret Service. I also had trouble figuring him out. He always sat very upright, an open, friendly face behind a pair of bright horn-rimmed glasses, always full of interest, in a way that seemed appropriate for a psychotherapist. Still, somehow I could not get rid of the feeling that his interest was not very deep. If I were to say the same thing a second time, he would always show the same animated but superficial interest. On the other hand there were these rays of light that streamed out of those smiling eyes, magnified by his strong lenses. If he took off his glasses, his face appeared as that of a somewhat tired old man.

I voluntarily took on a 40-day alcohol-free diet after my 50th birthday. I wanted to know if my consumption of alcohol had turned into a real dependence. No, not an alcoholic, although for years not a day had gone by without some consumption of alcohol. And strength enough to say "no," despite the occasional schemes by my environment to seduce me into drinking.

In our society alcohol has become a ritualized act of greeting and approval. You drank in society and felt sociable that way. But alcohol as a substitute for what? For true community?

Things had been balanced out that were not equivalent, but which should have been equal — to convince the other person and to force him to accede to our wishes! We drank together and so we shared emotions; it was as though we understood each other above all our different interests. This was something that came from business life, nothing more than a trick or a gesture made to even out opposing standpoints.

Alcohol had also become a calming and numbing agent against the forces of alienation in our everyday life. Particularly at the beginning of my work at the Book Fair, I had difficulties in ridding myself of the emptiness that I felt without some form of numbing. More and more I took tobacco, television and often a little drink. The enjoyment of alcohol was for me, as for many of my contemporaries, something of a hedonistic *ersatz* drug. We used trivializing diminutives like "It'll do me good," a "nice little wine," a "tasty little beer," a "little cognac to help the digestion," in order to free ourselves from the pressure of our conscience over a "small" indiscretion.

The man of our times was undoubtedly the man of the market. No longer the Biblical "yes-man" or "naysayer" or the Martin Luther type ("Here I stand, I can do no other!") but the man with his own identity! A man who found fulfillment and positive feelings in his "market value."

We all bared our teeth at cocktail parties, and pretended to pay attention to what others were saying. We listened to them in a distracted manner, but our overriding interest was *What impression am I making on the other person?* We did not experience any positive feelings of life from the roots of our being, from the depths of our experience, from peacefulness, or from any desire that we felt. Cut off from nature, floating around in the hurly-burly of daily life and taking our cues from whomever we happened to be with, what remained to us was the lust for power, success and recognition that was supposedly our own. And woe unto us if that power slipped away. We could no longer live with that empty isolation. The Minister President of Schleswig-Holstein, Uwe Barschel, who was forced from office and died in a Geneva hotel, was the prototype of this new man.

The painter Lorenzo in typical Ernesto Cardenal clothing was the opposite type. I gazed at him. "You don't need to look at me at all. You don't know me at all," he pounced on me. "I don't belong to the people around here." He looked suspiciously around himself, and then there followed a torrent of words of partially aggressive, partially contemptuous names for the people present.

Who could possibly have imagined that 45 years after the fact a German in a worn-out sweater sitting in first class in a giant airplane, shoveling in caviar and slurping vodka while reading Ralph Giordano's *The Second Guilt of the Germans*,[1] would be shuddering as he learned of the author's suffering, given in the form of incomprehensible statistics and correlations? Who would have thought that this suffering and the suffering of

---

1. Ralph Giordano (b. 1923): Jewish writer persecuted by the Nazis.

millions of others would turn out to be a mere historical episode, to be consumed sitting down in a well-heated airplane while crossing from continent to continent?

From Calle Maipú, a narrow one-way street full of noisy taxis and smelly jitney buses not far from Plaza San Martín, you go through a slowly opening automatic glass door and enter into a vaulted space paneled with dark wood and covered with lime green carpet—this was my beloved Hotel Dorá in Buenos Aires!

Stepping in from the wild, breathless city, I considered this warm, elongated room to be an oasis. On the right, in a middle niche, a clerk hunched over in front of the keyboxes. Next to him, the reception desk: another clerk behind the counter was constantly entering numbers into a large ledger. And then, higher by two steps, lay another niche, from which two elevator doors to the rooms opened just as slowly as the entry door.

Then came the bar with three barstools. Opposite it, barely separated from the rest of the room by two Spanish walls, stood four square tables with four chairs each. That was the restaurant of the hotel.

In the rear section, a few seating areas stood in front of a tall window that gave a view onto an inner fountain draped with stones and ferns. Along the right-hand wall was a bright green leather sofa, where the poet Borges always took his morning tea during my first visit in 1968, and two similarly colored heavy wingback chairs. I liked to sit in them if I was waiting for guests or for someone to interview. From here one could see the entire room all the way to the entrance.

At the rear left there was a small exit to the management office of the hotel, out of which a nattily made-up woman in her mid-40s, balancing on steep red stiletto heels, would come out, evidently a manager of the building.

The most important element of this hotel was its porters and bellhops. I still meet some of those who served me when I stayed here for the first time some 20 years ago. A little more bent over, a little grayer or balder than they once were, they bring today's guests the same friendliness and the same interest that they did back then. They let you know that they remember your past visits; they are pleased to see you and greet you like an old friend. This is not exaggerated customer service or even subservience, or even any bored arrogance or deliberate routine, as is often the case with people in this profession. They are your friends here; they are waiting for you and are ready to jump in at any occasion. When you walk into the Hotel Dorá, you are saved.

The Argentine driver, who took me to the Ezeiza airport: "You know, we here in Argentina feel a certain affection for Hitler, if not love. What an intriguing character, what a fantastic character!"

He pushed some invisible hair out of his face, "Just like when he brushed a lock from his face!" The friendly face of the taxi driver began to light up—"*Qué personaje hermoso, qué personaje hermoso!*"

1988—visiting the children in Córdoba. This woman was a granite ogre of humanity, who grew out of the iron love of Latin America. She was a new edition of her father Ramón, who was a legend in his own time. She was a dominant person, taking into account only the elements of her own confused thinking, feeling and will. Her thinking was abstruse and muddled, full of outbursts of emotion and unusual self-drama. I sat opposite her at the end of a whirlpool, in which I had once been the center. I belatedly got anxious.

On the next morning I was overcome by strong compassion for my two daughters—with Veronica, whom I had adopted as a daughter and who still loved me as a father in her quiet, reserved way, and with Anahí, this gifted child who longed for her absent father, because she was in danger of drowning in the wild being of her mother.

I flew out of this emotional Córdoba one day earlier than planned. My two daughters and this sweet little Noelia, my "little granddaughter," I would have gladly torn from this hurricane and taken with me. I kissed them, said goodbye with some pat phrases, boarded the airplane, and immediately fell into a deep but restless sleep.

Meeting with the Senegalese Mariama Bâ, whose first book *Une si longue lettre* was ...d—at the Book Fair when Africa was the focal theme—for publication in 14 languages.

The South African poet James Matthews with Jaime Smolovich, an Argentine ...irer of the Frankfurt Book Fair, whom we at first wrongly suspected of being a secret ...t of the Argentine military.

1980 The Maoist publishing house *"Rote Fahne"* [Red Flag] put up a sign, *Brezhnev the Hitler of Today, Block Brezhnev's Way.* This sign led to the intervention of the Sovi Ambassador Valentin Falin, who had the large sign removed through the action of tl Frankfurt state attorney's office.

1981 Gathering at an international book shop in Mexico City: (*left to right*) Hugo Set publisher of El Manual Moderno; Doris Oberländer, head of the international departm of the Frankfurt Book Fair; and Hermann Schulz, publisher of the Peter Hammer Ver

You have to let everything wash over you. The management of the Kodansha
Publishing House in Tokyo invited us to a meal in a *geisha* house, where we had to put on
traditional Japanese clothing. I appear here as a *samurai* with my companion Minette S.

1982 Opening of the Book Fair with plain "Mr. Schmidt," who one week earlier ha been Chancellor of the Federal Republic of Germany.

1984 When Federal Chancellor Helmut Kohl opened the Book Fair, everything revol around him. In the picture he is encircled (*from left to right*) by the general director of Publishers Associations, the press chief of the Publishers Association, and the Lord H Mayor of Frankfurt.

On the occasion of my 15th anniversary at the Frankfurt Book Fair, my colleagues surprised me with an ironic Superman poster, which of course I had to autograph at the end of the Fair. The poster reads: *15 Years of Making the Book World Tremble.*

1986   Guests from the book trade of developing countries. *Second from the left:* Jorg Barros, an outstanding publishing figure from the Chile of the Pinochet era.

1986   I always invited a group to a party at my apartment on the Saturday of the F This year I had guests from Bolivia, Mexico, Argentina, Cuba, Japan, Nicaragua and E Germany.

The Indian Minister Narasimha Rao and German Foreign Minister Hans-Dietrich Genscher on a tour of the Fair during the India theme year.

Rajiv Gandhi (*center*), Prime Minister of India, in the run-up to the focal theme for his country, on short notice granted me an audience. I flew to Delhi specifically for this. Two years later he was assassinated.

1987   Siegfried Unseld of Suhrkamp Verlag in the beginning constantly criticized o work, but later he was always very well-meaning.

1988   Annual visit of the delegation from the German Democratic Republic (GD East Germany): *(from left to right)* Norbert Mahn (Foreign trade book export), A Lange (GDR Central Committee, Culture Department), Jürgen Gruner (Chairman of Leipzig Publishers Association), Klaus Höpcke (Director of the Central Adminsitra of Publishing Houses and Book Dealers in the GDR Ministry of Culture), Hans B (General Secretary of the Leipzig Publishers Association).

The two waiters in the Palace Hotel in Turin circled around my table in an obnoxious pattern, pouring a drop of wine, a shot of mineral water, or perhaps straightening up something on the table, moving away again while still circling around, only to come back again in a somewhat wider arc. I fled from this nervous serving of guests.

Vanity that was tailored much more smoothly—the opening evening of the first Salon du Livre in 1988 in Turin, but the concept seemed to go over. In contrast to Bogotá, where the celebration of one's self by the organizers seemed to be the main point.

Afterwards to the Villa Sasci and the dizzying "middle-man" Inge Feltrinelli, flying from spot to spot when she would see such and such a famous personality whom she introduced to this one and that one and also to me, and then introduced me to them naturally with all the superlatives due to each one. Her glance flickered in the air without pause, always on the search for new sacrifices to her insatiable, lovable desire to bring people together.

I was in Paris and sitting on the sidewalk, no, naturally not—I was sitting at a table at a small restaurant on the sidewalk of Rue Surcouf on the Left Bank. A hard day of negotiations had just finished. In a hotel I had also just seen the defeat of our national German football team by the Dutch. Now I was sitting here, smoking my "perpetual" Wintermann cigarillo, drinking a coffee. Wine was still standing in the glass. A man in a tuxedo with a red embroidered handkerchief in his breast pocket sauntered over.

A sip of Beaujolais, a puff on the cigar... and 50 feet behind the man in a tuxedo his companion followed, wearing a fine blue silk dress, barefoot, her shoes in one hand. On the street along the banks of the Seine, only a hundred yards from here, locked in a traffic jam, hundreds of emergency police ready to set off in green buses.

I felt as though I were in a fine French film. I bit on a tasty piece of brown sugar, and took another sip of the wine. A little boy came running by and snatched the tip left by a guest on the neighboring table. His father, apparently a foreign worker, grabbed him, took him gently by the arm, and laid the tip back on the table.

I signaled to the waiter, *"L'addition, s'il vous plaît."* The waiter put it on the table, *"L'addition,"* effusively thanking me as if I had already paid. Someone on roller skates with a small pack on his back rolled by through the little street, very elated.

After my lecture at the Munich publishers club I went with F. to have another beer. He was a Berliner; he loved Munich, wrote novels, and managed a gift-book publishing house. "You should see those books! What we are doing is not so dumb!" He had built a house in Tessin with an idea of doing the writing that he had always wanted to do. He sat up from the table that we were sitting at, and, half crouching over, he made a gesture of looking into the distance by holding his hand over his eyes.

At such meetings I have often wound up with F., since he was happy to break off from the others, who always had a good time together. He was sober, consistent, mild, a very likable person. I just was amazed that every time I was in his company I was overcome by deadly boredom.

Ms. K. was a tall, attractive blonde woman, who suddenly appeared as an office assistant of the director of the German Publishers Association. She walked around with loud, clicking, brisk steps through the corridors of the Association, and because of her resolute manner, attracted the leering looks of the male employees who were passing by. Not one of them dared to get seriously close to her since they all feared a smart, sharp comeback that would put them in their place.

At first I paid little attention to Ms. K., since I had been living with my companion for the past six years. As far as any emotional involvement went, the work scene, and especially the German Publishers Association, was basically a taboo area. Having any romantic relationship seemed to me to be too dangerous because of the possibility of being detected, leaving me open to real pressure.

Nonetheless, on one sunny morning in August, when most of the employees of the German Publishers Association were away on summer holiday, I called up the office of the head o the company to get his agreement on some trivial matter. Ms. K. had been assigned to mind the shop on this blue summer day; otherwise there was no one in the office. We started chatting, and since there seemed to be no end to this chatting on the telephone, I invited Ms. K. on the spot to have lunch in an Italian restaurant on Grosse Bockenheimer Street, popularly called the "glutton street."

Nothing had yet happened. I had invited her knowing that it wouldn't be a bad idea to do something to improve the atmosphere at the German Publishers Association, which would have so liked to dominate the Book Fair. We ate well and continued our conversation from the morning. Ms. K., whose face I earlier thought had traces of being quite hard, and whom I had assumed to have a masculine approach to things, turned out to be quite a feminine being with many gifts. She talked earnestly and openly, engaged and sensibly, and then again somewhat cheekily. The male traits, if they had ever existed, vanished from her face. She carried on the conversation with a dry grace that surprised me, and we finally continued it in the Apple Cider Garden on the Lohrberg. I often had sat there back in the early 1960s during my student days at the book dealers school, whiling away the evenings over cider and pork ribs.

We finally got up from the table after night had fallen. In front of the building of the German Publishers Association, where Ms. K. got into her little Honda in order to drive home to Mainz, I gave her a little kiss on the cheek as a goodbye. It was clear to me that despite all my intentions something was happening to me.

İstanbul, November 1988. It happens that time simply moves forward. I had retreated to a little room on the seventh floor of the old Pera Palas Hotel. From here I looked out over the Golden Horn at the Blue Mosque, the old city of Stambul and the Galata Bridge. It was November and very chilly. The heaters burning soft coal and the general air pollution allowed only schematic silhouettes of the minarets to be seen in a greenish yellow fog. The cold grabbed me from my legs all the way up to my neck. Still, I stayed put in İstanbul. I made no pleasure trips. At midday I went to the Refik, where I could choose what to eat in the kitchen. At the Jacob II, I still met a few friends in the evening, like the writers F.C. Delius and Aras Ören, the Turkish-German author, the publisher couple Atil and Füsan Ant, and my colleague Michael Fenderl, who was in charge of the German book stall at the İstanbul Book Fair. I looked in on the Book Fair, but unwillingly, because it always seemed to result in jobs for me to do.

I read—Haldun Taner's *Stories,* Pierre Loti's *Aziyadé,* Aras Ören's *Understanding Paradise* and Yaşar Kemal's *The Undying Grass.*

I waited. What for, I didn't know. Probably for time to pass. I felt burned out. My stomach hurt, my pulse pounded in my left arm, my neck was itching. I waited for calm to return, and the strength to move forward.

After a feverish cold, I suddenly got the first signs of stomach cramps on the trip over the Bosporus to a meal at the publisher Recai Akpul. I was writhing in pain after drinking down three large glasses of vodka. On the way home, very strong stomach pains overcame me, along with the well-known Turkish diarrhea, heavy sweating and fever. In the morning I was absolutely done in. I got a few pills from the *eczane* and climbed back into bed. I lay still and waited. Had I hit bottom? I had let go and was letting myself sink.

The view from the window—on the bridge over the Golden Horn traffic was jammed solid; nothing was moving. I discovered that being sick was not so bad. The world outside came to mean less and less. I concentrated on myself, on my body, and simply sank back into myself.

After taking a bunch of pills, I climbed back into bed, satisfied with myself. The Sultan Ahmed Mosque and the chains of yellow light on the Galata Bridge glistened exceptionally in a fog-free night. And still, I couldn't fall asleep. Thoughts, questions and images ran through my head.

I rested in İstanbul, and waited there for ten days. My heart was full of affection for Füsan and Atil Ant, for the publishing house Serhat Yayınları, for Kezban Akçali, for the author Nimet Tuna, and for Aras Ören as well—people with open, genuine emotions. After so much human warmth, I arrived in frigid Frankfurt in a bad mood.

What had happened in those months? My love for Ms. K. had grabbed me with dizzying energy. Pain and agitation became standard all week long, and the few hours that we had with each other were holy moments of a closeness that I had never known with any other person. Ms. K. was like a fountain that seemed to gush unceasingly from deep in the ground. She stood like a tree with deep roots in the prehistoric rocks of life, a mighty tree made of strong, hard wood.

To throw myself in her arms, I had to be free. I therefore gave up the delicate relationship with my girlfriend of the time M., something that pained her. That relationship had recently been smothering me. M. needed me; Ms. K. did not need me. She loved my gentleness, my physical warmth, my affection that enjoyed all of her. Ms. K. rewarded me with closeness. She let me get very close to her. In her anger M. had screamed, "It's your goddamn curiosity, your insatiable curiosity." I did not feel at all insulted by this comment, on the contrary...

The Weimar of poets and thinkers, of Goethe and Schiller, the place that gave its name to the Weimar Republic, was a magical time in German culture and in the German being, as Luise Rinser had claimed once in a lecture.[2] In those days I felt I had touched the core of Germanness, which still persisted in us West Germans who were otherwise shaped by modern economic forces and manipulated by new mass media in ways quite distinct from the days of Weimar.

Here in Weimar, East Germany, on the previous day I had still insisted on my fear of visiting the Buchenwald concentration camp, but then I went, along with Dr. Wagner, director of the Municipal Museum, and my colleague Ronald Weber. While I was there, my imagination for horror failed me. I could not fathom the suffering that had occurred there. Even the identification of the murderers as Germans, which had overcome me in my youth when I saw pictures of the concentration camps, did not affect me here.

I shuddered at the thought of what people are capable of,

---

2. Luise Rinser (1911–2002): Political activist and writer, author of *A Woman's Prison Journal: Germany 1944*.

especially in walking through the exhibit, though I did not feel any personal guilt for what had happened. I was able to look critically at the curious distortion of history in this museum, where only the Communist heroes were celebrated. I also felt quite uncomfortable with the bombastic Buchenwald memorial. It should have been a place for quiet, for reflection and contemplation, and not another monument about state power with grandiloquent "Never Again" claims. This was a place of weakness and of the helplessness of the individual, but above us the needle-nosed attack helicopters of the Red Army circled incessantly.

Siegfried Lenz: *This may sound strange. Auschwitz remains in our custody. It belongs to us, the same way as the rest of our own history belongs to us.*

This comment by the great German author, uttered somewhere in the middle of the 1980s, set off a heated discussion between my press spokesman and myself. His reproach, made for the first time during our Italian journey in Milan: that with my cultural work I would "dirty my own nest." These were our "people" [*Volk*], that one *Volk* is just like any other, and that he would not allow my critical remarks about "our *Volk*" to go unchallenged. He spoke of traditions, of "bloodbaths" throughout history, of new generations, who don't want to have anything more to do with "those events," who have "pride in their national heritage."

I was surprised, since I had gradually come to consider myself a patriot who charted our problematic fatherland from a critical distance. This seemed to me to be the only possible form of identifying with the impossible history of my country. Had it all been merely a chimera, a historical slip-up? Couldn't we today imagine other historical "bloodbaths" as familiar events, as if Auschwitz had never existed? How could one speak of a continuous German culture, one that led directly to Auschwitz or at least was unable to stop it?

The Nazis were not a party or movement that had its roots in German tradition. From my point of view they were a horde of disgruntled men with no vision. Their image of the future was a backward looking *Utopia*. For me they were petty bourgeois a class that in that particular economic situation was poised on the verge of collapse into the *Lumpenproletariat*. They never stood *for* anything, but always *against* it—against the dominant order, against the *bourgeoisie*, against the *Jews*. They were not able to build up anything. They needed war to hold on to power. They were destined to lose the war since their conduct of power politics had no end in sight. When they finally took power, all that came out of it was the death and collapse within.

Why had German culture, so rich in tradition, put up so little resistance? Why had the Germans not stood up to this necrophilic raiding party? I didn't understand this suicidal mechanism. Why did they all follow the Führer like lemmings and even enthusiastically fall into the abyss? When I look at pictures and films about Hitler and his charges, they appear to me like poor people in fine clothes, who even at the height of their power were not genuine and could not believe in themselves. They carried out their Chaplinesque routines with a hard-bitten earnestness because they were standing on stage, and the spotlight was on them.

Where were the educated Germans; where were the "honorable" power elites. . . ? Where was—goddammit!—the "self-conscious working-class"? Where was the German *Volk*? It celebrated and gently but firmly collapsed. Was that what we should focus on, that which at this fateful and decisive moment in history had followed the Pied Piper into ruin? Should we now bind ourselves to these freshly sanitized but failed traditions, which have proven to be not just unreliable but outright lies—should we again chain ourselves to these as if nothing had happened? Was Auschwitz really only a sidetrack of history, a dead-header with no ongoing rail, an end station for so many finite lives? Was it the historically negligible fate of the wretched, while the real train of history thundered past this godforsaken Polish town?

No and again no! Every German train from now on should stop here. Every German seeking his identity should get off and think about whether the direction that he was going was the right one. As long as I had the impression that our political locomotive drivers were tearing through here, I had no choice but to maintain a critical distance to this Federal Republic of Germany. If things should change, then we would no longer need these "trails of blood" through German history, and then the *Volk* would no longer be necessary for a mature speaker of the German tongue; we would then hopefully look out on a peaceful future as a free, humane entity side by side with all our neighbors near and far.

Under such circumstances, I had to ask myself, both personally and professionally, whether my creative energy would be sufficient to set out in a new direction.

Shortly before this I was to set up joint living arrangements with Ms. K., but just then—irresistibly and not at all unexpectedly—the ghosts of a past love appeared. How tightly we cling to such ossified fidelities, especially those mixed with a heavy dose of guilt and sentimentality. I too was not exempt from such surprise attacks of old feelings!

How vital, how viable, how flexible was the new feeling that we called our love? How ready were we to look into the future, and how ready were we to cast off what lay behind us? How much of the future did one have at age 50, and how much energy for creating new hopes?

We returned from an exhilarating, beautiful weekend in the Rhön, and we again had to part because I was flying to Paris. At that point a great sadness came over both of us, a sadness that lay like lead on our limbs. It was practically incomprehensible since we would see one another again in three days.

Something was happening. Something was drawing us together. A metamorphosis of our lives had begun, a transfiguration that we could not control, but had only to consummate. We were frightened, but also somewhat amused. It was like a dream. In only a few days we would be living together. Would we then wake up one morning, look at each other in pure astonishment, and ask how we had gotten here?

In the morning I wandered through the mile-long corridors of the impossible 6,000-bed Rossiya Hotel in Moscow, looking for a breakfast spot that was open. In English I asked the key lady, who watched over our floor, and she barked "Buffet, up stairs, downstairs,—eight o'clock, ten o'clock, I don't know!" Then she pointed to the right, up the hall, then left down the hall, then up, then down. I thanked her with an exaggerated *"Bolshoe spasibo!"* for this exhausting piece of information. When I finally found a disgusting corner buffet that was open, I got a coffee at one of the filthy little tables. The only other guest besides me, a Russian, sat down next to me at the narrow table and wordlessly began to chomp away at his limp little sausage.

Nothing had improved in Moscow. The people seemed desperate. The supply of foodstuffs had become even worse. There were shortages of flour, sugar and even of yeast. On television there were earnest discussions about the economic woes.

The six vacation days that I had arranged for myself in the Rhön over the Pentecost holiday again gave me an opportunity for reflection. How had my work defined me during the last 20 years? I had not worked at the Fair; I had *lived* it. At first it was a support, a scaffolding, a structure that held me in place, and helped me to overcome my wavering ego and my spiritual crises. But for my private, personal relationships, this attitude was a burden and could lead to catastrophe. The scaffolding gradually became an end in itself.

My love for Ms. K. and her love for me now changed the balance of this arrangement; it meant saying goodbye to the scaffolding. Love carried me. Love took care of the human being behind the scaffolding, a human being who was not merely director of the Fair. It was not Ms. K. who demanded this; it was the mere existence of this love, this sincere and unrestrained intimacy. At the same time the Fair, which before had been my only existence by a long shot, found itself in a severe crisis due to an unforeseen and unmanageable event.

The mighty U.S. publishers now took aim at our final authority in shaping the Fair, and a new process set in that showed I had run up against a roadblock. This monster developed fierce powers, which carried the seeds of its own destruction and that of the exposition. Wherever it became impossible to break through the calcified structures and to allow fresh air to circulate, it was there that particular interests arrayed themselves against the whole. The only conceivable outcome would be stagnation followed by the slow extinction of our central precept. This

Fair was an organism, made up of thousands of individual lives and individual interests all brought together into a living whole. Where such an organism no longer had a unifying will that would assure an even and lively evolution into an imagined future, only a brittle superstructure would abide briefly before collapsing under the weight of its own internal contradictions.

Such thoughts came to me in New York when I learned that the big publishers, such as Random House, Simon & Schuster, Penguin, Harper & Row and their ilk, had rejected our proposals for new locations and openly threatened a boycott. If we were to submit to this blackmail, that would be the end of our bargaining position, for at that moment there was unfortunately no alternative to the plans we had already submitted.

1989 at the Salon du Livre in Paris—the French Foreign Minister Juppé, whom I was guiding through the graphics by Grass at the exhibit, shouted out excitedly, "Günter Grass, there he is, and with Brigitte Bardot, no less!" I corrected him that this was not Günter Grass, but Gunther Sachs, and he had nothing to do with either graphics or literature. The thoughtful filmmaker Hans-Jürgen Syberberg later noted that this had been an unconscious gesture of friendship. The Minister had wanted to establish something connecting Germany and France, and his memory had played tricks on him.

Günter Sommer, the drummer from East Germany, told the story best of how in Iraq the excited Arabs, out of sheer gratitude, started singing the *Deutschlandlied* (the West German national anthem) in the East German Embassy. The non-plussed East German diplomats had to acknowledge the song, if only with restrained applause. I mentioned similar experiences of West German diplomats in Buenos Aires.

From Nicaragua I wanted to send a message from the Frankfurt Book Fair to the Latin Americans that would be understood over there. What happened in Nicaragua was registered by intellectuals in all of Latin America. The result was as desired My lecture in front of not more than 25 people in the audience on "The Cultural Shortness of Breath, or the Slow Suffocation of Nations—On the Business-Oriented End of the Enlightenment due to the Forces of the International Book Trade," was reprinted not only in many Latin American countries, but also in my hometown newspaper, the *Frankfurter Rundschau,* as well as in the *East-German Publishers Weekly* in Leipzig.

Ms. K. and I flew to Panamá via Madrid on Iberia Airlines. In Madrid we put up in the beautiful Palace Hotel, which I knew from an earlier era. At night we walked through Madrid's old city and ate Serrano ham and drank a glass of red wine. The next day we wandered through the Prado, and at 2:30 we finally left for the airport. The plane was scheduled to leave at 4:55 PM, then at seven in the evening, then at one in the morning. It seemed as though we were sitting on the plane forever, since there were "technical problems," but finally at 3 AM we took off. We reached Panamá at eight the next morning. We took a room at the Hotel Continental, swam in the many-branched pool of the hotel, made love, slept a little. At about five in the afternoon we left for Managua.

This time no one was there to pick us up. We went to the Hotel Mercedes near the airport—an ugly dark room (that's what Ms. K. thought). Exhausted, we fell asleep. The following morning we met Hermann Schulz, Lutz Kliche and Uwe Timm, and we contacted the German Embassy.

The next day at around 6 AM we got instructions that we were to be ready at 7 for departure to the Plaza. It was July 19, 1989, the 10th anniversary of the revolution, and as it later turned out, the last annual celebration. Celebration of the revolution in the glistening sun. Before that it had rained.

In the evening a reception by President Ortega in the Olaf Palme Convention Center. We never got to see Ortega. Annoying gossip from the self-promoter Freimut Duve. Hermann Schulz was suffering from the presence of his ex-wife. Helmut von der Lahr ran around setting up interviews.

On the next afternoon we set up our book stall at the book Festival. At 8 PM the book Festival opened. I was standing between Ortega and Cardenal, though not allowed to speak. A curious German teacher asked me about my feelings of standing between such famous personalities. I actually felt rather stupid, standing there without saying a word.

My political work was done, and now we wanted to get a few days of vacation that we paid for privately.

Dinner with Comandante Borge, the Minister of the Interior. Nothing had come of the vacation house that Borge promised in San Juan del Sur. Now he promised us a different holiday house. I thanked him courteously. By Saturday Ms. K. was totally fed up; she had had enough of official happenings and wanted to take a rest. Unfortunately even on Sunday we still did not have a promised vacation house. Definitely coming on Monday. Then finally the breakthrough with the "available" driver and car to Huehuete. Before that we had tried to change money everywhere in Managua—all in vain! The route went through remote regions to our longed-for destination of Huehuete. Here we were told, "Terrible mistake!" Everything was closed. Besides, the vacation home that was so praised by Borge turned out to be a barracks in a single dilapidated village. So it was back to Managua. On the way back the driver fell asleep at the wheel, and we ended up on the side of the road. For the final two hours to Managua I took the wheel.

Now I had had enough; we wanted to get somewhere quieter. Our destination was now Guatemala, but before Thursday there was no flight. The Sheraton Hotel, where we settled down in Guatemala, was really very loud. Hard to sleep. We rented an auto from Hertz. It kept raining. Like refugees, we left Guatemala City in a fast new Toyota, hoping to head to the Pacific coast. From 5,000 feet high down to sea level. We drove through flooded streets via Escuintla to San José (Puerto) on the sea. We arrived at a silted-up, filthy nest. We had reserved the Hotel Chulamar from Guatemala City, but because of the high water, we could not even get to San José. Ms. K. was furious. She wanted to get out, preferably to Miami. Even though I was very experienced in travel in Central America, I too was very irritated.

We kept driving toward Liquin. The vacation center there was flooded out. We turned back. Back over the flooded streets to Escuintla and from there on an adventurous rocky road up into the mountains toward Antigua. This region was guerrilla territory, but we learned that only after arriving in Antigua. There were no hotel vacancies to be had, but we simply sat down in the Ramadan Hotel and refused to budge. After a long discussion, we received a room with an unfinished floor at half price. It was quite cool in Antigua. The clouds were hanging heavy. Ms. K. was completely exhausted and couldn't tolerate anything. She hardly talked to me. She wanted rest and sunshine. She wanted to get out of there.

Every trip is always a trip into one's soul. In the Middle Ages, "trip" was a synonym for change, for development. Internal and external things would come together. On this trip, Antigua was such a point of clarification, a kind of small catharsis on the road we were taking together. Perhaps only a momentary breakthrough for us, but it helped clear the air. At night in bed we sought each other out in a long tight embrace.

The following day all the practical problems were resolved. After a beautiful, sunny trip through the Guatemalan mountains, we found a place to stay in Panachatel on Lake Atitlán, which satisfied Ms. K.'s need for relaxation. Here we became much calmer and collected.

This chapter of little stories, pictures, impressions, critical arguments, discovery of a love, serious things and amusing things from the 1980s unfortunately ends with a sad story.

On October 25, 2006, while I was still writing this chapter, I read in a Frankfurt newspaper: *Downtown. At the Taunusanlage commuter train station on Tuesday afternoon at 12:15 a 73-year old Frankfurt resident threw himself in front of a train on the S5 line. The man was run over by the approaching train moving in the direction of Bad Homburg.*

I had no idea that it was Jaime — Jaime, who had put a gruesome end to his muddled life (he had recently been convinced of the futility of it all).

Jaime Pacheco in the 1980s and 1990s had been our official photographer at the Fair and had been a friend of mine. Jaime came from Argentina, with his home territory being the small Andes city of Salta in the province of Jujuy.

It was there that my later wife Dora met him, the owner of a small photo shop in the town, when she asked him to photograph her. The woman was not yet a mature woman, but a young girl. Jaime ran about in his studio excitedly trying to find the right setting for his camera. He didn't find it, and after he had been adjusting his camera for an hour on the young woman, he gave up: "Go out for a while and live! And then come back—I can't find your true face!"

That was Jaime Pacheco, an inventive photographer who fought for every picture.

At the beginning of the 1960s a German film crew came to Salta, intending to make a light entertainment flick with the then well-known German actress Christine Kaufmann, set in a dramatic Andes landscape. It was obvious that Jaime, the only inhabitant of the town who knew how to use a camera, would have a job only during filming. On the days when they were not filming, Jaime with his motorbike chauffeured the German film star around the foothills of the Andes. They became friendly, and the actress tried to convince him to come to Munich, where with his talent he would soon be able to make his own films.

Jaime followed this seductive invitation. He closed down his little store in Salta and soon stood in the presence of the "great actress" in Munich. She didn't even remember her little adventure with the "Andes Indian." There he stood in the big city, with only a few dollars in his pocket, and didn't know where to go. With a small job as a waiter, he tried to support himself, and began studies at the Munich College of Film. Somehow this didn't work. The "scatterbrain" Jaime—as people tended to call him—had wonderful ideas for films, but he told them to anybody and everybody, who then stole some of his greatest ideas and made the films themselves.

The little man from the Andes was lonely and was looking for a woman. In the end he married a thin, tall blonde woman and was soon the father of two beautiful little twin girls. He gradually stopped dreaming about his goal of making films, and with a friend he opened an Argentine restaurant that offered exquisite steaks. I too ate there in the short period of the existence of the restaurant. Naturally it was in vain, since Jaime had typical South American generosity, especially when it came to his friends. The meals were formidable, but he didn't know how to calculate the costs very well. Bankruptcy was foreordained.

At midnight on a summer day at the end of the 1970s, the doorbell of our apartment on Emil-Claar Street in Frankfurt rang gently. Jaime was standing in front of the door. "Please, can I stay the night with you? I have left my family."

We were glad to take him by the hand and lead him into our apartment. He remained there till we moved to a house in the north end two and a half years later. Then he took over our apartment.

Jaime was truly a "scatterbrain," and had trouble being accepted by most Germans. What does it mean to be a "scatterbrain"? Was this a weakness in his character, a moral deficiency, as if elicited by some criminal energy? Absolutely not! When people said that Jaime was a "scatterbrain," this did not mean anything other than he was full of unresolved contradictions, and that he didn't quite fit into our well-ordered world. People did not forgive him for this. Jaime could not be categorized. If someone had just formed an image of him, he would destroy it in the next moment.

I got him a job at Southwest Radio, a not very well-paid job as a supervisor for sound with one of the filming teams at the station. He kept having disagreements with the other employees, who did not want to accept or to accomodate this "Third World scatterbrain." When a piece of equipment stopped functioning, the photography team stood around discussing what was to be done.

Pacheco came up and asked what was wrong.

"The part doesn't work."

"What's the problem? Just go to the storeroom and get another one," he advised.

"We can't do that, it's not completely broken. You don't understand!"

Pacheco took the piece in his hands, spun it around several times in front of his wide-open eyes, looked at it up and down, and then in front of his shocked colleagues he raised his arm high and threw it onto the tile floor, where it was smashed to pieces.

"Now it's completely finished. You can get a new one," he said.

It was clear that Jaime would not last long at the radio

station. Since I always needed quick snapshots of the events at every Fair for the press, we then set up at every Frankfurt Book Fair a small darkroom with its own staff. Shortly after the exposition had begun, we could give photos to interested representatives of the press. In addition, among the visitors to the Fair director there were always many foreign publishers, politicians and book people for whom it was important to have a memento or evidence of their visit.

Jaime Pacheco, along with the contact person appointed by the Police Commissioner Seibold and me, for a dozen years were an inseparable Big Three as we patrolled the Book Fair. Everywhere we went in three, and Jaime always attracted attention to himself very quickly as he climbed on chairs and tables, and often onto the curtains on the windowsill. Sometimes he would fall from some unstable support with a loud crash. This happened on an official visit of the Lord High Mayor Wallmann to the Fair Management and the Publishers Association. For anyone who had anything to do with Jaime, he was the "scatterbrain."

In my time in Frankfurt, and especially at the beginning, I was always surrounded by such "scatterbrains." I liked that. Federico Schopf was one such, as was the "really persistent" visitor, the Chilean photographer Theodoro el Saca, who lived for three months after the Fair in the waiting room of our office. My best press chief Helmut von der Lahr also had such chaotic tendencies.

When Jaime parked himself in our house, he was not a burden, as one might assume. He immediately made himself at home in our kitchen and with dance-like movements he would prepare the mid-day meal for the entire family.

Jaime was really quite lonesome. He sought out people who would accept him the way he was, particularly women. But here, in the strangeness of Germany, that was a difficult undertaking. As time went on, Jaime became ever stranger, and often very aggressive. His depression brought forth a negative image of life. He always called the Germans "Fascists," so that even well-intentioned and tolerant people finally abandoned him. In the middle of the 1990s he moved away from me and the Book Fair as well. I tried to get out of him what had happened. That he couldn't drag the heavy camera bags around the fairgrounds any longer was the short answer.

Since we had the need, I hired Ulrike Deuscher as a young photographer. Jaime no longer showed up since I now "had replaced him with someone else." That's what he said to me when we once met briefly.

At the end of the 1990s, I was just about to enter the book fair in Buenos Aires when someone from behind me called, "Peter!" I was really quite pleased to see him again. We went to eat and chatted about the good old times. I gave him my book that in the meantime had appeared in Spanish and wrote a dedication for him: "To my rediscovered friend Jaime Pacheco." Nonetheless, that too did not bring any revival of our friendship.

Shortly before his gruesome death, now in the spring of 2006, he called me up on the telephone, crying, "Peter," he said sobbing, "I just saw the dedication in your book again. What an ass I was!" I made an appointment to meet him at the Fair. We sat down at a little corner restaurant in Hall 6 where we had once thrown down a quick steak and a beer during the active periods at noontime. We talked for an hour. Jaime seemed very quiet. He said that he had not been able to sleep at night for years, and he wanted to put an end to it all.

"But Jaime," I said, " That's no solution." That's what people say in such a situation.

"Yeah, yeah," he answered quietly. "You can't understand, you look back on a successful life, you don't have anything to reproach yourself with. I look back on a life of negativity. I always said no!"

After that we said goodbye. I stood still for a while and watched as he went away, no longer with those dancing, bouncing steps—as I suddenly realized—that I had always loved in him. Without looking back even once, he disappeared into the crowd of Fair visitors.

The Collapse of Real-Existing Socialism

Eugen E., who in 1989 was in charge of our exhibition work, gathered us all together in the very modest rooms of the small hostel of the Catholic Academy in Hamburg. The location offered a sort of workers welfare atmosphere. The weather was dark, foggy, and bitter cold. Everything seemed unfriendly. Our counterparts from the German Democratic Republic (GDR— East Germany) had difficulty concealing their displeasure at the accommodations. For them, the traveling cadre of the disintegrating GDR, this day in Hamburg shortly before the collapse of their own real-life Socialist world was to have been for them a last escape from their bleak existence; it was to be a moment of blotting out reality, of being submerged in the glitter of Western Capitalism. Everyone had the feeling that this collapse was coming soon, and yet here we were offering them the atmosphere of an East German Communist Party boarding school. Trained to regard everything as political, naturally they saw partisan intent lurking behind this treatment. Actually, however, it was nothing more than Eugen's thoughtlessness.

Jürgen Gruner, my old friend, the ambitious director of the Volk & Welt Publishing House in East Berlin, the Chairman of the (East German) Leipzig Publishers Association, suddenly seemed old and unable to concentrate. Despite his phenomenal ability at languages, which I had always admired, in this New Age he was was starting to lose his grip on things. In the period of repression and lies in the GDR, his language facility had given him room to maneuver within the system without placing him in grave danger. In his many public speeches, he always circled around unanswered questions, which he quite naïvely posed but never answered.

Now his language fell apart. I had always admired his curiosity, but now he was merely puzzled as to how he had managed things earlier. Unfortunately, he had lost his knack for asking questions. Like the entire system, Gruner and his Latin were at an end. He was no longer able to jump onto the New Age Express Train. Though often quite skeptical, he had believed strongly in the Communist Party system—or rather the merits of Socialism. That was his identity, and now this identity was disintegrating.

On the day that the Berlin Wall fell, Gruner suddenly realized that his Volk & Welt Publishing House and the Wall depended on one another. After all, this was a publishing house that was essentially only a licensee, with hardly any original book rights to speak of. I met him for the first time in India in 1972, and ever since he was busy inviting the world into the closed system of the German Democratic Republic. Now the GDR was itself open to the world. On November 9 and 10, 1989, the East Berliners, their eyes popping out of their heads, streamed into the other section of the city, where they were jubilantly received by the West Berliners.

The last decade of the 20th century essentially transformed the world and the foundations of our lives, even if we in the West did not notice this at first. Communism, the so-called Second World, collapsed in on itself, though in a surprisingly quiet manner, given the enormous power and amount of weaponry that had been piled up. We in the West, who took part in this historical revolution only as observers, could only be astounded as we watched. In the previous decades we had expended a great deal of energy in trying to get around or to pierce what appeared to be impenetrable state borders, or at least impassable for active business and daily life. Now the borders suddenly disappeared without our having done anything.

Reunification caught us unprepared. We regarded the pre-1989 bombastic comments of some politicians about "our brothers and sisters over there" and about our common fatherland as empty phrases of people living in the past, who themselves did not believe what they were saying. The overwhelming majority had come to terms with the *status quo* of two divided German states, a situation that was a consequence of the lost war. Everyone who had anything to do with the East, whether in politics, science or culture, had invested their strength and fantasy in making this situation more bearable. "Peaceful Coexistence" and "Change through Getting to Know One Another" were the watchwords of the day!

No one could or would imagine the powerful changes that now occurred. There were those who later claimed they had always stood for this goal of reunification; they demonized the deluded visionaries of the Left who had tried to improve the exchange of information and people across the rigid boundaries. Those who claimed that they had always stood for reunification were nothing more than hypocrites and opportunists.

The borders all at once stood wide open, and the people in the erstwhile "People's Republics," staggering and numbed by the sudden changes, began to look around at their newfound freedom. They didn't have a lot of time because then the dam broke. In the West the kettle of capitalism—as it existed in the Western industrial states—was already at the boiling point. High productivity and unbelievable mobility of labor and capital, which were demanded by the imperative of productivity, stood ready to pour into these "new markets." Before them lay a virginal land of investment, no longer protected by any wall.

Over here a market wrung dry down to the smallest niche; over there, lots of shortages, low productivity and lack of mobility. It was like a mighty natural cataclysm. The "emancipated" capital took the form of an avalanche of greedy and rather unscrupulous profiteers and carpetbaggers coming into an empty, unoccupied space. At that point the people in the "liberated" countries of Central and Eastern Europe had no chance of articulating their long suppressed needs. They did not even quite understand what was happening to them as they were assailed. In no time at all the omnipresent market spelled out everything they should ever desire.

The products available were not necessarily the most valuable ones, but were rather items with misleading packaging and containing sub-standard goods, which in the nature of the capitalist market allowed high profits to be earned. After all, the successful art of the market economy does not create value; it merely opens a space (the market) into which products can be dumped and profit extracted.

Opportunities for free development on the market—that is, "needs"—abounded in the "freed" countries of Central and Eastern Europe, but unfortunately the means to respond to those needs were lacking. A so-called market economy had to be erected quickly in order to put those means into the hands of people. That meant creating purchasing power that could now submissively serve the new ruler, which was the market. As a result, armies of business consultants, preachers of the new way, gladly marched to the East to drum the "free market economy" into even the most alert of those who had just awoken. They set up seminars, workshops and educational units to proselytize and publicize the new religion. The new believers now unhesitatingly prayed to the new Trinity, "Marketing," "Productivity" and "Joint Venture," hoping to latch onto their divine power. It is probably superfluous to point out that these caravans of market messiahs included many adventurers and people who had failed in the West, all hoping to make a fast mark or a quick buck.

Dams were breached in the West as well. All precious talk about the benefits of our "socially-oriented market economy" just fell away. So long as our system felt challenged by the competing Socialist ideologies, so long as we scrambled to head off revolutions lest they be exploited by the "others" (the Communists), then by contrast the capitalist system seemed almost humane. The achievements of our post-war society–the social safety net, secure wages, higher purchasing power, shorter work hours, health insurance—were all presented as coherent evidence of the superiority of our "socially-minded" market economy. But now the game was up.

We in the West had not caught on to the fact that whatever was happening "over there" had real consequences. I was the same. We had grown up in the Western system, and had celebrated our modest revolts and small victories. In the end we were rather satisfied with our small and open Bonn Republic of West Germany. Of course there were places to cavil about, but only once, in the 1970s during the "German Autumn," did it come to an existential crisis. Now our anti-authoritarian streak of 1968 was long gone. We had gotten too used to prosperity, open borders, free media and worldly success. We just assumed that everyone "over there" was *used* to the fact that they could not afford "quite so much."

On balance, we allowed ourselves some grumbling dissatisfaction that perhaps our situation in life was not completely justified. This may have come from the unmistakable feeling that we did not completely deserve this magnificent way of life, and that as punishment it might be turned upside down by a war or something even worse.

We at the AUM (the Exposition and Fair Company) reacted with what lay close at hand—help for the new publishers in Eastern Europe in the way of advice and workshops of the sort we had extended to Africa, Asia and Latin America since 1980.

At the Frankfurt Book Fair we had carried on significant trade with the Socialist state book dealers. Overnight they had been deprived of their owner, the Socialist state power, and they visibly crumbled in the next few years. In Frankfurt we lost business associates and customers. Some publishers from Western countries began to grumble that Frankfurt was no longer worthwhile. These state book dealers of the Socialist East had actually held a significant percentage of the sales at the Book Fair, to the tune of some $30 million per fair.

I had to do something. So in 1990 I made a trip to the neighboring countries that were the most important for us: Poland, Czechoslovakia, Hungary—and East Berlin, as well. I visited some of the budding young publishing houses, which previously had carried on their work semi-officially or even underground, quite successfully so in Poland. People knew how new books are made, how they are created, but everywhere there was no understanding of how books are sold.

So in the end we too enlisted in the army of business advisers marching eastward, and in practically every capital of the old Socialist East and of the states of the new Russian Federation we put on workshops for marketing and management in the publishing industry. In 1992 we compiled these experiences together in a book under the title *Making Books in the Future—Marketing and Management in the Publishing Industry.* This book was put together by people who had gathered publishing and communication experience in the seminars over the years—our seminar team of the time, Holger Behm, Hermann Schulz, Jochen Wörner, with the help of Gabriele Hardt. Organizational leadership was provided by our long-time employees in the exposition area, Iris Klose and Bärbel Becker.

This book, translated into Russian, Polish and Hungarian, became the basic textbook for our workshops, attended by 25 or so publishers each year for three to four days in centrally located seminar venues in each country. We began the workshop series in East Berlin in 1990. Warsaw followed in 1991; Rīga, Moscow, Alma Ata and Budapest in 1992; then in 1993 and 1994, besides Rīga, Warsaw and Moscow there were Radziejowice (Poland), Kiev, Minsk, Sofia, Kishinev (Moldova) and Tashkent. And so it went.

I was convinced that these activities, which we invested great effort in, fit in with the hopes of the participants. Even today it happens that if I am on a trip to these countries, I am invited by past participants in these workshops to visit their impressive publishing concerns, where with great pride they show me what they have built up.

There was an important side effect of these presentations in Eastern Europe for our Book Fair, that is, making the acquaintance of the young, forceful publishing personalities, brought back home by Iris Klose and Bärbel Becker. We invited the best and most active of these to the next Frankfurt Book Fair at our expense. It didn't take long until some American publishers offered to reimburse us so that we would "lend" them some of these invited young publishers and book dealers from the East. The idea was for them to get to know the American book trade while they were at the Frankfurt Book Fair. After returning home, these up-and-coming publishers soon spread the welcome notion in their countries that "You can only call yourself a publisher if you have been to Frankfurt!" Within a few years, the level of participation of Eastern European publishers had reached the point that it had been at before the fall of the Wall, and eventually surpassed it.

In the 1980s I had set up very good, perhaps even friendly relationships within the organization for the foreign book trade in the Soviet Union, Mezhkniga, and within the general management of the Moscow Book Fair and the Goskomizdat, as the Ministry of Books and Publishing in Moscow was called. Twice a year I regularly traveled to Moscow. The point was to conclude a "stupid little game" that the authorities in Moscow played with us each time we attended the Moscow Book Fair. Time and again they tore down our official stall sign with the name of our country *"Bundesrepublik Deutschland"* (German Federal Republic), written in Russian as well. They just could not accept what *they* read as a sovereign claim over all of Germany. An alternate construction in the genitive case was supposed to be the remedy—*"die Bundesrepublik Deutschlands"* (The Federal Republic *of* Germany).

Clearly I was not going to be able to rectify this through friendly dialogue. I also wanted to understand what and who lay behind this nonsense so that I might be able to have some effect here. From our side, the Foreign Office was no longer prepared to accept this provocation, and had threatened to withdraw any support for our exposition work. I went to Moscow several times, where my visit always played out with the same ritual. The jovial and mischievous Igor Kasanski, director of the Moscow Fair, greeted me in a friendly manner at the general offices. His sympathetic German expert Tanya Simon served as translator, as she had done for years. After fruitless days of negotiations, she always invited me to the Bolshoi Theatre, where we saw the ballet *Giselle* at least three times. Kasanki's assistant Sasha Brik, with whom I had traveled to Kiev to prepare a German book exhibit and who always made somewhat ironic comments ("Everything here follows the road to Socialism!"), would be sent down to get some gifts for me, preferably vodka.

The next day we always had a meeting with the heads of the Soviet book industry, Ministers Boris Stukalin, Irakles Chikrishvili and Vassily Slashenenko, at the Goskomizdat. Usually fighting off fatigue, I had to put up with an unending torrent of figures about the unstoppable progress of the Socialist book industry. Then I would give similarly impressive results for the German publishing and book trade industry and of the Frankfurt Book Fair. We always had mineral water, sticky yellow lemonade and a large package of sweets. In the evening I was invited to a big meal at the Prague restaurant on the Arbat or in the writers' club, where we ate and boozed it up gaily. The barrel-chested Vassily Sitnikov was always there; I had even been invited to his house once (something rarely done in Communist times). Sitnikov himself spoke an excellent German and entertained the group with great jokes, some of them being really very political. After the fall of the Wall I read in *Der Spiegel* that Major Sitnikov was the director of the KGB department for disinformation. Even today I'm proud that they felt that I was important enough to require such high level political handling. In the end I found myself quite secure among these important associates of our Fair.

On the basis of this feeling of security, at the following Moscow book fairs I simply changed the sign on our stall, and had the following written in German: "An exhibition of 220 publishing houses of the German Federal Republic." On grammatical grounds the Russians went ahead and wrote "Federal Republic of Germany" in their own language. And lo and behold, everything was fine. A very annoying spat between our two countries had been resolved.

In 1990 these good contacts were ended for the time being. Besides that, the well-known publishing and book-dealing companies either had vanished or had new owners. We had to start from scratch, since our American friends were now complaining that with the absence of customers from the East, the Frankfurt Book Fair was no longer attractive for them. They were considering a gradual withdrawal from Frankfurt. That is the way it was formulated, naturally once again by Alberto Vitale of Random House.

Once again I traipsed back to Moscow to try to figure out what was happening. There I was helped very much by the director of the local Goethe Institute, Kathinka Dittrich, whom I had previously heard lots of good things about. I got along very well with her and her earthy Dutch husband Koos van Weringh, Professor of Criminology in the Netherlands. Kathinka had a number of Russian friends and advisers, whom she introduced me to right away. These included Boris Chlebnikov, translator from the German and staff member of the magazine *Foreign Literature;* Yuri Maisuradze, whom I knew from his earlier activity as department director in the Ministry for Publishing and Book Trade; and Vitaly Babenko, an employee of the Text Publishing House in Moscow (which had succeeded as a private enterprise) who also served as a moderator of a literature program on Russian television.

The Russian book publishing industry, which had been more strongly tied than other economic branches to party and state institutions, in the period of the early reforms showed itself to be remarkably adaptable to the conditions of the free market economy. All publishing houses, regardless of the form of ownership, were economically independent. Censorship was abolished, and ideological pressure disappeared. Even though up to the end of 1992 the state had frozen prices for books, paper and printing services, a number of private companies had found their niche with so-called "hot goods"—detective stories; adventure literature; Utopian, historical, or erotic novels. This sector showed up to 100% profit, but by the end of 1992 the market for this type of literature was saturated. In 1992 the proportion of *belles-lettres* sales stood at 56%. Naturally this occurred at a cost to other areas, whose production was more complicated and less profitable—scientific books, textbooks and reference works. The declining supply of "socially relevant" literature, on which the Soviet Union had always placed great importance for political reasons, was perceived as a national calamity.

The output of this belletristic literature reached its zenith in 1991 with 538 million copies; thereafter production steadily sank, even for children's books. On the other hand the number of translated titles had tripled since 1988. In 1993 some 4,872 translated books appeared, with a total edition of 540 million copies, including 2,286 titles from English with 253 million copies, 978 titles from French with 142 million copies, and 303 titles from the German, with 36.7 million copies.

Vitaly Babenko, in answer to my intensive questioning regarding this new situation for books and publishing in Russia, sent me a letter in English with the following, sharp-tongued ironic analysis:

You can hardly find any publishing programs still existing in Russia... since the situation on the book market changes almost every week.... At the same time a casual observer might think that the

Russian publishing industry is becoming more and more civilized "at least in the choice of good titles," or in any case more legally compliant (at least with the awakening of a consciousness of copyright). You might even say that the days of crazy and gloomy publishing are over.

There are still two book worlds in Russia, commercial and non-commercial books, but the distance between these two kingdoms is much greater than the distance between the empires of "trade" and "non-trade" books in the West.

What is a so-called "commercial" book in Russia? In the eyes of the customer, it is a sewn, solidly bound book with a bright glossy dust cover full of naked women or blood-smeared body parts or huge monsters or Van Damme/Schwarzenegger superheroes (actually the mélange of types is hard to distinguish, from thrillers to wartime fantasies). In the opinion of publishers, a "commercial" book is that book whose printing sells out within a month.

Approximately 90% of the books published in Russia are generally not produced for reading. They are made for profit, and the content of these books does not depend on the value of the published literature, but on an unspoken deal between the publisher as the lord and the wholesale dealer as his vassal. The reading public seems to take on the role here of the slave. It is no wonder that the book publishing industry and the book selling market in Russia is criminal to its very core. [...]

Thinking, standards, logic, thought processes — everything is different when we compare the publishing world in Russia with that of the West. I have to admit the idea of orienting the content to the needs of the reader is extraordinarily new.

A decisive difference exists between the concept of publishing in Russia and that of the West. Publishing in Russia is based on the principle of the book edition (if a book is brought out in a set number, then it is said to be published). If the total number of copies is sold out, either to a wholesaler, to a book dealer or to someone else, then the book is sold out and the publisher and the printer can forget about it forever. Usually there is no second, third, or other edition. A catalog of "books in print" does not exist in Russia. The concept of "books in print" is completely foreign to Russian publishers.

This or something like it was the information that we were receiving about the situation of the Russian book trade. We had to align our strategies and the content of the workshop that we were offering accordingly. The questions of advertising and marketing were of great interest to the publishers, since in the long period of the economy of scarcity the sale of books was administered strictly by the state.

I took one step further by opening our first permanent office in Moscow. Actually, it was a permanent German book exhibit that I set up, something that the Soviet book authorities had always urged me to do. I had refused to do so because I could not control what would happen with the mainly scientific books that would be on display. I feared that these so-called exhibits, to which hardly anyone came, were to serve the Soviet authorities as a way to get our books for free.

Now the situation was quite different. The Goethe Institute in Moscow placed at our disposal some very nice rooms, since the Institute had moved into the former East German Embassy. In the spring and in the autumn we sent collections of books there. The local groups in Moscow—I made Tanya Simon the director of the first Book Information Center (BIC)—were to display the German books at special exhibits or at regional fairs. Soon the BIC became a contact office for both book industries and an information office for the Frankfurt Book Fair as well.

The Foreign Office had previously denied any institutional support for anything other than a German book exhibit, but designating the BIC as a permanent book exhibit gave me the chance to request that they fund the Moscow BIC. Other Centers followed in Warsaw, Bucharest and Beijing. Later we saw a German Book Office (GBO) open in New York.

A few years later we used our experiences gained in the workshops to set up fellowship programs. To be sure, we drew on what others had done, and we copied the program that had been running successfully for several years at the Jerusalem book fair. This happened though with the express permission of my Jerusalem friend Zev Birger, the longtime director of that book fair. What turned out to be so successful for our programs in the East was the creation of emotional ties between workshop participants and our Book Fair over many years. The Fellowship Program followed the same principle.

I realized that successful work for the Fair did not mean

just sales and professional presentations at our book stalls. All kinds of services were requested so that Frankfurt would be indispensable for the publishing authorities of all countries and languages. In 1987 we began a series of presentations for the publishing rights directors of publishing houses. The invitees to the Rights Directors Meetings, held on the opening day of the Fair—that is, one day before the actual beginning of business—included everyone involved in the business of literary rights—literary agents, talent scouts, employees of licensing and rights divisions of the publishers, and journalists as well. The problems and difficulties of the rights business, but also the openings and the opportunities, were highlighted by people familiar with the various rights markets, such as the Spanish language market, the children and youth book market, the art book market and the Chinese, Arabic and Eastern European book markets. Even today, despite the relatively high cost of participation, these presentations arouse great interest in some 180 to 280 attendees.

Other seminars were well-received, such as those for the young foreign book dealers whom we invited. An example of the introductory workshop was "How Do I Best Use the Book Fair?" for first-time attendees from the so-called Third World countries. These workshops created emotional ties to our employees, to the organizers and to the Book Fair itself.

Such emotional factors became increasingly important for our Fair work. Once I gave a dinner for important British publishers in the London Durrants. After I had greeted the guests and we went to the table, my neighbor alongside me—I think it was the director of the mighty Octopus Publishing House—said as I sat down, "I really only came to ask you a question. If you can give me a satisfactory answer, I will pay you 10,000 pounds on the spot."

"So what's the question?" I responded, full of interest.

My neighbor sighed deeply and said, "Can you tell me how I can prevent all my leading employees from being convinced every year that they absolutely have to go to the next Frankfurt Book Fair?"

I knew then that our offers to the international book trade were exactly right.

In the year after the fall of the Wall, together with the German Publishers Association we organized a sponsorship program for some 300 East German book dealers. The West German publishers agreed to assume housing and *per diem* costs for the people who came. Everyone would come to a party at the Fair to celebrate being together.

In the very first year we sponsored a workshop in East Berlin for the first newly founded publishing houses in the former East Germany, including the LinksDruck publishing house. Christoph Links, until then an assistant manager of the Aufbau Publishing House, had even during the times of the German Democratic Republic attempted to get a license for his own publishing house. In the new age this went very quickly. The Ch. Links Verlag is a stable, medium-sized publisher, still standing on its own legs after 17 years; it publishes nonfiction books on politics and contemporary history, biographies, research on the society of the German Democratic Republic, and literary criticism (and the German edition of this book!)

Out of all the other small publishing houses that I visited in East Berlin shortly after German unification, all of which celebrated with surprising euphoria the "paradise" for publishers under capitalistic freedom and care-free society, the only one that I am aware of that remains is that of Dr. Matthias Oehme. To be sure, under the new conditions he was not able to stabilize the UVA Verlag, founded in 1990 for high-quality modern literature. He had a good nose for publishing, and he took over the Eulenspiegelverlag and the publishing house Das Neue Berlin when they went bankrupt. The programs of these two publishing houses were oriented principally to the public in the old East Germany. Oehme: *The books that my predecessors in these companies made were original and beautiful, but they had made the great mistake of thinking that they were for the market in the West. However, they appeared in a publishing house of the East, and had just about no sales.* After seven months, the radically changed program, which was oriented to the East, reached its sales targets.

I value very much the literary work of the East German publisher Jürgen Gruner in his Volk & Welt Verlag, which lost over 90% of its employees. The chief editor Dietrich Simon, a feisty sort, sought to save the publishing house once again. Some 50% of the titles came from Eastern Europe, of which Russian literature made up the largest part. Simon: *Whoever was reading the Russians at that time was not surprised about perestroika and glasnost, since with the Russians you had to read a lot less between the lines than you did with our authors. However, what was in demand in the 1980s for its insights* [into Russia], *after the opening of the Wall was hardly of any interest for any East German.* Simon started out by trying it out with a British author. Lionel Davidson's *Kolmysky Heights* gained attention by selling 6,000 copies in the West. In the East, Rolf Hochhuth's *West Germans in Weimar,* in which the author took a stand for the East Germans and thus showed a sensitivity for the feelings of the new German states, still found 1,400 buyers. But in the end, the editions in small numbers that had been the custom of the largest publishing house in East Germany could not survive. The publishing house closed down, and Simon went back to a management post of the S. Fischer Verlag Foundation.

The only success story of the old East German publishing houses was written by the old flagship enterprise for East German literature, the Aufbau Verlag in Berlin. Actually, in a double sense. The last manager of the Aufbau Verlag in East German times, Elmar Faber, left the publishing house and with his son founded the successful Faber & Faber Verlag, specializing in well-done coffee table books, contemporary literature and art books.

The Aufbau Verlag itself was purchased by the Frankfurt real estate mogul Bernd F. Lunkewitz, who in his youth in 1968 had been a Maoist but had later come into money. This witty and awkward new publisher threw himself into publishing and tried to have the Aufbau Verlag compete with the big boys of West German publishing, like Rowohlt, Fischer, Heyne, and Droemer Knaur. He did this by hiring experienced marketing and publishing people, like Norbert Schaepe as head of marketing and later René Strien as director of the firm.

Guests of Honor

The public reception of our India theme had frustrated me to no end. After this debacle in 1986, it was clear that we could not go on like this. Either I must bring an end to what was really a fine program, or I would have to promote it in a way that would not be so burdensome to those of us in Frankfurt. At the same time, we had to maintain fidelity to the special character of the foreign cultures and literatures that we wanted to feature.

ITALY (1988)

It was the Italians who spurred me to develop the new concept of national focal themes, in particular the author Umberto Eco and the Italian Ambassador to Germany, Luigi Vittorio Ferraris. At the opening of the Book Fair in 1987 Eco gave a very significant address, though since it was given in Italian, hardly anyone understood what he was talking about. Still, everyone was quite convinced that it had been an outstanding speech. This gave me an inkling of what was to be expected from Italy. Ambassador Ferraris spoke an excellent German, and often published perceptive articles in *Die Zeit*. He called me up shortly after the 1986 Book Fair devoted to India, and suggested to me that we move forward in the alphabet after India and make Italy the focal theme for 1988.

I was quite pleased to take up this suggestion, even though a number of alterations had to be made to the running of the focal theme presentations. Italy would have to bear the costs and the responsibility for organizing the cultural and literary program. Frankfurt would take care of the PR, the advertising and the space for activities at the Book Fair. Later on, as a token of appreciation, we would hold a book exhibit for each guest country titled "Books about..." the country, thus in this case *Books about Italy*. The exposition was put together in our office. We ordered about 2,000 to 3,000 books about Italy and translations of Italian authors from all the international publishing houses that participated at the Book Fair. The exhibit would be shown in Frankfurt as part of the year of activities celebrating that particular country, and afterwards the books would be sent as gifts to the institutions of the guest country for their own use.

Italy agreed, and a new presentation series at the Book Fair was born, one that was successful from the very beginning. France, Japan and Spain almost immediately registered their interest for future years. For 1992 I was already negotiating with the Soviet Union. We could thus cheerfully switch from a two-year cycle to an annual thematic presentation. We were relieved of the pressure of success hinging on our strength alone. The particular guest country would now be responsible for success or failure, and usually this meant the government, though sometimes it meant the publishers' organizations.

This new arrangement led at times to sharp public debates in the guest countries, often to parliamentary debates, and always to heated battles in the public media. We in Frankfurt stood on the outside. At first, there naturally was the question for the guest countries of doling out hard cash to finance the programs. Italy put together 29 million Marks from various state and private sources. What then followed each time was a controversy about the state of the country's own contemporary literature and culture. Once the majority had found consensus, then authors and other arbiters of culture went into battle over who was to present the cultural image of the country.

I remember in Italy being invited to a dinner to dicuss financing. It was held in a vaulted cellar restaurant in Rome. All of the attendees, some 40 of the most influential personalities in Italian society, sat around a large rectangular table and talked, at first politely and good-naturedly, as suited Italian hospitality. But then, in the interim with the inevitable pasta course, voices grew louder and more heated. An excited duel of words developed between a state secretary from the Foreign Ministry on our side of the table and the president of Italian television RAI just opposite. Since this was in Italian, I couldn't follow the arguments exactly, but the verbal swordplay became ever more brazen. From what I could piece together, it was a matter of 1 billion lira that Italian radio wanted to add to its foreign budget for Frankfurt, but this was money that RAI had already been allocated by the same government for foreign enterprise.

The tension grew. I was tickled by such typical Italian ambiance. Then the debate became even more theatrical. Suddenly the state secretary jumped up, pushed his chair aside, and ran around the corner of the table with his napkin in his hand! A few noodles were still dangling from the corner of his mouth. Ambassador Ferraris, who was sitting next to me and thought that I was alarmed, laid his hand on my arm and whispered, "If they actually touch each other now, we have won!"

And in fact, it looked like the debaters would come to blows, but they fell into each other's arms. The problem was solved; each of them now returned to the exquisite main course which had been served; relieved, they offered each other a toast.

The month-long run-up to the appearance at Frankfurt, naturally accompanied by loud chatter from the guest of honor's national media, was a unique marketing campaign for the Frankfurt Book Fair. We had never done better in reaching the publishers, book dealers and other friends of the book in these countries. Each guest country year saw an increase in participation A large number of the new exhibitors later remained faithful to the Frankfurt Book Fair. For the Fair itself this new portion of the program meant a continuation of the focal themes, where we presented the content of the books on display, something that was later called "event culture."

The following summary was issued at the end of the Italian business year in the official and somewhat awkward prose of the Information and Publishing Office of the Prime Minister of the Republic of Italy: *The three goals set by Italy for itself have been achieved. These were the promotion of Italian publishing, a 'leap forward' of the Italian 'cultural product' on the European market, and cooperation among institutions, businesses, intellectual and professional societies.*

The organizational result was apparent in the over 200 presentations of the Qualified Initiative Program, before and after the Fair both on the fairgrounds and in the city of Frankfurt a well as in five other cities. It also could be seen in the building of the sensational Italian cultural pavilion at the fairgrounds, designed by the film designer Mario Garibuglia from Cinecittà, the film center in Rome.

With cardboard and imagination spread out over 35,000 square feet, Garibuglia used the old meeting hall on the fairgrounds left over from the 1950s to make a playful presentation of Italy's cultural self-image. The center was dominated by a forum, a meeting place with the 71 Italian authors and translators who had come to Frankfurt to meet with publishers, representatives of the press and Fair visitors. This was the first time that such a thing had been done at the Fair, and later the concept of a forum became a requirement for many book fairs throughout the world. Around the arena stood four towers and two doorways outfitted with exhibitions, all in the style of classical Italian architecture. There were also special exhibits in historically appointed rooms, places for meetings and rest periods, and stands to distribute brochures that had been printed especially for this occasion. On the upper gallery of the hall, you entered the "Mirror Café," a reconstruction of the most famous literary café in Italy, where naturally they served espresso, *gelato* and other Italian specialties. In addition to the exhibits, there were set props from the film *The Name of the Rose*, which included a full-scale reproduction of a Benedictine monastery library.

One fascinating event was the exhibition of "Alma Mater librorum" on the history of the book, prepared by the oldest European university, Bologna, on the occasion of the 900th anniversary of its founding. Other exciting presentations included a gala in Frankfurt's Old Opera House and the presentation of the latest Fellini film by Federico Fellini himself and his wife, the film star Giulietta Masina.

Italy as the land of the book created a recipe for how to exhibit at the Fair. The countries that followed had to take notice of their predecessor. As early as the opening press conference, I couldn't resist expressing myself with a certain effusiveness:

During the year in which we were preparing this Italian presentation in cooperation with our Italian colleagues, with government offices, and with organizations, diplomats and individuals, I was taught a lesson on how one should develop foreign cultural policy. This creativity, this energy, this dizzying activity, this courage to decide and to be responsible, but also this love of controversy in the planning and setting up of the Frankfurt program helped me, as an astonished Teuton, to move forward in my dreams, in the dreams of a fair as a giant festival of life, where we may all meet joyously, dispute with each other in a peaceable manner, listen to one another, and astonish one another.

FRANCE (1989)

The focal theme of France came along as a reciprocal double event. At our exhibit at the Paris Salon du Livre from May 18 to May 25, 1989, titled *L'Allemagne par ses livres* (Germany by Its Books), we tried to put on a book and literature festival similar to the one that the French promised for Frankfurt in October (October 11–16, 1989).

The decisive political initiative for this year of France originated at the "Frankfurt summit talks" in 1986. François Mitterand, President of France, and Helmut Kohl, the German Chancellor, agreed to have an exposition of the German–French book week during the 9th Parisian Salon du Livre in the anniversary year of the French Revolution. Thanks to this high-level connection, the cultural section of the Foreign Office gave us the means necessary to put on an ambitious presentation of books and literary people.

This German–French book week in Paris was integrated into the Parisian Salon du Livre. As expressed in the invitation by the President of the French Publishers Association, Alain Gründ, "This cultural event had enormous attractions;" the book week served "to deepen German–French literary exchanges."

In the end the result was exactly the opposite. For us, the Paris exhibition was a continuation of our series of presentations that we had begun successfully in the German Book Fair in 1983 in New York, and then continued in 1985 in Madrid with the *Semana de Libro Aleman*.

Unfortunately, there were differences of opinion between the French publishers and their association. Publisher President Gründ was pushing for rigorous internationalization of his fair, and had moved the Salon du Livre, which until then had been mainly a Francophone affair, from the classic glass domed building of the Grand Palais to the more modest fairgrounds at the Porte de Versailles. The French publishers built their stalls there, but then they boycotted their own exposition when all the decision-makers remained at their own publishing offices in the center of Paris.

"Literature is like politics and prospecting for gold. You have to go through a huge pile of worthless rubble before you get to the precious metal," said Foreign Minister Hans-Dietrich Genscher at the opening. Some of our publishers looked up their French colleagues in their offices in Paris, but the others limited themselves to smug comments in the German mass media and the professional press.

We ourselves concentrated on the many exhibitions, evening affairs, matinées, translator conversations and rounds of discussions, all of which we had scheduled together with the Goethe Institute. All of these were well-attended. We offered a very convincing representation of German cultural life by bringing some 30 authors, including the following: Günter Grass, Hans Magnus Enzensberger, Anna Langhoff, Herta Müller, Fritz J. Raddatz, Peter Härtling, Lothar Baier, Peter Stephan Jungk, Martin Lüdke, Marcel Reich-Ranicki, Golo Mann, Eva Demski, Gudrun Pausewang, Uwe Timm, from East Germany Helga Königsdorf, Christoph Hein and Stefan Heym, and Paul Nizon from Switzerland. Our press director Helmut von der Lahr was very much involved in contacting the press, and hardly any interregional French newspaper went without special sections on German literature and reflections and reports on the presentations in Paris. The most extensive and most thoughtful of these was a 30-page extra section titled *Pages d'Allemagne,* which was published jointly by *Le Monde* in Paris and *Die Zeit* from Hamburg.

There is no doubt that Parisian understanding of German literature was well-served by our efforts. That this general atmosphere could not be converted into hard cash was due to the circumstances I noted above. Our French colleagues recognized the problem and its source. As a kindly gesture of apology—though obviously no one called it that—the following year I was appointed "Officer of the Order of Arts and Letters" by

Minister of Culture Jack Lang, and received the appurtenant medallion.

As to Frankfurt, at first Mitterand "naturally" wanted to come, but then Chancellor Kohl had to make do with Culture Minister Lang because Mitterand was away on a state visit to Ecuador. Jean-Pierre Angremey, General Director in the French Foreign Ministry, opened the "French Autumn" at the 41st Frankfurt Book Fair. Given a budget of 10 million francs, France wanted to present herself as a literary and cultural center, and to create an intellectually ambitious atmosphere, to distinguish her contribution to the Book Fair from that of the Italians, who intentionally included advertising for tourism. French publishers, authors and exhibits used more than 20,000 square feet of exhibition space in their blue pavilion to show off installations on the history of the book in France, the Bibliothèque Nationale, the planned Bibliothèque de France, and the reading habits of the French public. The emphasis was to be on French literature as dealt with by young authors, who interested themselves in topics like "The Intellectuals and Europe," "Franco–German Misunderstandings," "The Man of the Future," and "The Rights of Men, The Rights of Women."

Some 78 presentations by the French guests took place, 26 at the fairgrounds and 52 in the city, including theatrical productions and an opera. Another 100 expositions were to follow in other German cities in connection with the Fair. Alain Lance, director of the Institut Français and himself a poet and translator, along with Michèle Bouchez, were the contact people for the organizers of the shows at the Book Fair.

French literature had always had it tough in post-war Germany, even more difficult than German authors in France. It was very prestigious for German publishers to publish French authors, but this desire abated when, with very few exceptions, these brought only losses to the publishers. It was characteristic that the work of Nobel Prize winner Claude Simon appeared from three publishing houses, but classics of the century, such as André Malraux and François Mauriac, were not successful. Julien Green, who had been written about by Walter Benjamin and Klaus Mann (*i.e.*, as early as the 1930s), found his readership in Germany only after a period of some 60 years.

Japan (1990)

The following theme year was dedicated to the Japanese. Yasuo Shimada-san from the Kodansha Publishing House had long been my close friend. I first met him at the bedside of the legendary publisher Shoichi Noma of Kodansha, the only really internationally active publishing house in Japan. The two of us traveled together through Africa in 1984 for the Noma Award.[1] Every time I came to Tokyo, Toshiyuki Hattori-san, the chief information office of Kondansha, had arranged a stimulating meal in a *geisha* house, where many times, to the great amusement of the Japanese hosts, I had to dress up as a Japanese *samurai*, and my companion, as a *geisha*. Every year Shimada-san and Hattori-san reserved at least a half an hour of my time at the Book Fair in order to question me about the state of the European book trade.

Kodansha took on the task and was able to convince the Japanese government to commit itself to a significant investment in Frankfurt. The organizers were able to spend around ¥2 billion, equivalent to DM 20 million at that time, to create a spectacle arranged meticulously down to the finest detail.

My colleagues and I, who were in charge of the preparations for the Japanese appearance from our side, did however have to sit through four- to five-hour meetings with the Japanese planners, who questioned us repeatedly and constantly on the same topics and events over and over again. Always with the same earnestness, we had to give information on the social impact of literature, on our advertising, on the size of the rooms, on the sources of light, on the amount of power available, *etc.*, even though we had already done that the previous time and the time before in as great detail as possible. We were beginning to doubt our ability to communicate, because after a few weeks another meeting was called and the same questions were posed. We were at our wits' end. This went on for a long time, until finally a few weeks before the Book Fair the Japanese associates brought the final plans, worked out to the last detail. At last our nightmare was at an end.

Hajime Hasegawa, the assistant director of the Japanese

---

1. The *Noma Award* is a yearly prize for outstanding new books by African writers published in Africa.

advertising agency Dentsu, who was responsible for the preparation of all the Japanese programs, explained to me the background of these enervating meetings. For the preparation of the Japanese focal theme there was an endless list of honorary members, special consultants, and consultants appointed by his Imperial Highness, Prince Takahito Mikasa, the patron of the committee for the "Year of Japan," to say nothing of the cabinet members and the presidents of cultural institutions, and of printing and publishing houses. In addition there was an organizational committee, which itself was subdivided into four subcommittees. Each decision was discussed in the group in order to motivate all of the members. Everyone was supposed to see what they did and to understand why. "Nobody was to be harmed." This iron law of delicacy, deriving from the Buddhist tradition, had to be observed.

The Japanese organizational structures, while immensely efficient back home, in their work with us clashed with a completely different work ethic, one fixated on quick decisions. And if that weren't enough, the four Japanese subcommittees also had to keep in contact with the 114 representatives of the 500 publishing houses who were represented by the Japan Book Publishers Association. There was no general agreement either among the 114 representatives or among the 500 others. By the time the Book Publishers Association could give its approval, the Fair deadline had gotten very close, a situation that made us quite nervous. Hasegawa had no choice other than to alter the imported structures on the spot, which meant circumventing the authority of the representatives. But with his staff of 125 plus 25 more in Tokyo, he decided to act directly and without hindrance from the subcommittees and the publishers association. Ever since that time, Hasegawa has walked around with a smile on his face. Needless to say, the Japanese business associates reacted in an irritated and insecure manner, since none of them were accustomed to such a way of working. "For one person to take over responsibility is quite strange to the Japanese," he noted.

I learned one more amazing thing from my guests, the Japanese authors, while I was sitting with some of them at a meal and discussing the possibilities that existed for the tran lations of the works of the writers gathered here. They listened to me attentively and earnestly, but then one of the gentlemen, I believe it was the writer Kenji Nakagami, carefully put his hand on my arm. He thanked me laboriously for my interest in Japanese literature, but then said, almost in an embarrassed manner, "Mr. Weidhaas, we are really grateful to you, but you must understand that we don't want to be translated; we are Japanese, and no one here understands us."

At that point I thought about Kōbō Abe, the great Japanese author, whose world-renowned novel *Woman in the Dunes* had so fascinated me. Did I understand him correctly? Had I really understood anything of Japanese culture?

Spain (1991)

Spain's contribution was built on sand. I had begun preparations for this focal theme with the then Culture Minister Jorge Semprún, and then with his successor Javier Solana, who later played such an important role in the politics of the European Union as a quasi-foreign minister. The next Minister of Culture Jordi Solé Tura finally completed the project, and dedicated it together with the Infanta Elena. What was presented at the Spanish Pavilion in the Congress Hall of the Frankfurt Fairgrounds greatly agitated the Spaniards who were present. Was this Spanish pavilion, with its tons and tons of beach sand that had been carted into the Congress Hall, a success or a "disaster"? You could hear a few unflattering comments like: "This is the Estremadura of Spanish publishing!" Or, "This is a bullfighting ring for books." "We wanted to give an image of the modern Spain, beyond the clichés, and someone brought us sand from the bullring and from the beach!" Quite often designer ideas that stoke the imaginations of those in charge can have this effect.

On the other hand Eduardo Arroyo received unrestrained praise; he had designed the logo of *Hora de España — The Hour of Spain,* a portrait of the 17th-century poet Quevedo with red hair. More than 5,000 posters were glued up in Frankfurt on advertising pillars and distributed to book dealerships. The demand was immense for the special bags that bore a picture of

Arroyo on the front and one of Juan Miro on the back. Portfolios and carry bags were practically ripped out of the hands of the people handing them out them. Pablo Martínez, program coordinator from the Spanish Ministry of Culture, commented, "I plead with you to never again give away such items for free. Nobody benefits from this onslaught!"

More than 10,000 plastic bags and portfolios were distributed; the various newspapers that had been prepared on the occasion of this focal theme were practically sold out; the catalogs of the exhibits, the books, the program of presentations, the Spanish authors, and the panorama of Spanish publishing found countless interested people. There were always about 300 to 400 people at the podium discussions, and there were never enough seats. All in all, 75,450 visitors attended the sandy pavilion.

When these results became known, all the whining stopped. The number of visitors reached the same level as that of the Italian thematic program. Italy had once and for all set the pattern on how to do things.

MÉXICO (1992)

We had a signed contract with the Soviet Union to be the guest country for 1992, but this state no longer existed. What to do? A year without a guest country? That would mean breaking the rhythm. But where could we so quickly get a well-known substitute topic? Usually each country needed at least two years of preparation. In a democratic discussion process, the preparation of the necessary financial means demanded a great deal of time and effort from the active organizers in the guest country. Where was there an available country where decisions could be made of such a basic and costly nature from top to bottom?

I remembered one of my colleagues whom I was friendly with, the president of an impressive state publishing house, and who alone seemed in a position to make the kind of decision that I urgently needed in a very short time. He was the director of the Fondo de Cultura Económico, the former President of Mexico, Miguel de la Madrid, who still had enough influence in his country to put through the decision that we needed. I had met de la Madrid at numerous international book expositions and book fairs. Once—it was in Bogotá—I sat with him on the podium with the then Colombian President Belisario Betancur Cuartas, who also was now active in the world of books, to discuss the situation of the Latin American book. Contrary to general opinion, the Latin American potentates were very well-educated and deeply involved in books.

I called him up and openly discussed my emergency situation. I then offered to Mexico the guest country spot for 1992. He calmly listened to me, and asked me a few practical questions about the scope and the costs for his country. Then he ended the discussion with a comment which became clear to me only later, that 1992 in particular was a significant year for Mexico because it marked the 500th anniversary of the meeting of our two worlds. He asked for two weeks' time for an answer. His remark referred to the "discovery" of America by Christopher Columbus in 1492. Not quite two weeks had gone by when Miguel de la Madrid called back—Mexico would be the guest country for 1992!

There was hardly any public discussion about this matter in Mexico, as had been the case in other countries or would be the case in such countries as Holland or Poland. On the other hand, there was a bitter controversy between two Mexican star authors, each of whom had access to a cultural periodical in which they really went at each other. The two authors were Octavio Paz[2] and Carlos Fuentes.[3]

Both of them I knew rather well, and would have liked to have the two of them in Frankfurt, together. The issue was which of them would represent the "Mexican" in Frankfurt. In this affair between two such outstanding personalities, only one could win. It was Octavio Paz who finally gave the opening address at the Frankfurt Book Fair, while Carlos Fuentes stayed home. He came the year after that; there was no Octavio Paz.

Although my description of the origin of the Mexican focal theme may suggest otherwise, for a number of years I had worked for some participation in Frankfurt to reflect the signifi-

---

2. Octavio Paz (1914–1998): Writer, poet; 1990 Nobel Prize in Literature.
3. Carlos Fuentes (b. 1928): Novelist, essayist and professor of literature.

cance of the Mexican book. I had traveled more than a dozen times to Mexico, giving lectures and speaking so often to the people in charge at the book association that I was welcomed there like a distant cousin. I also met Octavio Paz any number of times. In his opening address, Paz had this to say:

From the very beginning Mexican literature has been distinguished by the appearance of two contrasting characteristics that make up its essence, the tendency to universalism and the tendency to withdraw into itself. Wings and roots. Our literature, like the other American literatures, began as a dialogue with the Spanish tradition, which was experiencing its golden age at that time. Out of that dialogue a multilateral and passionate discussion grew with the other European literatures. A lively relationship, which sometimes led to polemics and breaks, and sometimes even to monologues and lonely adventures. During all these mutations and changes a dual tendency arose that split our literature and at the same time united it with itself: the love for the universal and then the strong desire to pull back and to retreat into one's innermost particularity.

This duality came out as early as the work of Juana Inés de la Cruz, the first truly great female writer that our continent has produced. Her poetry oscillates between the baroque of the 17th century, full of echoes of the classics, and the vernacular language. Another characteristic of Mexican literature, particularly of modern literature, is the constant presence, though not always visible, of the non-European reality of Mexico. For us this Indian reality is both our past and the present, a phantom that does not let us sleep; it is always something in the present and asks us questions. A secret, hidden, forgotten, and buried present, which suddenly emerges with the power of printed publications. When we speak to that tradition, we are speaking to ourselves.

When hearing these words by Paz in his opening lecture, I had to think of that most Mexican of all Mexican authors, Juan Rulfo and his novel *Pedro Páramo*.[4] Unfortunately, Rulfo had died in January 1986, and was not able to be present at this festival of Mexican literature in Frankfurt.

This was a worthy opening address by a great book person,

---

4. *Pedro Páramo* was first published in 1955 and had a critical influence on Latin American writers and the development of Magical Realism.

who went on to discuss the status of literature in the West. As the opening speaker, Octavio Paz was the correct choice. I could stop holding my breath; once again a difficult Fair had been put on the right track. Now this 44th Frankfurt Book Fair could find its way with the guest country topic of *Mexico: An Open Book—México: Un Libro Abierto*.

Flanders/Netherlands (1993)

When I ran into the three *Stichting* women from the Dutch and Belgian Frankfurt Association who were responsible for the preparation of the Fair, Pauline Sarkar, Anette von Soest and Bärbel Gerke, I thought I detected a certain coolness in their attitude to me. The three women were blaming me for the pressure and a whole host of problems that they were being subjected to, due to the demands of princely protocol from the sponsors at our opening cocktail party. It was clear that our arranger, Mr. Koudele, had made certain promises to some sponsors, such as to the master chef Cas Spijkers, the sponsor of our opening cocktail party, that he could give a copy of his recently published cookbook to the prince; but this would have been impossible on the basis of the restricted protocol. At the planning stages, such a development could not have been foreseen. Much more supposedly conservative countries, such as Spain, had not posed a fraction of such protocol demands that the so-called liberal and open societies of Holland and Belgium were presenting.

For me the situation looked like this. An outdated system such as that of the monarchy, which because of its anachronistic nature and its lack of any real significance in an open, democratic society, had to be protected and acknowledged by very stiff ceremony. At this Book Fair it ran into the reality of today's world, which is marked by a free-for-all attitude. These were two worlds, two principles that collided here. A conflict was preordained.

We could reproach ourselves for not having recognized early enough this complex situation. For this, we didn't have enough experience, and where we did, such as with the Spanish Infanta, the expectations of the court did not appear so clearly. Later we did learn here of a certain disgruntlement of the Infanta, which she shared with her cousin, the Prince of Belgium. Perhaps this was the reason for the heightening of the demands of the Belgian court.

Another element in this conflict was the highly sensitive relationship of the two countries, the Netherlands and Belgium, here made acute by the representatives of the two royal houses. The Dutch court had left all the security and protocol questions to be settled by the Belgian court, something that opened the way for the increased requests for maximum demands and guarantees.

To allow just as much regimentation as necessary, but also to allow as much leeway for free movement for people and for individual needs as possible—these had been my organizational principles for the Book Fair in the practically 20 years of my responsibility. This had served an exposition based on a large variety of interests because of the flexibility and the ability always to create free spaces. The risks lay between too strict regimentation on one hand and on the other a slide toward chaotic and unmanageable situations. Taking strong steps on one side might tend to create chaotic outcomes elsewhere.

Had we recognized the conflict earlier, the clash would not have been so nerve-wracking for us. We might have been able to dispense with the sponsors' legitimate wish for self-advertising, or we might have worked towards not having a visit by the royal houses, though the latter would have meant giving up some good publicity—and perhaps would not have been something that we could do. In this case we had to accept all of the demands of Dutch and Belgian protocol, whereupon one of our important sponsors dropped out, something that in turn led to extra costs for the opening evening of around 40,000 Marks. So the game played out this way—I had to arrange for a reduction in the size of the cocktail reception in order to reduce the financial loss.

Later, at the opening, the extravagant princely protocol could not be maintained, as we had foreseen. The princes simply did not follow the careful choreography of their handlers, and thus the chaos of our exposition once again won out. However, the two princes were very affable young men and really enjoyed themselves. The opening was successful, as was the entire focal theme which the Dutch and Belgian organizers had arranged for us, often interspersed with humorous interludes. One argument between Harry Mulisch[5] and Cees Notteboom[6] over who would take the significant role of the opening speaker for the Dutch—an argument similar to the one that the Mexicans had—was fought out forcefully in public. Harry Mulisch finally won.

The Fair was opened by Mulisch and the princes, who said nothing but who shone by their mere presence, and by impartially chosen Belgian and Dutch ministers, who naturally had to take the podium. There then followed a week of fireworks and exhibitions, in which humor was used as a mighty grease for communication. We took a chance, and people opened up to the messages from the Low Countries. It was one of the most successful theme years at the Book Fair.

Brazil (1994)

Brazil, on the other hand, did not go as I had hoped. Three good friends worked for this guest country. Up front was Alfredo Weiszflog, the Brazilian publisher of German extraction from São Paulo, who as president of the Brazilian book dealers chamber was responsible for the entire participation of his country. Then there was the go-getter literary agent Ray-Güde Mertin from Bad Homburg, who was especially devoted to Portuguese language literature. I had met her as early as 1971 at my German book exhibit in São Paolo when it was still in that city. The final person was the Frankfurt book dealer in Portuguese language literature, Teo Mesquita, from the former Portuguese colony of Goa, now India, who for over 20 years had been trying to find a customer base in Frankfurt for Brazilian and Portuguese authors.

I had great expectations for the Brazil team based on the commitment of these three wonderful book people. It's also true that the Brazilians had not spared on investment. As Alfredo told me later, there was even a deficit of $750,000 that

---

5. Harry Mulisch (b. 1927): Dutch writer, author of *The Assault*.
6. Cees Nooteboom (b. 1933): Novelist and author of *The Following Story*.

the book dealers chamber had to carry for a few years. Everything had been really too bombastic—the Brazilian pavilion and the half-dozen carefully edited representative picture albums about Brazil, which in part arrived only after the Book Fair in Frankfurt. These books, each in an edition of more than 1000 copies, must have cost a king's ransom. Still, the appearances of the Brazilian authors had good attendance. There was interest, but any highlighting of a particular aspect of the content or a particular author had been forgotten. There was Paulo Coelho, just following the enormous success of his 1988 book *The Alchemist,* translated in 40 countries, over 5 million copies sold, topping bestseller charts around the world. Still, people were not able to agree on some really scintillating Brazilian author to speak at the opening. They wound up with a rather colorless professor Josué de Souza Montello, who delivered an academic address about the influence of Goethe on Brazilian literature and its authors. The speaker was a rather amiable gentleman who in a very mild voice told this kind of anecdote: ...*at that very moment a lady came up to me at the entrance to the National Library and with her shaky hands wanted to give me a big package. She said, "I am a German, the widow of Dr. Juliano Moreira. I heard about this exhibit and I'm bringing you this gift—a bust of Goethe, which used to sit on my husband's desk."*

This was well-meant, but it was not appropriate if one wanted to inspire a German public for things Brazilian. I am convinced that this choice of the speaker was made by the Brazilian government, which was very heavily involved financially. We learned that it is the opening of the Book Fair that determines how strongly the public latches on to a topic.

AUSTRIA (1995)

The most remarkable thing in the Austrian year was without a doubt the round pavilion thought up by the architect Adolf Krischanitz. The glass exterior was enclosed in a citation in white from Robert Musil,[7] and it was visible from all sides and from all the halls, standing as it did in the middle of the fair-

---

7. Robert Musil (1880–1942): Austrian Modernist, author of *A Man Without Qualities.*

grounds, embracing the fountain with its stele. Here everything was offered, from the Hotel Dependance and its Café Sacher with its "little brownie," and then the Original Sachertorte down to the liveried waiter—it all provided a real Austrian ambiance. The unconventional pavilion had become necessary because the Congress Hall, in which the countries usually exhibited, had been torn down and was being reconstructed.

With the challenging Robert Menasse[8] featured as the opening speaker, the Austrians had done well. Menasse spoke about historical progress, about the sense and the purpose of history: *It makes no sense merely to utter beautiful words and to hope for something like a beautiful Utopia that would apply effectively worldwide. This week at this Fair we are experiencing something like that—a peaceful and productive coming together of people from all nations, languages and cultures.*

I also personally profited from this theme of the year. I got a new press spokesman with Rüdiger Wischenbarth, the director of the Austrian theme for the Fair, who had done his job very well. The previous director of our press office, Holger Ehling, had resigned to pursue a career as a freelance journalist abroad.

I also received a decoration as big as my fist, "The Great Badge of Honor for Services to the Republic of Austria," which was so impressively baroque that it could have been awarded by the Emperor Franz Joseph himself before the First World War. It wasn't, but it was from "The Federal Chancellor of the Republic of Austria exercising the functions of the Federal President by decision of...." The Austrian Chancellor, Dr. Franz Vranitzky, who had already visited the Book Fair several times, could not come because the threatened breakup of his ruling coalition in Vienna kept him away. In his place the political representative of the Austrian focal theme in Frankfurt, the Federal Minister for Science, Research and Art, Dr. Rudolf Scholten, pinned the stately decoration on my "honored" breast.

IRELAND (1996)

Irish President Mary Robinson attended an enchanting dancing and music soirée that took place at the old opera house follow-

---

8. Robert Menasse (b. 1954): Viennese writer, author of *Wings of Stone*.

ing her opening of the Book Fair along with German Chancellor Helmut Kohl and the Irish Nobel Prize winner Seamus Heaney.

The Irish had had a brainstorm. Since they did not have a lot of money available, they rented the Austrian pavilion and set up a typically Irish pub there. At the opening they served Irish stew to the honored guests and poured out the Guinness, something that did a lot to hinder the understanding of the speech of the Irish Minister of Culture, Michael Higgins, about the "rich Irish literature" and the necessity of fixed book prices in the EU. A 30-foot-tall inflatable Gulliver stood at the entrance to the fairgrounds.

Lar Cassidy, who was in charge of the theme "Ireland and its Diaspora," had more than the duty of energizing the Irish diaspora in England, America and Australia. The branches of the Guinness Brewery in Germany and in Ireland had decided to be a co-sponsor of the Ireland theme, and Cassidy therefore had called on the Irish "pubs" in some 500 German towns and cities to put on a "Day of Irish Life in Germany" during the Fair week. These included Irish music, Irish dance groups, and readings by the 30 Irish authors who had come to Frankfurt.

This is the first time that we completely spilled over geographically with the Frankfurt Fair theme into the whole country, with small Irish festivals everywhere. We got excited reports from Marburg, Aachen, Wiesbaden, Mainz, Cologne, Hamburg, Duisburg, Koblenz, Heidelberg, Bremen, from Moers on the Lower Rhine, from Biberach, from Bad Berleburg, though hardly anything from the East, regarding readings by Patrick McCabe, Irish poet Nuala Ní Dhomhnaill, by Hugo Hamilton, Colum McCann, Frank Ronan, John McGahern, Eoin McNamee (from Belfast), Edna O'Brien, Maeve Binchy and Roddy Doyle.

"Ireland is perhaps a small country in Europe, especially if you look at its population, but culturally we belong to the 'giants' of the world," Lar Cassidy had claimed at the opening press conference. At first this struck us as a bit of an exaggeration, but as we worked with the Irish literary figures and publishers who came, some with unusual and often unpronounceable names and experienced readings and the lively discussions in pubs, all of a sudden it dawned on us that we had hit a literary gold mine

"The Irish genius," writes Umberto Eco in his *Public Work of Art*, "moves constantly on the borders of lunacy, always on the level of provocation and collapse." This comment seems somewhat stylized, but it does touch on the core of the double role of Ireland as a teacher to the West and a dissident there.

In relation to its number of inhabitants, Ireland in the past 400 years had produced more great writers than practically any other country in Europe—Jonathan Swift, Oliver Goldsmith, Oscar Wilde, William Butler Yeats, Sean O'Casey, James Joyce, Flann O'Brien, Samuel Beckett.... Contemporary authors were groaning a bit under the burden of their ancestors. Still, a bestseller like Frank McCourt's *Angela's Ashes* proved that Irish literature had not necessarily missed the boat, but could stand on the terrain of international *belles-lettres* on its own. The literary gene of the "typical Irishman" could also be seen in the new generation, in Dermot Healy, Colm Tóibín, Neil Jordan and Roddy Doyle. This Ireland, the one that so few of us had been aware of, was a true discovery.

Lar Cassidy, a friendly Irish public official, gushed at the end of the Fair in very loud tones about the Irish Festival in Frankfurt, and was even "sure that this really positive conclusion would reverberate at home [in Ireland] in a clear improvement of the image of Germany." Unfortunately this was the last time that Lar could be so excited in an unrestrained way. Back home in Dublin, he died shortly after the Fair.

Portugal (1997)

Portugal had stood on our list of guest country programs for a number of years, and suddenly we received good news from Lisbon. They wanted and could take over the next topical year, but only this one, 1997, no other. Our Portuguese colleagues received the green light from their government for such a program in Frankfurt to function as preparatory advertising for the World Expo that was to take place in Lisbon in 1998. There was money for that. We had however promised this year to Hungary, and now I had to travel to Budapest to convince the local authorities and committees, which had already started preparing eagerly, to postpone until 1999.

For the Portugal year, the architect Luísa Pacheco Marques built the pavilion for them, a controversial mixture of "black box and sinking ship." That's how the Portuguese Minister of Culture Manuel Maria Carrilho explained it to Dr. Jorge Sampaio, the President of the Republic, and to the German Federal Republic President Roman Herzog. Inside it was dark and somewhat narrow. This, however, did not make any difference to the President of the Federal Republic of Germany. He took his seat at a chair that had to be grabbed from somewhere else in order to eavesdrop on the President of the Republic of Portugal, his Minister of Culture, and the Fair director as they were surrounded by people who were filming, snapping pictures, writing, sipping drinks, munching away—the usual scene at such occasions. "Ugly on the outside, practical on the inside"—that's the way the PR person for the focal theme summarized the impression of this black, angular building. About 12,000 visitors were said to have come to the pavilion every day, as many as in the previous year to the Irish focal theme.

Here the Portuguese Fair model was not "collapse" or *Mayday, Mayday!*—which might have been portended by the incline of the building—but rather "Ways into the World." This slogan aimed to describe the historical role of this country and the ambivalent heritage of its history—Portugal as the pathbreaker for European expansion, starting with the travels of Vasco da Gama to India some 500 years ago, coupled with an examination of the post-colonial identity of Portugal. More than 40 Portuguese writers came to Frankfurt to present their work, and we intentionally included the Portuguese language authors from Africa and the Americas among them. There were lectures about Portuguese film and screenings of such films, translator workshops sponsored by the Gulbenkian Foundation with poets like Luís Filipe Castro Mendes, Fiama Hasse Pais Brandão, Fernando Pinto do Amaral, all whose very names seem poetic. And of course there were exhibitions on Fernando Pessoa[9] and on topics like "Portuguese as a World Language." These latter included José Eduardo Agualusa from Angola, Germano Almeida from

---

9. Fernando Pessoa (1888–1935): Modernist writer and Portugal's most celebrated poet.

Cape Verde Islands, Mia Couto from Mozambique, Teolinda Gersão from Portugal, and João Ubaldo Ribeiro from Brazil. The most popular and most heavily attended were the purely literary discussions, such as the roundtables led by Curt Meyer-Clason on Portugal—"Poetic Reflections of a Country" with Pedro Tamen, Fiama Hasse Pais Brandão and Manuel Alegre; then, moderated by Ralph Roger Glöckler, the reading of "Place and Country" with Mário de Carvalho and José Riço Direitinho. There was the introductory theme, "Lisbon—A Literary Portrait," a reading and discussion with Lidia Jorge, João de Melo, Maria Velho da Costa, and moderated by Wilfried F. Schoeller. There was a reading as though in dialogue, led by Ray-Güde Mertin, of "Paths of the Contemporary Novel," as trod by Agustina Bessa-Luís, Almeida Faria, José Saramago and Maria Velho da Costa.

José Saramago was already on the way to the airport when the news reached us that he had won the Nobel Prize for literature that year. We sent someone chasing after him and his wife, who were intending to fly home, and were able to catch them just before check-in. He returned to the Fair. We improvised a press conference, which was heavily attended by the world press and many international television groups, all wanting to interview the new Nobel Prize winner. In the evening this writer and everyone interested in Portuguese literature celebrated this extraordinary event with great gusto. This was a fabulous conclusion to the Portuguese guest country program at the Frankfurt Book Fair.

Switzerland (1998)

"*Tschiel vast—Val Stretga*" (Broad Skies—Narrow Valley) was the subtle motto of the Swiss appearance in 1998, expressed in the Romansh language.

The Swiss were very much into understatement, at least in Hall 7, to which the public was directed by a banner spread across the street with the notation, "Switzerland is right next door." Switzerland presented itself in a spartan and reserved ambiance. People spoke very subtly of the "traffic chutes" and the "richly contrasting changes in color" of the rather sad curtains lining the walls of the hall. Behind these lay a labyrinth leading one way to "Henry von der Weid's Reading Machine," an astounding multimedia installation, and in the other, to the studio of Swiss Radio, with two auditoriums for readings and discussion with 100 to 150 seats. Christoph Vitali, long-time director of the Schirn Kunsthalle Frankfurt, the unconventional exhibition site near the cathedral, was the project director who developed the guest country design of "Swiss appearance."

On the very first evening the television station 3sat presented a star quartet for its broadcast of the "Literature Club"—Adolf Muschg,[10] Peter Hamm, Gert Heidenreich and Andreas Isenschmidt, debating five new publications, as moderated by Cohn-Bendit.[11] No less interesting was the discussion titled "The Other Life of Books: Literatures in Translation," with the publishers Inge Feltrinelli and Michael Krüger, conducted by translator Ilma Rakusa. A conclusion of the discussion might be what Krüger observed—basically people do not take seriously Swiss literature in the four languages: "Cendrars[12] is for the Germans not Swiss, but a Frenchman!"

At the evening opening the two national presidents, Flavio Cotti of Switzerland and Roman Herzog of Germany, flanked by Frankfurt Lord High Mayor Petra Roth and the ever-present project director Christoph Vitali, scouted the offerings of the Swiss hall, the Biblio-Thek, and all around on the walls, set up high, the mighty cross section of Swiss literary offerings.

The polyglot country had set out its book offerings on its Biblio-Thek, color-coded according to the particular language and arranged according to subject areas. The numbers were these: 63.6% of the Helvetian output was German, 19.2% French, 7.6% Italian, 0.6% Romansh and 8.9% in other languages. In accord with the statistics, 54 German authors were represented at the Book Fair, 21 French, 12 Italian, 8 Romansh and 10 writing in other languages.

---

10. Adolf Muschg (b. 1934.): Swiss writer and professor of literature.
11. Daniel Cohn-Bendit (b. 1945): French-German politician, *"Dany le Rouge"* of 1968 fame.
12. Blaise Cendrars (1887–1961): Swiss-born, French modernist author and poet.

Hungary (1999)

For a number of years the Hungarians had been my favorites. Ever since I had arranged the first German book exhibition in 1971 in Budapest, Szeged and Debrecen under dramatic conditions, an emotional tie to my colleagues there had formed that lasted for over 30 years, and still exists today.

András Tömpe, the former Hungarian Ambassador in East Berlin, now demoted to president of the Hungarian Publishers and Booksellers Association; his successor Ferencz Zöld; the solitary intellectual Paul Schweitzer, the great scholar of Thomas Mann, who, when he was in a depressed state, always introduced himself as 'No-no Paulie'; Péter Zentai and István Barth, director and president of the publishers and booksellers association after the collapse of the Iron Curtain; the writer and President of Hungary Árpád Göncz; the authors György Konrád and Péter Esterházy; the writer and former director of the Hungarian cultural house in Berlin György Dalos; the author Imre Kertész (winner of the Nobel Prize in Literature in 2002); the poet, essayist, and playwright István Eörsi; the publisher Tamás Miklós and the previous director of the International Book Festival Budapest that was set up by Katalin Balogh of our Frankfurt Book Fair team. An emotional, friendly relationship bound me to all these people.

First of all, Ferencz Zöld. Ferencz took over the post of director of the Hungarian Publishers and Booksellers Association in the 1960s. He was a tall, handsome man, who in his youth had worked as a model in fashion shows. Later he became a passionate lover of old books before he took over the administrative post in the booksellers' association. I often visited him in his office on Vörsemarti Place in Budapest. Then we would go out to eat, with the meal often degenerating into a friendly carousal. A number of times we laughed uproariously about Peter Meier of the Leipzig *East German Publishers Weekly*, who had been assigned to me by the East German secret police, and who could only with difficulty defend himself against our joint Communist–Capitalist teasing.

Hungarian state security had Ferencz watched by his predecessor Tibor D., who did not confine himself to watching, but conspired to aggravate his successor with a whole series of blackmail attempts. I knew nothing of this unofficial private war between the two of them, and always invited them together to a meal, as it turned out. When I later learned what was going on and asked Ferencz why he had not given me the slightest sign, he answered in his inimitable Hungarian German with a counter-question, "Am I a gentleman?"

He was a fine human being, too fine, or perhaps better, too sensitive for what happened to him in the "freedom" of the capitalist market economy. Ferencz was the director of the best and finest publishing house in Hungary, the scientific press Akadémiai Kiadó. As was common under Socialism, this company had a very large body of employees, with over 100 scientific editors, technical consultants, graphics people, pressmen, secretaries and other employees. In the course of the takeover fever, a large Dutch publisher grabbed the Akadémiai and immediately asked about productivity. Zöld within one year had to reduce the number of employees to around a dozen. He had no choice. A portion of the rights of the Hungarian publisher were later transferred within the international concern to other companies. Ferencz would have been able to leave the firm in great haste, but for him that would have been a betrayal of the Hungarian publishing industry and of Hungarian academic production. He was fired after he had completed the gigantic reduction in personnel and had gotten involved in publishing a scientific encyclopedia, for which the latest profit forecasts the company found to be not well-calculated.

Using his settlement, he bought a small bookstore in an out-of-the way section of Budapest. But he did not withstand that year without other effects, and as a result of the tremendous stress he was suddenly confronted with a health problem, which practically destroyed his ability to act as a book dealer. A sudden detachment of his retina left him almost completely blind! A book dealer who cannot read is like a bird that cannot fly. Day after day Ferencz stands in his little bookstore, lovingly supported by his wife, who reads off the books aloud to him.

With all this going on, and because it was my last year for national exhibitions, and because this was the year that rounded out the century and the millennium, Hungary was for me a very moving and very emotional thematic program.

Hungary makes an impression with charm and grace, with cosmopolitanism and a healthy self-regard, with an extremely varied exhibit program. The effect of any initial strangeness is quickly blown aside and turns into pure affection.[13] "Hungary unlimited"—thus went the Fair slogan—came to Frankfurt with 94 publishing houses and more than 10,000 books.

Naturally, Hungary enticed authors who already were well-known—Imre Kertész, György Konrad, Péter Nádas, and Péter Esterházy, who was brilliant with a saucy opening speech. This squad of "writer stars" was introduced by the Hungarian President Árpád Göncz.

One presentation that drew special attention was "10 Years after Opening the Borders—50 Years of the Federal Republic of Germany," the title of the roundtable discussion in the Pest-Buda Café in the Hungarian pavilion. Participants included the Hungarian Prime Minister Viktor Orbán, the former holder of that office Miklós Németh, and the then German Foreign Minister, Hans-Dietrich Genscher.

Despite all the turbulence that took place at the Book Fair after I left, the series of guest countries continued. In 2000 it was Poland, which I had prepared; then Lithuania, Russia, the Arab countries, Korea, and then India, which on its second appearance in Frankfurt was much more convincing and was greeted enthusiastically. Planning continued for 2007 for the cultural region of Catalonia; for 2008, Turkey; for 2009, China; 2010, Argentina—all interesting and enticing countries and regions, which would galvanize the book world at the Frankfurt Book Fair.

---

13. *German Publishers Weekly* 84 (1999).

Where Do We Put Everybody?

The early 1990s exacted a string of compromises in the principles that the Frankfurt Book Fair had stood for all this time. How much responsibility for the new restrictions lay with the historic changes of this era I cannot quite say. In retrospect, it was no accident that so many basic conflicts came together; the aggravations stemming from global political crises and indomitable macroeconomic forces could not help but play out in the world of business, even in the modest book trade. It was clear to everyone that the calm that we had enjoyed before was lost forever.

Or perhaps it was the sudden appearance of a new generation of managers, who were more specialized and thought more narrowly than the generation that preceded them. Perhaps this earlier generation had a broader outlook, and—also looking back longingly—had tarried longer over things that were more basic? "Professionalism" was a word that seeped into general usage at the end of the 1980s. Anyone who was "professional," someone who honed in on the target of his task, could not afford to be thoughtful and reflective, judicious and decent. These values were now thoroughly obsolete. What was considered professional, what was considered good, was to achieve the goal of one's business by the simplest and most direct route.

The Frankfurt Book Fair still functioned under a set of principles set up by the founders that even in those days had an influence on decisions. A characteristic image of the Frankfurt Book Fair for decades had been shaped by a certain equality and treatment of all exhibitors, no matter what their rank and no matter what share of the book market they held. This principle had been laid down in 1949 by men like Alfred Grade, Heinrich Cobet, and the members of those committees that were responsible for the first Frankfurt Book Fair, as well as by their successors—namely, that all exhibitors, large or small, would have the space of only two exhibit stalls. That way it could be assured that the small publishing houses, with their often very important publications, would not be marginalized by the dominant firms.

On the occasion of the 25th Frankfurt Book Fair, Alfred Grade was asked why in his view this approach had been successful. In his answer he pointed to the positive effect of this arrangement: ... *the technical limitations forced on us by the space issues of St. Paul's Church, and demanded of us by the democratic spirit of our activity—this democratic spirit so to speak—was the root of success for the Frankfurt Book Fair.*

It is true that in the following 40 years many concessions in this regard had to be made due to changing circumstances. For example, there were finally five different sizes of stalls ranging in length from 2 to 10 meters that a publishing house could rent. The big concerns could also help themselves by renting one stall for each "imprint," that is for each of the publishing houses that they had purchased but that still put out books under the original name.

Despite all this, the principle inherited from the founders endured; it was the guiding principle of many of our decisions. For instance, the price list for stalls was arranged so that the larger stalls gave a subvention to the smaller ones. We set up a progressive and non-linear set of fees in which, for example, the maximum stall consisting of five units was much more expensive than the sum of the cost of five individual units. Or if a mighty publisher thought it important to show that he was special by building his own stall and did not use our materials, that publisher was in no way reimbursed, although we as an organization saved on costs. He had to pay the same price as for a fully equipped stand.

This approach also appeared in the restriction that powerful publishing houses in their advertising in the Fair catalog or on the fairgrounds were not to be given opportunities for publicity that the smaller publishing houses could not afford. Naturally we observed this principle of equal treatment particularly in the location of the stalls, something that always brought us into significant conflict with the market leaders, who demanded the best places for themselves. This applied to individual publishing houses within the various exhibit groups as well as the groupings by country, where we always tried to mix in the less powerful book dealers, say those from the Third World (or later from the states of Central and Eastern Europe), with the ten to twelve largest book firms.

Over the years we had to withstand a large number of heated disputes over this policy, but we stuck with it. In the end we were able to get the market leaders to abide by our organizational dictate, even if they grumbled about it. I am even today convinced that this organizational principle, which placed certain restrictions on free market development, contributed to the integration of many marginal exhibitor groups into the Frankfurt Book Fair, so that in the end this Fair became a global meeting place for all branches of the book trade. This is something that we in the German book trade were very proud of.

Now I had to learn the hard way how times had changed. People were no longer willing to accept our long-standing policy without a fight. I would like to present this disagreement in some detail, a disagreement that stretched over several years and brought on heated discussions among wide circles of the international book trade. In my opinion, these changes constituted a fundamental break in our overall *modus operandi* for the Fair. This is painful for me because up until the end of this conflict I fought for the principles that I had long cherished, and in the end I had to suffer defeat despite all my efforts.

This was of course not the only battle that I was engaged in during those days. In the "Rushdie Affair," taking place at the same time (discussed in the following chapter), it was also a matter of what was basic for our Fair, namely a struggle for freedom of speech and freedom from censorship, all tied up with our relationship to a Third World country: the Islamic Republic of Iran.

The unexpected appearance of Leipzig as the site of a book fair, in what before had been an uncontested German market, again drew us into basic discussions about the meaning of our policies and the market for expositions in our category. The emergence of a large British-American-Dutch concern, Reed

International, which bought up whatever it could of the international book fairs, also challenged our leadership of the international market.

It was a period of heated battles in which I suddenly understood that with my convictions as to what Fair policy should be, I stood practically alone. The old-timers who would still lend an ear to those basics had left the governing committees, either because of their age or for other reasons. This group included people like Friedrich Georgi, former chairman of the German Publishers Association and head of the Parey Verlag, Hamburg; the cultural pessimist and DTV publisher Heinz Friedrich; the former chairman and Frankh publisher Rolf Keller; and even the social conservatives like the Stuttgart science and textbook publisher Wulf D. von Lucius. Now the decision-making committees were completely taken over by "professionals" like Frank Sicker, Klaus G. Saur and Gerhard Kurtze, people who were less hindered by having to reflect on their actions.

In addition, conflicts arose everywhere that were seldom about the matter in dispute. For one thing, people were settling old scores; for another, they were forming coalitions to advance their own agendas. Jealousy and a know-it-all attitude played great roles here. This goes for both the members of our Supervisory Board as well as the honorary and full-time staff at the German Publishers Association, all of whom fought vehemently for this parent company to control our decisions in the Fair Company. It was a difficult period, and often I got the feeling that what my predecessors and I and our staffs had built up and given life to was being torn asunder. I had the impression that this fair, an institution with its strengths and internal contradictions, had now gotten out of control; its old ways were no longer expedient.

Because of my deep and decades-long engagement in the Frankfurt Book Fair and my identification of it as a part of myself, as my life's work, these challenges and battles affected me personally, a situation that did not exactly promote in me a detached and flexible approach.

In 1984, after the completion of the new exhibition Hall 4 on the fairgrounds of the Frankfurt Fair, we gave up the halls on the west side of the fairgrounds, behind the railroad line, and made what we called the "Fair of the Short Paths." This was a compact area in a U-shape, formed by Halls 3 (two levels, totaling 11,129 m²), 4 (three levels, 42,201 m²), 6 (four levels, 35,542 m²), and 5 (two levels, 21,946 m²).

We gave a very good position in the largest and most attractive hall, the newly constructed Hall 4, to the international exhibitors, who competed very sharply with each other on the trade in licenses and co-editions. The German groupings of Belles-lettres and Textbooks, Youth and Children's Books, Maps and Travel Guides, Religion and Science-technology were spread over Halls 5 and 6. Art, Art Gallery releases and Special Editions took up the entire Hall 3. This was all in all a very good allocation, which in the second half of the 1980s gave us quite satisfactory marks from our exhibitors.

A fair, however, is not something static in which an arrangement can be made for all eternity. Some groups grow faster than others, and in some sub-areas there are reductions. Naturally all the exhibitors wanted to occupy the same location every year, since they felt comfortable from the previous or other years on the campus, and they wanted their business associates to find them at the same place as before. In this way defined user structures, streams of movement, themes, and action-oriented arenas were formed, which were opposed only by the people who were dissatisfied at the time. Those who were satisfied defended themselves tooth and nail.

As organizers of the Fair, we were always quite pleased when the changes within specific groups were not so great as to force us to make new arrangements on the fairgrounds. After all, any conflict with the exhibitors would likewise mean picking a fight with the press, which was only too happy to oblige its paying advertisers by printing any and all libel they could turn up against the Fair management. This usually took the form of accusations of not only idiocy but arrogance.

This became a sort of a ritual over the years, in which everyone played his role, and that is why one could get around the first, second, fifth, tenth regrouping, although it was always unpleasant and strenuous, often leading to some really ugly behavior by disputants. Nonetheless, we had always prevailed against the various militant individual interests and were able to structure the Fair so that if not all the participants, then at least the overwhelming majority, were satisfied. The steady growth of the exposition supported us.

The positive fact of this unbroken growth was what drove us inexorably to the next conflict over restructuring.

From 1984 to 1988 the proportion of international exhibitors had grown disproportionately by 1,421 new exhibitors, or a total of 32.1% of the 5,859 exhibitors (as opposed to "only" 20.7% growth from Germany), and the trend was continuing. Hall 4 was bursting at the seams; every square inch was assigned, and waiting lists could no longer be resolved. The challenge of the hour was to expand the area for the international exhibitors. At this moment we were aided by the completion of a new exhibition hall at the entrance area of the fair near the city, Hall 1 (with two levels and 18,036 m²). Admittedly, this hall lay some 100 yards from the next closest, Hall 3, the inner circle of the Book Fair, and its use would interrupt what was at this point our best layout of "the short paths." In no way could we simply put the foreign newcomers into the new hall and simply leave everybody else in the old one.

Moreover, the international arena was not a homogeneous one, but one divided into Anglo-Saxon, Romance, Slavic, and other language areas. Here there was a more sensible balance than in the German groupings. The new arrivals came from all language areas and had to be assigned to groups. It was also absolutely essential to maintain a balance between the strong and weak book trading countries.

After we had worked out a series of placement alternatives and had discussed them in detail, I decided to expand the international exhibitor area from Hall 4, which lay directly next to Hall 3. It was a matter of who would have to leave the beloved and centrally located international Hall 4 and move to Hall 3.

I could have made life easier for my colleagues and myself by leaving the eight strongest book trading countries in the hall. All the others, which did not have an especially strong lobby, could be jammed together in Hall 3—the then existing Eastern bloc countries, the Scandinavians, the Portuguese, the Australians, the Irish, and the have-nots from the Third World. It was just that this clashed strongly with my view of the organizational principles of the Fair, as I have already explained. I would then have created a "mainstream" center, and all the other foreign exhibitors would have been marginalized.

I hit upon the idea of taking out of Hall 4 the exhibitors who clearly constituted the opinion leaders in our line of business; namely, those from the United States. They would also exactly fill up Hall 3. It was clear to me that the publishers from America were primarily at the Frankfurt Book Fair in order to sell (not to buy), not that this made asking them to move any easier. Still, once the new structures had been accepted and new centers and streams of visitors had formed, the balance that would arise between the two areas seemed to be a good idea.

Admittedly, a move of the art exhibitors into the new Hall 1 would be necessary, something that meant another disturbing moment. So far, nobody was familiar with the new hall, but based on encouraging advice, I was convinced that we would be able to withstand the imminent storm reasonably well. To expand space in Hall 6, I planned to transfer the small exhibitor groups like Maps–Travel Guides–Globes into Hall 1 as well. In no way did I wish to touch Belles-lettres and Textbooks, since these groups included the most sensitive and most combative customers. And too much was too much. You couldn't upset all the exhibitors at the same time. Nobody could survive that kind of clash.

I knew that the then chairman of the Supervisory Board, in his professional role as publishing head of the Bertelsmann concern, was quite involved in an American venture, and I therefore early on made him privy to my ideas. He was in charge of the supervisory board of Bantam, the largest paperback publishing house in the United States, and had just taken over for Bertelsmann the old established American literary publishing house of Doubleday Dell. The company wanted to increase the stock of publishing rights for Bantam, but primarily it wanted to solidify the Bertelsmann reading clubs for its American subsidiary. In this activity the gentleman had missed the point that at the time of the takeover, Doubleday Dell was not in good business shape, and that with the exaggerated purchase price of almost $500 million, he had apparently acquired a "turkey," something

38 Opening press conference in the Gallery of the fairgrounds. Each year 7 to 8 thousand journalists reported on the Fair.

The newly erected reading tent on the fairgrounds of the Book Fair was well-liked the public on the weekend. From then on it formed a part of the annual program.

1988 The Italian star author Umberto Eco presented his new book *Foucault's Pendulum*, which appeared the following year from the Hanser Verlag.

1988 Inge Feltrinelli (*right*) was one of the Italian publishers who remained true to Fair for decades.

Robert Jungk was also involved in the Society for the Promotion of Literature from Africa, Asia and Latin America.

"Pancho" Gonzalez, president of the Spanish publishers association, was pleased at the award of "Friend of the Frankfurt Book Fair." He proudly wore the insignia on his lapel every day.

1988 Gioconda Belli, poet from Nicaragua, with her German publisher Herman Schulz of the Peter Hammer Verlag in Wuppertal.

1988 Ernesto Cardenal, poet and Minister of Culture of the Sandinistas in Nicarag with the promoter of Latin American literature Michi Strausfeld and the Nicarag publisher Erik Blandon at a discussion in Frankfurt.

The opening of the Second Festival of the Book in Managua made headlines in *Barricada*, the central organ of the FSLN. I had sketched out the plans for this festival with Ernesto Cardenal in a Frankfurt pub. It took place for the first time in 1987 in Managua and in 1989 for the last time.

The Spanish author and Minister of Culture Jorge Semprún (*center*) at the German stand at the Madrid Book Fair.

1990   The year of Japan at the Frankfurt Book Fair coincided with the 80th anniversary of the large Kodansha Publishing House, Tokyo. The anniversary was celebrated with the Japanese ritual of cracking open *saki* barrels.

1991   Meeting of fair organizers: (*from left to right*) Carlos Franz, book fair director Santiago de Chile, Marie Carmen Canales, co-director in Guadalajara, Michi Strausfeld the Latin American scout for Suhrkamp, Margarita Sierra, co-director in Guadalajara, and her successor Nubia Macias.

(*Left to right*) Frankfurt culture consultant Linda Reisch, Robert Jungk and his wife. (*In front*) Wolf Biermann, East German poet and singer, after a presentation in the Frankfurt Römer town hall.

German Federal President Richard von Weizsäcker on a hurried tour of the Fair.

1992 Trade journalists in each other's company: Fabrice Piault (*center*) of the French trade magazine *Livre Hebdo* and Paul Schweitzer (*right*), editor of the Hungarian book trade magazine and also an outstanding student of the work of Thomas Mann. Left, Ingrid, later my wife.

1992 Ringing out the Fair with colleagues from the business office, including long-time colleague Irmgard Hasselbach (*second from left*).

that amused people in the American publishing industry very much.

The chairman of the Supervisory Board had been "burned" by the American book market, and so had lost his appetite for risk and was looking to play it safe. As a result, it did not surprise me that he agreed to my suggestions only after some hesitation, but he also demanded that the Americans be informed before the final decision and that their objections must be listened to. That sounded very reasonable, but in fact it was not! Rather the old contradiction came into play here—the members of the supervisory board of the German Publishers Association who had exhibit stalls always had to weigh their own interests against the needs of the Fair. We were all naturally interested in its success, but I, as the person in charge of the development of the Fair, found myself in the painful position of having to combat the legitimate wishes, opinions and decisions of the Supervisory Board, or to get around them.

This was the backdrop for many upsetting arguments that were repeatedly aimed at me personally by the executive committee of the Supervisory Board and of the German Publishers Association standing behind the Board. I was considered difficult and incorrigible. Every one of the disputes that were carried on by the German Publishers Association against us always had the goal of neutralizing my authority and "getting control of me." I also assumed that they did not want to get rid of me, since they valued my successful management, but they overlooked the fact that this success was closely connected with my insubordinate behavior.

In this particular case I was not playing the expected role based on my past behavior; I really was doing what I was told. In the 40 years of the existence of the Frankfurt Book Fair, not one of my predecessors nor I had ever consulted the people affected by a decision before it was made or even informed them of what was being considered. We could never prevail if they thought there was the slightest chance that an imminent change could be aborted.

I therefore went against my convictions and did what the chairman of the Supervisory Board asked because I could hardly reject such an unambiguous and direct instruction from the chairman. I also acted obediently because in the past seven years of his chairmanship of the Supervisory Board, he had acted very strenuously and supportively on behalf of the Fair Company and the Book Fair, and because I understood what kind of dilemma he was in. Finally, I knew that at Bertelsmann he was on the defensive in a conflict with Mark Wössner, chairman of the management board, apparently brought on by the blunder at Doubleday. This was all to lead to his resignation from the company that very year.

Had I pushed harder and somehow convinced the chairman, then the whole affair would not have developed so virulently, and I would have saved myself many battles. After one or two years the Americans would certainly have accepted the new situation, just as hundreds of other outraged exhibitor groups had done before them.

At the end of January 1989 I set off with Franz-Josef Fenke, technical director of the Book Fair, and Helmut von der Lahr, press chief and director of the public relations department, for five days at the Algonquin Hotel in New York, where we set about our explanatory campaign among the New York publishing houses and marketing firms. And then things started to happen.

We spoke with all the right people in all the important publishing houses and in all the publishing and book dealer organizations. And as expected with most of our discussion partners there were some for and some against our intention. What was common to all of them was the great anxiety on the other side of the Atlantic concerning European integration. The American publishing houses cherished the wish of being neither physically nor geographically separated from the rest of the English-speaking world. We played at least a bit part in this wish, in that we drew all the English-language exhibitors closer to the Americans and thus had created a cohesive English sector.

The three of us returned to Frankfurt with the consciousness of having fulfilled our mission. As we expected, the American publishers were not excited about what we were doing, but in the end we were able to reckon on their acceptance. To be sur we had played a little trick here in that at no time did we drop a hint that the decision on displacement could still be changed because nothing had been absolutely decided.

The only people who would soon know better were the two people from Bertelsmann, Alberto Vitale and Alun Davies of Bantam Books. Not long after our visit in New York, but still before the decisive meeting of the Supervisory Board on February 22nd, Vitale had called up the chairman; and so he learned that there was still room to shake things up. That is what set off this power-hungry man of action to become the spokesman for the opponents of this entire displacement of the American exhibitors at the Frankfurt Book Fair. He must have laid down the law to our chairman in his conversation, telling him that this decision in no way was to go through.

At the next meeting of the Supervisory Board, after I had presented my plans, to everyone's astonishment the chairman unexpectedly pulled a little slip of paper from his jacket pocket and explained that on the trip to the meeting he had thought up an alternative plan, which he would now like to present.

The minutes of the meeting remark on this singular event: *The chairman of the Supervisory Board outlined an alternative plan, based on the idea of not interrupting established structures that function well* [obviously for the Americans], *and at the same time based on the notion that one should not try to dupe the dominant market* [!] *and the strongest exhibitors involved in international licenses by treating them as maneuverable masses to shove into unappealing areas. The entire Supervisory Board agreed to the decision, despite the vehement protest of the Fair director, after a long and intensive discussion, that...*

And then came the so-called alternative plan, whose most important element was that the Americans would remain in Hall 4. Every other group was apparently arbitrarily placed. The contentious "Belles-lettres group" was divided between Halls 5.0 and 1.2, which lay at least 150 yards apart—this was the most serious displacement *faux-pas*. These exhibitors observed their location and the location of their competitors with almost feverish jealousy, and utilized any supposed locational advantage of another party for an immediate argument for the improvement of their own situation.

Dutifully, I informed the Americans and the other foreigners, those whom I had met in a recent trip to the U.S., by fax, and all the others by letter. In addition, faxes went out to the British, U.S., French and German professional news outlets. Jubilation among the Americans, confusion and irritation among the others. The first protest letters started floating in, starting with the Dutch. Some publishers of *belles-lettres,* who were to be moved to Hall 1.2, now exerted strong pressure to be placed in Hall 5.

Quite apart from the questions of content, a new problem arose with regard to the allocation of the expansion rooms. These in the most part were plentiful where we did not need them, and were lacking where we did need them.

Another problem originated in Hall 1, which would be available to us only three days before the beginning of the Fair. Thirty percent of the Belles-lettres exhibitors, slated by the new plan of the Supervisory Board to be housed there, had their own building to do. Some of the self-builders had already told us that in this short time they were unable to complete the construction and were therefore withdrawing from the Fair. Among the art book publishers and editions there were scarcely any self-builders. We would not have had any such problem with our logistically well-planned mode of building our own stall units.

It turned out that a restructuring on the fairgrounds could not be improvised. Finally, we in the director's office laid plans on the table that we had worked out after many hours of discussion. I was so angry over the behavior of the Supervisory Board, who were not bothered by any doubts about who knew best, that I was tempted to implement this ridiculous plan. The protests coming in from the exhibitors made it quite clear that this new structure of the Fair could not be implemented. Besides, it seemed that in ignoring the negative opinions of the Dutch and Scandinavians, we had created a second class among the exhibitors in the "mainstream" group.

As the rumors in the publishing world swelled, the protests became so loud that they could no longer be ignored. A rump Supervisory Board of members who happened to be in Frankfurt at the time for other meetings finally made this announce ment on March 9, 1989: *Technical, organizational, and deadline problems that have occurred in relation to the new Hall 1 on the fairgrounds have caused the Supervisory Board of the Exposition and Fair Company to delay by one year implementation of its decision on the restructuring of the 1989 Book Fair. For these reasons the Book Fair in 1989 will maintain the same mode of placement as in the previous year.*

Everything remained as it had been in 1988: No expansion of the occupied fairgrounds to Hall 1. Retraction of some approvals for expansion of stalls in the international area. Ongoing pressure on Hall 4. Predictably long waiting lists that could not be resolved. But—calm—a whole year in which to prepare the first absolutely necessary restructuring of the Book Fair that had failed this year.

The 1988 Book Fair ran quite peacefully. We created a publishers center for the publishers who found themselves on the waiting list for the international area. The Americans breathed deeply and increased their business by 10.2%. The English did not want to lag behind and expanded their already impressive presence by another 5%. Everybody was basically satisfied that they could stay where they felt comfortable. Somehow this heated discussion of the past months became a sort of "publicity" campaign with quite positive results, as the number of exhibitors in the next year rose.

Nonetheless, it was precisely due to these positive results that we could not continue the way we had. The pressure on Hall 4 increased. Now exhibitors from other countries were thronging to Frankfurt, and oldtimers wanted to enlarge their stalls. You couldn't simply ignore the demand. We had to make room for growth available. The international area had to be expanded!

We just didn't know what to do after these events. Practically every route had been blocked for us due to the negotiations and poor decisions of the past two years.

On January 15, 1991, there was a special meeting of the Supervisory Board of the Exposition and Fair Company. We laid out two clearly unacceptable alternatives. The third alternative that we put up for discussion was the one that we liked in-house. It picked up on the failed plans of 1989, though it had two very severe handicaps. First of all, the Art group had to be subdivided into two groups of Illustrated Books and Art Editions, of which the latter was destined to remain in Hall 1. Secondly, as in 1989, there was no way out of placing the contentious Americans in Hall 3.

I was convinced that I really had to try one last time to regain my authority over the physical shaping of the Fair. I still wanted to be the person in charge of structuring the Fair and not only its moderator. It was my opinion that a gigantic undertaking like the Frankfurt Book Fair needed leadership in order not to be overtaken by the chaos of market forces and led astray. I am of the same opinion today, and therefore look back on this period with a feeling of resignation and sadness.

At that time I had to give up the idea of shaping the Fair according to my own notions, and thence had to capitulate in the face of legal authority within the institution. I cannot, therefore, make any individual responsible for what happened; it was the circumstances as described here that changed. On the other hand, it was also a result of my waning support among the decision-makers in those days. What could I have done? At that time it would have been more realistic just to give up on my test of strength with the Americans. But wouldn't I have then given up my last chance at taking control?

The Supervisory Board approved the new "old plan." The gong for the last round of the placement battle was rung. Initially the sharp reactions to the very serious changes did not occur. Even the Americans did not put up their expected outcry when we informed them in February 1991 of our recent decisions. In addition we had now put forth the "security argument." The First Gulf War was fully underway, and it was true that we could have better protected the Americans from any possible threat that was recognized early in Hall 3 rather than in Hall 4, which was open on all sides. Meanwhile the American publishers had entrusted their dealings regarding the Frankfurt Fair quarrel to the hands of their federation. It was here at a meeting of the international division of the Association of American Publishers in New York that a decision was to be made as to whether the American publishers should boycott Frankfurt, o how they should deal with this "insubordinate" management group at the Fair.

I once again traveled to New York and offered to explain to this meeting the reasoning behind our decision, but somehow people over there had become weary of the whole topic. Only after the meeting of their own committee on the Frankfurt Book Fair was I summoned, where I met with a dozen quite fatigued representatives of publishers. They tried to make clear to me how contemptuous they found our plan to once again drive the American publishers into a "ghetto," when we supposedly had promised never to do this again.

Their threats made in the name of publishers who were not present did not sound very convincing. They even threatened either to boycott the Fair or to reduce their stalls and staff in Frankfurt by at least 50%, especially by the large publishing houses. That way there would be enough room in Hall 4 so that a move would not be necessary.

I was quite familiar with the atmosphere within the American publishing industry, where each person jealously watched each step of the others. I knew that these "sharks" would never come to a meeting of the minds, unless of course they all faced the same emergency at the same time. That appeared to be unlikely.

All the same, the American book trade at that time was in a painful recessionary phase, and some of the publishing houses were quite happy to play around with the idea of a "protest reduction." It was obvious, as everybody knew, that companies like Simon & Schuster and Random House invested up to half a million dollars each time they went to Frankfurt, and that they could not pull back on this engagement without raising suspicions that their publishing houses were on the way down. There was a certain risk here. I was willing to consider a moderate size reduction for the large stalls, particularly since I saw in this more a correction in the market rather than damage to the interests of the Frankfurt Book Fair. Purely competitive concerns might justify an over-extension of the participation of the large American publishers who were presumably faced with a precarious cost–benefit analysis, but might there not be some bad side-effects, which could only result in total Frankfurtphobia? At first, the problem took care of itself; the American publishing houses registered, despite the expected placement in Hall 3. Only Simon & Schuster asked for a smaller stall.

The Book Fair ran absolutely smoothly in 1991. The American publishers in conversation seemed quite resigned to the situation. When the Fair was over, only about 30% of the American exhibitors expressed satisfaction with their location (previous year: 75%). In addition, satisfaction with business dealings unexpectedly sank from 92% in 1990 to 87% this year. Since these evaluations were still quite strongly dependent on the personal moods of the people making the evaluations, we could take some comfort in assuming that business was just as successful as in the previous year when everyone was satisfactorily housed in Hall 4. It was more an emotional problem that we had to deal with here.

Nick Veliotes, the president of the Association of American Publishers (AAP), for a whole year had skillfully kept himself out of the events preceding this discussion on placement. I don't know what moved him suddenly to take the initiative. He circulated notes and questionnaires to all his members in order to tease out a readiness to do battle, an attitude that had otherwise been waning for quite some time. He excused himself in a somewhat embarrassed fashion by saying that he had to represent the interests of his members, but somehow I have the suspicion that he had some ulterior motives. His sudden discovery of the members' needs was all too virulent to have been initiated merely from ongoing interest in representing them.

The field of battle that was prepared in an especially offensive manner during the first four days of the Book Fair by Barbara Meredith, the "field marshal" of the AAP, was a previously planned closing discussion with some American publishers on the Saturday of the Fair, where I had declared that I would be prepared to hear about their experiences and to take heed of the need for some improvements in the next Fair. This did not occur with "a few" publishers. In the end 80 American publishers insisted on letting me know of their displeasure.

On Saturday, October 12, 1991, I got up in front of a grim

group in the Blue Room of the Festival Hall. Those present were the chairman of the Supervisory Board, the technical director of the Book Fair, Mr. Fenke, and my assistant, all of whom, with the exception of one statement by the chairman, did not do any talking. It was very still as we just sat opposite each other in the room. Nobody wanted to start the slugfest. I got up and said, "Who will cast the first stone?"

And then the brickbats started flying in from all directions. These included the well-known accusations, brought forward many times before, of ghettoization, damage to business, poor air, inferior infrastructure in the hall, the supposed lack of knowledge of the Fair management regarding the international publishing rights business, the discrimination, the disadvantaged position of the U.S. publishers versus the Brits, *etc., etc.* After two hours everything had been said that could have been said. We were divided into two sides with deflated feelings and were not a bit more satisfied. The AAP had succeeded in provoking a sharply negative attitude in our clientèle, an attitude that eliminated any room for reconciliation.

I went back to my office, conscious of having put up a brave resistance, but in the back of my mind I knew that this last attempt to preserve our prior Fair policy had failed. Politics, including politics at the Fair, is the art of the possible. It would not be responsible any longer to continue to frustrate these outraged "preferred customers" with the long-cherished principles of our Fair.

Decision of the Supervisory Board at its 99th meeting on February 24, 1992: *The exhibitors from the United States will again be placed in Hall 4. The following exhibiting countries (all East European countries, publishing houses from the Third World, East and Southeast Asia, Austria, Switzerland and Scandinavia) are to move to Hall 3.*

Death to Rushdie!

On February 14, 1989, an extraordinary newsflash startled the world: the aged leader of the Iranian revolution, Ayatollah Khomeini, announced a *fatwa* against Salman Rushdie, the Indian-born British writer!

What had happened? What was a *fatwa*? What had the scowling Ayatollah to do with a British citizen named Salman Rushdie? These were the questions puzzling a confused Western world and its intellectuals.

Once again, in our unspeakable ignorance of the region, we in the West were completely taken by surprise, were shocked — indeed horrified. Just as we had been taken by surprise at the collapse of the Shah's apparently impregnable regime and the emergence of the venerable religious leader, and just as we had been shocked by the face of the bloody fratricidal war with Iraq, fought by the Ayatollah's followers with a fanatic sense of martyrdom, so now were we astonished by this recent turn of events.

My view was reinforced that we in the West really only talk and listen to ourselves. Nor do I exonerate our own "world" book market in Frankfurt from this tendency to self-absorption.

What did we, in fact, know about Iran and its people? Had we any idea why, in 1979, the Persians — the businessmen and university graduates, women and children, farmers and soldiers — turned their backs on the comic opera monarchy of the Shah — a regime which had so well suited us in the West? Why did they turn to a malign and medieval "reign of terror," clad with religious pseudo-legitimization? Apart from a few political scientists in university seminar rooms, who amongst us was aware of the larger political circumstances surrounding this turbulence in the affairs of an ancient and civilized nation?

It was not until two years later, at the outbreak of the First

Gulf War, that our media were moved to seek out the few specialists with some knowledge of the region—Islamic scholars and political scientists—and began pressing them for in-depth analyses. In fact, even these efforts to shed new light on the situation were swiftly subsumed by a deluge of typical war-related reportage that was rife with every imaginable distortion.

I cannot, however, entirely agree with Salman Rushdie's view on the subject of the *fatwa*, that it was purely and simply a case of gangsterism and nothing else. He made this comment in 1992, during the third year of his persecution. He appeared unable to comprehend that he had unwittingly become an instrument and a symbol in a global political conflict; and he was unable to free himself from the clutches of this situation.

Nor was this a situation rooted entirely in religion. The fact that the ailing Iranian Ayatollah had imposed a death sentence on the writer was based on Rushdie's apparent rejection of the requirements of *Shariah* or Islamic religious law that regulates public and private life, as opposed to the Koran, which only threatens punishment in the hereafter for those who have abandoned the tenets of the Islamic faith. But the fact that the Ayatollah had extended his *fatwa* to include any and all individuals involved in the dissemination of the offending book—the majority of whom were of completely different faiths—was another matter entirely. This new pronouncement effectively included translators, publishers and booksellers throughout the entire Western world. Salman Rushdie and his book *The Satanic Verses* had been deliberately molded into an ideological explosive that could be hurled into the inner sanctum of the hated West.

On the basis of our concept of literature, Rushdie's novel is a fascinating work. Having read the book twice, as well as having studied a great many reviews, I was totally enthralled by the visionary force of the author's narrative, and I have not been able to find a single review which has ever questioned the author's powerful literary creativity.

It was even a pleasurable read. Had I been a reader who knew little or nothing of Islam, the Prophet Mohammed, or of the Koran—the sacred book of revelations whose contents cannot be subject to interpretation as they represent the unalterable words of Allah Himself—I would have been more than happy to savor and enjoy the book in its entirety—including the "blasphemous passages." In other words, I would have read it for what it is and—according to the author—for what it is meant to be: a tale of the lost identity of those Muslim émigrés who, like Salman Rushdie himself, have been torn from the cultural context of their Indian and Pakistani homelands and have found themselves in the unexpectedly strange and forbidding new world that was London in the 1980s.

While it is entirely possible to read the novel on those terms, there can be no doubt that it was not read in that light by those who saw it as a deliberate provocation—and most certainly not by those who chose it as a weapon to be used for their own purposes. And, indeed, as soon as one makes the effort to take an objective view, it does appear that the author had every intention of being as provocative as his detractors had claimed!

In the chapter titled "Mahound," Rushdie makes use of the abusive names given to the Prophet Mohammed by (Christian!) colonial rulers in the Middle East, and embarks on a highly profane and derogatory interpretation of the 53rd *sura* of the Koran. It seems that the author genuinely relished the opportunity to deliberately attack the dogmas of Islam.

In a book review by Jochen Hieber, writing in the *Frankfurter Allgemeine Zeitung,* an attempt is made to clarify the process for us by offering an equally vituperative treatment of the characters in the New Testament: *Jesus Christ is only referred to by the use of pejorative nicknames. As well, vulgarly graphic details of his conception are presented and his preaching is reduced to cunning tactics. What's more, Mary, Martha and Mary Magdalene are represented as high-class whores in a brothel.*

In the light of all this controversy, it was virtually inevitable that the Frankfurt Book Fair would be drawn into the fray. This annual gathering included many of those who were the target of the medieval edict issued by the Imam: the publishers, booksellers, translators, to say nothing of the author. Here a crucial aspect of the self-designated character of our event was suddenly called into question, namely, its function as a forum for the unrestricted worldwide exchange of information based on cultural and scientific content.

Despite having been so vigorously defended over the years by both my predecessors and myself and by the respective supervisory committees, the Fair's guiding principle of absolute freedom from censorship was suddenly not merely being challenged by dispute or demonstration, but by the very real threat of terrorist violence against the lives of our participants. Freedom of speech, that most time-honored and acclaimed right within our Western culture, was being called into question by an accusation of blasphemy and offense to religious sensibilities.

In actual fact, however, something quite different was also happening at the same time—a fundamental, historical conflict between an oppressed and aggrieved culture, on the one hand, and its putative or actual oppressors, on the other, was being brought directly into the heart of one of the dominant centers of this exploitative imperialist culture. Initially, it was perceived as something entirely beyond comprehension, which gradually gave rise to repugnance and finally to fear.

The fact that a book should be chosen as the vehicle for this important and historic clash may, in fact, be related to the intrinsic character of Islam, which is the religion of the book *par excellence*. Annemarie Schimmel, a well-known German specialist in Middle Eastern and Oriental Studies, once suggested that the term "inlibration" should be used synonymously with Islam, in the same way that "incarnation" is applied to Christianity. In Islam, the Word of God was not made flesh, but was made a book. The "People of the Book" (*Ahl al-Kitāb*) play a key role in Islamic theology. For this reason, even today, the status of a book is quite different within the sphere of Islamic culture.

While we in the West have come to see a book as a commodity available for consumption on demand, in regions shaped by Islam (including those not given to fundamentalist excess) books are still viewed with something akin to the attitude of our forefathers, influenced as they were by the sacred character of the Book and reverence for the written word—an attitude which was prevalent in the days of handwritten books and medieval *incunabula,* and in the early days of the Age of Gutenberg.

This could also represent a certain asymmetry of historical

development, which may stand in the way of genuine communication on a worldwide scale as happens at the Frankfurt Book Fair. And yet, with its countless masses of books to be picked up and examined, its throngs of people coming together with a common purpose, with its opportunities for integration and communication, its challenges and its potential for development, the Frankfurt Book Fair exists in the here and now, offering a forum for every kind of encounter. In the case of Rushdie and the *fatwa,* it came face to face with a challenge it could not afford to ignore. It had to respond accordingly.

At this juncture, I will refrain from making any attempt to decide on the rights and wrongs of that response. It goes almost without saying that the handling of this matter subsequently gave rise to a great deal of wrangling and differences of opinion among the Fair's management board as well at the German Publishers and Booksellers Association. I shall therefore confine myself to describing the course of events during a crisis, which, for a variety of reasons, cast doubt on the fundamental principles of the policies applied to the Fair up to this critical time.

On September 18, 1988, an assistant of the Muslim Indian MP Syed Shahabuddin read an interview with Salman Rushdie in an English-language daily. His boss, after being informed of the contents, immediately spotted an electioneering opportunity and decided to call for the banning of *The Satanic Verses,* which was distributed in India by Penguin. Without ever having read the book, two days later, on September 20th, Mr. Shahabuddin launched his campaign to have the book banned.

On October 3, 1988, Mr. Islam Hijjaz, described as the Secretary-General of the Islamic Foundation, an organization financed by the Saudis in Madras (now Chennai), sent a telex to Faizuddin Ahmed, head of PR at the Islamic Foundation Publishers in Leicester, England (a company also operating with Saudi backing), reporting on the success achieved in luring voters away from the governing Congress Party as a result of demonstrations supported by Mr. Shahabuddin.

In the telex, Mr. Hijjaz also suggested that this might be a good opportunity for pro-Saudi operations in Britain to regain ground lost to the Iranians after 400 "believers"—mainly Iranian pilgrims—were killed during the Gulf War as a result of Saudi Arabian police intervention.

On October 5, 1988, Rajiv Gandhi—following the counsel of trusted advisers—made history by becoming the first prime minister of any state to ban the book in his country. Gandhi's advisers were basing their recommendation solely on a brief extract published in the weekly *India Today*.

At the same time that Penguin/Viking's top man in New York, Peter Mayer, received a telegram from New Delhi ordering the cessation of sales in India, the Islamic Publisher's PR man in Britain, Faizuddin Ahmed, was summoned to Riyadh. Presumably this came as a result of the photocopies of selected passages from the book that he had sent to 45 embassies of Muslim countries and more than 400 organizations around the world.

These, then, were the events leading up to the vitriolic campaign launched against Salman Rushdie and his book. The protagonists of certain politically motivated short-term interests which had nothing to do with literature seized upon this opportunity to advance their own ends. The Indian electioneering strategists were set against the competing forces of Saudi and Iranian Muslims to gain a dominant position of influence over Britain's extensive Muslim community.

Once the secular non-Muslim Rajiv Gandhi had banned the book on political and democratic grounds, what action was to be expected three months later from an Imam who laid claim to the spiritual leadership over all the Muslims in the world?—This was the question posed in the *Index on Censorship* (April 1990) by Adel Darwish, to whom I owe the details of most of the events I have outlined above.

Other Islamic states now followed the example set by Gandhi; South Africa also followed suit. On January 14, 1989, the book was publicly burned during a demonstration at the British Muslim center in Bradford.

Fourteen days later, while I was in New York with my colleagues Josef Fenke and Helmut von der Lahr, sitting in the office of the already agitated head of Penguin/Viking, Peter Mayer, *The New York Times Magazine* published its lead story on Rushdie and the threat against his life.

Two weeks later, disaster struck in Pakistan when five people were killed during a protest demonstration against the book. A hundred more were injured when the police were called in to defend the American Cultural Center in Islamabad against the onslaught of a fanatical mob. Then came the *fatwa* on February 14, 1989. Suddenly everyone who had had anything to do with the book remembered having read news items they had barely bothered about until that moment. The death squads of the Ayatollah had already liquidated 30 of his opponents in the Western democracies over the course of the previous five years. Lending particular weight to his threat, on February 15th the formidable Imam set a price of several million dollars on the head of Salman Rushdie. An unprecedented wave of hysteria and fear gripped publishers and booksellers throughout the Western world. Reports of attacks on bookshops in Britain resulted in the removal of the book from window displays everywhere. Publishers who had been planning translations of *The Satanic Verses* from the original English postponed production. In the end, the Italian publisher Mondadori was the first to decide to take a stand in the face of the fearmongers and brought out its own edition in Italian in March 1989. Christian Bourgois held the rights for the French edition, which appeared four months later in July 1989 and included the following statement: *Published with the support of the Ministry of Culture and Communication of the Republic of France.*

In Germany, concerns for people's safety led Kiepenheuer & Witsch Verlag to waive their rights to the book, which provoked an unprecedented outcry in the arts pages of the German press. In response, sixty high-profile German citizens, many of them publishers, authors and journalists, established a society which they christened "1989 UN Charter Article 19," with the intention of using this name for purposes of publishing the book. The German edition did, indeed, appear in late October of 1989, although it was too late for the Frankfurt Book Fair, which had already taken place. The names of the approximately 320 members of the society—including my own—were listed individually in the front pages of the novel with the intention of spreading the personal risk factor.

At the beginning of March 1989, 44 newspapers in 20 different countries had published a so-called "World Statement" from the International Committee for the Defense of Salman Rushdie. The names of the first 250 to sign ranged from Denmark to Bangladesh and included Tankred Torst, Hans Magnus Enzensberger, Hans Werner Schwarzer, Peter Ripken and Peter Weidhaas from the Federal Republic of Germany. The only German institution on the list, our Society for the Promotion of Literature from Africa, Asia and Latin America, joined those calling upon *all those in positions of political responsibility everywhere in the world to reject the death threat against Salman Rushdie and those involved in the publication of the book and to take concrete steps to ensure that these threats are withdrawn.*

In Britain this statement was published in large format and free of charge in almost all of the top-ranking newspapers, but in Germany, only Berlin's *Die Tageszeitung* was willing to print it. Later that year, even after the publication of the German edition of *The Satanic Verses,* all other German newspapers steadfastly refused to print any advertisements—paid or unpaid—due to fear of reprisals.

We at the Frankfurt Book Fair were already well-acquainted with Iranian militancy. In 1982, Iranian opposition students connected with the organization CISNU had wrecked the official Iranian stall at the Fair, after holding a hunger strike in front of the stall the year before. Finally in 1986, followers of Ayatollah Khomeini stormed a stall run by the opposition People's Mujahedin of Iran in the outdoor area, and four of the people manning the stall were so badly injured that they required hospitalization. It was only thanks to the swift intervention of the police that five of the attackers were arrested and charged. It turned out that four of those arrested were, in fact, official staff members of the Iranian Embassy.

Then and there I made the decision that both the official Iranian stall and that of the opposition must be closed for security reasons. At the end of the day, with the help of some of my immediate staff, I personally cleared out the Iranian's official stall, where we found garrotes and other suspiciously unsavory items.

I also resisted the angry protests of the Iranian Ambassador until the final day of the Fair. When I discovered that the Iranian

Foreign Minister had planned to make a brief visit to the Iranian stall while traveling through as the head of a delegation of Iranian Members of Parliament, I realized that this eventuality had to be prevented at all costs, and came up with the solution of closing the stall early. The backlash followed a few days later, hard on the heels of the Book Fair, when an "enraged" mob attempted to storm the German Embassy in Tehran with shouts of "Revenge for Frankfurt."

Taking into account all that had occurred up to this point, I came to the conclusion—although not without considerable misgivings—that we should abandon what had once been an ironclad principle of our Book Fair policy. It was a long-established cornerstone based on the belief that absolutely no one should be excluded from the Fair—no country, no religion, no ideology, no regime, however cruel or oppressive.

For decades we had tolerated the right-wing elements among the publishers at home as well as abroad. What's more, we had tolerated East Germany, the Soviet Union and the entire Eastern Bloc. Greece, Indonesia, North Vietnam, Argentina and Chile had all been controversial exhibitors at the Book Fair when those countries were governed by military dictatorships. There were vehement demands for the exclusion of exhibitors from Franco's Spain and of South Africa during the time of *apartheid*. The People's Republic of China called for the exclusion of Taiwan, Yugoslavia for the exclusion of Albania and the Nova Hrvatska publishing companies. Later the Spaniards demanded that official Catalan representation be banned, and Canadians objected to Québec being allowed to set up its own separate stall.

In retrospect, there are countless other examples, but the sole criterion for admission to the Frankfurt Book Fair remained constant. Books or other printed items had to be exhibited, and the only demand made of the exhibitors and the public was that debate concerning the exhibits must be conducted along democratic lines and in verbal form in accordance with Fair regulations. This was the guiding principle that had made the Frankfurt Book Fair all that it is to this day—a worldwide forum for ideas, for opinions, for debate with those of disparate views and ways of life, a marketplace for information and discussion.

At the 87th meeting of the Fair's Supervistory Board on February 22, 1989, I broke with that principle, because I took the view that in this most difficult and fundamental of disputes that we in the book trade had ever experienced, the Frankfurt Book Fair had to send a clear signal. The Board unanimously accepted my suggestion that Iran be excluded from future participation and passed a resolution that the Fair would hold this official position: *Until such time as Tehran's call for the murder of Salman Rushdie is withdrawn, Iran will not be admitted to the Book Fair.*

In the months between the Board's decision and the opening of the Fair the following October, there was a steady stream of new and horrifying reports of acts of violence, attacks on bookstores and anonymous threats against publishers. As early as February 1989, two bookstores were hit by bombings in Berkeley, California, as well as the New York warehouse of a newspaper that supported Rushdie. At the beginning of March, an arson attack destroyed the entire stock of books and some of the fixtures at a Mondadori bookstore in Padua. On the evening of March 29th, 36-year-old Abdullah al-Ahdal, a Saudi Imam at the Brussels Mosque, was gunned down together with the mosque's 48-year-old librarian. Although the cirumstances of the killing are still murky, at the time everyone immediately traced the motive to an interview given by Ahdal on Belgian television, in which he expressed the view that the Ayatollah's death sentence against Rushdie flouted certain rules of Islamic justice.

At the beginning of April, bomb attacks devastated two London branches of Dillons and Penguin Collets. If the sale of *The Satanic Verses* was not discontinued, declared a representative of the Muslim Youth Movement, further attacks would follow. During an anti-Rushdie demonstration in London involving 30,000 people on May 28th, British and American flags were burned. Before it was over, seventy people were arrested and twelve policemen injured.

But, in spite of the turmoil, the book was selling well. For weeks it topped the American bestseller list, and within a relatively short time Penguin/Viking were putting out a second printing of 300,000 copies. In spite of this, profits were negligible when set against the costs of the security precautions the publishers had been forced to put into effect. There was talk, at the time, of the sum of three million dollars in expenses incurred by the publishers for the installation of electronic surveillance and metal detectors plus the use of additional security services.

In Paris, the Presse de la Cité building was under guard around the clock, although Christian Bourgois was beginning to show signs of reluctance about proceeding with publication of the book. The old villa which was the head office of Kiepenheuer & Witsch Verlag at 5 Rondorferstrasse in Cologne was transformed into a virtual fortress, with barriers blocking the entrance and a surveillance camera mounted at the front door.

As preparations were underway for the Frankfurt Book Fair, we too turned our attention to the safety of the publishers of *The Satanic Verses*. The police suggested that all the publishers concerned should be housed in a separate hall, which would facilitate a full-fledged security check. This solution, however, was so contrary to the spirit and the statutes of the Fair that we felt compelled to reject it, and instead settled upon a general plan that signaled our concerted commitment to security but without actually making any guarantees of personal safety.

The fact that the Book Fair takes place in a public arena meant that a blanket security system, regardless of what it entailed, would be in complete contradiction to this reality.

During the course of the Fair, we therefore limited ourselves to checking people at the entrances and making direct observation of the stalls of all publishers associated in any way with the book. Unfortunately, even these moderate security measures were bound to affect the smooth running of our Fair, which was the reason behind the pre-emptive apology I made at a press conference marking the opening of the 41st Frankfurt Book Fair: *The death-threat by the leader of the Iranian Revolution has already been taken up by zealous emissaries in Great Britain. Events in the British Isles have had their effect on Frankfurt as well. For this reason, visitors to this year's Book Fair must expect to be confronted with the consequences of increased security measures.*

Furthermore, I was not only intent upon making a public apology, but also on making it clear to the outside world that we had taken extensive precautions and that any sort of attack on our participants would involve a considerable risk for any would-be assassins: *As the organizers of this Fair for the worldwide book industry, we regret the necessity for extraordinary measures more than anyone, but no one can be more convinced than we are that these security measures are vital. The Book Fair should be and must and will be a safe place for all concerned—trade professionals, exhibitors and the general public—in defiance of any and all dire conspiracies!*

Luckily, that robust pronouncement did not prove false. The Fair went off quietly, although those in positions of responsibility felt an unremitting nervous tension. The "International Committee for the Defense of Salman Rushdie and His Publishers" made a presentation during this 41st Book Fair on behalf of the persecuted author. Although Klaus Wagenbach, Otto Schily, Gerhard Ruiss, the Iranian Bahman Nirumand, Bernie Rath of the American Booksellers Association and Helmut von der Lahr of the Book Fair participated, the public at large hardly paid attention.

In a further statement made at this same press conference towards the end of my remarks, I admittedly went too far in my personal commentary on the events surrounding the Rushdie affair, particularly in the light of subsequent developments: *We should like Iran to take part with us again at the 42nd Frankfurt Book Fair, but I also declare my steadfast intention that this will not happen as long as this death threat remains in place.*

It was this final closing sentence in my speech to the press at the 1989 Book Fair which was seized upon two years later—by the German press in particular—when I was accused of having "broken promises."

A New Design and the Results

After the disaster with the Americans in the matter of moving them around, we certainly couldn't touch them or any other strong book-dealing country. The Americans had succeeded in knocking us out of the saddle. Any other strong exhibitor country willing to take a gamble could absolutely achieve no less than the Americans. The only alternative that we had was to shift the small and weak exhibitors, who we knew by experience could not defend themselves, from Hall 4 to Hall 3. This contradicted the organizational principles and the policies of the Fair that I had strongly defended for 15 years on behalf of the poorer representatives among the book trade countries.

Over three brainstorming sessions each lasting several days, some at my country house in the Rhön, our top staff worked through a total of nine alternatives planned out in detail by our colleagues JK and Franz-Josef Fenke. Nothing worked. Finally the moment came when we were totally exhausted by the fruitless discussions. We swept everything we had done from the table and settled on a solution based on completely new premises.

Nonetheless, the suggestion that we now came up with was not exactly new. In 1984, when we had to carry out the big move into the newly constructed fairgrounds, we had discussed this solution thoroughly, but we had rejected it since we preferred to give priority at the Fair to the professional public and with it the model of the "Professional Fair of the Short Paths." The model that now raised our spirits promised to get around all the painful spots that we were experiencing, even though it began with the premise that we would divide the professionally oriented exhibitors from those oriented to the public. The idea was to put all the exhibitor groups interested in the general public, that is, primarily the German-speaking ones, on the ground floor level of all the halls. The professional Fair for commerce carried on between the exhibitors would be pushed upwards from the lower floors of all the halls.

In order to make the free space as attractive as possible for all the people coming just to browse, we planned for a reading and activities center and a marketplace, where publishers could follow their fancy in the display of advertising, and where dealers would be able to offer souvenirs for sale at market stalls.

To be sure, two conditions imposed by the fairgrounds worked against the integrity of this enchanting model. For one, we would have to stock the somewhat distant Hall 1 on the first and second floors with publishers catering to the public (books for children and youth, religion, art, and maps and travel guides). The second issue would be that the entire public, both from the city in the east and from the parking lots in the west, would have to use the moving walkways ("Via Mobile") on the second floor to reach the center of the Fair. Our task was that when the general public came from behind Hall 1 or when they reached the central fairgrounds, they had to be separated from the professional public and directed to the ground floor. For that, there was only one way to go about it—to get the general public to where we wanted had to be done through incentives and a directional system.

At a special meeting of the Supervisory Board on September 28, 1989, the Board voted for this "horizontal" division (by levels), and thus the new horizontal division of the Fair was set for 1990. Traffic congestion points were unsnarled and doors were set up to achieve a logical approach to the Fair for the general public. Till then we, like most of our exhibitors, had long regarded this public of browsers as a necessary evil that we had to put up with. All prior attempts in this area had been stuck at the starting line. Was there now a chance to give real information to this public through the books that were displayed, and not simply to have them shuffle through the literature area like an undulating mass?

Nobody in his wildest dreams had any idea how much care and work such a total rearrangement would demand. We worked like dogs. The technical department directed by Franz-Josef Fenke in particular was subject to enormous loads, since there were no existing plans to draw on for reference. Practically every one of the over 5000 stalls had to be measured anew. Then the stalls had to be renegotiated with the exhibitors and placed in a new site—a gigantic expenditure of effort, which could be accomplished only by extraordinary work of all the employees putting in hundreds of hours of overtime.

We still had decisions to make regarding the shape of the open area which would be the central point of the "Fair for the general public." We worked out plans for thematic books in special tents, on electronics, poetry, religion, children's books, a library of new releases, an authors' café (meeting place for and with authors), a "Book Mountain" (which was to stimulate the public to present its own activities, and whose stage was also available to publishing houses for presentations). There was a canopy area for possibilities for future focal theme countries, a speaker's corner (not only for authors, but also for visitors and prominent personalities), for presentations in cooperation with the city stages ("Literature Live"), the construction of a book boulevard, on which the manufacture of a book from typesetting to binding could be shown.

In addition to the attractions, we had to have information, which, though not going hand-in-hand with the exhibits, would have to be communicated by means of a large video wall, in addition to information kiosks, flyers, and a custom-made directional system.

These were all plans that could hardly be completed in the first year. We did not have enough time or money or even any insight on how to do it. Our hope was that we would somehow get through the first year so that in the following year all our strength could be thrown into completing these programs for the general public.

Hanns Lothar Schütz, editor-in-chief of the *German Publishers Weekly* from the 1970s until his death in 1993, was a passionate news editor. He dreamed of making the *German Publishers Weekly* into a real discussion forum for the trade, but he kept running into these picayune requirements for publicity by various sectors of the industry, or by interest groups, or by self-absorbed individuals. One look at the *German Publishers Weekly* from 150 years ago in 1856 shows that this was nothing new: *The comment of the deceased Friedrich Perthes from more than a half century ago that there was really no economic group to match the book dealers in their lack of knowledge and their unwillingness to perform their duties. If a person would just take the trouble to look through a few volumes of the* Publishers Weekly, *he would see the mutual disparagements, the ignorant questions, the ridiculous suggestions, the failed efforts. It is striking that those complaints are still justified today.*[1]

Schütz exposed his work to this audience twice a week. He held fast to his understanding of himself as a journalist, to his intent of making the *German Publishers Weekly* into something more than a narrow house organ—and for that he was scolded and reprimanded. Like a whipped dog, he let the criticism flow over him. Twice a week, for 15 whole years. In that time, the man Schütz gradually became a nervous wreck, a body always on the defensive; a man whom no one trusted, who more and more soared along eccentric paths of his own, and then suddenly pulled his head in while awaiting the righteous indignation of the leading committees or of the management board.

In 1978, when I was not yet battle-weary, the publicly-led humiliation of Hanns Lothar Schütz by the representative assembly of the German Publishers Association so outraged me that I couldn't avoid writing an indignant letter to the chairman of this assembly, the Bonn book dealer Herbert Grundmann.

The grounds for the rebuke that Hanns Lothar received from the assembly of delegates, standing before them with head bowed, was his having reprinted from *Der Spiegel* magazine a vicious review by Schulz-Gerstein about the reigning pope of German literary criticism, Marcel Reich-Ranicki (of the *Frankfurter Allgemeine Zeitung*). In light of Reich-Ranicki's being a Jew, the article was labeled anti-Semitic. As has often been the case, here I was enraged by the hypocritical reprimand from this committee, which rebuked the editor-in-chief in such demeaning terms because they were afraid that such an article would be "bad for business" and would bring about attacks from their own ranks as well as from the public. I wrote to Grundmann, chair-

---

1. *German Publishers Weekly* 1 (January 2, 1856).

man of the assembly of delegates (with a copy to President Rolf Keller of the German Publishers Association): *I accept... that the current executive committee issues a reprimand if an error is considered to be a grave one. It seems to me macabre that one also demands from the person being punished that he lay bare this wound in the very newspaper that he edits, thus exposing himself to all the world and demeaning himself. This is very much like a public whipping. Such a man is done—he loses credibility among his colleagues, journalists, and his readers. [...] Would it not have been enough for him to publish in the* German Publishers Weekly *his regrets and possibly his apology? [...] I ask myself why such things are not kept in perspective. I also ask myself why the actual content of this affair did not merit a single word in the delegates' assembly. Was no one conscious of the embarrassment involved in this discussion about the size of the type in which the decision was to be printed? [...]*

I am convinced that in this case the dignity of a human being was violated as much as that of the other person involved in the incriminating article. Shouldn't the punishment fit the crime?

It's not worth repeating Grundmann's counter-arguments. Only one sentence with which he concluded his reply seems important to me because it throws such a characteristic light on Hanns Lothar Schütz: *In this case I don't see the 'dignity of an individual' affected at all. This was made clear to me by a call from Mr. Schütz on the morning of September 14th. He was thankful that in addition to the assembly, even individual critics had spoken to him personally afterwards and had expressed their faith in him.*

So this was Hanns Lothar, who was punished for his journalistic commitment and afterwards licked the paws of those punishing him. He had lost his feeling of self-worth and his pride.

The episode described here was not his first degradation and was not to be his last. Hardly a month went by in which he was not disciplined or slapped into shape. Anyone who had eyes to see experienced the dismantling of his personality.

Hanns Lothar continued to follow the exigencies of his ambition; that was praiseworthy. But at what price? He leaned very heavily on the support of the general manager of the Publishers Association, who promised to protect him. He feverishly followed the fortunes of the rival periodical *Buchreport* (Book Report), which in his opinion did exactly what he was not allowed to do. Anybody who had any contact with the *Buchreport* found a place on his blacklist.

His own editorial staff suffered from his moodiness. He began to drink, went through withdrawal, and then the cycle repeated. He was suffering; you could see it. His personality was held together by an extraordinarily correct exterior, and as a result lots of people were deceived. Hanns Lothar Schütz took his own life on September 6, 1993, by throwing himself in front of a subway car.

All of us who knew him on a daily basis could not help him. I had gotten to know perhaps before everyone else where his problems lay and what he was suffering in this organization. I reproached myself that in the past I had not sought out Schütz as a person and addressed him as a fellow human being. With regard to the Schulz-Gerstein article, it was only years later that I told him briefly about my letter of protest. He absorbed the information without commenting on it.

The last big set-to that I had with Schütz occurred after the newly structured Fair in 1990. *Restructuring of the Book Fair: The facts swept under the rug.* That's how the editor's column in the *German Publishers Weekly* opened in the edition of October 12, 1990, reporting on the Fair. The article began with the comment that just begged to be negated: *I am really stupid.*

In order to clarify whom he considered to be stupid, he skillfully set the scene to point out the person who had made outrageous comments and against whom people should direct their outrage: *That's the way it is—the Fair director Peter Weidhaas will say.* To remove any hint of being merely speculative, he quickly claimed: *What do the words 'will say' mean here? He's already done it. What's going on? Naturally it's the distribution of the book stalls in the new halls.*

And now he showed what he really meant to say. First he put himself in the place of the public: *I don't understand how such a red carpet in front of the ground floor of Hall 4 should signal to me that I am in the area for the general public....*

And in general, I can't make any sense of my having to come here in a trip taking hours in order to, let's say, look in on the twelve most important German publishing houses of belles-lettres.

What's more, for more than a dozen years the management of the Fair—which has always been pretty good in philosophy—has been talking about the Fair of the short paths. I had understood this as a compelling argument against the bellyaching about the Moloch of Frankfurt, about the 'gigantomania.' Now this philosophy has been turned upside down. By having the supposedly logical subdivision of the Fair into a general public area and a professional area, the Fair of the long paths is now perfect. That seems to be the new philosophy and therefore O.K. Or is it?

One more thing. Let me imagine that I am a publisher of children's books (and also an art book publisher) in Hall 1, and now I'm cut off from the rest of the book world—I am someone who finds it especially important to have contacts with foreign colleagues. How is it that I am 20 minutes away from the French—which, by the way, is the amount of time that it takes the Frankfurt intra-city railroad to go from Frankfurt to the Taunus mountain suburbs or for the inter-city train to go to Wiesbaden?

The article finally came to an end with quotations from publishers, who all shared the opinion of Hanns Lothar Schütz expressed in this way: *Dear Mr. Schütz, You are not stupid at all. All of us here have been double-crossed.*

A real hatchet job by the editor-in-chief, presented as a polemic that would gather up all the opponents of the restructuring of the Fair, provocative in its tone, overall quite emotional—hats off for cunning!

When I got the article in my country house in the Rhön, where I had repaired the day after the closing of this very strenuous Fair, I wasn't concerned with the literary analysis of this sorry effort. I was really irritated, and I wondered how this article could find its way into the *German Publishers Weekly*.

That this could have been the malice of this man, who here once again was working off old wounds—that was not a thought that I entertained. Or that he was serving people who undoubtedly were among those who were affected in this restructuring. There were always people who were affected whenever there was a change at the Fair.

That's the way it probably was—Hanns Lothar was here

sticking a knife into someone in the same way that people had always stuck a knife into him. Here he could at least once be on the side of those who were outraged. And there definitely was outrage among some well-known representatives of the Publishers Association.

The urge to hunt the hare is hot! And so if the hunt is now on, I have to strike some blows and perform some pirouettes so that the eagerness for the hunt does not fade too quickly. That's how I began my response titled *The Structure of the Fair: On Rabbits and Attack Dogs and the True Problems of the Book Fair*, which I pecked out the next day on my old Olympia typewriter in my house in the Rhön. I tried to clarify as well as I could what lay behind the planning and behind all the slogans. I didn't cover up any mistakes (such as in the numbering of the various groups in Hall 1). Of course, I couldn't refrain from including a certain polemical return fire in my opening sentence: *The attack dogs in the pack of hounds, obviously obeying their natural instinct to attack below the belt, should be forewarned. When you're out in front like this, you too easily lose sight of the general picture. But the general picture should be the one that the head of such an "information" organ as the* Publishers Weekly *should take to heart, even if some other approach generates a lot of merriment.*

The editorial board of the *German Publishers Weekly* had this opinion article accompanied by some voices of outraged publishers under the title *The Fair Management Comes Up Helpless*. The real answer to my article appeared some two issues later in the form of a long letter from a reader, *Criticism of the Sun King*, from a certain Dieter Curth, by profession a literary adviser and literature scout. As far as I could tell, he was not known to anybody in the industry. I therefore assumed that this letter had been engineered, perhaps even written, by Hanns Lothar himself, or at the very least arranged or ordered by him, since the author, like Hanns Lothar, miraculously touched on a host of points for which one needed to have insider knowledge.

In all the years that I had belonged to this Association, I had never once experienced a situation where somebody from the industry poured out such malice as did this letter to the editor, purportedly from Mr. Curth.

Regarding my comments about the use of Hall 1: *What*

trivial chatter about a fantastic buck that the Exposition and Fair Company has bagged.

Regarding discussions with foreign exhibitors: *Here our honored Fair director zooms from stall to stall, asking, "Hello. How are you doing?" "Quite well, thank you," and then he hurries off to the next stall to get a similarly acute positive response.*

Regarding the book retailers: *On the next day he should have been able to connect with a book dealer who wanted to order. Then our esteemed Fair Director would have gotten a taste of his own medicine by seeing what the working people of the Fair have to go through. Yet, how could you stand to spend all day with such a pompous stylist?*

Regarding informal discussion in the bars in the evenings: *Perhaps he met one of the hundreds of glory-seeking foreigners, who after the fifth glass of beer had forgotten his aching feet and all the deadlines that had been missed, and didn't exactly know whom he was chatting with.*

Regarding the German Publishers Association Center and the exhibitors from East Germany: *Sensitivity and flexibility don't seem to characterize the Frankfurt apparatchiks, best represented by Mr. Weidhaas, people who are mired in self-satisfaction.*

And regarding the general public and in general: *And how would our Sun King of the Exposition and Fair Company respond to criticism? A quick prayer to Cologne, Dusseldorf, Berlin and, amazingly enough, to Leipzig, which in general should pose a much more imminent threat to Frankfurt. After all, the book fair companies would like to have a coherent design for a professional book fair, a design that has no use for souvenir bags and brochures that have proved so attractive to people living in neighboring countries.*

This letter to the editor didn't contain anything concrete—it was just a very emotional roundhouse punch! A person completely unknown to me, a professional involved in the Book Fair (if he actually was such), and not really an exhibitor who was affected, poured buckets of aggressive criticism over me. What interests of his had I harmed? Who could react in such an exaggerated manner? Didn't some deep pain flash across the skies here?

The fact is, Hanns Lothar had this letter to the editor waiting in the pipeline on the day prior to a business meeting of the management of the German Publishers Association, where we were trying to make sense of his "Am I stupid?" article; we were trying to have a discussion to clear the air. At that time he did not utter a single syllable about the "Sun King" letter to the editor.

It was also a fact that on the day after the appearance of the letter I received a note of apology that was so typical of Schütz's behavior: *Dear Peter: After the meeting on Monday we parted— shall we say—amicably. At that time I was already regretting the publication of the letter to the editor from Dieter Curth. And I really want to point out, something I want to emphasize, that I do not share and do not stand for the contents of the reply by Curth. There is really no truth to the claim that is going around that I instigated this letter. I know Mr. Curth only slightly, and I have not spoken to him or seen seen him for a number of years.*

Now came the true grounds for this unholy campaign unleashed by Hanns Lothar: *It certainly doesn't make much sense to rehash again and again what has happened in the past...but we should recall what happened some time ago. It so happened that the editorial board and the Fair Company, represented by you, were "one heart and one mind." After all, I occasionally participated in your meetings, and I was even once invited to your company Christmas party. Those were the times—and please, don't misunderstand this as pure nostalgia—when we learned from the competing* Book Report, *that it was just this very publication you displayed in Leipzig on your stand. And you did not look to our* German Publishers Weekly *to find out what the editors thought about the course of your fair.*

He could not have said this more clearly. He felt that we had not taken him seriously enough, and besides that, at the Leipzig Book Fair in 1990, we had allowed the *Book Report,* his arch enemy, to publish material about what was happening in our society.

Whatever the reasons for Schütz's behavior in this affair, with the semi-official *Publishers Weekly* taking a position on changes in the Fair, he had presented the arguments of those exhibitors involved in this set-to with the Fair management. Nobody was prepared to be "double-crossed," even if we ourselves vehemently rejected this notion. After all, even the official organ of the organizer had recognized what was going on!

It is true, as we admitted, we had neglected in our plans to give a description of the reshaped design for the fairgrounds that was truly comprehensible. That still did not justify attacking the new arrangements with a few arid catchwords like "division of the exhibit levels" and "we are rolling out the red carpet for the public." The "new Fair" could not be experienced as a true improvement either by the users or by the visitors to the Fair.

The temporary disadvantages that always arise with a required restructuring and that included organizational mistakes and inconsistencies, as formulated by the *German Publishers Weekly,* began to dominate the discussions. We had very little to defend ourselves with, since we did not have any experiences from the past, nor could we grab hold of any positive picture for this new arrangement of the Fair.

Did we still have any chance of making up for what we had missed?

No, we had no chance any longer! Because of the explicit formulation by the *German Publishers Weekly,* this problem was taken out of our hands and moved into the sphere of the association politics. We no longer had any possibility of solving the conflict with our own means, as shown by the letter from the Mme Chairperson of the German Publishers Association to the chairperson of our Supervisory Board on December 19, 1990:

... the average member does not understand this battle of gladiators, since the Exposition and Fair Company and the German Publishers Association are understood to be the same institution. This discussion is seen as a failure of the management board of the Publishers Association, which does not seem able to create a uniform mode of proceeding to achieve its goals, and thus to give evidence of its competence. This entire affair affects not only Mr. Weidhaas, but also the Supervisory Board of the Exposition and Fair Company and indirectly the board of the German Publishers Association.

The Neverending Rushdie Affair

We at the Exposition and Fair Company gradually began to prepare what later filled the pages of the newspapers under the title of "The Rushdie Affair at the Book Fair." The other media followed suit, and this entire experience was soon to pose a severe existential threat to the Frankfurt Book Fair and to me personally.

On February 21, 1990, the Supervisory Board of the Fair Company reaffirmed its resolution that *Iran should be excluded from the Frankfurt Book Fair until the threat of assassination against Rushdie and his publishers and book dealers is withdrawn.* I made a suggestion that went even further to the effect that the domestic and foreign publishing houses at the Frankfurt Book Fair should be urged to make a statement of solidarity with Salman Rushdie and solicited to support the exclusion of Iran. The members of the Board were skeptical about this suggestion and did not approve it, since the reactions might be counterproductive. Apparently the Supervisory Board feared that if the Book Fair were as a whole to take on responsibility for the exclusion of Iran, this would set a precedent for many other requests for exclusion that had come in.

The Supervisory Board at this time did not know that the director of the Culture Department of the Foreign Office in Bonn, Dr. Barthold C. Witte, had several times asked me, albeit somewhat hesitantly, to change our policy toward Iran. In addition, the Iranian Embassy had telephoned me several times to protest the exclusion. On May 9, 1990, Dr. Witte asked the Supervisory Board of the Fair Company to rethink its negative attitude regarding Iranian participation in Frankfurt, especially in light of the changes noted by the Foreign Office in Iranian behavior since the death of Ayatollah Khomeini in 1989. On May

21, 1990, the Supervisory Board took up this letter. It welcomed the declared softening of the previous hard line of the Iranian representative, but at the same time it emphasized that it would have to wait awhile to observe the promised new behavior. That is the sense of the response that was sent to Dr. Witte the next day.

On June 13, 1990, the cultural attaché of the Iranian Embassy, Mr. Faridzadeh, came to see me together with a Dr. Amirplio, who acted as a translator, in order to discuss the lifting of the exclusion order and the possible participation of Iran in the Frankfurt Book Fair in 1990. It is worth providing details of this particular conversation since all the subsequent conversations with Iranian officials, including those held in Tehran, hardly differed from this one.

At the very beginning, the bearded Mr. Faridzadeh declared in the name of the Islamic Republic of Iran its interest in participating in the Frankfurt Book Fair in 1990: "Allow me to point out in this connection that five West German publishing houses have exhibited at the Tehran Book Fair, and that Iran itself has been invited to and has participated in other cultural events in London and Paris, as well as at film weeks in France, Switzerland and Italy."

I answered: "My dear sir, you know as well as I do what the problem is that has led to the exclusion of Iran from the Frankfurt Book Fair. We shouldn't beat around the bush! It is the threat of murder hanging over Salman Rushdie, which continues to be in force.

"Through this threat against Rushdie and his publishers and book dealers, Iran has not only made a decision that is counter to Islamic tenets, but has also created a set of circumstances that affects the basic principles of our culture, namely, the freedom of expression. In this century the Frankfurt Book Fair exists in a country that has had the bitter experience of having once suffered the loss of these principles, and it brings a special sensitiveness to this situation. The resolution of our Supervisory Board, which is still in force, says that Iran will be excluded from the Fair as long as the official call for execution against Rushdie remains in force. On the other hand, I won't try to conceal the fact that on our side there is a great interest in finding a solution that will allow Iran to participate in the Frankfurt Book Fair as soon as possible."

My counterpart smiled at me and leaned over slightly: "Since you, my dear sir, refer to historical events, allow me to point out that the principle of freedom of expression is hardly to be attributed to a particular cultural area. The tolerance represented by Islam is unparalleled in the history of the West. I only have to refer to the Crusades to show how the Western world of that time behaved in such a vile manner."

He leaned back onto my pale leather sofa, while Dr. Amirplio translated into flawless German the arguments just given. His dark and penetrating glance, though not an unfriendly one, did not leave me for a moment. "What the Rushdie case involves," he continued once again leaning forward, "I would not like to discuss with you here at length, since that would be a discussion about Islamic law. I consider that to be irrelevant to a political decision, which is what I consider the decree of the Frankfurt Book Fair to be. Besides, the Rushdie affair does not exist as a political problem for Iran.

"If people on your side are going to weigh in for freedom of expression, shouldn't you then give Iran the opportunity to state its position at the Book Fair? That's the only way that one can assure a true exchange of opinions. Or do you think otherwise?"

Although on this one point I basically agreed with Mr. Faridzadeh, he went on, without waiting for an answer. "In this connection, Mr. Weidhaas, I can assure you that we abide by German laws absolutely and this..."

I dared to interrupt him at this point, "But that has not always been the case in the past!"

Unperturbed, he continued, "...and will continue to do so in the future. Besides, I would like once more to point out that Rushdie is a British citizen, and the London Book Fair has invited Iran to participate. There is consequently no reason for the Frankfurt Book Fair to exclude Iran."

I looked over at my assistant Klaus Stahler, who was then bent way over his writing pad in order to keep an exact record of this conversation. I was familiar with this type of two-sided monologue from my numerous negotiations with the Eastern

Bloc, particularly in the former Soviet Union, and now from my side started in on my answering monologue. "Mr. Faridzadeh, as I already pointed out to you, as a German institution, the Frankfurt Book Fair has a special responsibility in light of its own history to maintain freedom of expression and freedom of publication. The decisions of other book fairs cannot therefore serve as a guideline for our internal considerations.

"It also is a fact that any change in our decision at this time will meet with great misunderstanding among the book dealers and publishers who also have been affected by the threat. They too would identify any possible Iranian bookstall unambiguously with the death sentence."

The cultural attaché became very animated. "I think, Mr. Weidhaas, that you are confusing the issues. The Ayatollah Khomeini pronounced the legal decision not as the head of state, but as an Islamic scholar. That means that the opinion that he has pronounced as a scholar continues to stand and may not be retracted. That however does not mean that the government of Iran as a country has sentenced Rushdie to death." And then the cultural attaché suddenly sat upright on my sofa. His voice lost his diplomatic restraint as he added. "Or do you think that if someone really wanted to kill Rushdie, then wouldn't it simply have been done, and the affair kept secret?"

I was suddenly overwhelmed as images shot through my head, but I attempted to continue the conversation with that same stoic composure that an exchange of this sort demands. "The dichotomy that you make here between state and religion, between Khomeini as an Islamic scholar and Khomeini as head of state, is really only a theoretical point. It is obvious that Iran has in no way distanced itself from this threat; to the contrary, the threat has been approved both by Khamenei[1] and by Rafsanjani.[2]"

"Here once again you are misinformed," my interlocutor interrupted me. "There never was an express confirmation, but only a response to a hypothetical question that was posed

---

1. Grand Ayatollah Ali Hoseyni Khāmene'ī (b. 1939) became the Supreme Leader of Iran in 1989.
2. Ayatollah Ali Akbar Hāshemī Rafsanjānī (b. 1934): Politician, writer former President of Iran (1989–1997).

to them. Both of them merely said that they considered that Khomeini's legal comment was correct.

"Moreover, the Islamic World Conference has explicitly confirmed that Salman Rushdie is an apostate, which *de facto* is a death sentence. Anyone with any experience in Islam can confirm this. And one more thing. The problem exists that Khomeini's verdict has been pronounced and can no longer be retracted."

The sophistry of this line of arguing put me in a tizzy. Wearily, I dug in my heels. "Mr. Faridzadeh, none of this alters the fact that you as a state have not distanced yourself from calling for a murder of a citizen of another state, something that is contrary to international law. Exclusion from our Book Fair affects you as the state of Iran." I didn't see any sense in continuing the discussion any longer and brought it to a conclusion. "Mr. Faridzadeh and Dr. Amirplio, let me in closing give you a vision, my wish for the future. My wish would be to organize an open discussion at the Frankfurt Book Fair between Salman Rushdie and a high-ranking Islamic scholar."

As he slowly rose from the sofa, the cultural attaché of the Iranian Embassy concluded with words that surprised me, but which were really quite absurd, given the actual situation. "We are not so very far from that. Iran can certainly consider such an event!"

After this statement, I stayed in my office with my assistant, but I was absolutely at a loss for words.

Iran was not admitted to the 43rd Frankfurt Book Fair in 1990. In the meantime, however, the game of using the author as a political football continued. At Christmas, in 1990, Rushdie made a desperate attempt to get his head out of the news by distancing himself from the "blasphemous" statements in his *Satanic Verses*.

Dr. Hesham El-Essawy, chairman of the Islamic Society for Religious Tolerance, expressed the view that Rushdie's declaration had under Islamic law "wiped the slate clean," but on December 25th the official Iranian news agency rejected the attempt at reconciliation and said that the death sentence was irrevocable."

At the same time, Rushdie's Western supporters reacted

quite angrily. With this gesture he had sold himself to the devil of these "potential murderers" and had betrayed his friends by "embracing a bigoted religion," one that called upon its supporters to kill a writer for what he had written. The English playwright Arnold Wesker called Rushdie's attempted reconciliation a victory for religious terrorism. The greatest sensation came in the reaction of the viewpoint of the former Oxford Professor of Law Francis Bennion, who resigned from the Rushdie defense committee. He called Rushdie a coward and a traitor to intellectual freedom, and proclaimed that a man like Rushdie was "not worth defending."

Rushdie gave up the attempt to reconcile with his persecutors, but he also lost the support of the Western literary commentators. Even the attacks on the Japanese and Italian translators of *The Satanic Verses* in the early summer of 1991 only merited short notices in the newspapers of the Western world.

It was only our admittance of several Iranian publishing houses to the Book Fair in 1991 that revived the public discussion about the Rushdie affair. Here is how it came about—In January 1991, we at the Exposition and Fair Company ran into a problem of authority that at first glance had nothing to do with the Rushdie affair. For several decades the management board of the German Publishers Association had a consulting subcommittee for foreign commerce, which found its role in setting up and administering a program required by the Foreign Office titled "Export Promotion Program for Eastern Europe." Deliveries to the Socialist state trading agencies were supported by public subsidies in the form of a 15% discount from the retail price, a program intended to expand the import of German books by those centrally managed commercial institutions by 15%.

Now that the Eastern European system had collapsed and the central purchasing organizations had been eliminated, this program was no longer feasible and had to be scrapped. This robbed the foreign trade committee of its most important task, and an internal discussion about its mission and purpose began.

Until now the Exposition and Fair Company had looked after practically 80% of all foreign activities of the German Publishers Association. The sitting chairman of the committee, Claus

Michaletz, who was the CEO of the scientific Julius Springer publishing house, was of the opinion that all the foreign activities of the German Publishers Association should be concentrated in the Exposition and Fair Company, since the company's required foreign experience and knowledge of languages could be used for foreign work. In the end Michaletz got his way.

Henceforth I was the person responsible in the German Publishers Association for the work of the foreign trade committee, and in my new function I traveled on January 21, 1991, to the Foreign Office in Bonn in the company of Mme Chairwoman and Claus Michaletz of the German Publishers and Booksellers Association. We were to negotiate an alternate use for the almost 2 million Marks that were now available after the cancellation of the cultural promotion program.

It was not a complete surprise that Dr. Witte opened the meeting with a question about the participation of Iran in the Frankfurt Book Fair in 1991. He made it quite clear that the Foreign Office would "very much welcome" the re-admittance of the Iranian exhibitors. If you are not familiar with the way diplomatic language is used, here is the message loud and clear: the Foreign Office was striving for an improvement of relations with post-Khomeini Iran, and the attitude of the Frankfurt Book Fair was an obstacle on the path to completing a very important opening for economic policy, an obstacle that had to be removed. This situation gave the perfect opportunity. The German Publishers Association had arrived as a supplicant.

I had not gone into this meeting completely naïvely. Once again, it was the classic conflict between the Exposition and Fair Company and the German Publishers Association over the Frankfurt Book Fair. The Association never faced up to this situation, and as a result the arguments involved always took a personal tone. The solutions that were sought for these conflicts therefore always missed the point entirely.

In thinking over the delicate situation and the analysis of the course of the Rushdie affair, I began to consider the most important factors (which I broached with my executive colleagues) to be the following:

- Boycotting Iran had in no way changed Rushdie's situation.

- The general media had lost interest in Rushdie.
- The principle of absolute freedom of opinion at the Frankfurt Book Fair had been broken.
- With the boycott of Iran, we ourselves were boycotting all those Iranians who did not identify with the *fatwa*.
- Could a relaxation of relations move the state of Iran to distance itself from the *fatwa*?
- Would a visit to Iran, perhaps to the Tehran book fair, be useful for discussions with governmental authorities?

Speaking with hindsight, I don't want to make the decision seem better than it was. The ideas listed here allowed us to maintain that our acquiescence to the wishes of the Foreign Office was not an inevitable retreat from our philosophy of the Fair, but instead strengthened our belief that another path must be taken that could fulfill our commitments to Rushdie and to international public opinion. It was obvious that we could not avoid a conflict of interest. I therefore suggested (in the presence of the chairperson and the chairman of the foreign trade committee) to the gentlemen of the Foreign Office that we not admit the state of Iran, but that instead we would not refuse permission to "private publishing houses" that applied for admission.

Since the Iranian Vice-Foreign Minister was expected in Bonn in a few days, I needed to get the written agreement of all the members of the Supervisory Board to this suggestion (there was no time for a meeting). I informed them on January 22, 1991, in a note that included the following comment: *The executive management of the Exposition and Fair Company approves the readmission of private exhibitors from Iran. We will continue to prevent participation of the state itself, that is, a large Iranian national book stall, in order not to completely lose our credibility.*

It is true that the death sentence continues to be a fact—and, as you know, on theological grounds it is apparently irrevocable—still, for a number of months more moderate tones from the Iranian officials have been perceptible....

With the sole exception of Ulrich Staudinger, head of the Schneekluth Verlag, all the members of the Supervisory Board immediately agreed to this solution. Mme Chairwoman, who had discussed this issue with the head of the publishing committee, also signaled her approval. If necessary, one of the members of the Supervisory Board would even allow in the Iranian state publishing house. After a truly lively discussion on February 20, 1991, the 95th meeting of the Supervisory Board supported the written resolution that had been submitted. Mr. Staudinger once again registered his "decided protest."

As if on cue, the Foreign Office on March 14, 1991, sent me an invitation to travel to Tehran with a high-ranking German delegation. Ministerial Counselor Dr. Witte informed us that the two Foreign Ministers in Bonn agreed on closer relations between Germany and Iran, in particular in the area of cultural and scientific cooperation. He wanted me very much to participate in the discussions, along with the president of the Goethe Institute and the representatives of the German Academic Exchange Service and the Archaeological Institute. On April 27th we flew to Tehran. On April 28th I met with the Assistant Minister of Culture Zangeneh to discuss the topic of "Rushdie," which was so important to me. The Minister was surrounded by a whole group of bearded men, mainly younger ones, among whom I recognized only Mr. Karbaji, who was responsible for the Tehran book fair.

The relatively free conversation proceeded in a similar fashion to the one I described above with the people from the embassy. We devoted ourselves for more than three hours to the Rushdie Question; nothing was left out. The cultural attaché of the German Embassy, whom I had invited to be present as a witness to this conversation, that evening confirmed to the head of our delegation my "courageous addressing of all the problems relating to Rushdie." Nonetheless, my hope of achieving some kind of distancing of the Iranian state authorities from the *fatwa* was disappointed. And not only my hope, but also that of Salman Rushdie, whom I had talked to at the beginning of April regarding my imminent trip and who had advised me in a subsequent telephone conversation how to go about it.

The problems were clearly stated, and it is true that I did not come only as a supplicant, but I also offered something in return. Still, nothing moved. I was quite frustrated and considered leaving early. On the next day, however, my resignation turned to anger when, before the beginning of the discussions in the Ministry, I received a draft of the minutes of the discussions that we had held the previous day. I decided not only to leave, but also not even to sign this paper. The text here was of common problems that we had discussed. Not one time did the contentious word "Rushdie" appear, even though the entire conversation had revolved around him.

At the end of another five-hour meeting in the Ministry, chaired by the less influential Mr. Karbaji, who was primarily interested in getting an agreement about his own fair completely wrapped up, I informed them that I was leaving that same evening.

At 8:30 in the evening, negotiations started up once again in the lobby of the Esteghlal Hotel, in which our delegation was being put up. We continued to discuss my signing the minutes that had been set up by the Iranians. What happened on that evening is among one of the most unpleasant encounters that I have ever experienced. It was not only the opposing side that I had to watch out for! I began to feel sorry for Mr. Karbaji, who clearly was under great internal pressure and was acting ever more nervous and agitated. The heads of the German delegation, Dr. Witte and Dr. Truhart, prowled around me. They didn't want to put any direct pressure on me, but they made it absolutely clear that my behavior in this situation would have a decisive influence on the success or failure of the mission. And what would Mr. Rushdie care if he was named or not named in an official German–Iranian position paper? I found myself in a ticklish situation. I had walked along the path to an opening to Iran, and had allowed myself at least partially to be part of German foreign policy (on whatever grounds). I had not come one millimeter closer to the goal of my engagement.

Time was running out. The taxi was standing at the door to take me to the airport. I saw my counterpart standing there sweating, the pages of the minutes in his hand. I knew that Mr. Karbaji had no authority to change the current version of the minutes. At a distance I saw the gentlemen from the Foreign Office waiting anxiously. I ripped the papers out of Karbaji's hand, signed them, and stormed out of the hotel meeting room

It was midnight. At 1:50 AM I left Tehran, and at 7:20 AM the plane landed in Frankfurt.

In May, I sent my colleague Helmut von der Lahr to Tehran to undertake a technical analysis of the book fair there. He did it with the energy so characteristic of him: structure, flows, logistics, exhibit halls, attention to exhibitors, advertising details, catalog—all of these had to be reviewed and discussed. An ordering and purchasing process that was absurdly complicated had to be simplified. From weaknesses and glaring defects in the electrical system through floor coverings down to the directional system—all these had to be set. Many hours were devoted to the aspects of advertising and exhibitor information as well as to the quality of the services at the fair.

More than my own brief contacts, often limited to officials, Helmut's descriptions of the hunger of the Iranian intellectuals for enlightenment, which he ran into at this fair, strengthened our notion that a partial opening to Iran could not be limited simply to the Frankfurt Book Fair. His impressions were similar to the experiences of the international exhibitors, a group which included large delegations from such publishers as Elsevier, Kluwer, McGraw-Hill, Prentice-Hall, Simon & Schuster, and Springer. It was clear that such an opening would have to be worked into Iran with many products of Western publishing houses.

What was later mocked scornfully by the press as a mere defensive argument on my part—namely, the reference to the dire cultural situation of people who had been educated at German universities—stemmed from descriptions by the German Embassy in Tehran, but even more from the impressive report from von der Lahr. The people whom he met were primarily scientists and physicians, who complained bitterly about the Federal Republic of Germany: "We were worth millions and billions to you when you gave us higher education. *Now you are letting us starve culturally!*"

After my report on the trip to Tehran, on June 5, 1991, the Supervisory Board again approved the path that we had carved out to a partial opening to Iran. Once again, Mr. Staudinger bowed to the vote of the executive committee only under protest.

Nothing changed in the mainstream media. Even the deadly attack on the Japanese translator of Rushdie, Hitoshi Igarashi, and the similar attack two weeks earlier on the Italian translator Alberto Capriolo, fortunately without mortal result, were mentioned only in passing by the media. We prepared ourselves for the next Book Fair, conscious of the fact that the entire Iran–Rushdie problem had been reduced from our many earlier experiences down to the "Third World" problem set. Eugen E., press spokesman for the German Publishers Association, arranged a protest letter from the president of the Association to the German Foreign Minister Genscher regarding the attacks on the translators, and this proved a welcome opportunity to once again call in the Iranian Ambassador. However, none of this changed the generally uninterested climate of opinion.

It was at that time that this same Ambassador, his Excellency Seyed Hossein Mousavian, came to my office with two other persons on August 19, 1991. We were particularly astonished upon greeting them when he intentionally ignored the outstretched hand of my assistant Susanne Schulz, who was in charge of taking minutes. At the end of the conversation he expressly begged our pardon, but "on religious grounds it was not possible for him to shake the hand of the assistant to the director."

In an attempt to salvage something from this not very impressive conversation, I asked the Ambassador to send us in writing some of the key points that he made there. These came to us the next day by fax.

In point one of the letter, the Ambassador repeated the arguments that we were already familiar with, that the "legal judgment" had nothing to do with Iran as a country, but then the essential points came:

1. *The Islamic Republic of Iran is of the opinion that states and peoples should mutually respect each others' opinions and should avoid forcing their own opinions on others.*
2. *Our international relationships rest on the following principles:*
   – *Respect for the provisions of the rights of peoples*
   – *Respect for the internal laws and regulations of each state*
   – *Non-interference in the internal affairs of other countries*

- *Mutual respect for the opinions and convictions of people, and avoidance of any insult to the values and religions of other peoples*

3. *The Islamic Republic of Iran was the first victim of terrorism in the world and decidedly opposes any type of terrorism in the entire world. In the past ten years many senior political and religious personalities in Iran, including the president of the state, parliamentary representatives, several ministers and hundreds of citizens, have been victims of terrorist attacks.*

Signature: S.H. Mousavian. (Seal of the Embassy.)

Was this the promise that Iran would distance itself from the *fatwa*? Was His Excellency simply lying, or did he not know better? Was all of Western public opinion simply on the wrong track? I could make neither rhyme nor reason of this, and simply filed the letter away.

At the end of August, Jürgen Schultheis, a freelance journalist who also wrote for the *Frankfurter Rundschau*, showed up at our office. Schultheis was known to us as a careful researcher and a serious author, and so I had no special reservations about discussing the topic of the year and Rushdie with him as he desired. I thought that a slow preparation of the public for the Fair, which was so unpredictable, could be of use in this month and a half before the event.

The article appeared on August 30, 1991, in the *Frankfurter Rundschau*, under the title *The Book Fair Readmittance of Iranian Publishers*, followed by the sub-title, *although the death sentence against Rushdie is still in effect*. In his article, Schultheis tried to get the opinion of various persons, whom he then cited: the publishers Klaus Wagenbach and Michael Naumann, the later state minister, approved the decision of the Fair management, while the political scientist Claus Leggewie spoke out loud and clear in favor of the boycott. The most fateful position, however was that of the vice president of the German PEN Club, Carola Stern, who did not restrain herself merely to sharp words of disapproval in the newspaper, but immediately sent a notice to all the members of the German PEN Club and to the newspapers on her distribution list. She demanded the exclusion of the Iranian publishing houses from the Frankfurt Book Fair that year. As she put it in the letter: *As long as the death sentence against Salman Rushdie is not revoked, any business with official Iranian publishers has the moral equivalence of arms dealing.*

Ms. Stern attacked me personally as the director of the Book Fair, and warned against regarding the Fair as simply an economically useful exposition for the book market. Every year many countries who practiced censorship and repression against authors and publishers were in residence at the Fair. In that sense nobody could talk about a fair with complete freedom of opinion, but state terrorism in the form of an expressly globally valid call for execution could not be the background for good business relationships, and would be a total novelty in the history of the Frankfurt Book Fair: *If this were to occur, the rich tradition of a meeting of literature, science, journalism and politics would give up its moral authority.*

With that formulation, the pugnacious lady struck at the heart of my understanding of the Fair. For decades I had carried out successfully a difficult balancing act between the economic success of the Fair and the culturally and politically ambitious consciousness of its participants.

The focal themes on Latin America, Black Africa and India, my attempts to draw the information-poor have-nots of the Southern and Eastern worlds into this highly commercialized book fair, the founding and maintenance of the Society for the Promotion of Literature from Africa, Asia and Latin America, my personal intervention for persecuted and jailed authors and publishers, some of whom I was able to get out of jail—all these things were aimed at a goal of creating an image of this hard-nosed business fair that would allow its participants to see themselves as part of an open, international communication process, and to see this as a value in itself. This was not simply a hypocritical front, but something that actually occurred, though with certain restrictions that have already been addressed.

I was deeply hurt. After all, this concerned the essential self-image of our Fair as a cultural and business meeting place for all those people in the world who concern themselves with the creation and publication of the printed word.

I had always been of the opinion that the successful image of this fair had to be formed in two places, in the profit and loss statements of the exhibiting publishers and in the heads of those people who created public opinion. That is why, since taking over responsibility for this unique instrument, I had always acted and thought on two fronts for its further development—on the one hand, for an improvement of business functionality through the new directional systems, creation of special interest centers, shortening of paths within the fair area; and on the other, the building up of the Fair's own expert press office, the presentation of topics of public interest not directly linked to special business interests, and broad cultural programs.

Later, when the controversy that was now brewing really came out in the open, some people from the German Publishers Association reproached me with the accusation that I had interfered in the publicity affairs of the Association. It was said that I had declared independence from any authority and had conducted "a self-centered and aggressive campaign to exclude the German Publishers Association" (direct quote from the spokesman of the Association).

This background story, and the knowledge that the campaign unleashed by Ms. Stern involved an attack on the cornerstone of our Fair policy, should make clear why I did not step out of the line of fire by simply referring everything to the German Publishers Association. Besides, there was nobody in the Publishers Association who could now handle such an explosive topic. There was simply nobody else familiar enough with the Rushdie question and who had a very strong opinion about it.

In hindsight, everybody knew that perhaps we should not have gone about it in this way. Twice during the debate I asked the general manager where the management board stood on this affair. Twice I was answered unambiguously that the president had no opinion on the matter! Well, there was no other way of going about it. In addition, the newspaper articles that now appeared were directed almost exclusively at me as the director of the Fair, whom they correctly assumed to be the originator of the decision to readmit the Iranian publishing houses.

The fireworks began on September 5, 1991 with a commentary in the *Frankfurter Allgemeine Zeitung* (FAZ) by Frank Schirrmacher, who classified my attitude toward Rushdie as part of the public ritual of an appeal meant merely to salve one's conscience. It was deemed improper to question such an attitude, but he, Mr. Schirrmacher, was now doing so, and very publicly at that.

On September 12th, Rolf Michaelis followed with an emotion-laden article in *Die Zeit: Rushdie is still being hunted, while Iranian publishers are in Frankfurt—The shame of the Book Fair.*

This article was extremely influential on further developments of the affair because it completely emotionalized the argument, and in a similar emotional manner made the German Publishers Association and the publishers all equally guilty. "What is the name of those putting on the program?" asked Michaelis disingenuously in the first line of his article. He then went on to give the answer himself: *The German Publishers and Booksellers Association is called the Börsenverein.* ["Verein" in German means association and "Börse" also means purse.] *Suddenly its true character is revealed. It's the money* [Börse] *that counts. Books and literature and perhaps morals? The German publishers and book dealers don't give a damn about such lofty things once they come out of the Frankfurt St. Paul's Church, having soothed their consciences.... I would have expected a different attitude from German publishers. Naturally book publishers have to know how to read not only books but also financial statements. Naturally they have to do good business—even with a state that declares a death sentence on writers.*

I was quite appalled. Had I at that time known what I know today, that such an emotional public expression of opinion can no longer be influenced or modified, then I would have said to myself, "That's the way it goes—let it be," and would have taken myself out of the media discussion.

Nevertheless, we at the Fair Company still believed that our own arguments were convincing. All we had to do was to get a hearing for them in the media. Our press chief Helmut von der Lahr was burning to get into the ring with Rolf Michaelis. On the very next day he presented me with an article and response which was not much less emotional than Michaelis's exposé. *Die Zeit* was ready to publish it in its next issue.

I found the article really worth reading and quite appropriate for its literary rigor and substance, an article that would serve as a tough wedge against the moralizing platitudes of Mr. Michaelis. Even though Lahr's answer verged on being over the top, I was convinced that one could not neutralize Michaelis's challenge with a balanced, relativistic reply, as is often done in public answers. War was being declared, the only way we could get equal time in the public media for our arguments.

The battle never materialized, at least not in *Die Zeit,* since in the meantime Eugen E., press spokesman for the management board of the German Publishers Association, which felt itself challenged, claimed its prerogative for the riposte. I withdrew von der Lahr's article and promised my disappointed fellow warrior that I would get his article published as soon as possible in the opinion column of the *German Publishers Weekly.* Helmut soon had the opportunity to test his strength against Michaelis on television (Hesse Radio Channel 3), something that he did with bravura and conviction. The only drawback was that hardly anybody watched that latenight show.

All the while thunder sounded and lightning flashed in the world of the media. Von der Lahr and I were interviewed daily for several hours by the radio, television, newspapers and magazines. The German Press Agency DPA published the PEN Club opinion of Ms. Stern. There was hardly a member of the media in Germany that did not get involved in reports and commentaries on the admission of the Iranian publishing houses.

We fought on, but from day to day it became clearer and clearer that the two initial emotional formulations by Carola Stern and Rolf Michaelis had won the day in the court of public opinion. We didn't have a chance. Our morale plummeted, so much so that many times, after difficult and exhausting days of studying the press, we asked what actually had happened to us. Whatever we put out to clarify the criteria for decisions by the Fair was met the next day by torrents of indignation in the press.

We did not stand exactly quite alone—the chairman of the Writers Federation, Uwe Friesel, publicly distanced himself from the opinion of the PEN executive committee. In the name of his federation he made it clear that the decision to admit the publishers was correct, perhaps even necessary, and that impermissibly two principles had been mixed together in the argument. Klaus Wagenbach threw the term "hypocrites" at the discussants. Michael Naumann in the FAZ and Peter Schütt in *Die Zeit* tried to moderate the bitterness of the discussion. Rainer Hoffmann attempted to clarify things in the *Neue Züricher Zeitung*, while Jürgen Schultheis presented our arguments in the *Frankfurter Rundschau*.

It was typical. Michael Naumann was torn to pieces by Ulrich Greiner in *Die Zeit;* Peter Schütt was defamed in *Die Welt* as a former member of the Communist Party. *Die Welt* took a "party line," exemplified by Jürgen Serke's editorial on September 28th: *The arguments of the people putting on the Fair come out of the old tired box of East–West relaxation of tensions. Fair director Weidhaas talks about the need for the 'free flow of books,' to the Bahr–Deutsch proposal of Change through Rapprochement.*[3] *And how could it be otherwise, since Weidhaas has on his side the association that in the years before the fall of the Berlin Wall discredited itself, the German Writers Federation. The Board of Directors of the Writers Federation jumps up to side with the producers of the Fair, saying that one should not dis-invite the Iranian publishers. The noble gentlemen of the management board pour out crocodile tears about the 'obscurantist reflex of a medieval theocratic mania,' but they believe that the German Publishers Association has to stick with the principle of 'change through rapprochement,' something that once upon a time ended the Cold War.*

Actually, one could sometimes think that everyone was using the affair to settle accounts with supposed or actual opponents.

In the meantime, startled by the Carola Stern paper, other well-known authors woke up and began to provide their own declamatory contribution for the salvation of Western culture and civilization:

---

3. *i.e., Ostpolitik*—the efforts of West Germany to normalize relations with Eastern Europe.

Günter Grass: *I'm not going to Frankfurt because I consider it disgusting and lacking in solidarity to lift the boycott of the Iranian publishing houses without a credible reason for doing so.*[4]

Hans Magnus Enzensberger: *The fact that the Frankfurt Book Fair is now welcoming Iranian publishing houses, which participated in the murderous witch hunt against Rushdie, can only lead to the conclusion that the Fair direction and the Publishers Association are both of the opinion that sales are more important than the lives of the authors.*[5]

Carl Amery: *Anyone who deals with such publishing houses puts himself on the level of arms dealers and supports the very system that has declared a death sentence on Rushdie.*[6]

Franz Xaver Kroetz: *It is simply indecent to mess around with an indecent, thoroughly theocratic regime, even if only in cultural matters.*[7]

Gabriele Wohmann: *I am shocked how Fair Director Peter Weidhaas has now talked himself into the new situation. He has descended to the level of pure business interests.*[8]

The situation finally came to a head when the big publishing houses of *belles-lettres*, vexed by more than three weeks of an ongoing press campaign, formed a united front and publicly threatened a boycott of the Frankfurt Book Fair. Old Mr. Piper of the Piper Verlag in Munich took the initiative.

Ten days before the opening of the Fair, the president of the Publishers and Booksellers Association received a letter signed by the following: Dr. Wolfgang and Dr. Hans-Dieter Beck (Beck), Dr. Karl H. Blessing (Droemer-Knaur), Ernst and Daniel Brücher (Dumont), Dr. Reinhold Neven DuMont (Kiepenheuer und Witsch), Dr. Klaus and Dr. Ernst Reinhard Piper (Piper), Dr. Michael Naumann (Rowohlt) and Dr. Siegfried Unseld (Suhrkamp):

The undersigned publishers and members of the German Publishers and Booksellers Association find it unbearable that in light

---

4. Günter Grass (b. 1927): Novelist; 1999 Nobel Prize in Literature.
5. Hans Magnus Enzensberger (b. 1929): Novelist and poet; author of *The Consciousness Industry*.
6. Carl Amery (1922–2005): Writer and environmental activist; author of *Capitulation*.
7. Franz Xaver Kroetz (b. 1946): Playwright, actor and director.
8. Gabriele Wohmann (b. 1932): Novelist, short-story writer and essayist.

of the ongoing threat of death against Salman Rushdie and all the translators and distributors of his work The Satanic Verses, *repeated a number of times, that such Iranian publishing houses may be able to exhibit at this year's Frankfurt Book Fair. These publishing houses, directly or indirectly, stand behind the sentence of death; they have supported it and have themselves disseminated it. As far as we are aware, these publishing houses are known to the German Publishers Association or should be so known.*

We, the undersigned publishers, find it impossible to accept in our minds and on the ground any kind of fair collegiality with a country that has decided to mercilessly hound to the very death a writer who with his work has stood for enlightenment and tolerance.

In the name of our ideals of the responsibility of our publishing profession, we therefore urgently ask of the leadership of the Exposition and Fair Company to exclude from the Book Fair any of the Iranian publishing houses incriminated in the Rushdie affair.

The battle was lost! At the moment that this letter surfaced, it was clear to me that our policy had failed and that we would have to beat a retreat. The publishing houses specializing in fiction had always been the public backbone of the Book Fair, quite independent of their economic significance. More and more publishing houses joined in with these opinions and initiatives. The call of the hour was for retreat. We had to save the coming Book Fair. If this attitude were to spread among the publishing houses (and signs were increasing that this was coming to be), the next Book Fair would descend into chaos. Besides that, a kind of whipped up publicity campaign had pre-programmed this storm against exhibiting by the Iranian publishing houses. It should be emphasized here that we had sought out these particular publishers because they belonged to the critical and opposition groups in Iran.

I cautiously began to prepare the policy of retreat, in which I gently dropped some clues that the moment for allowing in the Iranian publishing houses had still not arrived. Each one of my statements in those days brought forth a torrent of commentaries.

A discussion on the crucial topic "What now?" took place at a meeting on September 23rd of the executive committee of the German Publishers Association. The vote that then took place gave a surprising one-vote majority to maintain the admittance of the Iranian publishing houses to the Book Fair. People did not want to be blackmailed by the vagaries of public opinion. At the same time the committee criticized itself. This related to the decision of admitting at least a few Iranian publishing houses, which was considered to be correct, but they had neglected to review this decision properly after the murder in Japan.

At the meeting of the Supervisory Board of the Book Fair Company the next day, September 24, 1991, exactly the opposite happened. Now, by the same slim majority, the members of the Supervisory Board voted in favor of exclusion of the Iranian publishing houses.

On September 26th, the Thursday of the so-called festival week (since one meeting followed the other at the Publishers Association), we arrived at a final decision. Following the meeting of the representatives of the German Publishers Association, a decision was taken by the executive board of the Publishers Association and the Supervisory Board of the Book Fair Company: *In order to assure the ability of the Book Fair to continue in 1991, the Executive Board and the Supervisory Board have decided to revoke the permission given to the Iranian publishing houses to participate in the Book Fair.*

The Book Fair was saved, though a lot of crockery had been broken. Many wounds had been opened among the protagonists in this argument. A perhaps faulty Fair policy had been straightened out now, but many conflicts of interest had been brought to the fore.

Press commentary started to melt away, though once again a bewildering sort of publicity acted like irritating sand in our eyes. Even in the last phase of the hectic public debate, before the public decision of the executive committee in the German Publishers Association, the reproach of a "broken promise" by the Fair management to Salman Rushdie grew louder in the press.

On August 25th, a week before the appearance of the Schultheis article, I asked Rushdie's agent to call me back in Frankfurt in order to tell him about the imminent participation of the Iranian publishing houses in the coming fair. Naturally one could not call him directly, and his return call on August

26th came when I was not in the office. As I had arranged beforehand, Helmut von der Lahr told the writer what was about to unfold.

According to von der Lahr, Rushdie during this conversation expressed his understanding of our decision, but asked us to do everything in our power to prevent the Iranian officials from having any possibility of turning this action into an approval of the Iranian policy toward him.

At a presentation on Fair Saturday that had been planned earlier, we still thought that we could have a public back and forth between the two viewpoints about the Rushdie matter and the cautious opening toward Iran. Frank Berberich, editor of the *Lettre International,* unexpectedly pulled a photocopied letter from his briefcase in which he expressed to the editor his discontent that we had admitted the Iranian publishing houses against his expressed desire.

We had named the presentation "Drawing the correct moral—What now in the Rushdie affair?" It was moderated by Wilfried Schoeller from Hesse Radio, and included Jürgen Schultheis, Klaus Wagenbach, Michael Naumann, Uwe Friesel and Carola Stern. The Iranian poet Mahmoud Dowlatabadi gave an introduction regarding his personal situation as one living and writing in Iran, with a quite sophisticated explanation regarding the invitation to the Iranian publishers.

I spent many weeks trying to get our critics to participate in this presentation—Günter Grass, Hans Magnus Enzensberger, Rolf Michaelis and the nine publicity "matadors" had given us the brush-off, and now, partially resigned but also partially quite angry, I also personally withdrew from this program, which was intended to be the close of the affair.

I saw the "Rushdie letter" for the first time when Carola Stern unfolded it from her pocketbook at a pre-debate meeting in my office of all those participating.

Then on October 11, 1993, the Norwegian publisher William Nygaard of Aschehoug Publishers in Oslo was shot three times on his return trip from the Frankfurt Book Fair. Nygaard, who had published *The Satanic Verses* in Norwegian, was severely wounded.

A year later Nygaard posed some very uncomfortable questions at a press conference at the Book Fair: *How long can democratic countries overlook terrorist activities in their own territories? How long will these countries continue to carry on business activities with those states that control or even tolerate terrorist activities? Is it not the case that ongoing business contacts legitimize terror by the fundamentalists?*

Having been schooled very early on in this business of making the *fatwa* against Rushdie a political football, I was concerned with the politics following the events of September 11, 2001. Could one make an entire people or religious community responsible for the religious terror of specific individuals? If that were the case, one would have to exclude half of mankind, that is, the entire Islamic world. The use of the boycott and of shunning terrorism were very blunt weapons, weapons which did not affect the root cause, but instead affected those people in environments that themselves suffered from terrorism. In this case the enemy was no longer a state or a state community, which is why one could not declare war against terrorism. The common people were not affected by terrorism; only the leading citizens were. Even today, with the lurking fear that Islamic terrorism could take all of mankind hostage, I still think that our decision at that time to seek out a discussion with the Iranian intellectuals and book people was the correct path to tread. Calls for a boycott lead only to the self-satisfaction of those rabble-rousers, who honestly believe that they have accomplished a heroic deed when in our relatively safe public media they denounce the people who think otherwise as "arms dealers."

Of these, I must of course except William Nygaard. After an experience like his, any reaction is understandable. Remember, though, that he had not been a participant in that painful campaign that preceded his awful experience.

Reform by Coup d'état

At three o'clock in the afternoon on March 5, 1992, a vote at a meeting of the publishers committee was taken, ending with 14 ayes, 2 nays and 3 abstentions. The question of the replacement of the Supervisory Board of our Exposition and Fair Company with the executive committee of the German Publishers Association was taken off the table. A request was made that any changes be proposed as part of a package of structural reform.

I could hardly believe it; I did not trust myself to raise my gaze from my hands, which lay folded on the table. I thought how many members of the publishers committee would be looking over at me. I didn't want them to see what was going on in my head at that moment. I also wanted to spare the losers the expression of triumph in my face. And, to be honest, I was dubious that this really spelled the end what had been a grueling five months of extraordinary demands and stubborn resistance. Was this really the end of the siege? I forbid myself any hint of victory.

So much concentrated effort by my opponents in the Publishers Association! So much work in planning, meeting and persuading! Only one week earlier, on February 25, 1992, Mme Chairwoman of the German Publishers Association had attempted in a nine-page letter to beseech "all colleagues" of the delegate assembly not to reject her effort to turn over the Fair Company to the German Publishers Association. This letter marked the final collapse of her efforts. The treasurer reviewed the position of the executive committee of the Publishers Association and once again presented a resolution:

1. *After the end of the current period in office of the members of the Supervisory Board of the Exposition and Fair Company, the executive committee is to turn over the functions of the Supervi-*

sory Board to the following six to seven members of the executive committee: The three members of the executive committee who are publishers and the chairpeople of the specialty committees.
2. The chairperson is to take over the role of chair.
3. The bylaws of the Exposition and Fair Company are to be changed accordingly.
4. This resolution is to be delayed pending the agreement of the Publishers Committee at its next regular meeting and the clarification of the tax implications.

It went on to say that the Rushdie affair in particular had made clear that the communications between the executive committee of the German Publishers Association and the Supervisory Board of the Exposition and Fair Company must be improved, and public relations work in particular needed to be coordinated with each other (the old conflict about relations with the press). Despite the independence of the Exposition and Fair Company, the public relations work was the responsibility of the Publishers Association and therefore had to be taken over completely by the Supervisory Board.

Here it was in black and white. There had been an attempt to rescind the accomplishments of 1964, when the publishing personalities Witsch, Georgi and Metzner wrested control of the Frankfurt Fair office from the narrow-minded, local interest group that was the German Publishers Association. There was no doubt that a restoration of the Association's managerial authority over the Book Fair would ordain that decision-making should proceed according to the "relevance for the Association," and not the real needs of the Fair. For the management of the Exposition and Fair Company and for me personally, this would have been an unforgivable defeat.

The prior Supervisory Board chairman, who had been in office for years, had not accepted this *coup*, and therefore had resigned on December 10, 1991. I too believed that with this new arrangement I would no longer be able to do my job, which is why both internally and in the public press I had made the retraction of this plan a condition for my remaining in the leadership post.

Anyone familiar with the practices of this association knew that this was not a place where people tore each other apart, but rather where people always sought consensus through compromise. That is why at the beginning it was so difficult for me to comprehend the intensive, earnest and issue-oriented discussion that led to a resolution rebuffing all the efforts of the executive committee. All of this is revealed in the minutes of the meeting. It also became clear at that time that the structural reform and the associated plans of a holding company for the other companies of the German Publishers Association would collapse because of insufficient attention to tax issues.

For me the battle was over. The Exposition and Fair Company would remain in the form it had been in previously. I had publicly insisted on three core points to allow me to stay with the company, and every one was accepted. We had won all along the line. This affair was the latest and most vigorous attack on the independence of the Fair Company, whose basic responsibility continued to be the successful development of the Frankfurt Book Fair, no more and no less.

Looking back now with some distance on the autumn and winter of 1991–92, I can better interpret those events, and evaluate the power relations and underlying causes more calmly and more exactly. The historical background is much clearer to me now, as is the personal role of people active in what was in the end a very dramatic showpiece. Certain events, personal sensitivities and contingencies had to come together for a long-standing quarrel over the public relations activities of the company and over other matters to degenerate into a campaign that finally spun out of control.

Once again, here are the rules of governance for what was almost a classic power clash for organizations of our sort:

First of all, there was a national professional association, which sponsored the founding of the Fair, for which the goals were to bring together the domestic economic sector of producers and salespeople; they were to exchange information and to carry out commerce with one another.

Surprisingly, foreign actors began to take a big role in the Fair, and at that time the leading members of the Association—though not without protest from its own members—took the Fair out of the Association and set it up as a company on its own. People were afraid—and rightly so!—that the Association, focused on the particular interests of its members, might stand in the way of the further international development of the Fair. Admittedly, an attempt was made to retain unlimited control over the newly founded company by means of explicitly having the Supervisory Board subject to the Association and by means of a 100% ownership of the company.

They also decided not to give up control of the press and public relations messages of the new child. This was done mainly to save money, but it also served to retain control over the new company. The press department of the Association would continue to be responsible for the public relations work of the new Fair Company! From the point of view of the work of the Fair, this was a halfhearted solution, which later turned out to be completely dysfunctional.

Naturally, the Supervisory Board came to a resolution by unanimous vote. Even today it isn't clear to me exactly what was the source of this manic fear of independent public relations work by the marketing people in our office on Grosser Hirschgraben Street. Apparently it was a deeply entrenched lust for control, coupled with the knowledge that they would have a very poor hand to play if they gave away this trump card.

It was however evident that the activities of the two entities had very different requirements. It was also obvious that the publicity work of the federation could not fulfill the public relations needs of the Exposition and Fair Company, and that the two would eventually conflict. Any reasonable arrangement would therefore have to be based on extricating the press activities of the Exposition and Fair Company from those of the Association. Any success in the press by the Frankfurt Fair Company would automatically accrue goodwill to the benefit of the Publishers Association as the ultimate promoter! On the other hand, a poor image in the press for the Book Fair would automatically give a black name to the entire industry and naturally to the Association as well.

I found this to be the situation existing in 1975, when I took over direction of the Fair. In the meantime I learned that this poor image was not due to the stupidity nor the superficiality of the insiders who leaked information from these meetings to the outside. It was also not for lack of positive themes at the Book Fair. There were piles of interesting and important topics. But why weren't these topics taken up? Why instead did people just run after the bestsellers? One could then properly denounce this state of affairs as a sorry effort of commercialization!

It was the press—actually all the media—which had given political and cultural relevance to the politicization of the Fair that the students of 1968 had provoked, a relevance that it had not had previously. By 1972 the students had completely disappeared from the fairgrounds, but the journalists stayed. The number of exhibitors grew, but the topics that had been forced through by the students failed to materialize. The manipulated glitzy bestsellers, "compatible with the press," were taken up; otherwise one stood helpless against the "monster" Book Fair.

Two conclusions were to be drawn from this insight in 1975. First, cultural policy had to be made relevant to the media, and not just topics of economic interest. The focal themes were born beginning with the general topic of "Latin America." Secondly, the press had to be looked after not just at the Fair but over the course of the whole year. I had to insist on the construction of our own press infrastructure, for otherwise the quite finely tuned system of the Book Fair would have wound up wrapped in knots. Success proved me right.

The Publishers Association, for reasons totally irrelevant to the Book Fair, attempted to prevent such an outcome. I had fought a battle for over 20 years to develop this press infrastructure, which was so vital for the Book Fair. I had no other choice—either disaster at the Book Fair or confrontation with the German Publishers Association!

Countless intrigues, jealousies, defeats on both sides—the two press departments, and often the management of the two groups, were implicated in such matters over press work for the Book Fair. It came to a kind of trench warfare between the two groups. Any slight gain of territory by one side became the site of a counterattack by the other at the next meeting. My active press person, acting almost "underground," had his existence sanctioned only after years of arguments. The meeting place for journalists (the Press Center) enjoyed increasing satisfaction, and in the end the responsibility for this center too was disputed.

if it were to be allocated to the Fair management and consequently managed by the "press associate" of the Fair Company, then according to the notions of the Publishers Association this position would have to be subordinate to the press spokesman of the Association. Or was the journalists' meeting place to be subordinated directly to the press department of the Publishers Association? The discussion about who would do what was a very frequent subject of dispute between the Fair management and the press department of the Publishers Association. Naturally, the people involved in this hacking and slashing could play either an inciting role or a calming role.

Scrolling through the rolls of the German Publishers Association, we find the following occupants of the office of Association spokesman:

Alexander U. Martens did not get on with somebody over here in the Germans Publishers Association. He had to go.

His successor, Dr. Schachermeyer, from the very beginning never hit it off with the powers-that-be in the Association or with the head of the company. He was more for us than against us. After a short time he disappeared from the scene.

Then came Dr. Jörg Seelbach, a capable individual, who had enough sense of self to avoid sticking to the letter of the law. We had discussions with him, which seldom got as far as the executive committees. A kind of friendship even developed between us. We maintained this *status quo* for several years on the basis of this friendly relationship, and we made slight gains in the direction we wanted to take things.

When Seelbach left and the short interim period of his successor Dr. Johannes Willms was over, in came Peter C., a poorly organized individual, who from the very beginning depended on the head of the Association. Now the conflict came out into the open. Compromises that had been achieved were questioned. Finally Peter C., quite unnerved, gave it all up (not on our account, it seemed to me).

Klaus Kluge arrived on the scene, an outstanding PR and marketing man, who bequeathed to the German Publishers Association a series of fantasy-like reading and PR activities, just at the time when this type of social game was in vogue. However, he too at the beginning did not feel very comfortable sitting in the chair of the press spokesman. Acting diplomatically to all sides was not something that he knew how to do, and he also showed little interest in our ongoing dispute. It was during his period in office as press spokesman that we almost achieved our goal of independence. On June 26, 1989, Dr. Friedrich Georgi determined during a meeting of the Supervisory Board that the Exposition and Fair Company was the institution that put on the Frankfurt Book Fair, and as such its press spokesman should be in charge of the opening press conference. For one thing this had a clear internal logic, and for another, it was hard to explain to the journalists who came that their contact person during the Frankfurt Book Fair and during the entire year was not their contact person during the opening press conference.

After Klaus Kluge there followed Eugen E., a Bavarian journalist from Lower Franconia. After his training and a short period as an editor with a Munich tabloid, he had served the mayor of his hometown Würzburg faithfully for ten years as spokesman and chief cook and bottle washer. Then in 1986 he applied to be a department head in our exhibition department. The first months of his activity were quite satisfactory. I oriented Eugen E. to his work, and took him along on various trips. I took pleasure in his many ideas, and soon was discussing with him strategies for the Fair and even general political questions and problems of all sorts. This occurred not only during working time, but sometimes during holidays on the terrace of my apartment over a bottle of wine.

Suddenly many difficulties began in his department, which grew greater and greater until one day the entire department refused to tolerate his "authoritarian manner" any longer. I stood behind him, and, in a somewhat authoritarian fashion of my own, demanded of each employee a declaration of loyalty to his or her supervisor and the willingness to take on work assignments. This succeeded after some threats of termination. The department was reined in, but my confidence in Eugen was no longer as unshakable as before.

And then one fine afternoon in May in 1990, he told me that in July he would stop working for us and in September would begin as press speaker "on the other side," working for the director of the German Publishers Association. He said that this director, who had convinced him to change jobs, had suggested that the Exposition and Fair Company should continue to pay his salary until September since "over there" they couldn't afford to take him on until then. I was really astounded.

I now discovered a completely different Eugen E. than the one I thought I had known, a Eugen E. who ingratiated himself with his superiors but who stepped all over his subordinates if he thought he could get away with it. Now, however, it was not toward me that he insinuated himself, but to the director of the German Publishers Association. This was a man who always felt himself somewhat threatened and therefore succeeded in surrounding himself with sycophants. This other Eugen E., completely new to me, now became the sixth press spokesman of the German Publishers Association, in the midst of the culmination of a dispute that had lasted for decades. In order to make his new master happy, he readily agreed to the one-sided, resentment-laden outlook of the Publishers Association.

One can ask oneself what a new chairwoman of the German Publishers Association could do, a person who was chosen for this voluntary position in the Association, a person without insight into the deep relationships of the many interlocking organs of this institution. She had to trust her own "mine canaries." Despite all my criticism of this first female chairperson in the history of the Association, I don't believe she ever had a chance. It is true that if she had been another type of person, then in her term of office (starting in 1990) things would have gone forward as before, and she would have had to recognize that it wasn't only facts that were being laid before her, but deep personal resentments that were being worked out as well.

The chairwoman was a friendly person, quite different from the other candidate for the chairmanship, someone whom nobody in our Grosser Hirschgraben office wanted, but on grounds that were not apparent to me. In the first real electoral battle that I had ever experienced in the Publishers Association, she carried off a much heralded victory. The label "reform chairwoman" was immediately attached to her; and as such for many people in the industry who took the German Publishers Association seriously, she was a true harbinger of hope. I would say that I also shared this view. However, she was unfortunately ill-prepared for the political game that was carried out to perfection in this Association by intriguers who had long practice in outfoxing others. She mistakenly identified her new area of activity with the modes of decision-making that existed in her own successful publishing house, and with great political naïveté and Swabian zealousness she set about fulfilling expectations that were given to her. Naturally she got caught in the clutches of the internal strategists, and not only those of the leading functionaries, but also of those who had ulterior plans within the institution. These were people whose decades of experience in the *nomenklatura* of the German Publishers Association had given them the necessary strategic and tactical tools for manipulation.

Some members now loudly called for reform of the Association, that is, the part of the organization financed by the membership fees, but this really poorly prepared proposal had been quietly put to death at the membership meeting in Leipzig in 1990. However, in order not to get the reputation of having choked off a desire for reform among most of the members, people now discovered another area that would be worth reforming, that is, those companies that belonged partially or, like the Exposition and Fair Company, totally to the German Publishers Association.

This was a master stroke of cabinet intrigue by the schemers in the Association, one of redirecting the sweeping calls for reform away from the Association itself and toward much less dangerous targets. In our case the familiar arguments regarding our relation with the press were dragged out of the old war chest. This ploy was the true reason that such a worn-out topic came back with a vengeance.

Mme Chairwoman acted with verve in her desire for reform. At enormous cost, a consulting firm laid out a plan for a holding company of all the businesses of the German Publishers Association, with the executive committee of the Association sitting in the chair over everything. This costly plan, however, disappeared at the end of the election period of the current executive committee just as quietly as did all the previous attempts at reform. In this case people had forgotten that the bewildering

1992   Miguel de la Madrid, formerly President of Mexico, still had so much influence in his country that within two weeks he could arrange for Mexico to appear as the guest country in Frankfurt. We desperately needed a replacement for the Soviet Union, which had been dissolved.

1992   The Mexican poet and essayist Octavio Paz and his wife. *Left:* Patricia van Rijn, Mexican children's book publisher.

1992 Greeting the Czech President Václav Havel at a German book exhibit in Prague.

1992 At the stand of the Hungarian publishing house Akadémiai Kiadó with (*left right*) the Polish publisher Grzegorz Boguta, the American publisher Robert Baensch a the Hungarian publisher Ferencz Zöld.

1996 The publisher Rex How, who was the first to organize the Taiwan Pavilion in Frankfurt. We became close friends. From 2005 to 2007 he was responsible for the book fair in Taipei, and brought out the Chinese-language editions of my books.

1997 Symposium for the development of the international book market with Taiwanese publishers in Taipei.

1995 For their appearance as a guest country, the Irish came to the Frankfurt Book F with a giant inflatable Gulliver.

1997 At the Fair dinner party in the Italian restaurant Da Piva: the authors Uwe Timm, Robert Menasse, and (*center*) the movie actor and author Mario Adorf.

1998 (*Left to right*) The director of the Jerusalem book fair Zev Birger with his wife Trudi, and Teddy Kollek, the one-time mayor of Jerusalem and recipient of the Peace Prize of the German Book Trade, at a meeting in Jerusalem.

1998   Meeting with Salman Rushdie at the Frankfurt Book Fair under tight security.

1999   Protest against the cultural policy of the Iranian government at an exposition the international center of the Book Fair. The sign reads: *Iran: You burn books and sta authors against the wall and persecute artists.*

Frankfurter Buchmesse

50 Jahre Buchmesse

Fröhliche Feier: Show, Musik und Tanz machten den Galaabend in der Frankfurter Festhalle zum Ereignis

Geburtstagsparty in der Festhalle

Beschwingt tanzten sie bis in die späte Nacht: Aussteller und Messeteilnehmer aus aller Welt. In die Frankfurter Festhalle eingeladen hatten Messechef Peter Weidhaas und sein Team. Dort galt es, 50 Jahre Buchmesse zu feiern. 4 000 Gäste gratulierten und genossen das Programm. Bestseller-Autor Ken Follett griff zur E-Gitarre, und Peter Ustinov erheiterte das Publikum mit einem Liedchen. Gegen Mitternacht brachte eine brasilianische Gruppe mit Samba-Takten und feurigen Tänzerinnen die Party in Schwung. Die Halle war dekoriert mit Aufnahmen aus der Geschichte der Buchmesse, Fotos, die auch als Poster über das ganze Messegelände verteilt waren.

Gastspiel: Ernesto Cardenal

Komisch: Peter Ustinov

Historisch: 1950 war die Paulskirche Ort des Büchermarktes

Samba: Messechef Peter Weidhaas tanzte mit

Excerpt from the *German Publishers Weekly:* "50 Years of the Frankfurt Book Fair." (*counter-clockwise from top*) *A happy celebration:* Show, music, and dancing made the gala evening in the Frankfurt Festival Hall an event to remember; *Birthday party in the Festival Hall:* 4,000 guests came to celebrate the occasion; *Historical:* In 1950 the St. Paul's Church was the site of the Book Fair; *Samba:* Fair Director Peter Weidhaas joined the dance line; *Comedy:* Peter Ustinov; *Guest performance:* Ernesto Cardenal.

1998 The group of international book fair directors at my little house in the Rhön: (left to right) Yang Jixiang (Beijing), Dana Kalinova (Prague), Marta Diaz (Buenos Aires), L Haifa (Taipei), Monika Bialicka (Warsaw), Katalin Balogh (Budapest), Francesca Ferra (Bologna)—partially concealed by Courtney Miller (New York), Samir Khalil (Cairo Zev Birger (Jerusalem). *Standing in the background:* Bertie Falck (Göteborg).

2000 Celebration on my retirement as director of the Fair. Shortly before that I broken my arm. My colleagues remarked that I obviously couldn't let go.

profusion of companies was based on tax advantages, and doing away with them in favor of a new holding company would have entailed enormous tax outlays for the federation.

Here lay the core of my criticism of the overly strong influence of the previous volunteer executive committee—they did not correctly understand what had gone on previously, and with a layperson's naïveté they had undertaken highly complex tasks. They assumed no liability for hazardous decisions and bore no responsibility for the outcomes; in the end they lacked any concept of accountability.

They did the same thing with Mme Chairwoman, during whose term in office these men, ready for the next heat, took control of the reins. They did this first by making this woman into an icon to be glorified everywhere, and then by letting her reign run out with the holding company reform that she proposed. New people always stood ready with new areas to work on—so went the history of this association.

Here once again is the analogy of those game plans. In October 1991, the assistant chairperson, his brow knitted with care, at the meeting of the Supervisory Board for the 43rd Frankfurt Book Fair, indicated that the chairwoman, who was not present, was very dissatisfied with the handling of the Rushdie–Iran affair. She wanted a discussion of the topic at a special meeting after the Fair. The extraordinary meeting of the Supervisory Board of the Exposition and Fair Company was thereupon set for December 10, 1991.

In November 1991 the "inner management group" of the German Publishers Association (general director, director of the retail division, director of the publishing division, the two directors of the book dealers federation and of the publishing house of the Publishers Association, plus their legal counsel) discussed the topic at a special meeting. Game plan: *How can the Exposition and Fair Company be brought back into the Publishers Association? What happens if the Publishers Association once again takes over the publicity work of the Exposition and Fair Company?*

People were not even afraid (quite intentionally, one should understand) of provoking the resignation of the chairperson of the Supervisory Board of the Exposition and Fair Company in order to replace him with the head of the Publishers Association.

On November 26, 1991, the chairperson invited the Exposition and Fair Company Supervisory Boardmembers Günther Christiansen, Heinrich Hugendubel, Gerhard Kurtze, Volker Schwarz, Roland Ulmer and Dr. Klaus G. Saur (but not the chairperson of the Supervisory Board) to a private meeting at the exclusive Frankfurter Hof Hotel. The invitation invited the addressees to "a completely personal consultation... so that we can speak with one voice at the meeting of the Supervisory Board." Why then, without the chairperson of the Supervisory Board of the Fair Company, who had been in office for nine years, a man with whom I had worked closely?

On December 1, 1991, I was admitted to the hospital emergency room for a hernia operation. A few days later I asked that the December 10th meeting of the Supervisory Board be postponed because of my forced absence, a request that was rejected by the director.

December 10, 1991: At the meeting, the chairperson of the Supervisory Board of the Exposition and Fair Company announced his resignation because of "a serious lack of information and uncoordinated activities between the executive committee of the German Publishers Association and the Exposition and Fair Company."

On December 16, 1991, the chairman of the Supervisory Board submitted a three-page letter to Mme Chairwoman outlining the reasons for his resignation.

January 14, 1992: Because of many requests for a personal conversation with Mme Chairwoman, I was given an appointment on January 14th at 6 PM in the office of the director of the Publishers Association. As I walked in, I found, in addition to Mme Chairwoman, the assistant chairperson, the chairman of the publishers committee and the treasurer of the Publishers Association. I expressed my reservations about the desired changes in the structure of the Exposition and Fair Company and indicated that if the plans were to be put in effect, I would resign.

January 16, 1992: Now for the first time, almost a month after the event, the German Publishers Association distributed a press release announcing the resignation of the chairman of the Supervisory Board of the Exposition and Fair Company: *Dissent at the Exposition and Fair Company*. At the same time he was thanked for his nine years of activity—with his expertise, his engagement for the tasks, and his personal authority he had earned the esteem of his colleagues (*sic!*).

January 16, 1992: DPA—German Press Agency—press report: *Controversy in the German Publishers Association—Tighter Reins on the Book Fair*. Following the resignation of the chairman, Dr. Klaus G. Saur was made temporary chairman.

January 18, 1992: A fairly well-researched, three-column-long article by the independent journalist Jürgen Schultheis appeared in the *Frankfurter Rundschau*. The speculation at the end of the article regarding the business direction of the Book Fair went somewhat too far—"whenever possible the attempt of Mme Chairwoman to eliminate Peter Weidhaas in order to divert attention from her own predicament." And beyond that—wasn't our joint visit to the Foreign Office on January 21, 1991, the origin of the partial retraction of the boycott of Iran?

January 21–22, 1992: The Working Group of Literary and Textbook Publishers (AGLSV), at its annual meeting in Munich on January 22nd, discussed the events in Frankfurt at great length. The newly named chairperson of the Supervisory Board once again presented the position of the executive committee of the German Publishers Association, and attempted to straighten out the incorrect claims of the chairperson who had just resigned. Outraged resistance and criticism of the behavior of the executive committee were expressed at the general meeting. Messers Schaper (Knaur Verlag), Dr. Kind (Econ), von Eichborn and Frederking demanded independence for the Exposition and Fair Company.

I was asked by several speakers to comment on the plans of the executive committee, but I asked them to understand that I had to refrain from public statements. To be sure, I had used the dinner on the previous day actively to explain our position in personal conversations as best I could to many participants at this meeting.

January 23, 1992: The letter of resignation of the previous chairman of the Supervisory Board, dated December 16, 1991, was published in the *Publishers Weekly* No. 7 together with an article of justification by the new chairperson. On that same day, an interview with the new chairperson on this topic appeared in *Book Report* No. 4.

I responded to the claims of the new chairperson with a three-page letter together with attached copies of the corresponding documents.

I received no response to the two letters.

February 8, 1992: I sent a four-page document to the Supervisory Board with suggestions on solving the current structural crisis of the Exposition and Fair Company. In that letter I included the request that the Supervisory Board might make some decisions at its meeting on February 11th which might make unnecessary further publications and outside discussions in the book industry. Here too there was no response.

February 9, 1992: Great agitation! On the television show *title–theses–temperaments* (TTT), Jürgen Wilcke did a piece titled "Hunting Scenes at the Fair Tower. How they would like to bag the head of the Frankfurt Book Fair."

February 11, 1992: The TTT film ran on Sunday evening on television, and on Tuesday the meeting of the Supervisory Board took place. The new chairman seemed completely at sea; all the other members of the Supervisory Board looked very grim. The inquisition began: Weidhaas and his press chief von der Lahr, who had aroused distrust long ago, were interrogated very sharply. *Who arranged this garbage? One of the two of you must have done it.*

February 13, 1992: From the pen of Helmut Schmitz in the *Frankfurter Rundschau* — a well-researched, well-written half-page article *How the German Publishers Association wants to take charge of the Book Fair*. Schmitz for quite some time had been a supporter of our work, though sometimes critical of us; he must have been given a good deal of information and articles to do this piece. I'm not going to speculate any further about who gave these to him. The result was quite other than the film that had appeared on TTT, a good piece of solid information in the midst of all kinds of articles that were really way off base on this issue.

February 21, 1992: An article by Iris Radisch in *Die Zeit*.

The communicating Executive Committee: The German Publishers Association and the Fair Company struggle over the Frankfurt Book Fair. This article too was relatively factual and portrayed the situation as it actually was. Ms. Radisch had called me up, and I reluctantly had given her information.

February 25, 1992: The nine-page defense letter of Mme Director to all the members of the delegate assembly.

March 5, 1992: The decisive meeting of the publishers committee and the end of the affair.

Even after that, there was still a small unfortunate echo. In the March issue of *Forbes*, Tilman Jens, in the muckraking style of the TTT show, once again took out after the pitiful chairman of the Supervisory Board and went through the entire register of suspicions. This went way too far, and did not match reality.

Once this whole affair was over, I just wanted to put the whole thing behind me. I felt it was high time that I moved on. I considered an early retirement, perhaps at age 60 as my predecessor had done. The conflicts of recent years had not left me unscarred. I was burned out. The constant clashes had taken a toll on my body and my health. I had overtaxed myself for too long, and retirement was the only alternative left for me. If I were to remain as director of the embattled Frankfurt Book Fair, I had no hope of relaxation or recovery.

I had to get out. But how could that be accomplished? The Supervisory Board had not succeeded in loosening the tight connections between me and the Book Fair; they had not neutralized me. Now I wished to do this myself, but I also recognized how my work and I had been fused into a unit. The Book Fair and I were as one. Separation could only be done with a very fine scalpel.

Losing Control of the Fair

The Fair grew not only in the mainstream areas, but also in the "marginal" business zones, and so after a few years we faced the same problem that had driven us in 1988 toward expansion in the international exhibitor area. This time, however, we had reached the limit of our ability to grow. Even in 1995 we could not find space for some 200 exhibitors, and for several years we had not been able to satisfy the desires of exhibitors (about 7% of them) to enlarge their stalls. We stood in the face of yet another rearrangement of the Fair.

I really didn't want that, but I had a feeling about what would come. I wanted to hold on to what existed, even if we would have to turn away some exhibitors who wanted to be in Frankfurt. The "short path" system that we had developed was still functioning very well, and in recent years we had had some very successful Fairs. "Don't change horses in midstream!" Wouldn't our value and our market position be stronger if publishers from around the world had to put out some effort to be with us? Couldn't we find criteria under which we could limit admission?

And then once again I had a sinking feeling in the pit of my stomach—would the challenge by the electronic media subject the entire book trade to necessary restructuring, and thereby unleash a world-wide crisis in the publishing world? What did that mean for our Fair work? Might not the prediction of growth, based on the euphoric development of the past 40 years, without reflection on other possibilities, turn out to be an inaccurate extrapolation?

The ten-year financial plan of my colleague JK assumed the same growth rates of the past ten years. How else could he have justified his calculations—with other assumptions that were tests of a more pessimistic outlook? The market in those years after the collapse of the Socialist system had a clear hold on all conditions of life and on the way we thought and did business. It had its own ideology; it demanded optimism and movement, not stagnation. It demanded expansion and not standing still. It promised relief only upon exhaustion of all sources of profit. The market is goal-directed; it is arrogant; it emphasizes success. Anyone who wants to succeed in the world of business has to go for more; otherwise the competition will win out.

I admit that thinking this way was contrary to what I believed and that I submitted to this ideology with great reluctance. I also recognized that if I did not conform to this system in which I was currently playing a role, I would be more and more a sort of heretic. That is why in the end I became hesitant and distrustful even of my own positions.

In the 1970s and 1980s, I set my own path and made my own decisions, which were both well-supported and vindicated by events. Now those times were over. All of a sudden I found myself, a person who had always been condemned as a "progressive," in the conservative camp. That was a strange discovery. I didn't want this expansion of the Fair, but I didn't have convincing counterarguments against this *Zeitgeist,* this mood of the times as dictated by the market.

JK, my assistant for many years, a man whom I suspected of picking the winning side before taking a position, that is, to support whatever was the strongest at the moment, took this opportunity to move to a decision. He negotiated with the lessors of the fairgrounds in order to get the necessary exhibit hall space for the time of our Fair. I had approved these discussions under the assumption that since this proposal required shifting around other fairs at the fairgrounds, there would be a delay of several years. By then, by around 1998, I would be somewhat clearer about changes in the book trade and would be able to decide how we should proceed.

However, the management of the Frankfurt Fairgrounds showed itself to be surprisingly flexible and agreeable, demonstrating peculiar market sensitivity and business acumen. It therefore immediately agreed to our arguments for expansion.

Within a short time all the pre-conditions for an expansion of the Book Fair were in place. Our *trousseau* was ready.

We set about planning the "Fair for the New Century." What came out of this was something that was hardly a big step into the future, but rather a return to a design that we had left behind in 1984, when we had moved from the "Fair of the Long Paths" to the "Fair of the Short Paths." We had redesigned the new buildings in the center of the Fairgrounds in order to concentrate all the exposition activities around Hall 4.

Now we were going backwards to the "Fair of the Two Communication Circles," with the predominantly German language "Marketing and Public Fair" in the center of the fairgrounds that we had had till now, and the "International Rights Fair" on the other side of the railroad line in the western part of the fairgrounds. We had won half a million square feet of newly granted exhibition space, but we also had to absorb walking distances of at least a half mile from one end of the exhibitor area to the other. And—a nightmare—practically every one of the 6,500 individual exhibitors had to be moved to a new stall location; that is, 6,500 individual interests had to be plucked out of their state of relative satisfaction and jolted awake. Our task was akin to knocking down a beehive, and then trying to persuade each bee one by one that this new nest was just as nice as the old one, all the while being stung violently.

We developed and calculated a dozen different designs for the floor plan. We had to take care that for every exhibitor group there was sufficient room for growth. Then we had to make sure that the group would be in close proximity to its contact person at the Fair. Finally, everything had to fit into a given exhibition hall space. This was a calculation with two impossible things for each three possibilities. Fixing everything perfectly would have meant squaring the circle. There can only be an approximately functioning locational system. All the exhibitor groups would have to accept changes, and improvement would come about only for those who had been waiting for some time to enlarge their stalls. The rest would just have to put up with it.

In addition to the conditions already noted, we had a lot of taboos that hindered our planning. So for example, the electronic media section could in no way be moved to a central location in the Fair because many of the classical book publishers had already become quite unsettled by the rapid growth of this area of the publishing business. The notion that the monopoly on creating opinion, which previously had been held by the medium of the book, was now to be shared with the other media still had not penetrated into the heads of all the people in the industry. And were the Americans going to misbehave this time if they were displaced once again? From day to day we were conscious that we had embarked on one of the most difficult tasks of our trade.

One more thing—it suddenly became frighteningly clear to me that with this movement we were placing in question the entire sense and utility of the Frankfurt Book Fair. Every one of the exhibitors, who were already complaining about the financial and personal costs of participating in Frankfurt, would now in earnest pose the question, "Does it still make sense to go to Frankfurt?"

This doubt caused me many a sleepless night, but there was no way back. Perhaps I should have resisted more strongly? But that wouldn't have helped much, for the Fair had reached a point in its development where a decision had to be made. The Fair in recent years had put on a lot of weight and had become much less focused. I wasn't responsible for that; that was a phenomenon of the time.

Were I to shout out from the gallery the infamous Kafkaesque cry of *Stop!,* I would have been labeled just an oddball outsider. I had to maintain my place at the center of decision-making if I did not want to give up leadership. From then on decisions would no longer be my decisions alone. I had moved from being the creator of this event to its moderator. The votes that took place afterwards in the Supervisory Board, which I lost one after the other after halfhearted resistance, confirmed the change that set in from this point on.

In the meantime, once again there was a clash with the Americans, who threw their market-dominance onto the scale. I kept holding on to our Fair principles of mixing the large and small, strong and weak, an approach that gave a certain protection to the weaker ones and lent a sense of comprehensiveness to the

Fair. I stubbornly insisted on moving the Americans and the British from their prior placement in Hall 4 into Hall 9, also a multi-level building. I wanted to set up all the other international exhibitors on one level of 300,000 square feet in Hall 8. Hall 9 did lie on the periphery of the fairgrounds, but with the 100-foot-wide glass gallery it formed a unit with Hall 8. According to the way we planned it, the Fair for sale and purchase of international rights would play out in this total area in two halls of the same size.

The Americans and the British were the biggest sellers at the Fair. All the other exhibitors only sporadically experienced such success when somebody got interested in translation rights or other rights for the books that they offered. These exhibitors were looking for rights business almost exclusively by obtaining interesting English-language titles to include in their own offerings. Their position only served to show off their own identity and to have a fixed address in the bewildering crush of this business arena. Since practically all the exhibitors tried to appeal to the opinion-leading Anglo-Americans, I was still convinced that exactly where the English-language groups were located was not of prime importance. People would seek them out in any case; the halls would fill up, and they had no losses to fear for their customers.

The situation was quite different for exhibitors from Asia, Latin America, and from Southern, Northern or Eastern Europe.

A Fair is an appointment, a coming together of people. It is based on a fine network of human interaction, and depends not only on economic factors, but in a very high degree on psychological factors. The exhibitor from a less well-known country believed just as strongly in his products, had costs just as high, and had to make great efforts in order to get to Frankfurt. He wanted to be taken seriously like everyone else, and he measured his success or failure in the attention that was paid to him, even though this could not be paid in hard cash.

In accordance with the principle of mixing all the exhibitors together, we had succeeded in the past in making the difference between strong and weak exhibitors not seem too obvious. If I were now forced to put the strong seller groups together and to separate the weaker ones, this could only be humiliating for the latter since their lack of significance and the weakness of their offerings would be crystal clear in the form of halls empty of people. It is likely that after a few desperate attempts to change the situation, they would withdraw from the Fair and thus deprive the seller countries of potential customers.

Perhaps I painted too bleak a picture of the situation. I feared that a decision in favor of the strong ones alone would gradually undermine our quite sensitive system of success. I was convinced that there was no getting around starting up again with the Americans—the Americans and the English had to be moved to Hall 9!

We worked very hard at launching the information about our repositioning plans in the right form. Before the Fair in October 1995 we published the plans in all their detail in the international professional press. At the Fair itself we wanted to bring our critics together at an open meeting and to explain our decision.

It was on Friday the 13th, in October, when three of us—myself, the technical director Franz-Josef Fenke and the new press spokesman Holger Ehling, the moderator of the event—sat in front of a rather unfriendly looking assembly, just as we had done four years earlier. Delegates from 71 of the exhibiting countries showed up, including representatives of the Association of American Publishers (AAP) and the British association (PA). To our surprise, this informational meeting proceeded rather smoothly. In hesitant English, weighing every word before I spoke, I did not give the gruff-looking representatives of the exhibitors cause for fundamental criticism. My colleagues were quite happy and thought that all the problems had now been overcome. I however did not feel overjoyed. Did I have an inkling of what was to come?

The day before that, Alberto Vitale of Random House came to see me, this same person who had made life so difficult for us the last time. Since I was on my way to a press conference to make the opening greeting, he went with me across the entire fairgrounds, talking incessantly, making it clear that the Americans were to be placed with the British in Hall 8, since this was more pleasant and brighter than the other halls. After all, the Americans and the British were the strongest and most important exhibitor groups. What had happened?

When Vitale learned of the new placement plan, he thought that he had the same little game of power poker to play that he had won four years ago. This stocky and arrogant publishing boss had an uncanny ability to find opportunities to feed his insatiable hunger for power and to place himself at the head of leading opinion.

On the previous day, Vitale had Franz-Josef Fenke show him Hall 9, where according to our plans the American exhibitors were to set up shop on the lower level. Then he wanted to see one level up where the British were supposed to go. Although this level had a lower ceiling and was not as attractive as the ground level, he announced with an imperial gesture, "This is my hall! This is where the Americans have to go."

Franz-Josef could hardly believe his ears. He nodded, "O.K., if that's the way you want it!"

On the way back from this excursion, the two of them unfortunately passed an open door of Hall 8. Curiously, Vitale walked in to look over this hall. "No, this is it. This is our hall! This is where the Americans and the Englishmen must be housed together!" This man had finally found what he was really looking for, a goal for his troublemaking.

On the very day of our informational presentation, Vitale rounded up a number of important American publishers and convinced them of his plans. He also had gotten the British publishing organizations behind him with the argument that companies like Random House, represented both in the American and British sectors by smaller subsidiaries, should be put together at the edges between the British and U.S. contingents in order to save money. This would be possible only in the one-story Hall 8.

On the afternoon after our presentation, Nick Veliotes and Jack Hoeft, president and chairman of the AAP, along with Ian Taylor and another representative of the British PA, showed up in my office. Veliotes impudently claimed that the AAP had received no invitation to the presentation, and that is why they were here now. This was a pure lie, since I had personally invited

Nick by fax with return receipt to his office. Without beating about the bush, the visitors now repeated Vitale's demands and reacted as though they were quite insulted when their demand was not immediately met by Fenke and me. After the Fair we received the same demands presented again in four or five more or less similar letters.

Then we had the bad luck that I had feared. Could we, did we, have to give way to the demands of the "strongest customers"? The generally prevailing market principle said *"Yes!"* My assistant JK, who figured that we could not hold out in this battle, said, *"Yes, we must!"* Cautious soundings at the executive board of the German Publishers Association and on the Supervisory Board suggested a majority for that view. Internally I screamed, *"NO, NO, NO!"* If we were to give in now, then we would have to kiss goodbye to our Fair policy of equal chances for all exhibitors, and we would have opened the door to domination by the strongest market forces.

People opposed me, saying, "But what's the problem, isn't that the way the world is? You are putting on a market affair, and you act like a *romantic*!" But haven't we always gone on the assumption that books are not just commercial goods, but also represent culture and the human spirit? Didn't the *set price*[1] rest on the same premises of the protection of the small publisher and thus of the multiplicity of actors in the book trade? Didn't this "inviolable" principle, the one for which the matadors of the German Publishers Association had fought so bravely, rest on the same anachronistic principles as my supposedly romantic ideas?

Time was short. I had to convene an extraordinary meeting of the Supervisory Board in order to get a final decision so that we could continue with our planning. On the other hand, I wanted to wait until closer to a point in time when nothing else would occur and the public discussion would be over, at least for this year.

It was once again the 13th of the month, this time in December, when the meeting took place in the gatehouse of the

---

1. By law, new books are sold in Germany at a set price; discounting is not allowed.

fairgrounds where we could look down from above on the halls that were at issue. As I had feared, the trend went strictly in the direction of giving in to the strong business interests. People saw all their desires as plausible, and did not feel they were acting selfishly. Wouldn't the Americans and the British, by being placed in Hall 9, be even further from the German participants in the center of the fairgrounds! After all, these two groups are the most important business associates for us Germans!

I braced myself against this view, which was really very enticing, with a very sharply worded reproach. In this space, I maintained, only the interests of the Germans and the Anglo-Saxons would be served, while the rest of the world would "stand waiting outside the door"! This was the attitude that earned me the reproach of being a "social romantic." Nonetheless, my objection was close to the truth.

The meeting moved forward, and one could predict that at the end the majority would take what I considered to be a "wrong" decision. Luckily, the chairperson of the executive committee interrupted the meeting for a midday snack. I quickly cobbled together a compromise with my colleagues who were present, Fenke, JK and Ehling, a compromise that was intended to save face for all concerned. The chairperson put that "compromise" to a vote even during the meal. It was accepted. Everyone was quite pleased that it had not come to a big blowup. I had been quite vehement and created an awkward situation, and now everyone hoped that with this solution the conflict would be over. The Americans were the only ones who got entry into Hall 8, while the British and the stronger European countries formed a strong Hall 9, with the other countries filling up Hall 8 with the Americans. Nonetheless, it was clear to me that I had done nothing more than get a temporary delay of what had to be a final solution. This was not the end of the controversy.

As expected, the American AAP and the British PA immediately protested. Both their letters shared the argument that this new situation was worse than what they had before. Finally, we received a letter of protest from the Dutch Publishers Association, which flat out refused to have the Dutch publishers situated on the second floor of Hall 9. In the meantime, the supervisory board regretted the "compromise resolution" and signaled its readiness to put an end to the discussion by giving in to the wishes of the Americans. I kept delaying the final vote in order to get to the regular meeting of the Supervisory Board at the end of January 1996, where I wanted to try once again to grab hold of the steering wheel.

I think the time has come to say a few words about my colleague JK, "Assistant Director."

The very existence of this person at the Exposition and Fair Company was the result of that turbulent meeting of the Supervisory Board in Düsseldorf in February 1978, where I was unable to be present due to illness. Depending on whose version one believes, one portion of the board wanted to give me some help through the creation of a new position of assistant director, while the other portion of the board wished to limit my "monopoly on power." Whatever the reason, the result of that six-month search process, including interviews with over 80 applicants, was JK, a short, thin man with extraordinary energy and encouragingly clear intelligence.

At first I had my feathers ruffled over this position of "Assistant" who was to direct the company in "collegial leadership" and on an equal footing to myself. Only a few months went by before the Supervisory Board was basically questioning its own decision due to JK's initially disappointing performance, and did not want any more from him, though he succeeded in preventing his termination during this probationary period. After that time we worked together quite harmoniously. JK worked with indefatigable energy, primarily in the area of finance and budget planning, and made himself irreplaceable. Over the years these assignments became ever more clearly his responsibility. I restricted myself to basic financial decisions after I had discussed these extensively with him.

But it was not only the finances that he took responsibility for. He was not afraid of any job involving the internal management of our operations. And so quite gradually, in a process of several years, he took on the role of head of administration and personnel. We were a pair that worked together extremely well, treasuring the abilities and accomplishments of the other and complementing each other. It was a happy combination that also manifested itself in a sort of friendship. Both of us knew what we had in the other and therefore moved forward very carefully and sensibly with goodwill, even "affectionately," I am not embarrassed to say.

And then one day I made an error that had very serious consequences. My predecessor Taubert had retired at age 60, and I too was gradually reaching that age. After almost 30 years of work at the Exposition and Fair Company, I was feeling a growing urgency to call an end to it. JK and I many a time had spoken about my desire, but we had always avoided the question of succession.

The time came when JK no longer danced gingerly around this topic, and said simply, "If it should really come to the point that you take early retirement, I'm going to apply to be your successor." He now expected my complete agreement to this suggestion, trusting as he did our harmonious working together for many years and his accomplishments during that time.

Somehow I did not react so favorably that day, and a relationship of pure sunshine that bound us together was suddenly no more. Increasingly, differences of opinion emerged between us, based mainly on our different personalities. I often found him too passive, too bureaucratic, too authoritarian. He suffered under my chaotic, intuitive, dominant ways. However, on the basis of our interests we had always worked together to lead the company; we had found ways of understanding each other that had made it possible for us to reconcile our differences and to arrive at a common view of whatever matter we were arguing about.

What I had never considered was that this common basis of shared interests would not stand up in the face of the question of my successor, and JK for the first time clearly stepped out of the shadow of this common approach and built himself up in opposition to me by implying, *"Look here! I'm the one! I am your successor!"*

I answered him quite cautiously, since I naturally understood that this was a minefield. I saw the role that he had played in all the years of our working together: "You should really think that over. You are a terrific assistant director. With a new person, as assistant director you would have much more influence than if you have to answer to the Supervisory Board and the outside world for the entire operation. You do know that standing out front as the representative of the company and pushing through programs are not exactly your strengths."

A shadow of anger flashed across his face as he burst out, "You're acting just like your predecessor Taubert, who had just as little faith in his successor as you do!"

Everything that I said from then on, in order to put what I had said in perspective and to reduce its effect, was useless. I had hit this person at the deepest spot of his ego and had wounded him. From that moment on, our relationship changed. JK now attempted to show me, himself, and everyone else that he had his own position and that he was an independent power factor in this company, one to be taken seriously.

Suddenly and without previous discussion, he began to make decisions that he told me about afterwards in a surly manner, as though they had nothing to do with me. At the Supervisory Board he spoke of "his" financial decisions as though there were no longer any director of this company. At the business meetings of the top administrators, several times we had some very loud disputes in front of a shocked body of colleagues. When I came back from trips, I got the brushoff from him with an assertion that nothing had happened while I was away.

My reaction to all this was to set up a *"jour fixe"* in which he had to report to me about projects that he had taken on. We furthermore tried to neutralize our conflicts that broke out here at an early stage, but that did not always succeed.

That's the way things were moving at the time of the pending decision. On the evening before the meeting of the Supervisory Board on January 31, 1996, the chairperson of the board wanted to know if all of my co-workers shared the opinion that I had expressed of placing the Anglo-Saxons in Hall 9, despite their protests. With JK present, I had to tell the truth that there was one exception, namely JK, still not knowing that on the next day this would bring about a major shift.

At the meeting I built up my arguments based on the fact that the critics in the U.S. and Great Britain found our compromise decision of December even worse than the initial situation of placing both contingents on the three levels of Hall 9. Once again, I presented three alternatives for debate, thus distancing myself somewhat from the December compromise solution, since this had pushed all those affected into opposition.

I argued for the initial solution of putting the Anglo-Saxons in Hall 9, since this made for equality of the seller countries (primarily the U.S. and Great Britain) and the other buyer countries, and since the vertical movement between the three levels of Hall 9 could be assured only through the relative homogeneity and strong attractiveness of the English and Americans. It's true that the solution of the "Anglo-Americans to the one-level Hall 8" would superficially satisfy two of the economically strongest exhibitor groups, but at the same time it would constitute the final loss of sovereignty over structuring the Frankfurt Book Fair to the Americans and the British.

I could feel how the opinion in the Supervisory Board was gradually shifting. More and more comments cautiously took up my arguments. Decisions in such committees are often very strongly dependent on group dynamics. All of a sudden I felt that what had been impossible at the last meeting in December might succeed today. A change in the dominant mood was imminent. I held my breath—*Don't make any mistake now!*

And then it happened. The chairman turned to JK: "Well, Mister K., let's hear your opinion, since it's probably somewhat different from that of Mr. Weidhaas, as I have been given to understand." JK had promised me that he would not express his opinion at the Supervisory Board. What does this all mean? Would he get out of a bad situation by making a short statement that in some points he disagreed, though in principle he shared the opinion of the director?

Not by a long shot. Called on by the Chairman and given a legitimate position, he could now finally step out of the shadow of his supervisor, who had prevented him from developing:

Gentlemen, I see the decision before us basically as a pragmatic question of economics and policy.... With regard to the equality between buyers and sellers, I would like to note that those buyers, who often are part of the weaker publishing countries, will continue to come to Frankfurt if the sellers find themselves comfortable. A relatively uncomfortable situation is acceptable to them if they are offered publishing rights, as a rule from the stronger publishing countries.

To acquiesce to the desires of the Americans and the British would therefore also be equal to meeting the needs of the other publishing countries.

I would also like to express my fears that this new variation cannot last longer than one year. Discussions with the British and Americans since the publication of the decisions of the last meeting of the Supervisory Board have shown very clearly that distributing the British and U.S. exhibitors over the three levels of Hall 9 is not a feasible enterprise. If it should turn out to be absolutely necessary to change the Fair layout once again in 1997, then the loss of reputation and negotiating ability of the management of the Fair would be complete.

That was it then! After this argument from the side of the "professionals," the Fair management itself, all doubts of the members of the Supervisory Board were swept away. Basically everyone threw themselves at the feet of the stronger parties. Taking a deep breath, since they had to know deep inside what was being expressed, they decided by a vote of 6 to 1: *For purposes of expanding the Fair area in 1996, the Americans and the British will be housed together in Hall 8. France, the Benelux countries and Scandinavia will be in Hall 9 on the first level; the rest of the Romance language world, including Latin America, will be in Hall 9, second level; Africa, Asia, and Central and Eastern Europe in Hall 9, third level. The center for literary agents will be in Hall 8.*

The New Gutenberg Galaxy

The written word, the culture of books, and the Enlightenment are woven together in a remarkable dialectical process. The written word and the culture of books tore away the one-time monopoly of the cloisters over knowledge and information; the printed sheet during the Peasant War of 1525 symbolized the definitive obsolescence of the cloister libraries, which had stored their regulated knowledge on parchment rolls and handwritten papyrus books. The development from the illiterate Wolfram von Eschenbach[1] to the author Walther von der Vogelweide,[2] from the unintelligible Sunday sermon in Latin to the more accessible German translation of the Bible by Martin Luther, from the cloistered copyist in his private order to the movable type of an urban bourgeois printers guild—these three changes marked a revolutionary *cæsura,* whose full significance only became clear after computers, the Internet and multimedia once again recast the ways we think, read and act on the world.

Like many others, I grew up in a more or less purely written culture. It socialized me, and I became a strong supporter of this book culture. I felt myself one with book people. This was one of the reasons for my pronounced professional engagement with books, as a book dealer, as a bookbinder, as a book manufacturer, and in my global interventions for a healthy and lively book industry in the developing world. I wanted to make my own small contribution to a world of reason and enlightenment.

That's why for a long time I remained quite skeptical and suspicious about the new media, which, according to McLuhan's law—"The medium is the message"—delivered quite a different

---

1. Wolfram von Eschenbach (*c.* 1170–1220): Bavarian epic poet and the author of *Parzival,* the work in which he boasts of his illiteracy.
2. Walther von der Vogelweide (*c.* 1170–1230) was one of the most outstanding Middle High German lyric poets.

message. This may have been due to my now advanced age, as formulated by one of my co-workers, "The old man has had his time, now let us have a go at it!" Or as my successor as director of the Frankfurt Book Fair, the Swiss Lorenzo Rudolf believed, "The Word, Mr. Weidhaas, is out of style—from now on the Picture rules!" Or was it a sudden spell of cultural pessimism that had taken hold of me?

"Not that either," I wrote in 1983 in my contribution to the book edited by Gerd E. Hoffman, *The Wired Man*:

The activities of the author who experiences a subjectively existing reality for himself and transfers that to speech and writing will encounter a reception that is both active and stimulating. More even than the author, the reader must develop creativity and sensibility in order to penetrate into the furthest corner of a text in trying to understand it. The imagination of the reader is essential to a very great extent if a text is to portray moods, sounds, colors, smells, weather or descriptions of people—these are demanded both by the art of Writing and by the art of Reading. A printed text should never overpower the reader; it should not catch him by surprise or dominate him, unless of course the reader willingly enters and voluntarily follows the author on a long and intricate expedition into uncharted territory. Written texts appeal to the reader, although they are not messages in themselves. The recipient must reach out to what is written and what is printed, but nobody can force him to do that.

The audio-visual media are different. They use very up-to-date forms of communication, which are impossible to get away from.... Images and sounds are intended to flatter us into a good humor; they play with our emotions, not wanting to make us better informed or to offer information, but to manipulate us and condition us for their message. How frighteningly agreeable, how enlightening is the newscaster when he (or she) clears his throat. The flat tone-image-façade is broken, and the artificial and the invented become clear, all hindering easy consumption.

Now, on top of everything else, come the "New Media"—that cold-blooded extension of the technology that stems from the myth that everything is possible, down to the very last glass fiber. This completely neglects how dangerous the accumulated side effects are. The "New Media" are all of the following: reliable, efficient, smooth, 100%, all-inclusive (they might become so), orderly, correct, punctual and "clean." So clean, so pure, that not a trace of suspicion of fallibility, weakness or being out of control sticks to this system. Elementary human traits are eliminated; and when the electric power is cut off, a situation that is the only conceivable weak spot, one becomes afraid that a host of needs will descend upon us.[3]

In composing this essay, I went back to the question from my youthful days of how the enslavement, without resistance, of a cultured people could have been possible, as occurred to the Germans during the Nazi regime. That is why I titled my essay, excerpted here, "In a *Putsch,* the Radio Station is the First Place to be Attacked," an idea that had been confirmed once again by the Romanian revolution.

Over time, I began to have doubts about the thoroughly positive definition of the effect of the print media and of reading as a purely human technology. Didn't the one-dimensional development around book culture also reveal a misanthropic attitude? If so, the straight-line acceptance of the uniform modes of thought by reading also signaled a cold and inhuman side of the Enlightenment. Wasn't it the Enlightenment—with us since Bacon, Newton, and the French *Encyclopédistes* and positivists—that brought us an overload of straight-line reasoning, of exclusive single definitions, of exactness, and of perfection? Wasn't there at the same time an Enlightenment of the loss of good sense as well as of righteousness, of humanity as well as of inhumanity, of progress as well as of regression?

To recognize this Janus face of the Enlightenment could really first occur only when people would recognize the finiteness of human control over nature. That *progress* could also mean *regression* was first totally understood through the existence of the atomic bomb (extinction of the human species) and through ecological catastrophes (finite ability to control nature). One-dimensional thinking, naïve notions of exponential growth curves, and the belief in human progress by ever better and more perfect technologies in the end became a common

3. Gerd E. Hoffmann [Ed.], *Der verkabelte Mensch* (Braunschweig: Westermann, 1983).

platform for both capitalism *and* communism. They differed only in the ideological and political-economic form that this one-dimensional Enlightenment should take.

It's true that you can bind between the covers of a book the Sears catalog as well as Dante's *Divine Comedy,* Hitler's *Mein Kampf* as well as a cookbook, a love poem as well as a physics treatise. Still, one can and must have a discussion of good and bad books, of useful and useless ones, for a book is not only a means; the medium will always remain a part of the message— that is, if the medium itself remains. By the 1960s the creative and stimulating intellectual anarchist Marshall McLuhan had already prophesied the death of the book. Had this event already taken place by the time of his own demise in 1980, with the explosion of New Media?

McLuhan understood all media as existing along a spectrum from *hot* to *cool*. "Hot media" are those—like film, radio and yes, *books*—that engage us completely by heightening a single sense and demanding linear, logical analysis and long attention spans. "Cool media," on the other hand—primarily *television*—are low definition and require the simultaneous comprehension of a complex whole, and leave slow reason to the side.

Is life "hot" or "cool"? At the moment a love poem is printed, does it lose its essence, its compressed sensory communication between I and Thou, just as the story loses its character when no longer told, sung, or rhapsodized, but read separately in a book? As McLuhan noted, "With print many earlier forms were excluded from life and art, and were given a strange new intensity... which engenders specialism and fragmentation in experience...."[4] Regardless of their content, books are expressions of this high-level division of labor in a society that is increasingly alienated due to the antagonisms between head and heart, between head and hand, between specialist and layperson, between ration and emotion.

When I was still representing the values of reading books in an uninhibited and one-sided fashion, I looked critically at the challenges and results of New Media. That was the basis of our

---

4. Marshall McLuhan, *Understanding Media* (New York: Signet Books, 1964), 37.

focal theme of the "Orwell Year—1984" at the Frankfurt Book Fair. Like me, many of the intellectual leading lights of the time were unsettled by the forward march of electronic media everywhere; it wasn't difficult to present an interesting, well-attended program that included all levels of society. Implementation of the focal theme was critical of society; in the media area, it was directed in particular against television. Computers and the Internet had not yet developed their all-encompassing power, though we thought we knew what the consequences would be. One big PR sideshow in the focal theme program of 1984 was the "Cultigator," a one-and-a-half-ton machine press dressed as a crocodile or dragon, which ate up old TV sets, and with great smashing and grinding spewed them out as square lumps of tin, steel and cables. The Berne metal sculptor Hans Knecht then spray-painted them and offered them up as pieces of work called "Cretis." The *Frankfurter Allgemeine* found the appearances of the "Cultigator" worth a few indignant comments, where the author angrily compared this procedure with a book burning. The infuriated writer, however, overlooked the fact that in the smashed together product we were dealing with a machine, and that all the used material was reshaped into a work of art, while we know that in the historical burnings the affair had nothing to do with the destruction of paper, but was absolutely about the annihilation of ideas.

The "takeover of power" by New Media got closer and closer. In 1986, I decided to switch our bookkeeping to a computer-based system, something that led to a multi-year learning curve with untold errors and the resultant anger from our customers. In the end, however, the change brought broad synergies and increased productivity. At the end of the 1980s we were amazed at the presentation of the editor-in-chief of the *German Publishers Weekly,* Hanns Lothar Schütz, when he showed us his recently acquired fax machine, over which he exchanged entire sets of galley proofs in a matter of seconds with the printing house of his newspaper in Aschaffenburg. At the turn of the decade, computers became a toy for the masses, and soon enough the cumbersome laptop became a new electronic appendage that was *de rigeur* at any meeting or business conference.

I too went straight away to a store without the slightest understanding of what I was doing, and got a Commodore computer, a contraption that reminded me of nothing more than a box of chocolates. I wanted to understand this new work of the devil with practical "learning by doing." Helmut von der Lahr was our press chief in charge of internal communications and in charge of coordinating all our organizational processes that came together at a particular time in the fall. I gave him the job of outfitting all the workplaces with computers and networking them. That was a process that took a year, with innumerable failures. Not only did it at first not lead to savings, it fact it entailed very high additional costs for extra expert personnel, whom we needed to fix bugs and save us from the inevitable computer crashes.

The discussion in the book trade about the sense or futility of new possibilities was a many-sided one, with the majority leaning to the old cultural technology of reading, and everything new be damned. Every year in the fall at the Book Fair the well-known lament filled the air—*Reading is dying!* The fanfare of the collapse of education was blasted loudly from the military outposts of cultural pessimism. The youth in particular turned their backs on the book and contented themselves with mindless computer games.

Nonetheless, "progress" marched on. A new medium, once it was invented, could not be driven out by so much moaning and groaning. Isn't that the way it always is? The group in power defends its traditional cultural technology by denouncing its successor. Had it ever happened before in history that a new mode of communication completely replaced another one? Had the invention of the telex and the radio telegram completely replaced writing letters? Weren't new media also supplementary to the old media, transformations of the old into the new? After all, is computer communication possible without reading and writing?

It was a thoroughgoing learning process that many had to go through, including myself, in order to overcome an ingrained, one-dimensional conviction of book and print. We had to be ready to land on new, albeit virtual, shores. In April 1992, I was ready for it. I returned from a trip to the U.S. and immediately called together the members of our management team to announce, "This is it! We are going to have electronics as a business field in our book fair!" *Frankfurt Goes Electronic* was our commercial slogan, which for the next three years rubbed the opinion makers and the book industry the wrong way. Helmut von der Lahr had come up with that pithy catchphrase, which later in altered form found widespread use in general advertising for completely different products.

It wasn't at all clear that we were going to be successful with this surge into the future. There were only a few classical book publishing houses that made use of the new technologies. The book trade completely refused to entertain the idea that the new media could be integrated into their distribution activity. In order to win over new supporters, we had to move forward into what for us was a new area of technology companies dealing with software and other experimental items, which were sprouting like mushrooms all over the place. These new companies did not feel comfortable amidst our book people. "Why should we bother bringing our highly innovative products to this medieval book fair?" I believe that the aversion was mutual. Even the book dealers and publishers could hardly begin to deal with these volatile newcomers, who seemed to have a quick solution at hand for any deficit of information.

We went about the matter pragmatically. We looked at the telephone listings and the catalog for the last MILIA in Cannes, a special fair that had enjoyed success for a number of years in the sector that now interested us.

For the first time we brought a marketing department into our operation. Until then I had considered such an institution to be superfluous. Marketing for the Book Fair previously had been done by the international appearances of the Fair director, by the activities of our international department (book exhibits, participation in book fairs, workshops) and through global press reporting. In addition, 80% of the exhibitors were repeat customers, who responded to our invitations sent out in February without any further request. Now, however, we had to work in a new international business arena against strong, well-established competitors (MILIA, CeBIT, InfoBase), and against internal resistance of our own industry at that.

Two employees very skilled in communications now took over the new marketing task. These two women had until now been active in the area of setting up the focal themes—Sigrid Mortiz as head of the department and Susanne Kilian for the newly created area of electronic media. Both of them took on their assignment with great verve. We had to find answers to some new but very practical questions involved in the planning—*Who were the lead actors in the area of electronic media? What were the interactions—that is, who did business with whom? What were the needs of the exhibitor groups? What would the consequences be for the Book Fair? What structures and what potential could Frankfurt offer?*

The circle of actors in the print arena was relatively transparent. Interactions and transactions were more or less exactly defined—Authors and agents delivered the contents; the publishing house delivered the product as a book; the printing house physically created it; and the marketing department distributed it. Internationally, the book was marketed primarily through the sale of the rights and licenses to foreign publishing houses.

In electronic media, however, the interactions were much broader, and many more actors played a role. Who delivered the content? In contrast to the book, the content did not consist of a completed manuscript. Multimedia productions consisted of many various components. In order to obtain the content, these various elements had to be brought together and the rights and licenses had to be negotiated with the particular entities offering them.

In computer programs, the suppliers of "authoring tools" were asked for all kinds of customizations. Individually developed programs or plug-ins were offered by "software developers," while for film and video games there were film companies, agencies, archives (perhaps museums), leasing firms, all of which appeared as owners of rights. Music publishing houses had to be considered for musical works. For recordings, there were "production music libraries," archives and record companies. For photos, the "Picture Libraries," the archives and other copyright holders were of interest. In texts, the partners were both authors and publishing houses.

Who created the products? These were the pressing firms (CD-ROM, CD-i), video producers and packagers.

And who delivered the products? These were publishing houses with their own multimedia production, software firms like Microsoft, Voyager, *etc.*, but also hardware firms with their releases, multimedia firms, film companies (the slogan was "value-added information"), game producers, and printing companies as suppliers of services for multimedia products and software.

Who marketed these products? Multimedia companies as a rule did not grant any translation rights for their productions. They didn't give a license for an English-language product to an Italian multimedia firm. The product was either originally made in several languages or was marketed in the original language in other countries.

Still, marketing partners came in to play as book dealers, software dealers, department stores and specialty stores, wholesalers and distribution firms, video marketing firms, shippers and hardware dealers.

One of the widespread phenomena of multimedia productions involved co-productions and joint ventures. Multimedia productions are expensive, time-consuming and labor-intensive. People looked for partners with whom one could divide the costs and risks, each of whom contributed one part of the product—investors (money), publishing houses (content, copyright), research and development firms (market research), multimedia firms (development and production), manufacturers (*e.g.*, pressing).

Consultants played a role in the big picture, especially for companies that were just starting up production and who often transferred project management to outside experts, who did market research, administered the budget, contacted the various service firms, and pulled all the threads together.

Like literary agents in the print area, an increasing number of agencies appeared in the multimedia branch, agencies that handled the ideas of multimedia developers by trying to find investors and partners for joint ventures.

The "creative ones," those who delivered ideas and designs, played an important role in the design and development of interactive multimedia. Connections might occur between two large software firms, but deals were also made between the distributors and the suppliers of finished products.

The print publisher wanted to see what chance he had of reformatting his content into multimedia products, and he reviewed the goods that were already on the market. He looked for an adviser who could tell him what market his content was best suited for and what medium was most fitting. What technical and content requirements would be placed on his product? He was looking for a company that would manufacture his product on commission. Eventually, he also sought partners for co-production or for a joint venture. Finally, the sale of rights and licenses interested him, as did the purchase of print rights to a multimedia production.

We created our own group for electronic publishing in Hall 1.1, which was really well-stocked from the opening moment. We seemed to have addressed the correct business associates in the correct manner! All in all, 167 new exhibitors from 14 countries showed up. Frankfurt experienced its takeoff into the electronic future. Brian Blunden, CEO of International Electronic Publishing Research Centre (IEPRC) in Great Britain, and his wife Margot Blunden gave out a lot of information on the new business sector in a specially created electronic forum. Some 55 professional exhibitors came from the skittish publishers: the directors of licensing departments, book dealers, librarians, document specialists and other interested parties.

In addition, either Christoph H. Bräuer or Klaus-Michael Borisch, head of Multi-Media Books, gave seminars and workshops in which they loudly proclaimed that the book trade would have to become a dealer in knowledge and information along electronic pathways; they explained in some detail how this might be done.

The two publishers Florian Langenscheidt and Peter Kindersley had already intensively incorporated new media into their publishing activities, and had supported other companies in this area. Together with them, I tried to bring just two modest messages to the many journalists at the beginning of the Fair of the New Age.

Electronic publishing did not mean forsaking the Gutenberg Galaxy; rather it was a part of it. I then referred to our intention to pass on to the entire book trade the synergistic effects of the new programs offered by the Frankfurt Book Fair.

Even the traditional publishing rights meeting on the day before the Fair dealt with the very complex and complicated theme of this sector. The technologies of electronic publishing seemed easier to overcome than did the associated questions of copyright.

And who was the scapegoat who had opened the barn door wide to New Media? Was the death of the book now inevitably preordained? Was the decline of the cultural technology of "reading" inexorable?

The publisher and one-time chairman of our Supervisory Board, Matthias Wegner, who some time ago had managed to get me into the director's seat at the Fair, wrote to all the concerned newcomers after our second, very successful presentation of electronics:

This time there was not one discussion among publishers that did not begin or end with a question about the future of electronic media. While software suppliers were brimming over with optimism, some fearful publishers of belles-lettres still expressed the hope that "this bitter cup might somehow pass us by." Most people, however, look forward to the new possibilities. [...] Prophecies of doom about the 'end of the age of the book' are simply evidence of panic; this is apparent by any look at the future of New Media. In this year alone, where visions of a future without books are easily found, highly sensitive new publishing shoots are sprouting from the soil. We don't know whether new publishing ventures will overcome the obstacles in their way—Klaus Schöffling and Joachim Unseld with their Frankfurter Verlagsanstalt, Arnulf Conradi with the Berlin Verlag, or Christoph Buchwald with his brand new Luchterhand Literaturverlag (apparently well-financed by the Munich attorney Bötticher). Nonetheless, the power of makers of books to reach for Utopia, the courage for a publishing and literary adventure—these things are unbroken. Just look at the example of Christoph Links and his small (East) Berlin Links Verlag, which is becoming more and more attractive. The book will survive into the next millennium, not only in large companies, but also in innovative individual publishing houses. Assuming the continued existence of the fixed price for books, the life of the book will not be hindered, not by all the mechanisms of the market and not by its obstreperous electronic siblings.[5]

The independently arranged electronic exhibitor groups were finally dissolved after five years, since by then almost all the important electronic firms had merged into the traditionally existing exhibitor groups, which are defined by content at the Book Fair. Electronics was no longer a separate display topic, since the publishing houses had taken up the trend. Until then electronic media had been presented as a group, no matter which target audiences they ultimately served. So linguistic software sat alongside an online encyclopedia, an interactive computer game next to a library database. In the meantime, the new media were no longer being treated as something exotic, but had become an integral component of the publishing program. Learning materials appeared at the schoolbook stall (2006: Hall 3.1); DVDs of teenager fad books appeared in the children and youth book section (2006: Hall 3.0); travel guides that were supplemented by online offerings were presented by the tourism publishers. And in the exposition of scientific and technical publishing and information management (2006: Hall 4.2), highly specialized online databases and digital libraries sat side-by-side with weighty tomes of legal and medical reference works or loose-leaf binder works. Some 30% of the offerings at the Frankfurt Book Fair in 2006 were digital products, 43.1% were books, and another 8.75% were magazines, newspapers and journals.

---

5. *German Publishers Weekly* 82 (October 14, 1994).

Asia

Those of us responsible for book fairs were quite unsettled by the new challenges we faced, challenges that put us under a great deal of pressure to expand our mission. There were competitors, but even more disturbing were the purchases by Reed International, a Dutch-British firm, of the fair of the American Booksellers Association, the book fairs in London, Tokyo and Paris, the MITCOM electronics fair in Cannes, and a film rights fair.

My previous efforts had been of a supportive nature, and in no way were they to be taken seriously as business projects to expand the market or the influence of the Frankfurt Book Fair. The challenge by Reed now had us rethink the expansion of our international business in the sale of rights. The indicators that we consulted, as well as our own experiences in Frankfurt, all pointed to the Asian market—a publishing rights fair in Asia for building up and expanding the Asian fair business could be just the thing!

Accompanied by my then assistant Thorsten O., I set out for my last big trip for the Exposition and Fair Company. This was to obtain information for the basis of such a project, and at the same time to advertise the Frankfurt Book Fair in Asia. Unfortunately, this time I did not succeed in really getting far away, principally because our Frankfurt office kept roping me into its quarrels while I was on the road. What had always fascinated me on these trips, being alone to confront new people, wandering by myself into the unknown and conquering my ignorance, and then coming back as a new person—that was denied me this time.

It was early on a Monday morning, July 14, 1997, when I arrived in Tokyo. Thorsten O. came in from Moscow. We put up at the

Imperial Hotel, but jet lag and the time change did not let me get to sleep that evening. At 3 AM (8 PM in Frankfurt) I woke up with a headache. In a daze, I tried to orient myself to my new surroundings. Japan was not totally new to me. I had been confronting the unique otherness of the Japanese since my first trip to Tokyo in 1972, and I regarded my arrival here as a homecoming, a homecoming into the fairy-tale land of my memories. What struck me in particular at this time was the Japanese love of detail—in eating *tempura,* in the fresh rose in the elevator, in the mirror in the hotel bathroom that had a non-steaming section, the taxi doors which open and close automatically, and in the motorized window curtains in the hotel room.

Our Ambassador Dr. Brümmer greeted me at the German Embassy: "We know each other from somewhere. You have been around for such a long time!" On the next day Thorsten and I, though hardly rested, began our work. The first thing early in the morning we looked up the go-getter Akiko Kurita in the Japan Foreign Rights Center, then went directly to the Tuttle-Mori Agency, and finally to the very well-known literary agent, the jolly, round Tom Mori in his chronically cluttered "office." Neither conversation brought strikingly new information, but we did get the impression of how and what to work with in these agencies. Money could be made with *manga,* the typically Japanese comic books, which also could be sold in China. Then in the evening, with my old friend Yasuo Shimada-san, we were off to the good-time sushi restaurant Hutaba Sushi near the fish market in Ginza. We ate *maguro, salba, tai, tako, tairagai, ebi, anago, awabi* and all those wonderful raw fish morsels, and washed them down with beer. Then we went on foot through the muggy, warm evening back to the hotel. Yashuo commented that it was cool today.

Mr. Hideo Aoki of Motovun Tokyo is a somewhat aloof gentleman, an intellectual type; and Motovun is an agency for art and illustrated books. He sat in the midst of a chaos of books and notes, telling us of the lack of interest of Japanese publishing houses in international business. He always came to Frankfurt and was quite satisfied (in Hall 8 with the Americans and not with the Japanese in Hall 9.3), although the growth of the Fair had made things difficult. He felt that there are hardly any conversations any longer, just rushing from one contact to another.

Then we too rushed, already somewhat fatigued, to the Book Fair information evening for Japanese publishers, arranged by Mrs. Korenaga in the Publishers Club. Some 100 people attended, and I was honored by the presence of Shimada-san and Hattori-san (age 84). My introduction and presentation came from Harry H. Idichi of Froebel-kan Publishers, while I was held back behind the door by an employee of the Publishers Association. Then both wing doors opened, and I made my grand entrance. My lecture, including translation by Karl Watanabe, lasted an hour and a half, and at least half of the group fell asleep. Somebody said afterwards that nevertheless every word was meaningful. *Well then!*

I couldn't get rid of the feeling that for most of the people present this was a required show of friendship rather than any need to do business. It was once again clear that foreign business for Japanese publishers was more of an obligation than it was an economic necessity, which was likely the reason for the collapse of all previous book fair initiatives in Japan, as well as the relative lack of success of the Tokyo book fair. People referred to their unfortunate placement at the Frankfurt Book Fair in Hall 9 (due to the Americans) only in a roundabout way and very reluctantly.

On the following day we had lunch with Franz Stephan von Dohosha, senior managing director and boardmember-international of Gruner + Jahr. Originally from the German publishing giant Bertelsmann, he had been sent here eight years ago. Once a Bertelsmann man, always a Bertelsmann man. He made snap decisions, was only slightly judgmental, and showed insight and knowledge; he was friendly and full of information. Basically, however, he only confirmed what we already knew.

In the afternoon we continued discussions with the President of the Publishers Association, Takao Watanabe, with his charming daughter as translator. Beside him, Director Goma—with his flat, bureaucratic manner—reminded me of the one-time East German leader Erich Honecker. Here too there was support for an Asian publishing rights market, but many difficulties were foreseen in the multiplicity of languages and forms of writing. A common script for the use of computer languages was being promoted by the Asian Pacific Publishers Association, to be created out of Japanese, simplified Chinese and Korean writing systems; it would be intelligible to at least all the East Asian peoples. Other than that, however, the copyright contract business was not developed enough. One still could not concentrate on the Asian fair. The word "Dignity" kept appearing, with each of the existing fairs having its own "Dignity."

In the evening, another thank-you meal with the faithful unsung hero Karl Watanabe, who over the entire day had translated my Teutonic English into Japanese. Toward the end of the day I was plagued by hot spells and dizziness, and felt pressure in my kidneys. I rushed back to get a good night's sleep, but slept only until 3 AM.

Saturday, July 19, 1997 — Taipei, capital of Taiwan. The outside temperature is even more uncomfortable than in Tokyo — over 100°F with extremely high humidity. After only a few minutes I was absolutely soaked with sweat, but then returning to our air-conditioned rooms or sitting in an air-conditioned car gave me a real shock!

The Taiwanese are marked by their frankness and incomparable pragmatism. That makes intercourse with them freer and more predictable than with the reserved Japanese. Tseng Farn-chian, the publisher president in Taipei, and both his employees Jennifer Hsu and Lu Haifa, along with a young Liau, son of the grand-dame Mrs. Liau of Senseio Publishing, who always appeared in a tall, broad-brimmed red hat, ferried us around from 9 AM until 7:30 PM in the company's minibus. They were anxious to show us all the tourist attractions of their country, starting with the northeast coast of Ilan and then traveling over the mountains back to Taipei. At every stop we were always referred in a friendly way to a particular "quiet little spot," where, with a reference to the long road still in front of us, we were sent off to pee — another expression of the particularly pragmatic way of life of these Chinese.

In the evening I was really worn out, and I would have loved just to go back to the hotel. However, that could occur only after another dinner with Mrs. Liau and our traveling companions, where we received a ten-volume history of Taiwan by Emma Chen. Those twice-a-day sumptuous banquets were really very difficult to get through.

Rex How was the newly-appointed general manager for Commercial Press. The next day we had a two-hour lunch in which he participated with lots of important information and very keen, probing questions. Rex (his Chinese name is Hao Ming-yi), had been crippled in his childhood by polio, and now could hardly leave his wheelchair. He had visited me every year since 1989 during the Frankfurt Book Fair, and over the years we became very good friends. He eventually founded his own publishing house in Taipei, but the book fair business continued to fascinate him; in 1996, and from 2005 to 2007 he was in charge of the book fair in Taipei.

I soon discovered the awkward side of Thorsten O. I was never successful at finding any point of view in common with him regarding all the strange things that we were discovering *en masse* on this trip. I was more and more annoyed by his personal peculiarities, which clearly pushed him in the direction of an elitist worldview. Still, he did all the tasks that were assigned to him during this trip; working together in common does not have to mean being compatible in all things.

Today was absolutely too much—twelve hours of strenuous work. First thing in the morning, we were picked up at 8:30 and were off to the Taiwan Government Information Office for a discussion with the assistant general director Frederic P.N. Chang, successor to Charles Wu, who shortly would become Minister of Culture. This was merely an exchange of polite pleasantries, nothing more, but then we had a two-and-a-half-hour, very intensive exchange of opinions with a group of experts at the Hyatt Hotel. Then a short break and a light lunch, and then another round with 30 publishers, television people and a few journalists, all of whom squeezed me like a lemon, a good 3½ hours. I was exhausted when I went to the next round of questions and answers with the Taipei International Book Exposition (TIBE) team. They were principally concerned with the focal theme of "Germany" at the next Taipei book fair.

I was able to pull myself together a bit at the closing banquet. At 10 PM we got back to the hotel, where it took me until midnight to pack. At 6:30 AM we were taken to the airport.

After a two-hour flight, we landed in Hong Kong on Tuesday, July 22nd. Immediately after checking in to the New World Harbour View Hotel, Thorsten and I took an orientation tour through the impressive convention center that had been built out into the harbor basin. We also looked at the book fair, which was still under construction. The Germans were the only Western publishers to have a stand.

At 4 PM we met a Mr. Traeger, the next general manager of the Hong Kong office of the Frankfurt Book Fair. He was a Sinologist, and we wanted to clarify the interests of each of the parties in the Hong Kong deal. We all took part in the cocktail party and the subsequent fair banquet in the rotunda of the convention center. The view through the broad picture windows out over the skyline of Kowloon and of the harbor disappearing into the mist at dusk was enchanting, like a film made in Cinemascope. I met a lot of old acquaintances from Beijing.

After the meal, the head of the fair in Hong Kong, Benjamin Chou, took us through the halls, and with great pride, but also with nervous anticipation, the copyright center on the sixth floor, where the only true publishing houses that stood out were the esoteric Ahriman from Tübingen and Xenos from Hamburg. This arrangement surely was not going to work!

The next morning we had a conversation about a possible rights fair in Hong Kong with Wolfgang Ehmann and Susanne Weiss in the German-Chinese Chamber of Commerce. Then we visited the fair itself. Discussions with Weijang, who wanted to open a Chinese copyright agency, due to his feelings that the centrally managed official Beijing agency was too ponderous and too bureaucratic. Then to lunch with Joyce A. of our international office in Frankfurt, who was in charge of the German stall here in Hong Kong. Joyce earnestly described the problems in our office, and the very poor atmosphere made worse in my absence by the pigheaded policies of JK. It wasn't the first time I had heard something like that.

In the evening we took the Star Ferry to Kowloon to eat in the Jade Garden restaurant. I was accompanied by Joyce A. and Claudia K., who was soon to be entrusted with our Beijing book information center, and who on her own initiative had flown over from the Chinese capital for these meetings here in Hong Kong. Thorsten was so tired that he remained at the hotel. Claudia K., who spoke excellent Mandarin, seemed to me to be a practical, hard-working person. After the meal the three of us strolled along the waterside, which was lined with brightly lit kites, a leftover from the ceremonies of the turnover of Hong Kong to China. Out there on the Hong Kong side the high-rise buildings were decorated with kitschy light chains, which in size and extent combined with the cruising junks, ferries and boats to create an unreal, theatrical scene.

We had a discussion at the Hong Kong Trade Development Council with the intelligent assistant executive director C.S. Lee and Francis Wong. For an hour and a half we discussed the Asian rights market and the Hong Kong book fair. We discussed "one country–two systems," a phrase applied to China and Hong Kong but clearly directed at Taiwan. Should Taiwan agree to this model, it would make possible a unification similar to the one that had taken place for Hong Kong, including peaceful and prosperous development with a great deal of autonomy. In that case, Hong Kong would lose its mediating role, since Taiwan could negotiate directly. Should Taiwan block this path or seek a way to independence, one would have to count on a tough, possibly even military reaction to the problem by Beijing. Military experts at the moment were observing the buildup of invasion troops within the People's Liberation Army.

I ruled out closer cooperation of the Frankfurt Book Fair with the Hong Kong Book Fair, and also concluded that efforts in the direction of a publishing rights fair were in vain.

The following morning I met with Rex How, who wanted to have the first volume of my autobiography translated into Chinese. Claudia K. was to get a copy of the galleys as soon as possible in order to look for a translator in Beijing. Rex would soon send me a contract. I warned him that he should first have some test translations done. No, no—what I had described would be enough. The book would appear simultaneously in

Taipei and Beijing, where his Commercial Press had an office.[1] In addition, he wanted to have me become editor of a series of international authors. I had to turn him down on grounds of lack of time.

Then I took a little time off, and with Claudia K. as translator set off in the hot and misty day to Lamma Island. This island was clearly not the Pearl of the Orient. Three large chimneys of a power plant, itself hidden by green hills, towered over this little locale, which was quite dirty and menaced by evil-smelling, brackish water. Nonetheless there were good seafood restaurants, and one could sit outside and enjoy nature. I truly enjoyed this freedom of the fresh air after the many days of imprisonment in all the ice-cold air-conditioned interiors.

We landed in Singapore. After the hectic pace of Tokyo, Taipei, and of Hong Kong in particular, this city on first impression seems out of the way, almost like a small town. At least things are more relaxed here. Well, it was the weekend, and our first day without an appointment. We were staying at the Excelsior Hotel, where I was able to turn off the air conditioning in the room, which relieved my neck pains. I spent a few hours in the morning at the little pool set into the cement building (in the shade), swam some, and thus adjusted to the climate.

In the morning at 9 AM we went to the central office of the Times Publishing Group, and there we met the industrious Ms. Shirley Hew, who brought along the senior vice president of the publishing house, H.H. Chiam. Both of them were enthusiastic supporters of Frankfurt. What was even more important was that Chiam had joined up with seven or eight publishers to form their own federation to support what was once called the Chinese Book Fair, from now on to be known as the World Book Fair. This Times Group was internationally very active, but more in the West than in the Asian publishing rights market.

---

1. After the book *Und schrieb meinen Zorn in den Staub der Regale* was translated, Rex How had it published in 1999 with Commercial Press. In 2003, he had an abridged edition in simplified Chinese done at the Commercial Press in Beijing. In 2005, he put out a translation of my book *A History of the Frankfurt Book Fair* through his own Net and Books imprint in Taipei, and in 2008 published the present book of memoirs in Chinese.

Shirley Hew was interested for us to have some discussions with the World Book Fair, and set up an appointment for us with the organizer in charge, Michael Hew—a relation perhaps?

Then at the Tanglin Club we met K.P. Sivam, a member of the tiny Indian minority and a member of many, many associatons. A friendly soul, he warned us about the World Book Fair, since the Times Group was involved and was pocketing the profit.

Thorsten and I walked back to the hotel, where at the Riverside we drank a beer and vodka. Completely soaked in sweat, I got back to my room and called the office in Frankfurt to follow up on several faxes that had arrived during the day.

On every trip there comes a time when you are completely fed up. That day was today. In the morning I had to think about the tricky situation at the company, about the head of the German Publishers Association, about JK, about the fact that here I am paddling around in circles—I asked myself whether the whole thing makes sense, whether what we are doing here is understood by anybody back home! Truly, we had already cleared up what we had wanted to clarify, and we were only halfway through our trip. What in God's name were we going to do with the rest of the time? However, there was no turning back; the planned trip had to be completed.

In a really bad mood, I began the day with Klaus Jürgen Scholz, the managing director of the Singapore International Convention & Exhibition center, a Swabian who showed us around some 300,000 square feet where the World Book Fair would take place starting the following year. This fair center was very well-organized and was very well-suited for our eventual plans. Nonetheless, it is rarely the official arrangements that guarantee a successful Fair, as we know all too well....

We then had an appointment at the Singapore Trade Development Board with Tham Hock Chee. Tham had studied in Germany and had worked in Frankfurt as well. He made an initial impression of being tired and surly, but then a lively discussion developed. The Trade Board was naturally very interested in a project for a publishing rights fair in cooperation with us. We went off to have a meal together. When the discussion came around to the events of 1968 in Germany, our Mr. Tham suddenly thawed out and became quite animated. He called himself a "fellow traveler" of that time, which he had experienced while in Hamburg.

At the Ministry of Information and Arts I spoke with the director for Information and Policy, Mohamed Ali Baksh, regarding questions of restrictions on imports, on taxes, and on matters of censorship. Naturally hard pornography and incidents like the Rushdie Affair were borderline cases that the authorities wished to discuss. Otherwise, one would have to create special rules for all kinds of cases for such an international fair. Here too there was great interest, and we got agreement for promotional support from the Trade Development Board.

Then came our Singapore appointment with Michael Hew (husband of Mrs. Hew of the Times Group), who was organizing the World Book Fair, and Seow Choke Meng of the Singapore Press Holdings, a nervous, agitated and scrawny individual, who immediately upon meeting us enlightened us with his entire history and his opinions on everything. These two people did not number among the most *sympatico* contacts on that trip, but they were the ones who a year ago in Frankfurt at the Fair had brought me together with the local Singapore representatives. Even at that time they had presented a proposal for a cooperative venture.

At this point Thorsten and I went to the famous Raffles Hotel to drink their well-known "Singapore Sling," a cocktail made of gin and pineapple, which didn't taste particularly good to me. We closed out the evening with a little supper in a cozy Pennsylvanian restaurant and a glass of vodka from my bottle in the hotel.

We were leaving an economic wonderland. Everything here seemed to be set up in the most advantageous manner—the cleanliness in the streets, in the houses, in the rooms. The traffic orderly and light (honking forbidden!), no traffic jams. Slowly we drove on freeways lined with brightly blooming bougainvillea bushes. At the airport we were astounded by the well-manicured orchid garden in the departure hall, which had little streams running through, with goldfish the size of carp romping about.

Our arrival in Jakarta was quite different, where we once again emerged into the chaotic and noisy Third World. In the taxi we were tormented by the slow-moving, pollution-laden stream of traffic. Traffic jams are a way of life in Jakarta—760,000 autos move at a stop-and-go pace, supplemented by another 61,000 each year. Only about 50% of all commuters use the meager public transportation system, while all the others sit in their cars or on their motorbikes. You have to reckon on hours to cover a distance of a mile or so. Often you can see the building that you are going to on the other side of the street, but there's no way of getting across. The car drives along for another quarter of an hour since there are no chances to make any turns, and then finally one can stumble back for another quarter of an hour on the destined side of the street. I am reminded of Lagos or Mombasa and of the metropolises of Latin America. We turned into the entry of our hotel, a skyscraper block with a powerful entrance lobby, which would be our glitzy but not very homey headquarters for the next few days.

In the afternoon we had our first contact with IKAPI, the Indonesian publishers association. We met Aida Joesoef Ahmad, a friendly but very talkative woman, and a one-time journalist, Dr. Alfons Taryadi, who never stopped writing down what I said, since he wanted to do an article about it. Indonesia would like to be a focal theme country, but on the other hand it wanted support for its presence in Frankfurt, since otherwise everything was too expensive. We missed the clear goal-orientation of the Chinese; here we met the grand, dreamy, self-satisfied chatter about the way things are. After two and a half hours we had everything done.

At noon the following day we charged into the Goethe Institute, after having spent the morning dealing with papers, messages and speeches. Dr. Barth, the director of the Institute, a very pleasant person (we had met once before in 1986 in Madras), had done a good job in preparing for our presentation. Thirty publishers had gathered in the lecture hall of the Institute, where first I showed a video about the Frankfurt Book Fair and afterwards gave a lecture. In a discussion we dealt with the same questions as the day before. The Indonesian book trade was still very weak. Pirated works continued to proliferate, even though the country had now signed the Berne Convention.² Fewer foreign authors were pirated than were domestic bestsellers. IKAPI was too weak to prosecute all these cases and to pursue them in court.

Once again we struggled through the traffic back to the hotel and refreshed ourselves in the Oasis Restaurant. This fancy restaurant is set up in an old Dutch colonial villa and is patronized in particular by business people. We ordered a typical Indonesian *rijsttafel*. After a clear fish broth with mushrooms, suddenly a dozen young women marched up to our table, all dressed the same in pink jackets over batik sarongs. Each one of them carried a porcelain dish from which we served ourselves. The rice came in mounds on the first plate, followed by crab omelet, fish fillet in a spicy sauce, steamed lamb in coconut milk, grilled chicken with chili and garlic, marinated lamb and beef, sticks of seafood and chicken and who knows what else, each of them proffered by a different young woman. Later there were candied fruits and coffee. We drank a California Cabernet Sauvignon, and really let go that particular evening.

The next day at 9 AM we were at the internationally notable Granmedia, the largest publisher in Indonesia. The director of the publishing department, Gabriel Sugianto, had rounded up eight of his employees. At Frankfurt they only bought rights, though they continued to come with 20 people. A publishing rights market in Asia? Maybe once in a while they would buy a book from Japan or Taiwan, but fairs elsewhere in Asia or anywhere else were not patronized. Frankfurt was enough for them.

Accompanied by the three women Siti Gretiani (Editor), Sri Reni Moerwaningsih (Rights Officer), and Listiana Srisanti (Head of the Fiction and Children's Book Section), we then visited two bookstores, followed by a Chinese meal at a shopping mall. We never did have a true discussion, though our questions were answered in a friendly and concise manner.

The lower part of town was a true purgatory, with the falling-down houses of the old Dutch colony of Batavia, and piles of

---

2. The *Berne Convention for the Protection of Literary and Artistic Works* is an international agreement governing copyright law, first drafted in 1886.

trash everywhere. A canal with stinking, slow-moving sewage. The traffic on the sides was energetic and noisy, but hardly moving; people were shoved together toward small dirty little stores, little peddlers' carts, with children playing in the dirt. Everywhere it stank of urine or worse. A mangy brown cat was scratching in the trash looking for something edible. A moist heat hovered over it all, accompanied by the roar of the engines in the stalled traffic. I had a vision of the future of a smothered life in a society undergoing the collapse of the capitalist system, robbed of all its resources and creative energies, with people left behind in this Dante's Inferno, with everyone retreating into their air-conditioned, antiseptic castles.

We retreated in exactly the same way by grabbing a taxi out of the halting traffic. We explained to the bemused driver where we wanted to go, someplace where he had never been. When we returned, we passed by giant pictures of Suharto and his guests, the President of Namibia and his wife.

The Café Batavia lay on a small traffic-buffeted square opposite the palace of the one-time Dutch governor. This is a place that actually hardly exists anymore—old dusty charm from the 1950s and '60s in a historic warehouse from the Dutch colonial period. Photos in dark frames line the walls up to the very high ceiling, showing actors, presidents, artists and authors. This continues on into the toilets, where Bernard Shaw looks down on you while you pass water over a grill opposite a gigantic mirror, over which the falling cascades of water cause your reflection to swim together with that of your neighbor.

In the semi-darkness was a bar in which essentially all the drinks in the world were available, from Caipirinhas to Margaritas to Stolichnaya vodka, which I ordered. I felt as though I were in Hemingway's Floridita in Havana. This was in astounding contrast to the life around us.

On Sunday, I spent two hours in the pool and then studied the documents for Kuala Lumpur. After that I slept a bit and watched television, just doing nothing. All of a sudden I started thinking about the office.

Since the ill-starred Rushdie Affair, I had become more reserved in my decisions and had turned over the actual course of company policies to the various departments, principally to my assistant director JK, while I retained for myself only the final sign-off on decisions. In those years I was only actively involved in activities around electronic publishing, such as the Rights-on-ROM catalog. I wanted to sort of slide over into early retirement, since I was convinced that I did not want to take responsibility any longer for the many decisions now coming up.

All of a sudden it struck me that I had lost the edge in the long war with the German Publishers Association. I no longer trusted my own estimates and evaluations of the situation. Somehow I had resigned myself to the ongoing attempts of people on the Supervisory Board and in the Association to limit my freedom of action. Chaos reigned in the office. Everyone thought that he could be in charge. Everyone was fighting for himself and against everyone else.

In Malaysia at first everything went along very pleasantly. The airport in Kuala Lumpur is quite large, without a lot of traffic. The taxi breezed toward the city. Suddenly, with our high-rise hotel already on the horizon, the traffic came to a dead stop. For an hour we moved forward only inch by inch. It was sticky and hot in the car, even though the air conditioning was rattling on. Outside, impatient people were scurrying back and forth, trying to see if their bus was coming. It was not.

At 9 AM we had an appointment in the hotel, but nobody showed up. So we took a hotel shuttle off to the government quarter in order to meet the person in charge of the National Book Council of Malaysia. We discussed their participation at the Frankfurt Book Fair in great detail, and we heard the lament that was expressed quite often in the discussions during this trip—people went to Frankfurt only to buy, but unfortunately were not taken seriously as sellers by the other participants.

We went to lunch together at a famous club, but it was closed because of a power outage. We went to another club that had no air conditioning, also because of a blackout, but at least they served a Chinese meal. We sat down to some spicy food in the sticky rooms where you couldn't even open any windows. Very soon we were all soaked in sweat.

Practically a quarter of a century earlier I had met the "friendly, but reserved" cultural attaché at the German Embassy in Bogotá. When we walked into the office of Harald N. Nestroy, the German Ambassador in Malaysia, the comment immediately came bubbling out of him, "We know each other from Bogotá!"

Nestroy immediately began talking about his work here in Malaysia—about a BASF deal for 1 billion dollars soon to be concluded, about the difficulties in negotiating conditions with the people in Malaysia, who even after signing a contract wanted changes; of the obligatory "donations" that were expected from any company that wanted to be taken seriously for a commission. So the Bosch Company, which in the previous month had wanted to celebrate the 35th anniversary of the founding of its local branch, had been happy to get away with a payment to the Minister President of "only" 500,000 ringgits "for social purposes."

Nestroy invited us to a nearby Thai restaurant for lunch. Since Thorsten still had to make preparations for the presentation in the afternoon at the Goethe Institute, he left early, allowing our conversation to be more personal. We talked like two old friends who had not seen each other for a long time, about our families, our life experiences and all kinds of things. Finally he said goodbye to me at the door of his official car, which he made available to me so that I could get to the Goethe Institute in time. "I have been carrying your business card all these years around with me, even though I usually cross off the contacts made at earlier postings. Why I did that I can't exactly say!"

Gerhard Engelking ran the local Goethe Institute like a caring innkeeper, always looking out for his guests. He acted very earnestly, though his ponytail, black clothes and the gold chain around his neck made one think more of a hippie. We had expected at the most 15 publishers at the meeting. Almost 40 people showed up, then patiently watched a pretentious video advertisement before listening to my 40-minute presentation. After half an hour of ponderous discussion, I invited everyone to a reception in the little garden café of the Institute. Everybody attacked the food that was offered.

One last day without any appointments before going off into the wide-open air. We were warned about the ongoing air pollution, apparently drifting in from the forest fires in Sumatra. Two short excursions in the area of the hotel convinced me that the air in fact caused a very unpleasant scratching in my throat, so I was reduced to spending almost the entire day in my hotel room.

Naturally nobody was at the airport when we arrived two hours late at about midnight in New Delhi—only the usual chaos, heat, and people trying to dragoon us into their cars. I succeeded in chartering a little bus with air-conditioning. At the Taj Mahal Hotel we were put up with all Indian hospitality in the luxurious Club-Étage. I don't know who had arranged that. Well, we finally had arrived.

In the morning, S.K. Ghai, whom I knew from my earlier trips to Delhi, appeared to push on me a list of appointments. Ghai was quite excited about the new New Delhi Book Fair, although it would bring in only a fraction of the exhibitors (250) that its sister fair in February had brought in, the New Delhi World Book Fair. When I asked him about the reasons for the creation of a second Delhi Book Fair, he put me off. The same thing happened later with the president of the publishers group and other publishers when asked about it. At one point it became clear that the Indian publishers had founded this fair because they wanted to have their say as to what would happen instead of being subject to the admittedly bureaucratic state Indian Book Council. The publishers all in all exhibited a childlike enthusiasm about this affair, as though they had put something over on an overbearing father. And it gradually became clear to me what role they had assigned to me—that of the great "Fair Guru"! At the opening ceremony, where I gave a short speech, Publisher President Narendra Kumar called me one who was "a legend in his own time," who by his presence was giving his blessing to the newcomer in the family of international book fairs.

At midday we had lunch in Hall 7 of the fairgrounds—in between all kinds of interviews in the corridors. In the evening, the 74-year-old Dina N. Malhotra had invited us to a special dinner in the India International Center. I had a long discussion with the Brit Clive Breadley, who was quite excited about his imminent retirement at Christmas time, and with Dina's son, Shekhar Malhotra, and his wife, both of whom were really very pleasant people.

First thing the next morning the photographer Cherian Thomas of the *Indian Express* posed me in the usual way—with a book, at a computer, looking out the window into the broad beyond. The interviewer came along, a friendly and intelligent, somewhat chubby young man, Sourish Bhattacharyya, and posed the right questions, and I had the impression that my message was getting across to him. I kept looking longingly out of my hotel room window while I was waiting for the next interviewer. The red sandstone buildings of the government quarter rose up out of a thick stand of trees, which were hidden by the skyscrapers of the high-ranking government officials. Swarms of small, long-tail blue cockatoos buzzed above the branches.

Later we went off to the fair, where we were to participate in honoring some well-deserving book dealers. The other honored foreign guests and I presented to the beaming book dealers three dreadful copper-molded Buddha trophies. Arvind Kumar, former director of the World Book Fair, suddenly clapped me on the shoulder. Arvind had been in Bellagio, but had then quit his post because his superior, a government bureaucrat, had been "an idiot" (he told him that to his face!). I was really happy to see him, since he is one of the really clear-headed people in India. Then Thorsten and I strolled through the halls, where the same people made us want to escape a tea party. I decided to skip the next cocktail party for "Meet the Foreign Delegates at the DBF," and we returned to the Taj Mahal Hotel.

I had to husband my strength. I canceled all my appointments for the morning, and went down to the swimming pool, where I thrashed around in the water like an imp. That felt really good after all the sitting of the past few weeks.

It was the last day of a trip that never seemed to end. We took a taxi to the fairgrounds, and started looking for the administrative center where my last lecture was to take place. We were sent on a half-hour trek in scorching heat across the fairgrounds, so that once again I arrived dripping with sweat. The members of the executive board of the association started screaming at each other why so-and-so had not picked me up at the hotel. There were about 20 people there, practically all "Frankfurt-goers," so I put my talk back into my pocket and for about an hour talked about new things that would be coming along, particularly Rights-on-ROM. Then one last press appointment—Smita Bhatia, correspondent of the *Telegraph*, interviewed me quite extensively in my hotel room.

It was then the appointed time to go to the Oberoi Hotel, where a luncheon had been set up for us by a worthy trio from the German Embassy, Ambassador Ute Banerjea-Komers, cultural attaché Wolfgang von Erffa and press attaché Peter von Wesendonk. The party also included an older, very interested, and quite open-minded woman, Salima Tyabji, and the editor of the magazine *India in the Present*, Dr. Sveta Dave Chakravarty, and the ever-present president of the Publishers Association Kumar, who here too arrived 45 minutes late.

Drawing Up the Balance Sheet

The "lead employees"—JK and I, plus the lawyer, the business manager of the German Publishers Association, and the public relations head of the Book Fair—had to leave the room. The Supervisory Board was going into executive session. Outside in the corridor I was overcome with a leaden heaviness, which I attempted to battle with some strong red wine that had already been laid out for the subsequent luncheon in our reception room. The process reminded me of an oral examination for graduation. JK was named business director; people congratulated him. The Supervisory Board later declared itself satisfied with the premature dissolution of my contract under the condition that the succession was in order before I left. For me that was nothing new. I was suddenly dead tired. The fatigue did not leave me in the evening, as I headed home with heavy heart and leaden limbs. I dreaded this last year of employment ahead.

Unless engaged in Cairo or Taipei, publishers and book fair people start their book year in Leipzig in March. Lots of people who plan on Frankfurt on the Main also show up in Leipzig on the Pleisse River, and the animosities between the two book fairs have long been laid to rest. Leipzig has found its place as the German springtime book fair, while the international autumn fair takes place in Frankfurt. We from Frankfurt made extensive use of the Leipzig site, where one could more calmly concentrate on dealing with book customers than was possible at home.

When the Leipzig Book Prize for European Understanding was awarded to the British historian Eric Hobsbawm and the Croatian publisher Nenad Popović, I was sitting between the chairmen of the two previous German Publishers' Associations (East and West Germany), Jürgen Gruner (East) and Günther

Christiansen (West). Gruner was visibly sinking deeper and deeper into his chair. During the applause, he twice ostentatiously and limply clapped his hands together. Too much was said here that no longer fit into Gruner's world view, which had been formed by the collapse of socialism, or was it perhaps that on the contrary he was enamored of the Marxist theses being propounded by the academic prize winner Hobsbawm, but thought that in this capitalistic world surrounding him he wasn't able to show it? When I ran into him later in a Fair café at a standup table with Elmar Faber, he snapped at me regarding the war in Yugoslavia as if I had personally instigated it. The old "comrades" in their nostalgic resignation yearned for the old days, and mixed everything together in their frustration. *First you finished us off, and now you are bombing our Serbs! And no one is protesting!* On the next day, however, when I passed by the Faber booth at the Leipzig Book Fair, he rushed over to me and apologized.

I won't deny that this experience gave me the impetus to start a project with Nenad Popović, a person who was deservedly awarded the Prize for European Understanding in Leipzig. During the war, he had dedicated himself tirelessly to his publisher colleagues and to authors from the other republics and provinces of Yugoslavia. This project related to the Serbs and to all other Balkan authors involved in this unholy war of Yugoslav secession. At the opening press conference of the Frankfurt Book Fair, after referring to a presentation on the situation in Iran, I said:

Another topic central to the politics of our time this year is the war in Kosovo and the process of social disintegration in the former Yugoslavia, which is still going on after ten years. Here the Book Fair has taken the initiative and has invited 16 renowned authors from all parts of the former Yugoslavia to a pre-fair conference and to a press conference tomorrow, the first day of the Fair. The goal of the initiative, which has the working title of "Group 99," is to re-create a way to talk to one another, a process that has been interrupted even among the intellectuals by the wars and the upheaval of recent decades, but that remains a prerequisite for new cultural and political beginnings, and for the creation or re-creation of freedom of opinion and a truly free cultural climate.

The conference took place three days before the Fair at a hotel in Kranichstein (near Darmstadt). On the first day, the entire group appeared at the press center. Several of the authors later were able to do public readings from their works at the international center.[1] The project was conceived as a kind of "Group 47," but it soon faded away when the Book Fair ceased supporting it after my departure. The authors met only once again in Montenegro at a meeting organized by Nenad Popović.

The Jerusalem Book Fair stood on my agenda for June. A visit every two years to the Jerusalem International Book Fair was always a special event for us book people. The absolute success of this special fair rested on two factors related to one another—the *Shoah* and the Fair director Zev Birger. The financial basis of the exposition was to a large extent assured by German participants. The Holtzbrinck Publishing Group and the Bertelsmann Publishing House rented oversize stalls that they could hardly use during the fair, and these two big publishers were also engaged through foundations and the financing of programs.

Birger played the instrument of forgiveness like a virtuoso. Everybody admired and loved him for that. Who of us from the successor generation to the Nazis would not have a warm feeling to be embraced by a survivor of the Holocaust and be called "friend"? Zev and his wife Trudi, who both called me their friend, wonderfully embodied human forgiveness and the love of a defiled generation, and as a result people were always ready to do everything possible for these two.

And so the German publishers of rank and renown all came personally—Reinhold Neven DuMont from Kiepenheuer und Witsch, Michael Krüger from Carl Hanser Verlag, Frank Wössner from Bertelsmann, Christoph Buchwald from Suhrkamp, Lothar Menne from Heyne, Viktor Niemann from Piper, Georg von Holtzbrinck and Monika Schöller from S. Fischer, great

---

1. The authors who came to the conference: From Kosovo: *Ali Podrimja* and *Shkelzen Maliqi*. From Montenegro: *Milorad Popović* and *Don Branko Sbutega*. From Croatia: *Slavenka Drakulić, Miljenko Jergović, Viktor Ivančić* and *Slobodan Šnajder*. From Bosnia: *Ivan Lovrenović* and *Semezdin Mehmedinović*. From Serbia: *Filip David, Drinka Gojković, Bogdan Bogdanović* and *Dragan Velikić*. From Slovenia: *Drago Jančar*.

publishing personalities, who, except at Frankfurt, never appeared together at any international book fair. In addition, this time Michael Naumann, the German Minister for Culture and erstwhile publisher of Rowohlt Verlag, came, as did the chairman of the German Publishers Association. And whenever so many decisionmakers get together, some deals are always concluded—transfers of titles, sales, plans for joint book projects. And so this Fair was not lacking in interest from a business point of view.

But here too in Jerusalem the quarrels from Frankfurt overtook me. Even though I had tried during the fair and at other occasions to keep as far away as possible from the chairman of the German Publishers Association, I unloaded some hot words on him on the terrace of Zev's house. During the course of that exchange I came out with everything that was bothering me about the behavior of the executive committee of the association and about the way my successor was being chosen. His answers, though not uttered in an unfriendly way, could in no way pacify me. The way the head of the Association was acting came right out of the whole organization's bureaucratic-*apparatchik* mindset. They never understood the essence of things! My anger over that unproductive conversation robbed me of another night of sleep.

The following day I was able to go back to the book fair. The general presentations of the Jerusalem Book Fair were of very high intellectual caliber. What struck me after a rather ironic speech by Michael Krüger was the thin-skinned nature of the American editors in any discussion about why so few foreign titles were taken for American production. Those who were being addressed felt as though they were forced onto the defensive whenever asked why in the United States a book that had not yet been written could possibly merit a huge advance on the basis of a two-page summary, while a book from another language could be turned down with the reasoning that one couldn't read it ahead of time because of the lack of language skills. This problem had to be addressed, since the American publishing houses only wanted to sell their own products, and showed scarcely any interest in taking up the offerings of non-American publishers.

On the basis of the somewhat resigned attitude that Krüger adopted in his talk, I thought I could see that he too no longer believed in an unlimited future for what he, as a publisher, stood for. However, that was exactly what it was that so moved me and many others at this fair—that just as this world of true publishers and friends of books seemed at an end, here in Jerusalem it seemed to live on. In any case, this fair embodied a book world which we often yearned for, which back home and elsewhere was already done for.

Book fairs are no medium for the future; they will soon disappear! Is this what was impending at the end of my engagement with the book fair? Was this wonderful medium really reaching its historical terminus? The Arabs had an old saying: *When an age dies out, a library dies.* Was it only my mood at the end of my tenure that presaged an end to book fairs?

A type of publisher originating in the United States had come to the fore, one that considered the making of books to be another business entirely, and who defined success by the highest possible sales numbers. Alberto Vitale, then CEO of Bantam, New York, was just such a type, someone who asked André Shiffrin if he was able to look at himself in the mirror in the morning if he made such poor books (meaning poor sales). Shiffrin in his Pantheon publishing house (an imprint of Bantam) was one of the few American publishers who was still involved in publishing true literature, and not the kinds of mass-consumption goods that Vitale wanted.

A few well-meaning publishers, with whom I discussed my fears, comforted me by saying that it was a good time for me to leave the sinking ship. Just then was the right time to go. What would come afterwards could only be doomed to decline.

I didn't believe them, but at that time, due to my personal and general melancholy, I did not have the appropriate arguments at hand. I was convinced that book fairs were still irreplaceable for all those people for whom the content of books was important, for authors and publishers of books of literature, science and technology, of art, books for children and youth, and above all—for the readers.

Book fairs as festivals of books are a marketing opportunity to bring the offered contents to the right customer. Once the press and the media in the 1970s rediscovered the content of books at book fairs, alternative reading material had often been made available to a broad reading public of engaged reporters, books that were produced by small publishing houses under very strong conditions of self-denial. Many book fairs that had developed in the book festivals, in Göteborg and Leipzig, in Guadalajara and Taipei, have become unique windows into spiritual and scientific development and into the daily life of those societies encompassed by these literatures.

In yet another argument—books have to cross boundaries; they must shed light on what others do, and they must awaken understanding and move us closer to what is Other. In the age of globalization book fairs take on the important task of distribution, of exchange between countries, between cultural regions, between various language groups. Not only on the grounds of solidarity with the Third World, and not only because I may have been a man of the Left, I had been active in getting translations from the countries of Africa, Asia and Latin America during my tenure at the Book Fair. How much knowledge had we gained about countries and people through their literature, and how that literature had helped us become part of the lives of others! What great discoveries we had brought to the Book Fair using our annual focal point presentations!

There's no doubt that there is a lively exchange of information throughout the world due to electronic media, but this exchange is fleeting and superficial. Besides that, the electronic means of storage are still really quite unstable. What I saved in the 1980s on diskette can no longer be retrieved; it is all lost! Technology has so developed that the old disks can no longer be opened. And now I hear that limited storage time is also true of self-burned CD-ROMs onto which we have entrusted so much that is worth remembering. The prognoses are between one and ten years, and then the data are gone!

Everywhere in the world new international book fairs are being founded, most recently in Greece, South Africa, and among the Arabs in Abu Dhabi and Riyadh. Where else but at a book fair can intellectuals, researchers, politicians, or simply interested people stay informed about what is going on without and within their countries? The book offers long storage times (at least 100 years) and deepening engagement with the content that is offered. The book fairs are an appropriate medium for distribution. Contents that are interesting for a country or a cultural region can make an appearance at a fair; translation rights may be purchased and brought into one's own market. Book fairs are, for books, the global medium for distribution, just as the Internet is for electronic information.

The old, almost blind Kazimierz Majerowicz before the turn of the century spent long years as the managing director of the Polish book dealers organization Dom Książki, and functioned as the top book dealer in Poland. Now he groped along near our fair stall at the Warsaw Book Fair. I often had dealings with him, and as he tapped by me, so helpless, I was hit by a strong feeling of the past. I thought of a sculpture by Rodin: *She who was the helmet maker's once-beautiful wife.* I said goodbye to my colleagues at the German stall and realized that something had come to an end for me. Melancholy rose in me, and I returned to the hotel in the rain.

One night in May I just couldn't relax at my house in the Rhön, and took out my pen and a few sheets of paper and went upstairs. Here, sitting in my comfortable wingback chair under the glow of the sofa lamp, I fought my sadness by trying to draw up a balance sheet of my activity at the Frankfurt Book Fair:

On the occasion of the 25th book fair under my directorship, and in light of my imminent retirement from the Exposition and Fair Company, I would like to make a report about the most important activities and innovations for the Book Fair and our work abroad that occurred during my service for the Ausstellungs- und Messe GmbH [Exposition and Fair Company, Ltd.] *of the German Publishers and Booksellers Association.*

I conceived the document as a kind of official finding regarding my 25-year activity as director of the Frankfurt Book Fair. I divided my activity into three distinct phases:

1. Dynamic development phase (1974–1989): Reworking and systematizing the organizational flows in technology and administration.
2. Reaction phase (1990s): loss of the ability to shape the Fair

to the market-dominant forces (U.S. publishers, concentration of ownership processes).
3. Future phase (end of the 1990s to the turn of the century): *Frankfurt Goes Electronic.* Introduction of electronic media as an independent exhibitor department at the Fair (1993). Virtual book fair. Transition from exhibitor group orientation to one of electronic media offerings (CD-ROM, online).
4. Drawing up the balance:
    – From 1974 to 1998 the number of exhibitors at the Frankfurt Book Fair rose 245% (from 3,903 to 9,545), and exhibitors with their own stalls grew by 288% (from 2,360 to 6,793).
    – Space occupied grew by 342% (from 54,000 m² to 184,590 m²).
    – The number of participating countries increased by 45 (from 60 to 105).
    – Visits by the public also increased from 150,000 to 290,000, some 193%.
    – The greatest rate of increase was that of the participation of public media, 349% (from 3,150 to 11,000 journalists).
    – In this time period six focal theme fairs emphasizing a subject and eleven focal theme fairs emphasizing a country, with a total of 2,340 individual presentations organized and given.

By the morning hours, I was holding this six-page document in my hands. I looked at the pitiful numbers of the balance of 25 years of a very strenuous existence. Was that what I was trying to do? Was that everything?

All of a sudden I remembered the experience of the "Berlin pit." Hadn't it all begun there, the drive that sent me through this life full of adventure, the drive to gather people together in order to create communities with them? Later on I had a specific clientèle in my sights, who felt bound to a common goal just as I did, that is, to create means of communication that would serve mutual understanding and would help bind people together.

On that night in May, I began to write this book—a book that really was not meant to serve as a justification, as I originally intended when I drew up the balance sheet. And so my late-night attempt at justification with an "Activity Report" turned into a recounting of all I had gone through in my wanderings amongst the exhibit halls of the Frankfurt Book Fair.

More and more often in that last year I sought to put distance between myself and my professional life by seeking refuge in my little house in the Rhön. It had been a remarkable summer, with thousands of snails in the meadows and in the flowerbeds, but no birds. The trees stood quiet and empty at dusk. Nothing moved. Where were they, those loud and active residents of my fifth room? The merry titmice that flapped around over the balcony in order to get at a spider or at some other prey. Where was the tail-wagging robin that sat on the fence to launch its hunt for insects? Where were the wagtails, who got under the gables of the house to have their brood? Where was the little wren, who at twilight would warble its mighty songs from the rafters of the barn? Where were the swallows that shot across the meadow like dive bombers? Where had they all gone? Not even one pigeon that had lost its way, no crows, no magpies. The single little bat that in previous summers had buzzed around our heads was nowhere to be seen. And the martens or the birds of prey, who during the day let out their sharp shrieks? Had they come earlier in the season, and I had just missed them, or would they come later? Somehow I found it unsettling; I felt myself quite alone.

(It later turned out that all the animals were hiding from a total solar eclipse of August 11th. The next day they were all back again!)

I look up from my writing implement. Outside it is storming. A ray of sun breaks through the rainclouds. I close the computer, climb the 80 steps from our bright maisonette in Mainz down to the poorly lit garage and get behind the wheel of my old Citroën.

I want to get some distance from the experience of these last years at the Book Fair. I am going to Frankfurt, to my barber Gino, who for some 40 years has been taking care of my thinning hair and exercising his artistry on my beard.

As I cross over the Rhine bridge and look out onto the mouth of the River Main, I think of those historical "market ships," which in Gutenberg's time made ten-hour towing trips to bring the traveling participants in the Book Fair from the left bank of the Rhine to the Main bank of Frankfurt. Today I am traveling the 40 kilometers in 40 minutes in order to visit my barber!

In Frankfurt I first go to the administrative offices of the Book Fair in order to take care of some details related to the Society for the Promotion of the Literature of Africa, Asia and Latin America, which I am still associated with. Some employees see me in the hall and greet me enthusiastically. We talk about old times and new times. Time flies by in a flash, and I have to hurry to be on time for my appointment with Gino, whose barbershop lies quite close to the famous *Buchgasse*.

Today I have no time to stop and linger. I hasten past the many alleys and down through Hauptwache Square. It is here—just now—that I come upon the unsuspecting couple among the sea of anonymous faces. He, a reader, like me. She, a young woman, like so many I've known. And the book—its name, peering out at me from the man's pocket.

I suddenly make sense of the title. The author is Trudi Birger. The book, *Facing Fire: How I Escaped the Hell of the Concentration Camp*.

I feel myself thrashing about in the sea of this memory. The last time I saw Trudi Birger, it was just before her sudden death. We were at the Jerusalem book fair in the spring of 1999, when she was together with Zev, who had been so happy with his wife. Trudi, who had superhuman life force and will to live, was the anchor of Zev's life, a fine and sensitive friend. Trudi Birger, born in Frankfurt as Trudi Simon, had in her book described the apocalyptic memories of her years in Auschwitz, where she and her mother had escaped the death ovens several times, due to her incomparable will to live. I had been friendly with Zev and Trudi for a few years. They had never spoken about their past, about their experiences in the concentration camps of Nazi Germany. They had kept quiet not only toward me, but toward all their friends, in Israel as well, and even to their closest relatives, including their children and grandchildren.

I have read a good deal about why Holocaust survivors speak to no one about their gruesome experiences, not even with anyone in Israel, after the horror that they were subjected to. They build a bourgeois existence, found families, and bring forth children, but they speak to no one. Some commentators have explained this behavior by saying that those affected were unable to integrate their experience into a "normal" life. In the light of the apocalypse that they lived through, it would not have been possible for them to participate in the mundane activities of everyday life. Other commentators reported on the "shame" felt by Holocaust survivors, precisely because they were the ones who had survived. Zev and Trudi Birger—in my opinion—were no exceptions to this "repression of experiences." An American, Jeffrey M. Green, who categorically wanted to understand the unimaginable, had dragged the story out of Trudi Birger and had brought her to the attention of an international public in that book that was sticking out of the pocket of the man near the Frankfurt police station. Zev, however, continued to maintain his silence.

At our second Bellagio meeting of directors of international book fairs in 1996 on Lake Como, one evening I went for a walk with Zev along the lake shore after a very intensive conference day. I told him about Bad Wörishofen, where I had had myself treated with a short cure for my poor health. Then Zev began to talk, at first hesitatingly, then ever more forcefully.

At the end of the war, Zev Birger was liberated from the concentration camp at Dachau and brought by an American officer to the military hospital in Bad Wörishofen. Due to hunger and typhus, his body was covered with pus-filled boils, and he weighed only about 75 pounds.

And then the little man began to tell me his story, which was so important for his survival—this man who was later the great international communicator, beloved by everybody, particularly by women, with his understated Jewish humor and his friendly compliments.

"Lying in my bed, I went in and out between dreams and wakefulness—everything was swimming together. When

I opened my eyes, I first saw a white jacket, and down below those frightening boots of German officers. I heard how that person standing right next to me said to another person, 'This case is hopeless!'

"Those words hit me like a knife between the ribs. I was completely out of it. Now, lying in a soft bed with bright white sheets, was I to be a hopeless case? Then I screamed at the German doctor: 'You are the one who is hopeless! This case is not hopeless! This case is going to live!'

"This experience gave me back my old, ornery will. The strength to survive had come back to me."

Mention of Bad Wörishofen had torn away the armor in which Zev had encased himself. He later told me that he then made a trip with one of his sons to visit the site of his suffering, including Bad Wörishofen. And a year later his book appeared, *No Time for Patience,* in which he once again related this depressing story. The book was published by several German publishing houses as a joint project.

Once again I had set up a three-week cure in the baths at Bad Wörishofen. My unstable health during my last year of work forced me into this; besides, I was greatly overweight. This time, despite the awful rainy weather, I pushed myself to consistently maintain the good health regimen that I had undertaken — bicycling, swimming, an extended nap in the afternoon, bathing in the spa waters, massages, special diet, and no alcohol.

After only a week of the cure I was feeling stronger. I was amazed at the return of my sense of smell. Eagerly I breathed in the air of the spa park, so full of the aroma of cow dung and pollen. There was also the fresh water air near the fountains, and the resinous fragrance of freshly cut tree stumps and the wild strawberry smell of flowering clover. I even eagerly took in the sanitarium's own mixture of the chlorinated swimming pool and the various spa aromas, such as hay stubble and other herbs.

The day before I had spoken by telephone with Stefan R., a publishing house employee from Berlin, who had many good traits for the director of a fair and whom I would gladly have seen as my successor. In the meantime he had been interviewed by a headhunter from the German Publishers Association and had "a good feeling," but after the negative reaction of his first conversation with the chairperson of the Supervisory Board, he had become cautiously skeptical. As soon as I found myself healthy and strong and felt that I could deal with the book fair problems with some distance, as had not been the case in the previous week, I could not conceive why I wanted to stop. In the previous 25 years I had been programmed exclusively for one goal, the Book Fair. Now I had no new goal.

I sought out quiet, and therefore once again before the Fair I went for a late summer weekend to the Rhön. I slept in my big Rhön bed, but every morning I was up at 4:30 AM. The immense efforts to put on the Fair hung over me, as happened every year at this time. I had stage fright, and it was as though I were standing again and again for an examination.

The press had always made the greatest demands on me, and I fought against their totally free access for many years. The interest of the media in me was seldom anything that touched on my role as director of the Fair. To the contrary, the media pursued me in all sorts of conceivable areas of knowledge and put me in the role of the All-Knowing. I was quizzed very little about that which I really knew about, meaning the events at the Fair. On the other hand, people asked me freely about anything referring to books or to culture, whether it be on China or the Balearic Islands. I was supposed to give information about German and European literature, to say nothing of literature from India, Africa or America, or in special cases about the life of the Chukchis, Japanese, or of the Bolivians. A number of reporters were also interested in the past or future of those literatures. On the literature on women in Islam, the literature of homosexuals and socialism, workers' literature of 1968, children's literature starting from age five—I was supposed have an opinion on everything!

I regretted this role of the All-Knowing. I wanted to use the press for the Fair. Still, the representatives of the media were just looking for original or provocative sound bites. Recently I had to do up to 70 interviews with television, radio, and the written press, mainly in German and English, with a few in

Spanish. I felt like a hen who had been set on a pot to lay eggs when the sign was given: "We have 1 minute 30. Please keep it short!" Favorite themes in the 1990s were especially the death of the book and the power of the electronic media.

In my public appearances, I wanted to give not just generalities, but as much as possible something with solid content. Therefore in preparations for openings and other scheduled public events I often used third parties, press spokesmen, assistants, or outsiders to draft speeches. Besides that, I read constantly throughout the year on international flights, in sleepless hotel nights, before falling asleep at home, all the while trying to keep up with things for the topics that were expected. Nevertheless, new questions often hit me in an unexpected way, and afterwards I had the feeling of having pronounced conceited nonsense.

In addition to all that, I thought myself responsible for everything that happened at the Fair, especially for any mishaps. My identification with this work had gone so far that I perceived as a personal failure the slightest error that might occur, a malfunction, a contradiction, or an unreasonable demand for our participant customers. The Fair was so big, the processes and possibilities for error so numerous, that I was no longer in a position to be responsible for everything. My method of shaping the Fair by using all of my creative powers had not been workable for some time. That was another reason why our parting was essential.

Now I yearned for the moment when I could again be outside in the Rhön and would have this last Fair behind me. That would be an immense sigh of relief!

Then it was all over. Even during the Book Fair I had experienced increasing relief, and only afterwards had noticed how much the responsibility for the Fair had weighed on me. What I had probably needed earlier was words of encouragement, of recognition, something that all of a sudden at this Fair I found in an overflow of friends and foes. Even the chairman of the German Publishers Association dedicated almost half of his press conference to an appreciation of my services. Although he didn't sound very convincing, it did me good.

And then the International Book Award, a prize of recognition from the international book community of UNESCO — lots of friends came to the presentation, including "Pancho" González from Madrid, Klaus Wagenbach and Inge Feltrinelli, who had God knows a million things to do at the Fair other than to plunk themselves down at what was, as the rule, a very pedestrian ceremony. And finally my beautiful Saturday evening, the dinner party, which as in previous years I put on with invitations to 50 or 60 guests in the Ristorante Da Piva, with all the international friends and the friendly comments.

After the Book Fair, I immersed myself in the diaries of a German intellectual, who had gone through almost the entire 20th century in Germany with his manic diaries and notebooks. On television a soap opera was running more or less based on Victor Klemperer's *Diaries 1933–1945*, which to be sure had little to do with his real sketchbooks, which I had been reading for months, more and more enthralled. In those long sessions of reading into the night, I followed day by day this professor of Romance languages, who had converted from Judaism to Protestantism, as he and his wife went through the Dresden of the Nazi period, 1933–1945. Based on the two thick volumes titled *I Will Bear Witness*, I became familiar with the life portrayed there, German life in this century. Then his years in the Soviet occupation zone and the newly founded German Democratic Republic occupied me, his diaries of 1945–1959, *The Lesser Evil*. Many, many names, which I can't even begin to enumerate, disturbed me, as did Klemperer's academic vanity and self-absorption. Nonetheless, this was an authentic, contemporary look into the period "over there" in East Germany directly after the end of Nazi rule, a look at that other Germany about which we know a lot less than we do about our own corresponding period.

I was fascinated by the desire of the old Klemperer to make his case, who in the face of the *memento mori* was hectically flaunting his own significance, showing off his lecture dates and his presidential offices, which he savored with an inconceivable possessiveness. Apparently this was a reaction to the enormous humiliation and disparagement that he had experienced in the Nazi era. In any case Klemperer's conversion to Marxism, his suddenly appearing Russophilia, his conviction in favor of the East German Socialist Unity Party, all seem to me to be of an overwhelmingly opportunistic character. They do not grow out of conviction and understanding. How could even such a clear-headed person like this Victor Klemperer be predetermined by his Being? But aren't we all products of our environment and our socialization? Doesn't our Being determine our Consciousness? It seems to me that I am reflecting here on my own life situation. Was I enthralled by the sketchbooks of this really estimable man Victor Klemperer because of his internal conflicts, his German life, which I had accompanied in my reading over half a century—didn't this resemble my own reflections at the close of my times?

The gradual rediscovery of the present was a refreshing finding that I experienced after my inner release from work at the Fair. I had already announced it—having arrived in "retirement," I wanted for the first time "to look back in some detail." Now I experienced sudden moments of complete orientation to the present. I was living here, at this moment, in this light, at this temperature, and I saw here in the Rhön the clouds and the colors of the autumn leaves; I smelled the air in the autumn. All of a sudden I found that life was good!

Afterword

Nonetheless, I felt isolated. Previously so many people had surrounded me. Had I become a world-wide "person collector" for the Book Fair? A longing for book people took hold of me, those people to whom I had so long devoted myself, those people who had been around me for so long and in such large numbers. I felt a great hunger for communication. Where were those people, those contemporaries, whose friend I had once been, who had sought me out, had supported me, had shielded me? Where could I find them? Only at the book fairs! I had to go back. I recalled an earlier project that I was still loosely connected with.

In 1994, the two directors of the Mexican book fair in Guadalajara, Margarita Sierra and Maria Carmen Canales, lit on the idea of inviting the directors of all the well-known international book fairs to a conference in Italy at a scholarly center on Lake Como. They had received money for such a meeting from the Rockefeller Foundation in New York.

    We colleagues of these two very active Mexican fair planners were at first not very excited about this plan. What did we fair directors actually have in common? Every one of us considered his fair to be the most important and the best. It was a given that Frankfurt was the biggest, but even so the others still came in second place!

    I too hesitated. What will they talk about? Did we wish to have an agreement on deadlines among the various book fairs? I had never been driven by a feeling of competition among our fairs. If someone wished, I always helped in the founding and development of the other fairs—most certainly with the FIL in Guadalajara; at Budapest, at the wish of the Hungarian publishing president István Barth and with Péter Zentai, the director of the Hungarian Publishers and Booksellers Association, I had founded that international book festival and had worked with it since then. In Taiwan and in Bucharest we gave ongoing help. In Madrid/Barcelona, Moscow and Beijing, the founding fathers had all consulted with me before beginning their fairs. I had always been of the opinion that most book fairs were obligated to a national and even regional book market, or at the least to their own language area, and so could not really be competitors of one another. A competitive situation could really occur only between the truly international working book fairs, such as Frankfurt, the children's book fair in Bologna, and the London Fair. On the other hand, so went my objection, one could protect himself very well by having the best on offer, the most polished fair technology, and the best service.

In the end, most of us showed up for the meeting.[1] As we took our places at the long conference table, some of us still apprehensive, it fell on me, the man of Frankfurt and the most senior, to lay out the topics for cooperation in a keynote speech.

I began with the question of who we actually were, and posed an answer to this question with my personal ideas on the drive to create communities. Slowly the colleagues sitting around the table were drawn in, and by their nodding heads and agreeing murmurs I could see that with all of them the same thing had appeared in their work, from the largest in Frankfurt to the smallest in Kenya. We had found items in common, and could now proceed to speak about all those things that oppressed us and for which we could seek solutions in common. A group of friends was formed—that was something that we felt sitting in the evening by the lakeside and drinking whiskey from a bottle while each person sang a song from his

---

1. Those present at the first Bellagio meeting in 1994 were the directors of the following book fairs:

Margarita Sierra and *Maria Carmen Canales* (FIL Guadalajara), *Francesca Ferrari* (Bologna), *Trish* and *Wilfred Mbanga* (Harare, Zimbabwe), *Peggy Barber* (American Library Association), *Marta Diaz* (Buenos Aires), *Miguel Laverde* (Bogotá), *Yang Jixiang* (Beijing), *NTS Chopra* (Singapore), *Zev Birger* (Jerusalem), *Péter Inkei* (Budapest), *Samir Khalil* (Cairo), *Charles Wu* (Taipei), *Robert Gasset* (Havana), *Peter Weidhaas* (Frankfurt), *Patrick Dubs* (Paris), *Alfredo Weiszflog* (Inter-American Publishers Group, GIE São Paulo), *Hélio Carlos Dias* (São Paulo), *David Unger* (FIL Guadalajara, secretary).

homeland. Even the shy and soft-spoken Yang Jixiang from Beijing could not hold out, and warbled a song from the Peking Opera.

From this initial meeting arose a network of international book fairs, in which today others are represented as well—Leipzig, New York, London, Göteborg, Prague, Warsaw, Seoul, Thessaloniki, New Delhi and Capetown. And I, as the only one without a book fair, still show up at every meeting, because I have been chosen by my colleagues as the "chairman" of this illustrious gathering every two years.

In the meantime, I have been repeatedly invited to book fairs as a so-called "consultant." That is exactly what was missing in my "retirement." Going to those types of book fairs has allowed me to cross paths with the lives of the book people. I can still give something to my other colleagues based on my extensive experience with book fairs.

That satisfies me very much. Yes, I dare even to use the word that very rarely appeared during my exciting lifetime experiences—I feel myself happy to be there!

Index of Names

Abe Kōbō, 233
Achebe, Chinua, 140
Achmet (MN), 72
Adorf, Mario, D-5
Agualusa, José Eduardo, 244
Ahdal, Abdullah, 275
Ahmad, Aida Joesoef, 362
Ahmed, Faizuddin, 270, 271
Ajneya, (Sachchidananda Vatsyayan), 177
Akçali, Kezban, 196
Akpul, Recai, 196
Albert, Leo, 157
Alegre, Manuel, 245
Ali, Muhammad, 49, 63, A-3
Allende, Salvador, 81, 129
Almeida, Germano, 244
Alonso, Alicia, 78
Amado, Jorge, 90, 91, 147
Amery, Carl, 95, 307
Amirplio, Dr., 290, 291
Anand, Mulk Raj, 177
Ananthamurthy, U.R., 174, 177
Anders, Günther, 131, 132
Angelis, Paul de, 155
Angremey, Jean-Pierre, 230
Ant, Atil, 196
Ant, Füsan, 196
Antes, Horst, 21
Aoki Hideo, 353
Arens, Gottfried, 94
Arndt, Rudi, 102
Arnold (DE), 40
Arroyo, Eduardo, 233, 234
Asturias, Miguel Ángel, 75

Bâ, Mariama, 140, B-1
Baader, Andreas, 106, 111
Babenko, Vitaly, 218
Baciu, Ştefan, 127, 128
Bacon, Francis, 342
Baensch, Robert, 157, 158, 186, D-2
Bahr, Egon, 306
Baier, Lothar, 229
Baksh, Mohamed Ali, 361
Ballard, Martin, 19
Balogh, Katalin, 247, D-8
Bamberger, Maria, 77
Banerjea-Komers, Ute, 369
Barbeitos, Arlindo, 141
Barber, Peggy, 387
Barbie, Klaus, 78
Bardo, Brigitte, 202
Barros, Jorge, B-6
Barschel, Uwe, 190
Bart-Williams, Gaston, 141
Bartels, Andreas, 155
Barth, Christian, 362
Barth István, 247, 386
Baumhof, Dr., 26
Bebey, Francis, 129
Bechler, Uli, 67
Beck, Hans-Dieter, 307
Beck, Wolfgang, 307
Beckenbauer, Franz, 63
Becker, Bärbel, 215
Becker, Jörg, 137, 149
Beckett, Samuel, 243
Beckmann, Gerhard, 96
Beer, John, 19, 20
Behm, Holger, 215

Belli, Gioconda, 129, 186, C-4
Benedetti, Mario, 129
Benedetto, Antonio di, 77
Benjamin, Walter, 230
Bennion, Francis, 294
Berberich, Frank, 310
Bessa-Luís, Agustina, 245
Bessie, Cornelia, 155
Bessie, Simon Michael, 157
Betancur Cuartas, Belisario, 235
Beti, Mongo, 129, 138
Beyer, Kurt, 104
Bhandari, Mannu, 178
Bhatia, Smita, 369
Bhattacharyya, Sourish, 368
Bialicka, Monika, D-8
Biermann, Wolf, C-7
Binchy, Maeve, 242
Bioy Casares, Adolfo, 77
Birger, Trudi, 372, 379, 380, D-5
Birger, Zev, 220, 372, 379–381, 387, D-5, D-8
Blandon, Erik, 186, C-4
Blessing, Karl H., 307
Blunden, Brian, 349
Blunden, Margot, 349
Bogdanović, Bogdan, 372
Boguta, Grzegorz, D-2
Borge, Tomás, 185, 204
Borges, Jorge Luis, 75, 92, 191
Borisch, Klaus-Michael, 349
Bötticher, Dietrich, 350
Bouchez, Michèle, 230
Bourgois, Christian, 272, 276
Brück, Wolfram, 105, 187
Brandão, Fiama Hasse Pais, 244, 245
Brandt, Willy, 21
Bräuer, Christoph H., 349
Braun-Elwert, Wilhelm, 107
Breadley, Clive, 368
Brecht, Bertolt, 59, A-2
Brezhnev, Leonid, B-2
Brik, Hugo, 186
Brik, Sasha, 216
Brücher, Daniel, 307

Brücher, Ernst, 307
Brümmer, Dr. (DE, JP), 353
Bruno, Giordano, 8
Buback, Siegfried, 106
Buchwald, Christoph, 350, 372
Bükey, Fahriye, 126

Canales, Maria Carmen, 386, 387, C-6
Capote, Truman, 178
Capriolo, Alberto, 300
Cardenal, Ernesto, 75, 92, 127, 128, 185, 186, 203, C-4, C-5, D-7
Cardenal, Fernando, 186
Carpentier, Alejo, 75, 81
Carrilho, Manuel Maria, 244
Carstens, Karl, 142
Carvalho, Mário de, 245
Cassidy, Lar, 242, 243
Castro, Fidel, 78, 127
Cendrars, Blaise, 246
Céspedes, Augusto, 92
Chakravarty, Sveta Dave, 369
Chamorro Cardenal, Pedro Joaquín, 127
Chang, Frederic P.N., 356
Chantiles, Nicholas, 157
Chávez, Hugo, 91, 92
Chen, Emma, 356
Chiam, H.H., 359
Chikrishvili, Irakles, 59, 62, 216
Chitre, Dilip, 177
Chlebnikov, Boris, 217
Chopra, NTS, 387
Chou, Benjamin, 357
Christiansen, Günther, 322, 370
Clifford-Simons (GB), 19
Clurman, Rodney H., 157
Cobet, Heinrich, 250
Coelho, Paulo, 240
Cohn-Bendit, Daniel, 246
Columbus, Christopher, 235
Conradi, Arnulf, 350
Coronel Urtecho, José, 186
Cortázar, Julio, 90, 92, 95, 147
Costa, Maria Velho da, 245

Cotti, Flavio, 246
Couto, Mia, 245
Cruz, Federico, 186, 188
Cruz, Juana Inés de la, 236
Cuadra, Pablo Antonio, 128

Dadié, Bernard Binlin, 141
Daki, Sammy, 19
Dalos György, 247
Dante Alighieri, 343
Daruwalla, Keki N., 162, 163
Darwish, Adel, 271
Das, Kamala, 177
Dasgupta (IN), 170
David, Filip, 372
Davidson, Lionel, 223
Davies, Alun, 259
Delius, Friedrich Christian, 196
Demski, Eva, 229
Desai, Anita, 177
Detha, Vijaydan, 178
Deuscher, Ulrike, 209
Deutsch, André, 19
Devi, Mahasweta, 178
Dhur, Bimal, 171, 172
Dias, Hélio Carlos, 387
Diaz, Marta, 387, D-8
Díaz, Roberto, 185
Direitinho, José Riço, 245
Dittrich, Kathinka, 217
Divinsky, Daniel, 94, A-5
Doderer, Klaus, 137
Donoso, José, 90–92, 95
Dos Passos, John, 32
Dowlatabadi, Mahmoud, 310
Doyle, Roddy, 242, 243
Drakulić, Slavenka, 372
Dubs, Patrick, 387
Duve, Freimut, 203

Ebert, Friedrich, 80
Eco, Umberto, 224, C-2
Ehling, Holger, 241, 331, 334
Ehmann, Wolfgang, 357
Ehrlich, Arnold, 28
Eichborn, Vito von, 323

Ekwensi, Cyprian, 141
El-Essawy, Hesham, 293
Elena María Isabel Dominica de
  Silos de Borbón, 233, 237, 238
Eliezer ben Nathan, 7
Eliot, T.S., 178
Emecheta, Buchi, 141
Engelking, Gerhard, 366
Ensslin, Gudrun, 106, 111
Enzensberger, Hans Magnus, 229,
  273, 307, 310
Eörsi István, 247
Eppler, Erhard, 151
Erasmus of Rotterdam, 8
Erbach, Kurt, 104
Erdmann, Horst, 147
Erffa, Wolfgang von, 369
Esterházy Péter, 247, 249
Ezekiel, Nissim, 178

Faber, Elmar, 223, 371
Falck, Bertie, D-8
Falin, Valentin, B-2
Farah, Nuruddin, 141
Faria, Almeida, 245
Faridzadeh (IR), 290, 292, 293
Fehr, Götz, 40
Fellini, Federico, 227
Feltrinelli, Giangiacomo, 23
Feltrinelli, Inge, 23, 24, 193, 246,
  384, C-2
Fenderl, Michael, 57, 196
Fenke, Franz-Josef, 41, 63, 114, 258,
  265, 271, 278, 279, 331, 332, 334,
  A-7
Ferrari, Francesca, 387, D-8
Ferraris, Luigi Vittorio, 224, 226
Fischer, Samuel, 123
Fitzgerald, F. Scott, 32
Franco, Francisco, 61, 274
Franz, Carlos, C-6
Frederick II of Hohenstaufen, 8
Frederking, Gert, 323
Friderichs, Hans, 60
Friedrich, Heinz, 253
Friesel, Uwe, 305, 310

Frisch, Max, 63, 74, 159–161
Fuchs, Gerald, 27
Fuentes, Carlos, 75, 81, 92, 235

Galeano, Eduardo, 90, 91, 94, 129, 186
Gama, Vasco da, 244
Gandhi, Rajiv, 176, 271, B-7
Gangopadhyay, Sunil, 178
García Lorca, Federico, 78
García Márquez, Gabriel, 76, 77, 81, 90, 147
Garibuglia, Mario, 227
Gasset, Robert, 387
Gauland, Alexander, 103
Geiser, Elisabeth, 28
Genscher, Hans-Dietrich, 229, 249, 300, B-7
Georgi, Friedrich, 17, 53, 253, 313, 318
Gerke, Bärbel, 237
Gersão, Teolinda, 245
Ghai, S.K., 367
Giordano, Ralph, 190
Glöckler, Ralph Roger, 245
Goethe, Johann Wolfgang von, 197, 240
Gojković, Drinka, 372
Goldsmith, Oliver, 243
Goma (JP), 354
Gombosuren (MN), 71, 72
Göncz Árpád, 247, 249
Gongor (MN), 186
González, Francisco "Pancho", 384, C-3
Gottlieb, Paul, 155
Grade, Alfred, 250, 251
Grass, Günter, 87, 158, 159, 202, 229, 307, 310
Green, Jeffrey M., 380
Green, Julien, 230
Greiner, Ulrich, 306
Gretiani, Siti, 363
Gröning, Fritz, 186
Gründ, Alain, 228
Grundmann, Herbert, 281, 282

Gruner, Jürgen, 210, 211, 222, 370, B-8
Guevara, Ernesto Che, 23, 75, 127
Guha, Dipak Kumar, 165, 168, 169
Gupta (IN), 169
Gutenberg, Johannes, 8, 9, 379

Haider, Qurat-ul-Ain, 178
Haley, Alex, 83
Hamilton, Hugo, 242
Hamm, Peter, 246
Hamm-Brücher, Hildegard, 137
Hardt, Gabriele, 215
Härtling, Peter, 229
Hasegawa Hajime, 231, 232
Hasselbach, Irmgard, C-8
Hattori Toshiyuki, 231, 354
Havel, Václav, D-2
Healy, Dermot, 243
Heaney, Seamus, 242
Hebsacker, Jo, 64
Heidegger, Martin, 132
Heidenreich, Gert, 246
Hein, Christoph, 229
Hemingway, Ernest, 32, 364
Henkys, Reinhard, 126
Hershan, Stella, 28
Herzog, Roman, 244, 246
Hew, Michael, 360, 361
Hew, Shirley, 359
Heyde (GB), 19
Heym, Stefan, 229
Hieber, Jochen, 268
Higgins, Michael, 242
Hijjaz, Islam, 270
Hitchins, John, 19
Hitler, Adolf, 8, 111, 126, 192, 199, 343
Hobsbawm, Eric, 370
Hochhuth, Rolf, 223
Hoeft, Jack, 332
Hoffman, Gerd E., 341
Hoffmann, Hilmar, 48, 59, 103
Hoffmann, Karin, 57
Hoffmann, Rainer, 306
Holtzbrinck, Georg von, 372

Honecker, Erich, 354
Höpcke, Klaus, 186, B-8
Hopper, Edward, 35
How, Rex, 356, 358, D-3
Hoxha, Enver, 73
Hsu, Jennifer, 355
Hugendubel, Heinrich, 322
Huxley, Aldous, 152

Idichi, Harry H., 354
Igarashi Hitoshi, 300
Ike, V. Chukwuemeka, 141
Inkei Péter, 387
Irele, Abiola, 141
Irving, John, 159
Isenschmidt, Andreas, 246
Ivančić, Viktor, 372

James, Henry, 178
Jančar, Drago, 372
Janorschke, Klaus, 47
Jens, Tilman, 181, 325
Jergović, Miljenko, 372
Johnson, Uwe, 23
Jordan, Neil, 243
Jorge, Lidia, 245
Joyce, James, 243
Jungk, Peter Stephan, 229
Jungk, Robert, 152, 153, C-3, C-7
Juppé, Alain, 202

Kafka, Franz, 74, 124
Kahle, Hans Hermann, 40
Kalinova, Dana, D-8
Kalow, Gerd, 153
Kaplan, Jeremiah, 155, 157
Karbaji (IR), 297, 298
Karry, Heinz-Herbert, A-2
Kasanski, Igor, 216
Käsmayr, Benno, 146
Kataev, Valentin, 127
Kaufmann, Christine, 206
Kehl, Daniel, 135
Keller, Rolf, 40, 107, 253, 282
Kemal, Yaşar, 196
Kertész Imre, 247, 249

Kezilahabi, Euphrase, 141
Khalil, Samir, 387, D-8
Khāmene'i, Ali Hoseyni, 292
Khare, Vishnu, 166, 178
Khomeini, Ruhollah Mousavi, 266, 267, 272, 273, 289, 292
Kilian, Susanne, 347
Kind, Gero, 323
Kindersley, Peter, 349
Kinski, Klaus, 63
Klarsfeld, Beate, 79
Klemperer, Victor, 384, 385
Kliche, Lutz, 185, 186, 203
Klose, Iris, 215
Kluge, Klaus, 317
Knecht, Hans, 344
Knef, Hildegard, 63
Kohl, Helmut, 228, 230, 242, B-4
Kolatkar, Arun, 177
Kollek, Teddy, D-5
Königsdorf, Helga, 229
Konrád György, 247, 249
Korenaga Yasuko, 354
Koudele (DE), 237
Kourouma, Ahmadou, 129, 141
Krischanitz, Adolf, 240
Kroetz, Franz Xaver, 307
Krüger, Horst, 153
Krüger, Michael, 246, 372, 373
Kumar, Arvind, 368
Kumar, Narendra, 367, 369
Kurita Akiko, 353
Kurtze, Gerhard, 253, 322

Lahr, Helmut von der, 57, 203, 208, 229, 258, 271, 277, 299, 304, 305, 310, 324, 345, 346
Lance, Alain, 230
Lang, Fritz, 179
Lang, Jack, 230
Lange, Arno, B-8
Langenscheidt, Florian, 349
Langhoff, Anna, 229
Lapide, Pinchas, 151
Laverde, Miguel, 387

Ledig-Rowohlt, Heinrich Maria, 23
Lee, C.S., 358
Leggewie, Claus, 301
Lenz, Siegfried, 198
Levi, Peter, 78, 79, 186
Lewis, Oscar, 81
Lewis, Sinclair, 32
Li Paotung, 70
Liau (TW), 355
Links, Christoph, 222, 350
Lins, Osman, 90
Linz, Mark Werner, 157
Liu Chuanwei, 67, 69, 70
Locke-Carey, Alice, 161
Lohle, Carlos, 128
Lohmeyer, Dr., 21, 22
Lollobrigida, Gina, 63
Lorenz, Günter W., 92, 93
Loti, Pierre, 196
Louw, André van der, 112
Lovrenović, Ivan, 372
Lu Haifa, 355, D-8
Lu Xun, 68
Luchting, Wolfgang A., 77
Lucius, Wulf D. von, 155, 253
Lüdke, Martin, 229
Lunkewitz, Bernd F., 223
Luther, Martin, 190, 340

Machado, Alfredo, 186
Macias, Nubia, C-6
Madrid, Miguel de la, 234, 235, D-1
Mahapatra, Sitakant, 178
Mahler, Horst, 111
Mahn, Norbert, B-8
Maisuradze, Yuri, 217
Majerowicz, Kazimierz, 376
Malhotra, Dina N., 176, 367
Malhotra, Shekhar, 368
Maliqi, Shkelzen, 372
Malraux, André, 230
Mandel, Ernest, 109
Manley, Joan, 157
Mann, Golo, 229

Mann, Klaus, 230
Mann, Thomas, 247
Mao Zedong, 66, 109
Markau, Heike, 187
Marques, Luísa Pacheco, 244
Martínez, Pablo, 234
Martens, Alexander U., 317
Martius, Götz, 23
Marx, Henry, 29
Marx, Karl, 109
Masina, Giulietta, 227
Matthews, James, 139, 141, B-1
Mauriac, François, 230
May, Karl, 73
Mayer, Peter, 28, 29, 271
Mbanga, Trish, 387
Mbanga, Wilfred, 387
McCabe, Patrick, 242
McCann, Colum, 242
McCourt, Frank, 243
McGahern, John, 242
McLuhan, Herbert Marshall, 25, 26, 32, 340, 343
McNamee, Eoin, 242
McNiff, Philip J., 33
Mehmedinović, Semezdin, 372
Meier, Peter, 247
Meinhof, Ulrike, 111
Melanchthon, Philipp, 8
Mello, Thiago de, 90, 92, 95
Melo, João de, 245
Menasse, Robert, 241, D-5
Mendes, Luís Filipe Castro, 244
Menne, Lothar, 372
Meredith, Barbara, 264
Mertin, Ray-Güde, 149, 239, 245
Mesquita, Teo, 239
Metternich, Prince von, 28
Metz, Johann Baptist, 151
Metzner, Alfred, 53, 313
Meyer-Clason, Curt, 77, 95, 245
Michaelis, Rolf, 304, 305, 310
Michaletz, Claus, 294, 295
Mikasa Takahito, 232
Miklós Tamás, 247
Miler, Kuki, 94, A-5

Miller, Courtney, D-8
Miller, Henry, 32
Miro, Juan, 234
Mitterand, François, 228, 230
Moerwaningsih, Sri Reni, 363
Mohn, Sigbert, 76
Mooij, Martin, 113
Moreira, Juliano, 240
Mori, Tom (Takeshi), 353
Mortiz, Sigrid, 347
Mousavian, Seyed Hossein, 300
Moutchia, Walter, 186
Mulisch, Harry, 239
Müller, Herta, 229
Müller-Römhild, Dr., 17
Muschg, Adolf, 246
Musil, Robert, 240
Muth, Helmut, 57
Mzee, Said, 138, 145

Nachtigall (*Nightingale*), 108
Nádas Péter, 249
Nakagami Kenji, 233
Narasimhaiah, Hosur, 174
Narayan, Rasipuram Krishnaswami, 174, 178
Naumann, Michael, 301, 306, 307, 310, 373
Nauta, Lolle, 112, 113
Németh Miklós, 249
Neruda, Pablo, 75, 91
Nestroy, Harald N., 366
Neumann, Volker, 105
Neven DuMont, Reinhold, 307, 372
Newton, Isaac, 342
Ngũgĩ wa Thiong'o, 129
Ní Dhomhnaill, Nuala, 242
Niedecken, Wolfgang, 185
Niemann, Viktor, 372
Nirumand, Bahman, 277
Nizon, Paul, 229
Nkosi, Lewis, 141
Noma Shoichi, 231
Notteboom, Cees, 239
Nygaard, William, 310, 311

O'Brien, Edna, 242
O'Brien, Flann, 243
O'Casey, Sean, 243
Oates, Joyce Carol, 159
Obama, Barack, 92
Oberländer, Doris, 57, B-2
Obiechina, Emmanuel N., 141
Oehme, Matthias, 222
Orbán Viktor, 249
Ören, Aras, 196
Orfila Reynal, Arnaldo, 80, 81
Ortega, Daniel, 185, 203
Ortiz, Adalberto, 90
Orwell, George, 152, 344
Ousmane Sembène, 129

Pacheco, Jaime, 205–209
Pacheco, René, 78
Pahlavi, Mohammad Rezā, 266
Palitzsch, Peter, 59, A-2
Parra, Nicanor, 129
Pasternak, Boris, 23
Pausewang, Gudrun, 229
Pawar, Daya, 177
Paz, Octavio, 92, 235–237, D-1
Perthes, Friedrich, 281
Pessoa, Fernando, 244
Peter, Franz-Wilhelm, 62
Piault, Fabrice, C-8
Pick, Charles, 19
Pielsticker, Karl, 107
Pinochet, Augusto, 25
Pinto do Amaral, Fernando, 244
Piper, Ernst Reinhard, 307
Piper, Klaus, 307
Plessen, Elisabeth, 82
Podrimja, Ali, 372
Ponto, Jürgen, 106
Popović, Milorad, 372
Popović, Nenad, 370–372
Postman, Neil, 152
Price, Dr., 26
Pritam, Amrita, 178
Puig, Manuel, 90, 92

Quevedo, Francisco de, 233

Raddatz, Fritz J., 159, 229
Radford, Michael, 91
Radisch, Iris, 324
Rafsanjānī, Ali Akbar Hāshemī, 292
Rakusa, Ilma, 246
Ramanujan, Attipat Krishnaswami, 179
Ramírez, Sergio, 90, 95, 129, 185
Rao, Narasimha, 169, B-7
Rao, Radsha, 174
Raspe, Jan-Carl, 106
Rath, Bernie, 277
Rau, Johannes, 126, 149, 188
Rauter, Rosmarie, 137
Reich-Ranicki, Marcel, 229, 281
Reisch, Linda, C-7
Reuchlin, Johann, 8
Reymann, Günther, 104
Reynolds, Russell, A-4
Ribeiro, João Ubaldo, 245
Riemenschneider, Dieter, 163, 164, 172, 174
Rijn, Patricia van, D-1
Rinser, Luise, 197
Ripken, Peter, 149, 273
Roa Bastos, Augusto, 75
Robinson, Mary, 241
Röder, Tom, 47
Rodin, Auguste, 376
Rodríguez, Ana María, 186
Roloff, Michael, 29, 45
Ronan, Frank, 242
Rosenberg, Mary, 27, 117
Ross, Martin, 112, 113
Roth, Karl, 104
Roth, Petra, 246
Rowohlt, Ernst, 123
Rudolf, Lorenzo, 341
Ruiss, Gerhard, 277
Rulfo, Juan, 75, 90, 95, 147, 236
Rushdie, Salman, 266–268, 270–273, 275, 277, 289–291, 293–295, 297, 298, 301, 302, 304, 308–311, 361, 364, D-6
Russell (US), 19

Russell, Bertrand, 111
Russell, Dr., 26, 29

Sábato, Ernesto, 75, 150
Saca, Theodoro el, 208
Sachs, Gunther, 202
Sahay, Raghuvir, 166, 179
Sampaio, Jorge, 244
Sánchez, Jésus, 81
Sander, Volkmar, 29, 154, 158, 160
Saramago, José, 245
Sarkar, Pauline, 237
Saur, Klaus G., 155, 253, 322, 323
Sbutega, Don Branko, 372
Schachermeyer, Dr., 317
Schaepe, Norbert, 223
Schaper, Peter, 323
Scheel, Walter, A-2
Schiller, Friedrich, 197
Schily, Otto, 277
Schimmel, Annemarie, 269
Schirrmacher, Frank, 304
Schleyer, Hanns Martin, 106
Schlotterer, Christoph, 155, 156
Schmidt, Emil, 104
Schmidt, Helmut, B-4
Schmidt, Ruppert, 90
Schmidt-Braul, Ingo-Eric, 42
Schmitz, Helmut, 324
Schnorr, Alfred K., 104
Schoeller, Wilfried F., 245, 310
Schoenberner, Gerhard, 126
Schöffling, Klaus, 350
Schöller, Monika, 372
Scholten, Rudolf, 241
Scholz, Klaus Jürgen, 360
Schoop, Kurt, 103
Schopf, Federico, 95, 208
Schubert, Reinhard, 47, 146
Schultheis, Jürgen, 301, 306, 310, 323
Schulz, Dr., 21
Schulz, Hermann, 96, 123–129, 133, 134, 146, 148, 149, 203, 215, B-2, C-4
Schulz, Susanne, 300

Schulz-Gerstein, Hans-Georg, 281
Schulz-Keil, Wieland, 29, 45
Schütt, Peter, 306
Schütz, Hanns Lothar, 280–287, 344
Schwarz, Volker, 322
Schwarzer, Hans Werner, 273
Schweitzer, Paul, 247, C-8
Scorza, Manuel, 90, 92, 95
Seelbach, Jörg, 99, 317
Seibold, Commissioner, 208
Semprún, Jorge, 233, C-5
Senghor, Léopold Sédar, 142
Seow Choke Meng, 361
Sepamla, Sipho, 139, 141
Serke, Jürgen, 306
Setzer, Hugo, B-2
Shahabuddin, Syed, 270
Shaw, Bernard, 364
Shiffrin, André, 28, 374
Shimada Yasuo, 231, 353, 354
Sicker, Frank, 253
Sierra, Margarita, 386, 387, C-6
Simon, Claude, 230
Simon, Diet, 57
Simon, Dietrich, 222, 223
Simon, Günter, 149
Simon, Tanya, 216, 220
Simonides of Keos, 9, 10
Sinha, Kabita, 179
Sitnikov, Vassily, 186, 217
Sivam, K.P., 360
Skármeta, Antonio, 90, 91
Skriver, Ansgar, 148
Slashenenko, Vassily, 216
Smolovich, Jaime, 189, B-1
Šnajder, Slobodan, 372
Snater, Fekko, A-5
Soest, Anette von, 237
Sofala, J.A., 138
Soika, Ruth, 28
Sokolov, Vassily, 84
Solana, Javier, 233
Sölle, Dorothee, 151
Sommer, Günter, 202
Souza Montello, Josué de, 240

Soyinka, Wole, 140
Spencker, Joachim, 67–70
Spijkers, Cas, 237
Springer, Axel, 158
Srisanti, Listiana, 363
Stahler, Klaus, 291
Starkmann, Alfred, 158
Stasiuk, Andrzej, 84
Stauber, Horstmar, 105, 187
Staudinger, Ulrich, 17, 40, 48, 59, 101, 102, 104, 296, 299
Steinitz, Dr., 28
Stephan, Franz, 354
Stern, Carola, 301–303, 305, 306, 310
Straus, Roger, 157
Strausfeld, Michi, 96, 185, C-4, C-6
Strauss, Richard, 78
Strien, René, 223
Stukalin, Boris, 216
Sugianto, Gabriel, 363
Suharto, 364
Suhrkamp, Peter, 124
Swift, Jonathan, 243
Syberberg, Hans-Jürgen, 202

Tamen, Pedro, 245
Taner, Haldun, 196
Tansi, Sony Labou, 141
Taryadi, Alfons, 362
Taubert, Sigfred, 16–18, 28, 41, 42, 45, 46, 54, 66, 336, A-1
Taylor, Ian, 332
Tchaikovsky, Pyotr Ilyich, 78
Tendulkar, Vijay, 179, 180
Tenzin Gyatso (HH Dalai Lama), 168, A-7
Teschendorff, Martin, 107
Tham Hock Chee, 360
Thomas, Cherian, 368
Thyagarajan, R., 177
Timm, Uwe, 203, 229, D-5
Timossi, Jorge, 188
Tóibín, Colm, 243

Tomasi di Lampedusa, Giuseppe, 23
Tömpe András, 247
Torres Restrepo, Camilo, 75
Torst, Tankred, 273
Traeger, Rudolf, 357
Troschke, Peter, 119, 120
Truhart, Dr., 298
Tseng Farn-chian, 355
Tuna, Nimet, 196
Tura, Jordi Solé, 233
Tyabji, Salima, 369

U Tam'si, Tchicaya, 140
Ulmer, Roland, 322
Unger, David, 387
Unseld, Joachim, 350
Unseld, Siegfried, 39, 40, 44, 156, 307, B-8
Uslar Pietri, Arturo, 92
Ustinov, Peter, D-7

Vargas Llosa, Mario, 90, 92, 95, 147, A-3
Velikić, Dragan, 372
Veliotes, Nick, 264, 332
Verma, Nirmal, 129–131, 134
Videla, Jorge Rafael, 94
Viera, José Luandino, 141
Viney, Nigel, 19
Vitale, Alberto, 217, 259, 331, 332, 374
Vitali, Christoph, 246
Vogel (DE), 63
Vogel, Dr., 166
Vogelweide, Walther von der, 340
Vranitzky, Franz, 241

Wagenbach, Klaus, 23, 156, 277, 301, 306, 310, 384
Wager, Dr., 197
Wallmann, Walter, 102, 103, 105, 208
Wang Chengchung, 70
Wang Yongshen, 67, 70
Watanabe Takao, 354
Watanabe, Karl, 354, 355

Weber, Ronald, 42, 197
Wechsler, Ulrich, 121
Wecksler, Sally, 28
Wedel, Peter Graf von, 104
Wegner, Matthias, 17, 350
Weid, Henry von der, 246
Weidenfeld, Arthur George, 19, 20, 24
Weiss, Susanne, 357
Weiszflog, Alfredo, 239, 387
Weizsäcker, Richard von, C-7
Werfel, Franz, 124
Weringh, Koos van, 217
Werner, Dr., 118
Wesendonk, Peter von, 369
Wesker, Arnold, 294
Wilchek (DE), 61
Wilcke, Jürgen, 324
Wilde, Oscar, 243
Willms, Johannes, 317
Wischenbarth, Rüdiger, 241
Wista, Howard, 28
Witsch, Caspar, 53, 313
Witte, Barthold C., 289, 295, 297, 298
Wohmann, Gabriele, 307
Wolf, Christa, 83
Wolfe, Thomas, 32
Wolff (DE/GB), 19
Wolff, Kurt, 123–125
Wolfram von Eschenbach, 340
Wong, Francis, 358
Wörner, Jochen, 215
Wössner, Frank, 372
Wössner, Mark, 258
Wu, Charles, 356, 387

Yang Jixiang, 387, 388, D-8
Yeats, William Butler, 243

Zahrnt, Heinz, 151
Zangeneh (IR), 297
Zea, Concepción, 80
Zeldin, Richard, 28
Zentai Péter, 247, 386
Zimmer, Dieter E., 94
Zöld Ferencz, 247, 248, D-2

A NOTE ON THE TYPE

This book is set in Galliard, designed by Matthew Carter and issued by Mergenthaler in 1978.

Galliard is based on the designs of the French typecutter Robert Granjon (*c.* 1513–1589), who worked in Paris, Lyon, Antwerp, Rome, and Frankfurt am Main.

The version used here, ITC Galliard CC, was issued by Carter & Cone in 1992.